Ius Gentium: Comparative Perspectives on Law and Justice

Volume 120

Ius Gentium is a book series which discusses the central questions of law and justice from a comparative perspective. The books in this series collect the contrasting and overlapping perspectives of lawyers, judges, philosophers and scholars of law from the world's many different jurisdictions for the purposes of comparison, harmonisation, and the progressive development of law and legal institutions. Each volume makes a new comparative study of an important area of law. This book series continues the work of the well-known journal of the same name and provides the basis for a better understanding of all areas of legal science.

The *Ius Gentium* series provides a valuable resource for lawyers, judges, legislators, scholars, and both graduate students and researchers in globalisation, comparative law, legal theory and legal practice. The series has a special focus on the development of international legal standards and transnational legal cooperation.

Marco Antonio Simonelli

The European Court of Human Rights and Constitutional Courts

A Study on the ECtHR Case Law

Springer

Marco Antonio Simonelli
Department of Political Science
University of Barcelona
Barcelona, Spain

ISSN 1534-6781 ISSN 2214-9902 (electronic)
Ius Gentium: Comparative Perspectives on Law and Justice
ISBN 978-3-031-71267-8 ISBN 978-3-031-71268-5 (eBook)
https://doi.org/10.1007/978-3-031-71268-5

This Springer imprint is published by the registered company Springer Nature Switzerland AG
The registered company address is: Gewerbestrasse 11, 6330 Cham, Switzerland

Contents

Abbreviations

ACC	Constitutional Court of Albania
BCC	Constitutional Court of Belgium
BVG	Federal Constitutional Court of Germany
CCB	Constitutional Court of Bulgaria
CCBH	Constitutional Court of Bosnia and Herzegovina
CCC	Constitutional Court of Croatia
CCCZ	Constitutional Court of Czech Republic
CCLT	Constitutional Court of Lithuania
CCLV	Constitutional Court of Latvia
CCM	Constitutional Court of Montenegro
CCNM	Constitutional Court of North Macedonia
CCR	Constitutional Court of Romania
CC RSA	Constitutional Court of South African Republic
CC UGA	Constitutional Court of Uganda
CCSB	Constitutional Court of Serbia
CCSK	Constitutional Court of Slovakia
CCSL	Constitutional Court of Slovenia
CEE	Central Eastern European
CJEU	Court of Justice of the European Union
CoE	Council of Europe
ECHR	European Convention on Human Rights
ECJ	European Court of Justice
ECtHR	European Court of Human Rights
FCC	Constitutional Council of France
HCC	Constitutional Court of Hungary
ICC	Constitutional Court of Italy
PCT	Constitutional Tribunal of Poland

PTC	Constitutional Tribunal of Portugal
SCT	Constitutional Tribunal of Spain
VGH	Constitutional Court of Austria

Chapter 1
Introduction

1.1 Setting the Scene. The Strasbourg Court and the National Constitutional Courts in a Space of Constitutional Interdependence

Marta Cartabia, former President of the Italian Constitutional Court, once described Europe as a space of "constitutional interdependence".[1] With this expression, Cartabia was pointing to the fact that European constitutional courts had become integral parts of a legal space much wider than the domestic legal system, characterised by legal pluralism and where national constitutions no longer enjoy supremacy above all other sources of law, in particular EU law and the European Convention of Human Rights. To explain the functioning of this intricate system of charters and courts, the term multilevel constitutionalism was coined, to express the idea of various layers of legal orders complementary to each other but whose legitimacy is not derived from one another.[2]

In the fundamental rights domain, the creation of this enlarged space entailed a multiplication of the legal avenues available to individuals to claim protection of their fundamental rights. National constitutional courts are no longer the ultimate guarantors of fundamental rights, as individuals may turn to the European Court of Human Rights ('the ECtHR') to seek protection of their rights, with the European Court of Justice sometimes also intervening in the process. This overlapping of jurisdictions also brought about an increased potential for institutional conflicts in case of disagreement on the content of a fundamental right, as all those tribunals aim to ensure the supremacy of the charter they are respectively entrusted to guarantee, and there are no codified rules to solve possible clashes. In fact, rather than on a coherent and uniform legal framework, the smooth functioning of the European

[1] Cartabia (2016), p. 1791.

[2] More extensively on the notion of multilevel constitutionalism see, Pernice (1999), pp. 709–715.

M. A. Simonelli, *The European Court of Human Rights and Constitutional Courts*,
Ius Gentium: Comparative Perspectives on Law and Justice 120,
https://doi.org/10.1007/978-3-031-71268-5_1

multilevel system for fundamental rights protection relies on the loyal cooperation between constitutional courts and European ones, which means, in the first place, the acceptance from both parties that the different systems for the protection of fundamental rights are complementary rather than competing,[3] and that what matters is not having the final say but rather engaging in a constructive dialogue.

From the Strasbourg standpoint, which is the one adopted in this book, one should not forget that the informing principle of the ECHR system—now reaffirmed by the Preamble of the Convention—is that of subsidiarity, according to which national judges are primarily responsible for guaranteeing fundamental rights and the enforcement of the ECHR. To comply with this principle, the ECtHR should show deference towards national constitutional courts' decisions in fundamental rights cases, especially when they demonstrate to have considered ECtHR-made standards in their reasoning.[4] Besides, the ECtHR does not govern the execution of its judgments, which is almost entirely dependent on the goodwill of national authorities. As a matter of fact, the extent to which the ECtHR's judgments are to be taken into account by national judges in many cases depends on the effects assigned to them by the national constitutional court.[5] For securing the implementation of its judgments, and thus the effectiveness of the whole Convention system, the ECtHR thus cannot prescind from cooperating constitutional courts. To put it otherwise, the European system of fundamental rights protection is a polyphonic one, and without harmony between its different voices, clashes inevitably occur.

At the same time, constitutional judges increasingly find themselves having to assess the compatibility of domestic law not only with the constitution but also with the norms of the Convention—which in Council of Europe Member States generally has supra legislative status -[6] and they naturally turn to the ECtHR case law to receive guidance. In this sense, a cooperating constitutional court is no more just the supreme domestic authority, as it shall also faithfully fulfil its role of "European judge", taking into account the ECHR in the interpretation given by the Strasbourg Court when required to do so, and accepting that Strasbourg has the last word on questions concerning the interpretation of the Convention. At the same time, constitutional courts realised that invoking the Strasbourg authority when adjudicating contentious issues, independently of the invocation of the ECHR by one of the parties of the proceeding, could reinforce the argumentative strength of its judgments and consolidate its position *vis-à-vis* other State institutions. This cooperation between constitutional courts and the ECtHR resulted in the breakdown of the relationship of the bi-univocal correspondence between fundamental rights and the

[3] Szymczak (2007), pp. 26–27.

[4] The same Strasbourg Court early recognised its subsidiarity with respect to national jurisdictions in the historic judgment in, *Handyside v. United Kingdom*, 5493/72, 7 December 1976.

[5] On the point see: Petrov (2018), p. 500.

[6] On the position in domestic legal systems of the Convention, the most comprehensive work covering all Council of Europe countries is that of Martinico and Pollicino (2010); where the authors note a convergence towards a supralegislative status for the ECHR. Also worth mentioning is the work by: Kelle and Stone Sweet (2008).

constitution, and its replacement with a dynamic relationship of mutual subsidiarity which,[7] despite inevitable tensions and conflicts, has led to the creation of a legal space that, up to the beginning of this century, was generally considered the most successful regional system for the protection of fundamental rights in the world.[8]

The relationship between the Strasbourg Court and national constitutional jurisdictions, however, cannot be reduced to its cooperative, horizontal, dimension, as there are aspects of this relationship that fit better in a narrative of subordination rather than cooperation. Since the landmark judgment in *Ruiz Mateos,* where the ECtHR for the first time applied Article 6 ECHR to constitutional proceedings, constitutional courts are indeed required to adapt their procedures to the fair trial standards flowing from Article 6 ECHR.[9] This means that the Strasbourg Court not only deals with the constitutional courts' substantive interpretations but also scrutinises their procedural performance. This tendency gradually evolved in such a way that it appears nowadays unquestionable the procedural subordination of constitutional justice to the exigencies of the right to a fair trial as resulting from the Strasbourg case law. Such a subordination appears with all evidence especially when considering the degree to which the ECtHR case law has been capable of affecting the functioning of constitutional justice systems well beyond the limits of the individual right to a fair constitutional trial, reducing the autonomy of constitutional courts to organise their procedure and functioning, affecting their deliberative procedures and imposing standards concerning the constitutional and legislative framework governing the functioning of constitutional justice.[10] Rather surprisingly, this significant expansion of the Strasbourg Court's competence was received without significant protests by the same constitutional courts,[11] and it seemed to imply the acceptance by constitutional judges of the role of the Strasbourg Court as a de facto European constitutional court.[12]

Yet, offering a fully optimistic description of the relationship between the ECtHR and national constitutional courts would be misleading as, especially in the last two

[7] See: Ruggeri (2011), p. 549.

[8] See for instance: Helfner (2008), p. 125.

[9] In *Ruiz-Mateos*, for the first time, the Court declared that the guarantees of Article 6 ECHR were also applicable to constitutional proceedings. See: *Ruiz-Mateos v. Spain* (12952/87), 23/06/1993. This tendency gradually evolved in such a way that through Article 6 ECHR the Strasbourg Court has been able to profoundly affect the functioning of constitutional jurisdictions, including by scrutinising their deliberative procedures. The extent of this rationalisation process will be analysed in Chapter 4.1.

[10] See for instance: *Avdić and Others v. Bosnia and Herzegovina* (28357/11), (31549/11), (39295/11), 19/11/2013; *Marini v. Albania* (3738/02), 18/12/2007.

[11] Such a circumstance has been noted by one of the fiercest critics of the applicability of the fair trial guarantees to constitutional jurisdictions, Favoreu (2004), p. 10.

[12] Actually, there is an ongoing debate in the academia concerning the constitutional nature of the ECtHR jurisdiction, which was particularly lively at the beginning of the past decade. See, below, fn 69.

decades, there have been signals that constitutional courts may have grown tired of the ECtHR's prominent role in the European legal space.

First, it is almost commonplace to affirm that during the past decade, the whole ECHR system entered into an "existential crisis" provoked by a resurgence of sovereignist tendencies and the rise of populist sentiment, especially in Central and Eastern European States. Those movements challenged the legitimacy of the European integration process as a whole, thereby including the ECHR system, epitomised by the Strasbourg Court. Constitutional courts of populist-ruled countries fully embraced this rhetoric, entering into harsh confrontations with European jurisdictions, often complaining about being subject to more stringent standards with respect to Western European democracies. These rebellions reached their maximum in Poland, where,[13] in 2021, the Polish Constitutional Tribunal went as far as declaring the unconstitutionality of Article 6 ECHR, inasmuch as it applies to constitutional courts.[14]

Second, this crisis was aggravated by growing resistance coming from constitutional courts of older democracies like Germany and Italy, which, in a different, more nuanced form, also challenged the interpretative authority of the ECtHR and the binding force of its judgments.[15] Those rebellions evidenced, if it was ever necessary, that the ECHR structural equilibrium is a very delicate one, and that one of its keystones is represented by the relationship between the Strasbourg judges and national constitutional courts.

Notwithstanding the aforesaid, in recent years the attention devoted to the issue of the relationship between the ECtHR and constitutional courts has been rather scarce. There are, of course, several works focusing on the relationship between the two European courts and national courts,[16] as well as studies of a wider scope investigating the interplay between the European legal order and national legal systems in general.[17] Yet, a book aimed specifically at illustrating the state of affairs of the relationship between Strasbourg and national constitutional jurisdictions is long missing.[18]

---

[13] Not to mention the case of the Russian Constitutional Court that repeatedly stressed the supremacy of the Russian Constitution over the Convention and declared the ECtHR ruling in *Anchugov* as non-executable. We will go back on the ECtHR judgment at a later stage. See, below, fn 68.

[14] Polish Constitutional Tribunal, Case K 6/21, Judgment of 24 November 2021. The text of the judgment translated into English is available on the website of the same Polish Constitutional Tribunal at: https://trybunal.gov.pl/en/hearings/judgments/art/11709-art-6-ust-1-zd-1-konwencji-o-ochronie-praw-czlowieka-i-podstawowych-wolnosci-w-zakresie-w-jakim-pojeciem-sad-obejmuje-trybunal-konstytucyjny. All the websites were last accessed on the 30 of June 2024.

[15] For a review of those cases see: Martinico (2016), pp. 59–78.

[16] See amongst many: Popelier et al. (2011).

[17] See for instance: Arnardóttir and Buyse (2016).

[18] In the past, the question of the relationship between constitutional courts and the ECtHR had interested in particular the French scholarship, where it is possible to find several contributions on different aspects of the relationship. See amongst many: Favoreu (2004); Berger (2011), p. 7; Burgorgue Larsen (2001). The most comprehensive work on this theme is the one by Szymczak (2007). In the English language scholarship, the work of Kosar and Petrov on the role of the

1.2 Why this Book?

Against this backdrop, this book seeks to fill this gap by providing an assessment of this relationship from the standpoint of the Strasbourg Court, more specifically, from the prism of its case law. Adopting an empirical methodology, all the judgments of the Strasbourg Court in which constitutional courts are cited have been collected and catalogued. From the mere collection of this large set of data—consisting of more than three thousand judgments—it has been possible to obtain statistical evidence about the presence of constitutional courts in the ECtHR case law, thus sketching out the quantitative dimension to the relationship. However, the scope of this book is not limited to photographing the relationship through numbers and figures. A qualitative analysis of this jurisprudential *mare magnum* was carried out in order to reach two distinct objectives.

The first is to provide a complete picture of the relationship between the ECtHR and each constitutional court of the Council of Europe. This analysis seeks to assess the ECtHR dialogic posture towards each constitutional court, as well as to give an overall assessment of the Strasbourg Court's role in the European legal order. The analysis has been conducted along the East/west divide to test the merit of criticism advanced by judges and politicians of Central and Eastern Europe—and shared by a part of academic scholarship-[19] according to which the Strasbourg Court is being more assertive towards constitutional courts of new democracies, and conversely recognises a wider margin of appreciation to constitutional courts of established Western European democracies.

Second, the book assesses the extent of constitutional courts' procedural subordination to the ECHR. This means, in other words, assessing how the Strasbourg Court applies Article 6 ECHR to constitutional jurisdictions. This analysis will allow us to identify the various components of the right to a fair constitutional trial as elaborated by the Strasbourg Court, envisaging to define the European standards concerning its minimum content and evaluate the degree of the rationalising process of constitutional justice undertaken by the ECtHR. At the same time, through an analysis of the applicability of Article 6 to constitutional jurisdictions, it is also possible to spot those aspects of national constitutional justice systems that are susceptible to falling within the scope of Article 6 and, conversely, what areas of constitutional justice, if any, still escape the Strasbourg's Court scrutiny.

1.3 Outline of the Book

Those objectives inform the structure of the book as follows.

---

domestic courts in the ECHR system can be mentioned, albeit it is not specifically focused on constitutional courts. See: Kosar and Petrov (2017).

[19] See in particular: Flauss (2003), p. 1632 and, more recently: Sap (2020).

Chapter 2 sketches out the relationship between the ECtHR and national constitutional courts in its qualitative and quantitative dimensions. First, by paying specific attention to the most recent jurisprudential developments, it illustrates how ECtHR evolved from a remedial jurisdiction whose powers were limited to awarding compensation in individual cases to a quasi-constitutional jurisdiction, and the reaction of constitutional courts to this evolution. Section 2.2 retraces the progressive expansion of the applicability of Article 6 ECHR to constitutional proceedings and its evolution from a provision simply enshrining an individual right, to a transformative tool of constitutional justice systems. Section 2.3 is instead devoted to photographing the relationship in its quantitative dimensions. With the support of charts, this Section presents statistical evidence concerning the presence of constitutional courts in the ECtHR case law and draws some preliminary conclusions from the observation of those data.

The central part of the book contains an assessment of the Strasbourg Court's relationship with European constitutional courts. In light of the sheer volume of judgments under consideration, an approach based on the individual analysis of the relationship with each constitutional court has been adopted for the sake of clarity. In particular, Chap. 3 is dedicated to the constitutional courts of consolidated democracies of Western Europe. Chapter 4 instead illustrates the relationship of the Strasbourg Court with the constitutional courts of the new democracies of Central and Eastern Europe. Each Section, which is accompanied by charts illustrating the citations' patterns, contains a brief explanation of the national system of constitutional justice, as well as an assessment of the relationship based on the most significant cases decided by the ECtHR.

Chapter 5 provides an overall assessment of how the ECtHR interacts with national constitutional courts. In particular, Sect. 5.1 identifies the factors shaping the relationship between the ECtHR and national constitutional courts. Section 5.2 creates categories to classify the various patterns and techniques followed by the ECtHR in the citation of constitutional judgments, whilst Sect. 5.3 assesses the extent of the procedural subordination of constitutional proceedings to Article 6 ECHR and defines the essential components of a fair constitutional trial. Section 5.4 instead considers the relationship outside the framework of Article 34 ECHR, and especially the potential of Protocol 16 ECHR to become the primary channel of dialogue between constitutional judges and European ones.

Finally, Chap. 6, taking stock of the jurisprudential developments observed, it illustrates how the ECtHR is currently framing its role vis-à-vis constitutional courts (Sect. 6.1). Finally, Sect. 6.2 speculates on the future direction of the constitutionalising narrative in the ECtHR case law, especially in light of the transformation of Article 6 into a meta-norm capable of informing all aspects of the constitutional justice system. Assessing wha will be considered, as well as the prospective impact of the entry into force of Protocol 16 ECHR on the relationship between constitutional judges and European ones.

1.4 Methodological Issues

As a final step before embarking on this task, it is necessary to briefly illustrate the methodology adopted to carry out the empirical research by clarifying the criteria used to delimit the pool of decisions and courts and defining all the practical aspects typical of an empirical study. The first methodological aspect to be clarified is which judgments of the ECtHR have been included in our research. Those are the judgments the Chambers and the Grand Chamber of the Court issued on individual complaints under Article 34 ECHR. In the context of Article 34 ECHR procedure, the Court may issue two types of pronouncements: judgments (*'ârrets'*) and decisions (*'décisions'*). However, neither the text of the Convention nor the Rules of Procedure of the Court expressly distinguish between these two types of acts. On the contrary, Article 45 of the Convention imposes the same degree of motivational burden on both.[20] Ultimately, the main distinguishing criterion appears to be that when the Court rules on the merits of an appeal, it always does so with a judgment, whereas decisions are essentially used for declaring the inadmissibility of applications.[21] For this reason, as well as the fact that judgments are usually more richly reasoned than decisions, the research has been conducted only on judgements.

Within the category of judgments, distinctions can be made with regard to the composition of the adjudicating body. The formations of the Court empowered to pronounce judgments are the Grand Chamber,[22] the Chambers of seven judges,[23] and the Committees of three judges, the latter bodies being an articulation of the

[20] Further blurring this distinction is the 'nonchalance' with which the Court has resorted indifferently to judgments or decisions in cases of removal from the register by friendly settlement. Even though Article 39 ECHR is unequivocal in stating that "In the event of an amicable settlement, the Court shall remove the action from the register using a decision limiting itself to a brief statement of the facts and the solution adopted", the European Court has often declared a *friendly settlement to* have been reached by a judgment. A search of the Court's database shows that since 1981, the Court has declared a case to be removed from the register pursuant to Article 39 ECHR 794 times by judgment. This practice of the Court does not appear to be justified in light of the Rules of Procedure which, in all its versions, have always required the adoption of a decision when a case is removed from the register to reach an amicable settlement of the dispute. For further details, see above, fn 1.

[21] Another minor differentiating element can be found in the Rules of Procedure, which allow judges to have their dissenting or concurring opinion annotated only to judgments. See Art. 74-2 *Rules of Procedure of the Court.*

[22] The Grand Chamber, whose composition is governed by Rule 24 of the Rules of Procedure, consists of 17 sitting judges and three substitutes. Members by right are the President of the Court, the Vice-President, and the judge of the nationality of the respondent State. The remaining 15 members are determined by drawing lots unless there has been a referral by a Chamber, in which case the seven judges of the Chamber will also sit on the bench.

[23] The Sections are the entities into which the Court's administrative structure is divided, thus not exercising judicial functions. Their composition, which must be balanced in geographical terms and reflect the different legal systems of the Member States, is fixed for a period of 3 years by the full Court—itself a body without judicial functions - on a proposal by the President of the Court. Each of them has a President who, in accordance with Article 25 of the Rules of Procedure, is responsible for drawing lots to select the judges who make up the Chambers. This draw is made on a rotational

structure of the chamber.[24] Concerning the three-judges committee, Article 28(3) ECHR provides that they may only rule on the merits of an appeal if the "question concerning the interpretation or application of the Convention or its Protocols at the origin of the case is the subject of settled case-law of the Court". This limitation, as well as the Committee's obligation to adopt its judgments unanimously,[25] inevitably results in a reduction of the reasoning apparatus to a mere reference to the Court's relevant precedents. Therefore, it was decided to analyse only the judgments delivered in Article 34 ECHR procedure by the Grand Chamber and the Chambers of the Court.

As a final point, since the research covers all the case law of the Court since its foundation, it is necessary to briefly illustrate the set-up of the Court before the entry into force of Protocol No. 11, which established the Court as a permanent jurisdiction. In a nutshell, and for what is most relevant here, the procedure before the *Vieille Cour* was characterised by the filtering function performed by the Commission, the only body competent to receive appeals.[26] Since the Commission only had the competence to declare appeals admissible or inadmissible,[27] in accordance with what was established for decisions in general, its decisions were not analysed.[28] As to the Court, there were only two court formations before Protocol 11: the Chamber[29] and the Plenary Court.[30] For the purposes of our research, the judgments delivered by both these compositions were taken into consideration.

basis, except for the judge of the nationality of the respondent State who, together with the President of the Chamber, is a member ex officio. See Mowbray (2012), p. 18.

[24] More in detail on the organisation of the Court and the court formations see: Mezzetti and Pizzolo (2013), p. 103.

[25] When no agreement can be reached within the panel, the appeal is forwarded to a Chamber. The procedure for dealing with the appeal, as well as an explanation of the reasons for the introduction of committees, can be found in: Mowbray (2012), p. 48.

[26] It is worth recalling that until the entry into force of Protocol No. 9 on 1 October 1994, claimants did not have the right to bring proceedings directly before the Court, whose jurisdiction, under former Article 44 ECHR, could only be activated by the Commission and the Contracting Parties. For a detailed reconstruction of the operation of the pre-Protocol 11 complaints procedure, see: Macdonald et al. (1993), pp. 605–801.

[27] For an illustration of the role and functions of the body, see: Schermers (1990).

[28] Moreover, the Commission's decisions, especially when considered in relation to those of the current Court, are characterised by the brevity of the reasoning, which is completely absent in admissibility decisions, since if the application was admissible, the Commission was later obliged to draw up a *report* on the merits of the appeal, which was forwarded to the Court or the Committee of Ministers. For more detail on the procedure before the Commission, see: Lodigiani (1969); and Monconduit (1959).

[29] The Chamber initially consisted of 7 judges and following the reform of the Rules of Procedure by 9, was the ordinary court of the Court. For more detail on the procedure before the Court see: Jacobs and White (1975).

[30] The Plenary Court, composed of 16 judges, was replaced in October 1993, through the amendment of Rule 50 of the Rules of Procedure, by a Grand Chamber, with the same functions but composed of 19 judges. See van Dijk and van Hoff (1998), p. 34.

The second preparatory step has been identifying which courts to include in our sample. In order to do that, we adopted a working definition of constitutional court as a body separate from the judiciary that exercises *exclusively* the judicial review of legislation with judgments having *erga omnes* effects.[31]

If we apply this definition to the constitutional and highest jurisdictions of the Council of Europe Member States, it is possible to come to a sufficiently clear selection. First of all, it is possible to exclude from our research the supreme courts of Cyprus, Denmark, Estonia, Finland, Greece, Ireland, Iceland, Malta, Monaco, Netherlands, Norway, Sweden, and the United Kingdom.[32]

However, there remain some cases of uncertainty, above all, the case of the Estonian Supreme Court. Under Article 148 of the Estonian Constitution, the Supreme Court is in fact the only court of last resort. However, the power of *judicial review*—granted to the Supreme Court by Article 152(2) of the Constitution[33]—is exercised by a specialised Chamber composed of nine members elected for 5 years by the Supreme Court *en banc*.[34] Therefore, it would not be entirely out of logic to claim, as some authors do, that it is a separate body.[35] Be that as it may, in order to avoid an arbitrary selection of the relevant cases, it has been decided to exclude the Estonian Supreme Court from our pool.

---

[31]This definition is essentially the minimal definition of a constitutional courts of the Kelsenian model, unanimously accepted in constitutional scholarship. Amongst many see: Cappelletti (1970), pp. 1050–1051.

[32]The exclusion of those courts, as well as other supreme jurisdictions such as the French Court of Cassation, from our research is not without consequences, as in many instances, the dialogue between those courts and the Strasbourg Court has been constitutional in nature. Sometimes, those dialogues have inspired constitutional courts: consider for instances the similarities between the 2009 *Horncastle* judgment of the United Kingdom Supreme Court and judgment 49/2015 of the Italian Constitutional Court, both essentially affirming that not every decision of the ECtHR is binding for national judges. More extensively on the point, see, Martinico (2012), in particular, pp. 421–423.

[33]According to which 'The Supreme Court declares invalid any law or other legislation or administrative decision that is in conflict with the letter and spirit of the Constitution'. All the texts of the Constitutions and Constitutional Court laws cited in the course of this chapter have been consulted, in their English translations, on the 'Codices' database of legislation and case law maintained by the Venice Commission (http://www.codices.coe.int/NXT/gateway.dll?f=templates&fn=default.htm), or alternatively on the official websites of the governments of the various countries.

[34]This peculiarity—a *unicum* in the panorama of European legal systems and closely reminiscent of the *Salas constitucionales* of Latin American countries - does not seem to be due to a conscious choice of the Estonian constituent, but rather to the fact that, at the time when the Constitution was written, there were not enough cases to justify the establishment of a specialised court. See Schwartz (2000), p. 253.; Sadurski (2014), p. 13.

[35]Sadurski even states that 'in the overall constitutional system and, for all practical purposes, the Estonian Chamber can be viewed as a separate constitutional court, like any other in the region'. See Sadurski (2014)

Conversely, there are no doubts, although the debate on its jurisdictional character has not yet died down,[36] as to whether the *Conseil Constitutionnel* should be included in the search, especially following the introduction of the "Question Prioritaire de Constitutionnalité", which gave the *Conseil constitutionnel* the competence to review the constitutional legitimacy of primary legislation also incidentally.[37]

However, adopting a purely normative criterion, looking exclusively at the constitutional courts' formal powers and competencies as resulting from the texts of Constitutions and other primary laws has the obvious limitation of not being able to take into account the political system in which the Constitutional Court is called upon to operate. Considering that within the Council of Europe a consistent number of countries cannot be considered fully democratic,[38] it appeared necessary to restrict our research to those constitutional courts that can exercise effectively their jurisdiction,[39] conversely excluding those that are just 'sham' constitutional organs.

This led us to the exclusion in the first place of the constitutional courts of Azerbaijan, Russia, and Turkey. With regard to the Turkish Constitutional Court, it was decided to exclude it from our sample, as a proper analysis of the relationship between the two courts implies, in light of the troubled history of Turkish democracy, a continuous contextualisation of the ECtHR judgments, an operation that is, however, beyond the scope of this work. Moreover, the authoritarian drift following the failed coup of 15 July 2016, watched helplessly by the Strasbourg Court, and the

[36] For an exposition of the thesis according to which the Conseil constitutionnel's control has a jurisdictional character and a contestation of the main criticisms of this assumption see: Badinter (2009), pp. 2–3.

[37] More on the functioning of the French incidental constitutional appeal, see: Carcassonne et al. (2015); Rousseau (2012).

[38] According to the 2022 EIU Democracy Index, within the Council of Europe, there are just 13 countries can be considered full democracies, with a majority of states that are flawed democracies (27) and 6 hybrid regimes. See: EIU Democracy Index 2022. Frontline Democracy and Battle for Ukraine, 5. Available at: https://www.eiu.com/n/campaigns/democracy-index-2022/?utm_source=google&utm_medium=paid-search&utm_campaign=democracy-index-2022&gclid=Cj0KCQjw8qmhBhClARIsANAtbodHv9zfpk1_Pp_J0C5BwgQ-sw1cU-e_B9g0S0ta93ok0aQI8e3kOeMaAs63EALw_wcB#mktoForm_anchor.

[39] This notion, the effectiveness of judicial review of legislation, has been developed by political and constitutional doctrine to assess the performance of a Constitutional Court, i.e., essentially, the compliance of political actors, and in particular the governing majority, with the decisions of the Constitutional Court. The parameters for assessing the effectiveness of a constitutional jurisdiction are rather debated in doctrine. One part of the doctrine holds that a constitutional jurisdiction can be said to be effective only if three conditions are met: (1) the willingness on the part of public and private subjects to have recourse to the Court; (2) the presence of adequately motivated constitutional case law (3) the acceptance by constitutional bodies that the meaning of the Constitution is determined at least in part by the interpretative activity of constitutional judges. See: Stone Sweet (2012), p. 826. Other authors propose instead to measure the effectiveness of a constitutional court on the basis of a more qualitative criterion, i.e. the degree of correspondence between the Court's decisions and the principles of the Constitution and good governance in general; as well as—and on this there is unanimity—whether the Court's decisions are actually implemented. See Harding et al. (2008), pp. 18–19.

arrest of the two constitutional judges,[40] constituted the last nails in the coffin of the constitutional court's independence and autonomy. As to the Russian Constitutional Court, from its very first days by then-President Yeltsin nipped its inpendendence in the bud, suspending its activities for some 17 months and then proceeding to '*court-packing*'.[41] The Russian Constitutional Court would never recover its independence. Similarly, it is also superfluous to analyse the relationship with the Azerbaijani Constitutional Court, as it essentially continuously operated in an authoritarian regime.[42] Similarly, the constitutional courts of Armenia, Georgia, Moldova and Ukraine will be excluded from our analysis. All these countries face threats of different gravity to their existence as independent states, and generally have a problematic record of human rights protection.[43] For these very reasons, the effectiveness of the constitutional courts' role as the ultimate guarantor of fundamental rights is, at the very least, doubtful.

Also, looking at the domestic situations of some Central Eastern European Countries, and in particular, Hungary and Poland, the government's desire to keep the Constitutional Court under pressure is manifest. In Poland, it all began in 2015 when the government prevented the publication of the judgments of the Constitutional Court for more than 6 months and subsequently curtailed its independence by appointing friendly judges.[44] In Hungary, since the landslide victory of Fidesz in 2010, the parliamentary majority has gradually eroded the prerogatives of the Court—which before the reforms of Prime Minister Orbán's reforms, was considered one of the most powerful courts in the world[45]—by removing numerous types

[40] The two judges were the first public servants to have been removed in execution of the emergency decrees of 2016. On this point, see: Perilli (2017), in particular p. 276; available at: http://www.associazionemagistrati.it/rivista/numeri/nm_5.pdf.

The author also emphasises the strong symbolic content of this decision as since 2013, the Constitutional Court had been trying to put a stop to the authoritarian turn attempted by President Erdoğan.

[41] A detailed and interesting reconstruction of the early years of the Russian Constitutional Court through the figure of its President can be found in: Scheppele (2006), p. 1757.

[42] According to Freedom House's 2024 report, Azerbaijan is a "consolidated authoritarian regime." The Report notes that ever since 1990 international observers have not considered elections credible or competitive and that in recent years civil liberties has been further shrunk by the Alyev' regime. See: https://freedomhouse.org/country/azerbaijan/freedom-world/2024.

[43] In the 2024 Freedom House Report, all those 4 countries, classify as "not free". See, https://freedomhouse.org/explore-the-map?type=fiw&year=2024.

[44] This situation was harshly criticised by the Venice Commission, that stressed how the refusal to publish the judgments negatively impacted on the independence of the body and thus on the rule of law. See CDL-AD(2016)026, *Opinion on the Law on the Constitutional Tribunal*, Adopted by the Venice Commission at its 108th Plenary Session (Venice, 14–15 October 2016), paras. 74–101. For an accurate description of the political climate created around the Constitutional Tribunal and its developments see: Szymielewicz (2016).

[45] This view, shared by a large part of the doctrine, referred as much to the Court's broad jurisdiction as to the breadth of the subjects who could address it, as well as to the concrete ways in which it exercised its powers, resorting to jurisprudential notions such as that of the 'invisible constitution'. See Blokker (2014), pp. 62–63.

of legislative acts from its review of constitutionality and restricting the avenues to go before the court.[46]

Even though the above circumstances undoubtedly impaired the ability of these courts to exercise a counter-majoritarian and fundamental rights protection function,[47] this does not diminish the usefulness of a research analysing the relationship between these courts and Strasbourg. First, because Hungary and Poland are Member States of the European Union, and this has insofar prevented the two countries from backsliding into fully-fledged authoritarianism.[48] Second, analysing the ECtHR judgments dealing with the precedents of those two courts permits assessing how the Strasbourg Court reacted to the capture of constitutional courts by populist majorities.[49]

In conclusion, the courts on which we will conduct our research are the constitutional jurisdictions of: Albania, Andorra, Austria, Belgium, Bosnia and Herzegovina, Bulgaria, Croatia, Czechia, France, Germany, Hungary, Italy, Latvia, Lithuania, Luxembourg, Montenegro, Northern Macedonia, Poland, Portugal, Romania, Serbia, Slovakia, Slovenia, and Spain.

Finally, the last step has been to address the research's practical aspects, such as the research engine and the keywords used, taking into account the Court's bilingualism. In fact, as most of the ECtHR judgments are drafted in only one of the two official languages, some adjustments were necessary.

The research has been conducted on the search engine of the ECtHR, HUDOC.[50] The research covered all the judgments delivered under Article 34 ECHR from the Court's first judgment in *Lawless v. Ireland (no.1)*, until the 31 of December 2022. For the sake of simplicity, the research has been conducted on each constitutional court included in the research separately, i.e. restricting the search to one respondent state at the time.

The main issue concerned the Court's bilingualism. In fact, although French and English are the two official languages of the ECtHR, the Court does not publish all its judgments in both languages, on the contrary judgments are normally published in just one of the two languages.[51] In order to obtain a complete set of data it was

---

[46] On the new structure of the Hungarian Constitutional Court and a brief analysis of recent case law, see: Paczolay (2015).

[47] Among the several academic contributions on the subject, a broad overview is offered by: Blokker (2014), pp. 62–62; for a focus on Hungary and Romania see von Bogdandy and Sonnevend (2015).

[48] Even though the European Union has been considered also a main propellent of populist rhetoric across Europe, even the fiercest critics of the EU approach to populism, concede that EU membership is a guarantee against a more severe authoritarian drift in the two countries. See: Adamski (2019).

[49] In general, scarce attention has been devoted to this issue, as the literature has focused more on the instruments that the ECtHR has to fight populist rulers. See, for instance, Zysset (2022).

[50] https://hudoc.echr.coe.int/eng#{%22documentcollectionid2%22:[%22GRANDCHAMBER%22,%22CHAMBER%22]}.

[51] Articles 57 and 76 of the Rules of Procedure indeed provide, unless the Court decides otherwise, for the judgment to be published in only one of the two official languages. The only exception is the judgments of the Grand Chamber that are published with the words 'Done in english and *french*'

therefore decided to carry out the search using both ‘constitutional court’ and ‘cour constitutionnelle’ as keywords. Yet, after a preliminary check on each constitutional court included in the pool, it emerged that in the judgments delivered in French with Portugal and Spain as Respondent States, the ECtHR uses the term “tribunal constitutionnel”.[52] It was therefore decided to use the term ‘tribunal constitutionnel’ as an additional ‘keyword’.[53] Conversely, and somewhat bizarrely, the term “constitutional tribunal” is never used in English language judgments. As a last remark, with regard to the France constitutional jurisdiction the keywords “conseil constitutionnel” and “constitutional council” were used.

References

Adamski D (2019) The social contract of democratic backsliding in the “new EU” countries. Common Mark Law Rev 56:623–665

Arnardóttir OM, Buyse A (2016) Shifting centres of gravity in human rights protection. Rethinking relations between the ECHR, EU, and national legal orders. Routledge, London

Badinter R (2009) Une longue marche “Du Conseil à la Cour constitutionnelle”. Cahiers du Conseil constitutionnel 25:9

Berger V (2011) Les Cours constitutionnelles et la Cour européenne des droits de l’homme. Les Nouveaux Cahiers du Conseil constitutionnel 32:7–17

Blokker P (2014) New democracies in crisis? A comparative constitutional study of The Czech Republic, Hungary, Poland, Romania and Slovakia. Routledge, New York

Burgorgue Larsen L (2001) L’ “Autonomie constitutionnelle” aux prises avec la Convention européenne des droits de l’homme. Revue belge de droit constitutionnel 1:31–64

Cappelletti M (1970) Judicial review in comparative perspective. Calif Law Rev 58:1017–1053

Carcassonne G, Duhamel O, Dufy A (2015) QPC. La question prioritaire de constitutionnalité. Dalloz, Paris

Cartabia M (2016) Europe as a space of constitutional interdependence: new questions about the preliminary ruling. Germ Law J 16:1791–1796

Favoreu L (2004) Corti costituzionali nazionali e Corte europea dei diritti dell’uomo. Rivista di Diritto Costituzionale 1:3–24

Flauss JF (2003) Faut-il transformer la Cour européenne des droits de l'homme en juridiction constitutionnelle? Recueil Dalloz 25:1638–1645

(*Fait en français et en anglais*), thus attributing the same authoritative character to both versions and also not allowing one to distinguish the language in which the judgment was actually written.

[52] Out of 245 cases in which the term ‘Tribunal Constitutionnel’ is used, only in two cases is the term ‘Cour constitutionnelle’ used instead: Cf. Pellote *Pellon v. Espagne* (45238/99) 25/07/2002; *Melo Taddeu v. Portugal* (27785/10) 23/10/2014. Quite inexplicably, the Polish and German Constitutional Tribunals are always referred to as the “Cour constitutionnelle” in the judgments written in French.

[53] Conversely, and somewhat bizarrely, the term “constitutional tribunal” is never used in English language judgments. Indeed, a search throughout the Court’s jurisprudence of the string ‘constitutional tribunal’ yields three results: two relating to a case of the Inter-American Court of Human Rights and another consisting of the citation of a passage from the law on the Polish Constitutional Tribunal. See *Baka v. Hungary* (20261/12) 23/06/2016; *Magyar Helsinki Bizottság v. Hungary* (18030/11), 08/11/16; *Kozak v. Poland* (13102/02), 02/03/2010.

Harding A, Leyland P, Groppi T (2008) Constitutional courts. Journal of Comparative Law 2:1–22
Helfner LR (2008) Redesigning the European court of human rights: embeddedness as a deep structural principle of the European human rights regime. Eur J Int Law 19:125–159
Jacobs FJ, White RCA (1975) The European convention on human rights, 2nd edn. Clarendon Press, Oxford
Kelle H, Stone Sweet A (2008) A Europe of rights. The impact of the ECHR on national legal system. Oxford University Press, Oxford
Kosar D, Petrov J (2017) The architecture of the Strasbourg system of human rights: the crucial role of the domestic level and the constitutional courts in particular. Zeitschrift für ausländisches öfentliches Recht und Völkerrecht 77:585–621
Lodigiani G (1969) La commissione nella convenzione europea dei diritti dell'uomo. Giuffrè, Milan
Macdonald RSJ, Matscher F, Petzold H (1993) The European system for the protection of human rights. Nijhoff, Dordrecht
Martinico G (2012) Is the European convention going to be 'supreme'? A comparative-constitutional overview of ECHR and EU law before National Courts. Eur J Int Law 23:421–424
Martinico G (2016) National Courts and judicial disobedience to the ECHR: a comparative overview. In: Arnardóttir OM, Buyse A (eds) Shifting centres of gravity in human rights protection. Routledge, London, pp 59–78
Martinico G, Pollicino O (2010) The National Judicial treatment of the ECHR and EU laws. Europa Law Publisher, Groningen
Mezzetti L, Pizzolo C (2013) Diritto processuale dei diritti umani. Maggioli, Rimini
Monconduit F (1959) La Commission Européenne des Droits de l'Homme.A.W. Sijthoff Leiden
Mowbray A (2012) Cases, materials and commentary on the European Convention on Human Rights. Oxford University Press, Oxford
Paczolay P (2015) The transformation of the constitutional court in Hungary. In: Szente Z et al (eds) Challenges and pitfalls in the recent Hungarian constitutional development. Harmattan, Paris, pp 167–182
Perilli L (2017) Stato di diritto, l'indipendenza della magistratura e la protezione dei diritti fondamentali: La tragica deriva della Turchia dal 2013. La Magistratura 1-2:239–278
Pernice I (1999) Multilevel constitutionalism and the treaty of Amsterdam: European constitution-making revisited? Common Mark Law Rev 36:703–750
Petrov J (2018) Unpacking the partnership: typology of constitutional courts' roles in implementation of the European court of human rights' case law. Eur Const Law Rev 14:499–531
Popelier P, van der Heyning C, van Nuffel P (2011) Human rights protection in the European legal order: the interaction between the European and the national courts. Intersentia, Cambridge
Rousseau D (2012) Question Prioritaire de Constitutionnalité. Lextenso, Paris
Ruggeri A (2011) Sovranità dello Stato e sovranità sovranazionale, attraverso i diritti umani, e prospettive di un diritto europeo "intercostituzionale". Diritto pubblico comparato ed europeo 2: 544–561
Sadurski W (2014) Rights before courts. A study of constitutional courts in Postcommunist states of central and Eastern Europe. Springer, Heidelberg
Sap JW (2020) Double standards. The political character of international human rights. NTKR, Tijdschrift voor Recht en Religie 2:197–214
Scheppele KL (2006) Guardians of the constitution: constitutional court presidents and the struggle for the rule of law in post-soviet Europe. Univ Pa Law Rev 154:1757–1851
Schermers HG (1990) The European Commission of human rights from the inside. Hull University Press, Hull
Schwartz H (2000) The struggle for constitutional justice in post-communist Europe. Chicago University Press, Chicago
Stone Sweet A (2012) Constitutional courts. In: Oxford handbook of comparative constitutional law. Oxford University Press, Oxford, pp 816–830

Szymczak D (2007) Ła Convention Européenne des droits de l'homme et le juge constitutionnel national. Bruylant, Bruxelles

Szymielewicz K (2016) Poland after November 2015: the end of the rule of law or a phase of radical democracy. In: Morillas P (ed) Illiberal democracies in the EU: the Visegrad group and the risk of disintegration. Cidob Edicions, Barcelona, p 55

van Dijk P, van Hoff GJH (1998) Theory and practice of the European convention on human rights. Kluwer Law International, The Hague

von Bogdandy A, Sonnevend P (2015) Constitutional crisis in the European constitutional area. Hart Publishing, Oxford

Zysset A (2022) Calibrating the response to populism at the European court of human rights. Int J Const Law 20:976–1005

Chapter 2
The Relationship Between Strasbourg and Constitutional Courts. Qualitative and Quantitative Dimensions

2.1 The Quest of the Strasbourg Court for a Role in the European Legal Space

During its first 30 years of activity, the role and nature of the ECtHR were not a matter for discussion, and in general, its trajectory was considered a 'success story'.[1] However, as it often happens, the Strasbourg Court was bound to become a 'victim of its own success'.[2] A turning point was undoubtedly the dissolution of the USSR and the subsequent former communist countries' rush to join the European Union and the Council of Europe: during this process, the Council of Europe almost doubled its size, with 19 Central and Eastern European States joining in a ten-year span, from 1992 to 2002.[3]

This enlargement of the CoE towards the East faced the Court with a whole new spectrum of human rights issues, completely different from those affecting the more consolidated Western democracies. The accession of countries with little to no democratic tradition indeed obliged the Strasbourg Court to deal with structural

Supplementary Information The online version contains supplementary material available at https://doi.org/10.1007/978-3-031-71268-5_2.

[1] Zwaak and Cachia (2004), p. 53; Drzemczewski (2000).

[2] The expression has been used by many authors to describe the crisis faced by the Court during the '90s. See, amongst many: Turnbull (1995).

[3] Those are: Albania (1996); Armenia (2022); Bulgaria (1992); Bosnia and Herzegovina (2022); Croatia (1997); Czech Republic (1993); Estonia (1996); Georgia (1999); Hungary (1992); Latvia (1997); Lithuania (1995); North Macedonia (1997); Poland (1993); Republic of Moldova (1997); Romania (1994); Russia (1996); Slovakia (1993); Slovenia (1994); Ukraine (1997). The dates of ratification and entry into force can be consulted at: https://www.coe.int/en/web/conventions/full-list?module=signatures-by-treaty&treatynum=005. All the links were last accessed on the 30 of June 2024.

M. A. Simonelli, *The European Court of Human Rights and Constitutional Courts*, Ius Gentium: Comparative Perspectives on Law and Justice 120,
https://doi.org/10.1007/978-3-031-71268-5_2

and systemic violations of human rights related to the ongoing processes of transition to democracy, like in the landmark judgement in *Broniowski v. Poland*,[4] and in some cases, with the manifest failures of such transitions.[5]

These historical developments were accompanied by a substantially continuous process of institutional reform affecting the Strasbourg Court, which formally began in 1994 with the approval of Protocol 11 ECHR, which transformed the ECtHR into a permanent court, simultaneously introducing the possibility for individuals to directly apply to the Court.[6]

The combined effect of the CoE's expansion and the introduction of an individual direct appeal provoked an uncontrollable growth in the number of applications received every year. If in its first 40 years of activities, a total of approximately 45,000 applications were allocated for decision, in the 5 years following the entry into force of Protocol 11—from 1999 to 2003—the applications allocated by the ECtHR were more than 90,000, i.e. more than double the figure for the period 1958–1998.[7]

To try to remedy this situation, a new Protocol (n. 14) was adopted in 2004 to give the Court the instruments to manage such a massive inflow of cases. First, through a reform of Article 35 ECHR, individual access to the Court was restricted by introducing the requirement that the application must show a 'significant disadvantage' allegedly suffered by the applicant, thus cutting out petty cases. Second, two new judging formations were instituted: the single judge to deal with clearly inadmissible cases (Article 27 ECHR), and the three-judges committee, entrusted to decide cases concerning matters where there is a well-established case law (Article 28 ECHR).[8] The capability of Protocol 14 to address the issue of the excessive caseload was immediately questioned, in the academia,[9] but also by its very drafters: already in 2005—5 years before Protocol 14 entered into force—the High Contracting Parties meeting in Warsaw set in motion a process for elaborating "a comprehensive strategy to secure the effectiveness of the [ECHR] system in the longer term".[10]

---

[4] *Broniowski v Poland* (31443/96), 22/07/2004. On the case law of the ECtHR concerning transitional justice see, Brems (2011).

[5] This is surely the case of Russia, where the failure of democratic transition became evident soon after the accession to the CoE. On Russia's membership in the CoE see: Bowring (2000).

[6] For a wider commentary on the content of this Protocol see: Bernhardt (1995).

[7] All the data were retrieved in the report prepared by the ECtHR for its 50 anniversary. See: European Court of Human Rights, 50 Years of Activity: *The European Court of Human Rights - Some Facts and Figures*, Strasbourg, 2010. Available at: https://www.echr.coe.int/documents/facts_figures_1959_2009_eng.pdf.

[8] More extensively on the elements of novelty introduced by Protocol 14 see: Beernaert (2004).

[9] See: Beernaert (2004), pp. 555–557.

[10] Warsaw Declaration of the Heads of State and Government of the Member States of the Council of Europe, 16–17 May 2005, in particular, para. 2. Available at: https://www.coe.int/t/dcr/summit/20050517_decl_varsovie_en.asp.

This impetus culminated in the adoption of Protocols 15 and 16, which entered into force on 1 August 2021 and 1 August 2018 respectively. Whilst Protocol 15 added, amongst other things, a new Recital at the end of the Preamble to the Convention explicitly recognising the principle of subsidiarity and the States' margin of appreciation, Protocol 16 introduced a new consultative procedure with which the highest national jurisdictions could ask the ECtHR interpretative questions.[11]

Those institutional reforms all seemed to indicate a shift in the functioning and role of the ECtHR which, at least in the idea of the High Contracting Parties, should have been less concerned with the task of redressing individual injustices, to focus on the most significant cases that contribute to the definition of European common standards.[12] This shift was in parallel accompanied by two developments in the Strasbourg case law, which form part of what has been labelled a 'systemic turn' in the ECtHR case law.[13]

First, the Court embracement of the renewed subsidiarity endorsed by the Brighton Declaration, by providing a new interpretation of Article 13 ECHR in the landmark judgment *Kudla v. Poland*.[14] The Court, after affirming the breach of Article 6(1) ECHR as regards the excessive length of a proceeding, went on to also declare the violation of Article 13 ECHR, insofar as no effective domestic remedies were deemed to exist for the applicant to seek relief for unreasonable delays of proceedings. The significance of this judgment is at least twofold.[15] On the one hand, *Kudla* may be interpreted as a Court attempt to shift the focus of its supervisory role from providing remedies in individual cases, to one in which its scrutiny is concentrated on assessing the adequacy of the system of remedies put in place at the national level.[16] But, more importantly, the Court held that the lack of effective national procedures for protecting ECHR rights may alone result in a violation of Article 13 ECHR, essentially affirming the existence of a procedural obligation inherent in all the ECHR Articles:[17] insofar as all the ECHR Articles can be

[11] On the functioning of this procedure and its potential for reducing the Court's backlog and improving the relationship with constitutional courts see: Lemmens (2019); Dzehtsiarou and O'Meara (2014); Voland and Schiebel (2017).

[12] Flauss (2003), p. 1638.

[13] Harmsen (2007), pp. 41–50.

[14] 30210/96, *Kudla v. Poland* (GC) 26/10/2000.

[15] The significance of this judgment, however, is not limited to this aspect, being also a fundamental decision in the field of prisoners' rights. On this point see: Tulkens (2004).

[16] Harmsen (2007), p. 44.

[17] According to some authors, the European Court of Justice in *Associação Sindical dos Juízes Portugueses* (C-64/16) carried out a similar operation. Here, the Court of Justice affirmed that Article 19(1)TEU contains positive obligation for Member States to ensure effective remedies in all the fields 'covered by EU law'. However, the Court of Justice insofar has not yet found a violation of Article 19(1) TEU caused by lack of effective remedies. For a commentary to the judgment focused on the procedural obligations stemming from Article 19(1) TEU see: Pech and Platon (2018).

considered as containing an implicit procedural obligation, all individuals shall be able to fully assert their rights under the Convention in the legal order of the Member States in accordance with the principle of subsidiarity hence, at least in theory, reducing the number of cases reaching Strasbourg.[18]

A second development is the introduction of the much-discussed 'pilot judgment procedure', aimed at dealing with structural problems in the protection of fundamental rights at the national level. This procedure has its legal basis in a 2004 recommendation of the Committee of Ministers.[19] Even though this recommendation fell short of constituting a solid legal basis,[20] the ECtHR promptly seized on the opportunity, delivering its first pilot judgment on 22 June 2004 in the case of *Broniowski v Poland*.[21] Albeit elements of uncertainties remain as to what differentiates a pilot judgment from an ordinary one, especially as regards their effects—which under Article 46 ECHR should be the same—the characterising element of a pilot judgment can be identified in the fact the Court does not limit itself to identify and sanction the problem that has given rise to a violation of the ECHR (in a high number of cases) but also prescribes the measures which the State shall implement to remedy the problem.[22] In essence, as Judge Zagrebelsky put it, the ECtHR with a pilot judgment asks the national government to "change the national system in law and in practice. Nothing more, nothing less".[23] It is thus evident that the pilot-judgment procedure cannot be interpreted just as an attempt by the Court to gain control of its docket, rather, looking at the greater picture of institutional and jurisprudential innovations, one is compelled to look at it as a part of a wider tendency towards a constitutionalisation of the ECtHR.[24] In the same sense, it has been observed how, also outside pilot judgment procedures, the ECtHR has progressively abandoned its classical approach to remedial measures,[25] focused on adjudicating an ECHR violation in a specific case, in favour of a strategy indicating to the Respondent State the general measures to be adopted in order to redress the violation and prevent future breaches.[26]

---

[18] Flauss (2003), pp. 1639–1640.

[19] Res(2004)3, *Resolution of the Committee of Ministers on judgments revealing an underlying systemic problem,* adopted by the Committee of Ministers on 12 May 2004, at its 114th Session. The text of the resolution is available at: https://search.coe.int/cm/Pages/result_details.aspx?ObjectId=09000016805dd190.

[20] Paraskeva (2003), p. 7.

[21] *Broniowski v Poland*, 31443/96, 22/06/2004.

[22] In more details on the functioning of the pilot-judgment procedure see: Glas (2016), p. 43.

[23] *Lukenda v Slovenia* (23032/02), 06/10/2005, partly dissenting opinion of Judge Zagrebelsky, para. 6.

[24] In the last two decades, the constitutionalisation of the European Court of Human Rights has been one of the central issue in the literature on the Strasbourg Court. See for instance Ulfstein (2021); but also Greer and Wildhaber (2012); Stone Sweet (2009); Flauss (2003).

[25] Kosar and Petrov (2017), pp. 590–591.

[26] Sadurski refers to this kind of judgment as 'semi-pilot', characterised by the fact that the general measures to be adopted are indicated only in the reasoning and not in the operative part. See: Sadurski 2021. fn 16.

A further indication of the increased 'constitutional tone' of the ECtHR case law, comes from a series of cases decided during the '10s, which seemed to confirm that the Court was actually willing to go down this path. Two outstanding examples are represented by the judgments in *Anchugov v Russia* and *Baka v Hungary*,[27] decided by the Grand Chamber in 2013 and 2016, respectively. In both cases, the Court declared the incompatibility with the ECHR of domestic norms of constitutional rank despite the national constitutional courts had previously affirmed the opposite.[28] The significance of this move was highlighted by the concurring opinion of Pinto de Albuquerque in *Baka*, where it solemnly affirmed "urbi et orbi" that the majority has conferred to

> the Convention's supra-constitutional effect, in order to override the contradicting domestic constitutional provision. In so doing, the Court affirms itself *as the European Constitutional Court,* with the power to declare domestic constitutional provisions devoid of any legal effects within the relevant domestic legal order.[29]

Albeit, the Court strictly speaking never claimed the power of striking down legislation, in subsequent cases concerning core democratic and rule of law principles, it has sometimes carried out an abstract review of the conventionality of national legislation, acting as a *de facto* European Constitutional Court.[30] For instance in its 2021 judgment in *Xeroflor*,[31] the Court affirmed the illegality, according to both national and ECHR law, of the composition of the Polish Constitutional Tribunal. The ECtHR, in its first ruling delivered in the context of the Polish rule of law crisis, did what the European Court of Justice has always refrained from doing, i.e. declaring in straightforward terms that Polish courts do not comply with the requirements of a tribunal established by the law, depicting its role as a court of last resort for the protection not of individual injustices but of European constitutional principles.

All in all, from this case law it clearly emerges the intent of the Strasbourg Court to frame its role in the European legal space as that of a *sui generis* constitutional

---

[27] See: *Anchugov and Gladkov v Russia* (11157/04), (15162/05), 04/07/2013; *Baka v Hungary* (GC) (20261/12), 23/06/2016.

[28] For commentaries on the two cases focused on this aspect see: Abashidze et al. (2017); Kosar (2018); Simonelli (2019).

[29] *Baka v. Hungary*, Joint Concurring Opinion of Judges Pinto de Albuquerque and Dedov, para. 1 (italics added). In another concurring opinion annotated to the *Al Dulimi* judgment—delivered by the Grand Chamber just 2 days before *Baka*—Pinto de Albuquerque further elaborates on the constitutional nature of the Convention, and its effects vis-à-vis the United Nations System For a comment on this aspect of the opinion see: A. Peters, "The New Arbitrariness and Competing Constitutionalism: Remarks on ECtHR Grand Chamber Al-Dulimi", *EJIL:Talk! Blog of the European Journal of International Law*, 30 June 2016. Available at:https://www.ejiltalk.org/the-new-arbitrariness-and-competing-constitutionalisms-remarks-on-ecthr-grand-chamber-al-dulimi/.

[30] For a more extensive analysis of ECtHR cases supporting this conclusion see: Arcari and Ninatti (2017).

[31] *Xero Flor w Polsce sp. z o.o. v Poland* (4907/18), 07/05/2021.

jurisdiction,[32] capable of reviewing national law of any rank and eventually declaring its incompatibility with the Convention. Leaving aside the question of whether such a claim can be considered well-founded,[33] this jurisprudential evolution has significant implications for the ECtHR relationship with national constitutional courts.

Most importantly, a narrative of constitutionalisation entails the establishment of a hierarchy amongst European judges, according to which the Strasbourg Court ceases to be just one of the actors in the European scenario, a *primus inter pares*, to acquire the role of a European constitutional court, hierarchically superior to national constitutional courts. This attempt to frame the relationship with constitutional courts in a vertical rather than horizontal direction relies on the assumption that constitutional courts accept the scrutiny over their decisions by the ECtHR and are ready to amend their case law if found incompatible with the Convention. Yet, accepting the ECtHR scrutiny would ultimately mean recognising the supremacy of the ECHR over the national constitution, something that European constitutional courts insofar refrained to do.[34] Also, in the trend towards a hierarchisation of the relationship, there is an inherent risk of shrinking the space for constructive dialogue between the two courts, which manifested with particular intensity with respect to the constitutional courts of new democracies.[35] As a matter of fact, the straightforward affirmation of the ECHR's superiority over the national constitution and declarations of unconventionality of constitutional judgments, have insofar regarded only Members States from Central and Eastern Europe.[36] In any case, given the impossibility for the ECtHR to quash national legislation, in order to have an unconventional norm expelled from the domestic legal system, the judges in Strasbourg have to trust that national authorities, i.e. the constitutional courts, will do that. To put it more bluntly, under the current ECHR Treaty framework, the ECtHR may transform into something closer to a European constitutional court only in the measure that national constitutional courts will allow this transformation to happen.

Yet, it comes as no surprise that this constitutionalising process was met with some hesitancies by national constitutional courts, jealous to protect their monopoly in the judicial review of legislation, and the supremacy of the Constitution, even if this may imply challenging the legal status of the ECtHR judgments in domestic legal systems and the same authority of the Strasbourg Court to interpret the Convention. The following pages will be devoted to illustrating those challenges, but also the concrete manners through which national constitutional courts may collaborate with the ECtHR.

[32] The expression is taken from: Flauss (2003), p. 1640.

[33] The academic debate on the topic is rather extensive. See, above, fn 74.

[34] Martinico (2012), pp. 419–422.

[35] This risk was already perceived almost 20 years ago by Favoreu, who criticised the Strasbourg Court for being excessively paternalistic towards constitutional courts of new democracies. See: Favoreu (2004) above fn 11,18.1.

[36] Conversely, it is striking to note the more conciliatory attitude of the Strasbourg judges in the confrontation with the Italian Constitutional Court. See, below, Ch. 3, 1.3.

2.2 The Constitutional Courts and Strasbourg. Between Loyal Cooperation and Judicial Disobedience

Constitutional courts occupy a prominent space in the European legal space, and especially in the ECHR system, as they are often responsible for determining the status of the Convention in the national hierarchy of norms,[37] for the transposition in the national legal systems of ECtHR-made standards, and for controlling in the first place the conventionality of State's actions.[38] In the narrative of European multilevel constitutionalism, constitutional courts are often described as the most important domestic allies of the Strasbourg Court, decisively contributing to an 'ever-closer' embedment of the ECtHR case law into the domestic constitutional architecture.[39] However, it would be misleading to depict European constitutional jurisdictions as a monolithic bloc of courts loyally cooperating with Strasbourg, as virtually every national constitutional court had episodes of confrontation with the ECtHR, and some more than others. As a first approximation, two macro attitudes towards the case law of the ECtHR can be identified[40]: the first is an attitude of loyal cooperation and mutual reinforcement; the second is an attitude of defence and challenge.

2.2.1 *The Constitutional Courts as Allies of the ECtHR*

First and foremost, constitutional courts may cooperate with Strasbourg in implementing and promoting ECHR standards. This kind of cooperation, one of the distinguishing features of the European multilevel legal system,[41] produces a twofold effect. On the one hand, the reliance on international and supranational standards strengthens the position of the national constitutional court *vis-à-vis* the political majorities, on the other, it enhances the effectiveness of the ECHR, as constitutional courts are the institutions that are best placed to secure the execution of the ECtHR judgments in the domestic legal system.[42]

[37] In some CoE Member States, it is the same national constitution—e.g. Article 55 of the French Constitution that precise the status of the ECHR in the hierarchy of the sources of law. For an overview of ECHR reception in domestic legal orders see: Keller and Stone Sweet (2008), pp. 3–28.

[38] Although it is improper in the context of the Convention system to speak of a conventionality control at the national level—as it is possible to do in the inter-American system—it is undeniable that constitutional courts are increasingly called upon to adjudicate on questions concerning the ECHR. Yet, a comprehensive investigation of the content and dynamics of conventionality control by constitutional courts is still missing. For a critique analysis of the conventionality control in IACHR system see: Tello Mendoza (2023).

[39] See, Kosar and Petrov (2017), p. 608; Sadurski (2009), pp. 397–398.

[40] For an overview of the constitutional courts' attitudes towards the Strasbourg Court see: Petrov (2018).

[41] van de Heyning (2013).

[42] Petrov (2018), p. 500.

A primary factor susceptible to influencing the relationship with the Strasbourg Court is the rank assigned to the ECHR in the national hierarchy of norms. In Austria, where the ECHR enjoys constitutional rank,[43] the Federal Constitutional Tribunal has a constitutional mandate to interpret constitutional fundamental rights in light of the Convention, it is thus unsurprising that the *Verfsassungsgericht* figures amongst the most engaged jurisdictions with the ECtHR case law.[44] An increased engagement with the ECHR can also be observed if the national constitution provides for a clause obliging to interpret fundamental rights in accordance with international human rights law, e.g. Article 20 of the Romanian Constitution and Article 10.2 of the Spanish Constitution, both affirming that the provisions concerning fundamental rights must be interpreted in conformity with human rights treaties ratified by the State.[45] Concerning the Spanish case, the Tribunal Constitutional, since its first judgments, interpreted this provision as attributing to the ECHR the status of a hermeneutic criterion of "decisive relevance",[46] thus making the ECtHR case law 'an outstanding benchmark' for fundamental rights protection.[47] Despite all that, the *Tribunal Constitutional* always refrained from affirming that the Convention may function as an autonomous parameter in constitutionality review,[48] whilst it conceded that international human rights, in general, constitute a constitutionally 'mandatory interpretative parameter'.[49]

Despite the lack of constitutional status, some constitutional courts have integrated the ECHR, as interpreted by the Strasbourg Court, in the parameters of the judicial review of legislation: the Belgian, Czech, German, and Italian constitutional courts have all elaborated doctrines allowing the ECHR to be employed as a constitutional yardstick to various degrees.[50] Particularly interesting is the technique adopted by the Italian Constitutional Court that, with the two s.c. 'twin judgments'

---

[43] In 1964 the Austrian Constitution was amended in order to confer the ECHR's constitutional status. Gamper (2016) p. 75.

[44] Grabenwarter (2013).

[45] A similar provision is Article 16 of the Portuguese Constitution, which affirms that "the provisions of this Constitution and of laws concerning fundamental rights shall be interpreted and construed in accordance with the Universal Declaration of Human Rights." However, since the provision only makes reference to the Universal Declaration of Human Rights, the position of the ECHR is less clear. On the point see: Cortes and Violante (2011), pp. 764–765.

[46] STC 22/1981, F.J 3. For a wider overview of the relationship between the two courts see: Ripol Carulla (2014).

[47] These citations are taken from the intervention of the President of the Spanish Constitutional Tribunal at the 2015 opening of the European Court of Human Rights judicial year. See: *Dialogue between judges, European Court of Human Rights*, Council of Europe, 2015, 50–51. Available at: https://www.echr.coe.int/Documents/Dialogue_2015_ENG.pdf#page=25.

[48] See in particular, STC 120/1990, *Fundamento Jurídico* 2.

[49] STC 140/2018, *Fundamento Jurídico* 5. For a summary of the position in the debate on the interpretation of Article 10.2 see, Alvarez Rodriguez (2021).

[50] For more details on the differences existing between these techniques see: Paris (2017), pp. 627–629.

of 2007,[51] interpreted Article 117.1 of the Constitution—enshrining a general duty of the Italian State to abide by its international obligations—as empowering the Court to review the constitutionality of national legislation using as a parameter a provision of the ECHR.[52] In the years following the 'twin judgments', the Constitutional Court decided several cases pending before it on purely European grounds, i.e. adopting as a sole parameter the ECHR, essentially invalidating legislation for being incompatible with the Convention, and only indirectly with the Constitution.[53]

In the same logic of cooperation, constitutional courts may engage with the ECtHR case law by entering into a dialogue with the Strasbourg Court.[54] The starting point is often a judgment in which the constitutional court departs from the ECtHR case law explaining the reasons for the departure,[55] whilst at the same time inviting the Strasbourg Court to reshape its own case law to secure smoother compliance with domestic constitutional principles. At its best, this judicial dialogue may result in a fine-tuning of the content of ECHR rights and reinforce the legitimacy of the Strasbourg Court, like in the famous *Hannover saga* involving the German *Bundesverfassungsgericht*.[56] Yet, it is easily understandable why an attempt at dialogue may rapidly evolve into a clash of jurisprudence if none of the two courts is willing to compromise with the other.

On other occasions, when the cause of the ECHR violation lies in a practice or a procedure of the constitutional court, the cooperation may also consist of the constitutional court correcting its own case law or procedural rules. This has happened with more frequency in relation to constitutional jurisdictions of new democracies, like the Albanian and Czech ones, which decided to change their practice in order to comply with Strasbourg's judgments.[57] This kind of cooperation is particularly significant since it denotes an acceptance by constitutional judges of the procedural subordination of constitutional justice to the ECHR procedural norms.[58]

---

[51] Italian Constitutional Court judgment nn 348 and 349 of 2007. An English translation of the judgments is available at: https://www.cortecostituzionale.it/documenti/download/doc/recent_judgments/S348_2007_Eng.pdf; and https://www.cortecostituzionale.it/documenti/download/doc/recent_judgments/S349_2007_Eng.pdf respectively.

[52] For an extensive commentary of the two judgments see, Biondi Dal Monte and Fontanelli (2008).

[53] For an empirical study on how the Italian Constitutional Cours deals with the ECtHR case law see: Groppi (2016).

[54] Petrov (2018), pp. 510–511.

[55] According to Martinico, the providing of justifications for the departure is one of the main distinguishing elements between an attempt at dialogue and outright disobedience. Martinico (2020), pp. 249–250.

[56] See especially the last ECtHR judgment in the saga, *Von Hannover v Germany (No.2)*(GC) (40660/08), (60641/08), 07/02/2012.

[57] See, *Gjyli v. Albania* (32907/07), 29/09/2009, para. 56; Judgment of the Czech Constitutional Court, 21 February 2012, Pl. ÚS 29/11.

[58] See, below, 1.2.

Finally, in some instances, constitutional courts instead of cooperating with ECtHR in the promotion of European standards may turn to Strasbourg to seek support and protection against the ruling majority.[59] This pattern characterised the relationship between the ECtHR and the constitutional courts of Members States formerly belonging to the communist bloc in the first years after the ECHR ratification, when those constitutional courts did not have a consolidated case law, and in order to enforce the values of democracy and the rule of law in the context of complicated democratic transitions were relying primarily on the assistance of CoE bodies, especially the Venice Commission and the ECtHR.[60] Thanks to this external support,[61] constitutional courts of this area managed to affirm themselves as important veto players in domestic policies,[62] and strong allies of European courts in the integration process.[63] However, as we will see in the next paragraph, at the beginning of the '10s this idyllic relationship came to an end.

2.2.2 *Disobediences and Rebellions. Constitutional Courts v. Strasbourg*

To begin with, after two more than two decades of activity, constitutional courts of Central Eastern European States had developed their own case law in the fundamental rights field, thus reducing their need to search for guidance in the ECtHR jurisprudence.[64] Second, the rise of populist politics emerged as a key disruptive factor in the relationship. The populist narrative depicts constitutional and international courts as an unnecessary and illegitimate check on the democratic will of the sovereign people, as they represent the principal obstacle populists encounter in the dismantlement of constitutional democracy and the consolidation of their grip on power.[65] Where populist parties obtained a governing majority, like in Hungary and Poland, the constitutional court constituted their primary target. The Hungarian Constitutional Court was essentially rendered powerless by virtue of a series of constitutional amendments,[66] whilst the Polish Constitutional Tribunal has been the target of a 'hostile takeover' by the ruling majority,[67] which completely neutralised

[59] For instance, the Czech and Italian constitutional courts explicitly adopted the ECHR as a yardstick for the review of legislation. Petrov (2018).

[60] For an overview of this period see: Motoc and Ziemele (2016).

[61] Bugarič and Ginsburg (2016), p. 71.

[62] Schwartz (2000).

[63] Piqani (2007), pp. 4–8.

[64] Kosar and Petrov (2017), pp. 616–617.

[65] Arato (2019).

[66] More in details on the transformation affecting the Hungarian Constitutional Court see, Halmai (2019), available at: https://www.diritticomparati.it/wp-content/uploads/2019/07/2-Halmai.pdf.

[67] Extensively on the Polish constitutional crisis see, Sadurski (2019).

its counter-majoritarian function.[68] Following this capture, the Polish Constitutional Tribunal composition was declared by the ECtHR in violation of Article 6 ECHR with the already mentioned *Xeroflor* judgment. As a reaction to this decision of the Strasbourg Court, the Polish Constitutional Tribunal declared the unconstitutionality of Article 6 ECHR, inasmuch as it is applicable to constitutional courts. This judgement constitutes the most serious challenge to the ECHR coming from a national judge, as not even the Russian Constitutional Court in 2015 went as far as declaring the unconstitutionality of the ECHR.[69]

Without going as far as the Polish Constitutional Tribunal, constitutional courts may adopt a variety of attitudes which more or less openly challenge the authority of the ECtHR case law. Those defiant attitudes may range from a mere reluctance to take into account ECtHR case law in constitutional adjudication, to different forms of qualified disobedience to the duty of faithful implementation of Strasbourg's judgments. If the disobedience consists of an open challenge of the ECtHR authority with no other scope than defending national sovereignty against external interferences, as in the reactions of the Russian Constitutional Court to the *Anchugov* judgment, it can be defined as "unprincipled".[70]

When instead the constitutional court seeks to enter into a dialogue with Strasbourg, aimed at reaching a better interpretation of the ECHR, which duly takes into account the peculiarity of the domestic legal system, the disobedience can be qualified as 'functional'.[71] This kind of disobedience can be rightly seen as a welcome consequence of a more thoughtful application of the principle of subsidiarity, as it fosters the constitutional court's role in the protection of ECHR rights and the determination of their content, but only as long as the constitutional court is ready to accept that is not going to have the last say in this dialogue, i.e. it eventually adopting the interpretation proposed by Strasbourg judges.

Frequently, the disagreement between the two courts resides in a different understanding of what constitutes a legitimate restriction, i.e. in a different application of the principle of proportionality. In those cases, when compliance means accepting the ECtHR balancing between the fundamental right in question and the countervailing national interests, constitutional courts tend to stick by their balancing, generating non-compliance with the ECtHR case law. The underlying cause of those clashes, which have interested the major European constitutional jurisdictions,[72] is the assumption that constitutional judges are better placed to assess

---

[68] Miroslaw Granat, a former judge at the Polish Constitutional Tribunal, actually argues that the Constitutional Tribunal now performs the opposite function of a constitutional court, as it mainly serves to provide judicial legitimacy to the decisions of the ruling majority. Granat (2022).

[69] On the significance of this judgment for the relationship between the two courts see, Ploszka (2022). Available at: https://doi.org/10.1007/s40803-022-00174-w.

[70] The Russia Constitutional Court in its judgment affirmed that the ECtHR decision was impossible to execute given its incompatibility with the Russian Constitution. More in details see, Dzehtsiarou and Fontanelli (2018).

[71] Martinico (2020).

[72] Probably the constitutional jurisdiction which had the harshest confrontations with the Strasbourg Court is the Italian one. Amongst the many episodes, the most recent is the s.c. *Varvara* saga,

the national interests at stake, as the nature of the proceedings before the ECtHR does not allow the latter court to fully consider the systemic implications of its judgments.[73] In essence, what is called into question by constitutional courts is the very idea that ECtHR judgments shall be mechanically transposed into the domestic legal system. Since no constitutional court of the Council of Europe assigns a supra-constitutional status to the ECHR,[74] and neither the ECtHR ever elaborate a doctrine of primacy of ECHR law, the transposition of an ECtHR judgment remains indeed formally subject to its compatibility with the national constitution.[75]

Further, it has to be recalled that the principle of the *erga omnes* effects of the Strasbourg judgments is not explicitly enshrined in the ECHR, which only affirms that the judgments are binding for the parties of the proceeding (Article 46), neither the ECtHR had never plainly affirmed that all its judgments have binding effects for all the Contracting Parties.[76] Henceforth, in cases of structural violation of the ECHR having their cause in a legislative provision, constitutional courts may easily devise tools to limit the *erga omnes* effects of Strasbourg judgments in the domestic legal system. This is exactly what the Italian Constitutional Court did in its judgment 49/2015, where it held that ordinary judges are bound to follow the ECtHR case law only when 'well-established' or contained in a pilot judgment.[77] Reacting to this judgment, the ECtHR affirmed that all its judgments have "the same interpretative

concerning the imposing of confiscation without a conviction judgment. For a detailed account of those episodes in the Italian literature see, Viganó (2019).

[73]This argument has been employed by the German Constitutional Tribunal to limit the effects of the ECtHR case law. On this point see, Martinico (2020), p. 264.

[74]In most Member States the ECHR has a legislative or supra-legislative status, with only Austria and the Netherlands assigning it constitutional rank. Of those two, only in the Netherlands, it seems plausible to affirm that the ECHR, as any other international law, enjoys supra-constitutional status. However, as well known, this is a peculiarity of the Dutch system strictly interrelated with the absence of a jurisdiction empowered to carry out judicial review of legislation. On the point see, Martinico (2012), pp. 404, 413–422.

[75]This means that, in the hardly conceivable hypothesis of a conflict between the ECtHR judgement and the constitution, the latter shall always prevail. In similar terms see, Judgment n.49/2015 of the Italia Constitutional Court, C*onsiderato in diritto*, para. 4. In this judgment, the Italian Constitutional Court held that ordinary judges are bound to follow the ECtHR case law only when 'well-established'. Even though the ECtHR quickly reacted affirming that all its judgments have the same interpretative authority and binding force, it is evident how the ruling could negatively affect the penetration of the ECHR in the Italian legal system by allowing national judges to selectively apply Strasbourg judgments. An English translation of the judgment is available at: https://www.cortecostituzionale.it/documenti/download/doc/recent_judgments/S49_2015_en.pdf.

[76]Arnardóttir (2017), p. 823.

[77]In the judgment, the Italian Constitutional Court elaborated a set of interpretative criteria to be taken into account when deciding if a precedent is well-established: (1) the creativity of the principle affirmed; (2) the presence of dissenting opinions annexed to the ruling "especially if supported by robust deductions"; (3) the fact that the decision was delivered by a simple chamber "without the endorsement of the Grand Chamber"; (4) the fact that the ECtHR had duly taken into account the peculiarities of the Italian legal system. For a commentary see, Mancano and Martinico (2016).

authority and binding force",[78] without however specifying that this binding force deploys effects *erga omnes*. Pinto de Albuquerque—after a convincing effort to infer the principle of *erga omnes* from the existing Strasbourg's case law[79]—concludes its separate opinion to the judgment by warning that judgment 49/2015

> threaten[s] to narrow the practical effect of the Court's jurisprudence upon domestic legal systems in a manner quite obviously deleterious to the continued operation of the entire Convention system.

Even though this formulation may at first appear too drastic, it simply reflects an accurate estimate of the degree to which the effectiveness of the ECtHR judgments, and thus of the whole Convention system, is dependent upon collaborative constitutional courts. Because, as we briefly illustrated, if constitutional judges are not willing to cooperate, they have at their disposal a vast array of arguments and techniques to challenge the Strasbourg Court's authority.[80]

In light of the aforesaid, one could reasonably expect that constitutional courts are capable of exerting a considerable degree of influence on the ECtHR case law, as the latter court should be always prone to compromise with constitutional judges to secure their loyal cooperation. Yet, previous studies that have investigated the role of constitutional precedents in the ECtHR case law have concluded that the Strasbourg Court instead tends to insulate itself from all kinds of inputs coming from national constitutional judges to assert its legitimacy and autonomy *vis-à-vis* them;[81] a conclusion that seems supported by the assertive stance assumed by the ECtHR in the line of case law going from *Anchugov* up to *Xero Flor*.[82] The difficulties in pursuing both goals emerge especially when the two courts disagree on the minimum prescribed content of a fundamental right: when the ECtHR declares a breach of a Convention right after a constitutional court, in the same case, found no fundamental rights violation, the ECtHR has to persuade the constitutional court to adopt its own balancing, even though this entails changing the constitutional content of that right.

---

[78] *G.I.E.M. S.r.l. and Others v. Italy* (1828/06), (34163/07), (19029/11), 28/06/2018.

[79] Ibidem, *Partly Concurring, Partly Dissenting Opinion of Judge Pinto de Albuquerque*, paras 72–77.

[80] In this sense, it is worth recalling the Italian example. In Judgment 166/2017, the Italian Constitutional Court deliberately refused to implement the *Stefanetti* judgment of 15 April 2014 (21838/10), (21849/10) et al. With the latter ruling, the ECtHR partially overturning its ruling in *Maggio v. Italy* (357/07), 17/05/2011, had affirmed that the retroactive modification *in peius* of the pension treatment of those who had paid social security contributions in Switzerland - thus benefiting from a lower rate - had violated not only the applicants' right to a fair trial, but also their right to the peaceful enjoyment of their pension protected by Article 1 Protocol 1 to the Convention. The Constitutional Court in the above-mentioned judgment drastically reduced the applicative scope of this ruling by stating that the principle had been affirmed "with specific and limited reference to the particular position of the new applicants" (See Judgment 166/2017, *cons. dir.* 4.1).

[81] Actually, academic literature has mainly focused on the influence of the ECtHR on constitutional courts, devoting lesser attention to the issue of the influence of constitutional courts on the ECHR system Szymczak (2007), p. 204.

[82] See, above, fn 32–33.

In this sense, analysing the ECtHR's case law citing constitutional courts allows us to analyse how the Strasbourg judges pursue those two partially contradicting institutional necessities, namely a solid partnership with national constitutional courts on the one hand and the protection of its autonomous interpretative authority on the other.

2.3 The Procedural Subordination of Constitutional Justice to the ECtHR

So far, we have considered the relationship between the Strasbourg Court and national constitutional jurisdictions only in its cooperative, dialogic, dimension. Yet, constitutional courts are not only the main interlocutors of the Strasbourg Court, as sometimes their performance can be scrutinised by the ECtHR. To begin with, when the legal system provides for the possibility of individual constitutional appeal, and this constitutes an effective remedy to be exhausted according to the Strasbourg case law—as is the case of the German *Verfassungsbeschwerde* and of the Spanish *recurso de amparo,* just to cite a few—the applicability of Article 6 ECHR to constitutional proceedings means that the Strasburg Court may review the constitutional court's procedural performance. Also, the procedural subordination of constitutional courts to Article 6 is not limited to concrete miscarriages of justice in specific cases, as the ECtHR may identify the cause of the violation of the right to a fair trial in the normative and jurisprudential framework governing the procedure before the constitutional court. In those cases, either the constitutional court itself or the parliament will be thus obliged to amend the contested rule in order to comply with the ECtHR's decision.

At the outset, it has to be noted that a reading of Article 6 ECHR does not allow to automatically infer its applicability to constitutional proceeding, as the text of the provision only refers to proceedings concerning "civil rights and obligations" and criminal charges. And indeed in the very first years of activity of the ECtHR, the European Commission on Human Rights excluded the applicability of Article 6 to inadmissibility decisions of constitutional courts, since those decisions did not concern "either a dispute over civil rights and obligations or the merits of a criminal charge".[83] In 1974, the applicability of Article 6 to constitutional trial, was excluded by elaborating a doubtful distinction between civil rights and constitutional rights,[84] excluding its applicability to proceedings concerning the latter.[85] However, during

[83] European Commission of Human Rights, *X. c. Allemagne* (441/58), 07/07/1959.

[84] Those doubts are shared by, Ibrido (2016), p. 14. Available at: https://www.rivistaaic.it/it/rivista/ultimi-contributi-pubblicati/renato-ibrido/intorno-all-equo-processo-costituzionale-il-problema-della-operativit-dell-art-6-cedu-nei-giudizi-dinanzi-ai-tribunali-costituzionali.

[85] European Commission of Human Rights, *16 Austrian Communes and Some of Their Councillors v. Austria* (5767/72) et al., 31/05/1974, para. 2 (The Law).

the '80 s, the idea that constitutional trial could fall within the scope of Article 6 started to emerge in the ECtHR case law, at least as regards the inclusion of the duration of the constitutional process in the determination of whether the national proceeding as a whole was of reasonable length. A first signal was contained in *Buchholz v. Germany*,[86] where the ECtHR, after excluding that the duration of the proceeding before the Constitutional Tribunal fell within the scope of Article 6 in the specific circumstances of the case, added that there was "no need to decide whether it might be otherwise in different circumstances", thus leaving the door open to a possible inclusion of constitutional proceedings within the material scope of Article 6.[87]

Five years later, when the Court had the occasion to come back to the issue with the judgment in *Deumeland v. Germany*, it seized the opportunity to do that.[88] Although no significant elements of differentiation from *Buchholz* can be found—as in both cases the Constitutional Tribunal declared inadmissible a complaint against a decision of a court of last instance—the ECtHR, with a clear—and unmotivated-[89] overruling of its precedent, held that to assess the reasonable duration of the national procedure under Article 6(1) ECHR, the proceedings before the constitutional court must also be taken into account, as "although it had no jurisdiction to rule on the merits, its decision was capable of affecting the outcome of the claim".[90] The applicability of Article 6 to constitutional proceedings at least from the angle of the reasonable duration of the proceedings was subsequently confirmed by a series of cases in which the Strasbourg Court refused to detract the time of examination of constitutional appeals from the period to be taken into consideration for evaluating the reasonable duration of the proceeding.[91]

The applicability of Article 6 to constitutional proceedings was however far from being integral, as the only guarantee that was held applicable to constitutional proceedings was that of reasonable duration, and only inasmuch the constitutional procedure was part of a more complex procedure. Indeed, this appeared only logical, as the decision of a constitutional appeal or of a question of constitutionality delays the definition of controversies pending before ordinary tribunals.[92]

A more far-reaching affirmation of the applicability of Article 6 to constitutional proceedings was the one contained in the 1993 judgment in *Ruiz Mateos v. Spain*, where the Court for the first time held that the substantive guarantees of the right to a fair trial apply to proceedings before the constitutional courts, and in particular to incidental judicial review of legislation. The case originates in the expropriation of all the companies of the *Rumasa* holding, established by a law decree and

[86] *Buccholz v. Germany* (7759/77), 06/05/1981.

[87] Ibidem, para. 48.

[88] *Deumeland v. Germany* (9384/81), 29/05/1986.

[89] Ibrido (2016), p. 30.

[90] Ibidem para. 77.

[91] See amongst others: *Bock v. Germany* (11118/84), 29/03/1989.

[92] Malinverni (1994), p. 391.

subsequently sanctioned by a law of the Spanish Parliament. The facts of the case are well known and there is no need to enter in much detail. The Ruiz Mateos family, owner of the holding, raised a question of constitutionality concerning this law in the proceedings before the Audiencia Nacional, which was declared admissible by the *Tribunal Constitutional.* During the procedure before the Constitutional Tribunal, the applicants repeatedly asked to be admitted as parties of the procedure, and all their requests were denied by the Constitutional Tribunal, which ultimately ruled against the Ruiz Mateos, holding that the expropriation law was not in breach of the Spanish Constitution.[93]

In its ruling, the ECtHR not only reaffirmed what is defined as a 'well-established case law', according to which "proceedings in a Constitutional Court are to be taken into account for calculating the relevant period where the result of such proceedings is capable of affecting the outcome of the dispute before the ordinary courts",[94] it also went on stating that even the other substantive guarantees of due process, such as the principle of equality of arms, apply to constitutional proceedings inasmuch as they are capable of affecting the content of the applicant's rights. By reading the judgment, the ECtHR however seems worried to limit its material scope, stressing that the applicability of Article 6 to the questions of constitutionality was a consequence of the specific circumstance of the case, namely the fact that the law under the scrutiny of the Constitutional Tribunal only affected the applicant. Yet, as observed by Judge Pettiti in its dissenting opinion, having affirmed the applicability of Article 6 ECHR on the basis that the constitutionality judgment concerned "a law which directly concerns a restricted circle of persons" appears to be a decidedly vague criterion, leaving unanswered the several questions concerning the applicability of Article 6. In particular, the affirmation that Article 6 applies to constitutional proceedings when this is capable of "affecting the outcome of the dispute before ordinary courts" seems to imply that the applicability may vary according to the features of each constitutional justice system and to the specific guarantees being considered. The criterion of the capacity of affecting the outcome of the applicant's dispute nonetheless becomes well-consolidated case law with the 2004 *Gorraiz Lizarraga v. Spain* judgment, where the ECtHR held that albeit "the proceedings before the Constitutional Court ostensibly bore the hallmark of public law" their capacity to affect the rights of the applicant subjected them to the respect of the guarantees of Article 6.[95] A further expansion came with the judgment in *Süssmann v. Germany* of 1996.[96] Here, the European Court of Human Rights applied the guarantee of the reasonable duration of the trial also to the admissibility phase of constitutional proceedings, even if those proceedings were not preceded by litigation before ordinary tribunals, provided that they were capable of affecting the applicant's situation.

---

[93] For a commentary of the judgment see: Chueca Sancho (1994); Castro-Rial Garron (1994).

[94] *Ruiz Mateos v. Spain*, para. 35.

[95] *Gorraiz Lizarraga v. Spain* (62543/00), 27/04/2004, para. 47.

[96] *Süssmann v. Germany* (20024/92), 16/09/1996.

In a nutshell, the type of procedure through which the constitutional court is seized seems to be irrelevant, the only relevant criterion to be taken into account being the capacity of constitutional proceedings to affect the outcome of the dispute on the applicant's right. The application of this criterion ultimately makes conditional the applicability of Article 6 to an analysis not only of the relevant legal framework but also of the specific circumstances of the case. At the same this implies that all types of constitutional procedures, with the obvious exception of abstract appeals of constitutionality introduced by public authorities, fall within the scope of Article 6, as long they are capable to affect the outcome of the dispute on the applicant's right. In the year following the *Süssmann* judgment, the ECtHR gradually held applicable to constitutional courts various aspects of the right to a fair trial, such as the right to an independent and impartial judge,[97] the right to a public hearing,[98] the right to an adversarial proceeding,[99] and also the right to access to a tribunal.[100]All in all, nowadays it is possible to safely affirm that in principle all the components of the right to a fair trial as resulting from the ECtHR case law are applicable to constitutional proceedings.

Despite having conducted constitutional proceedings within the material scope of the ECHR, the Strasbourg Court has always been well aware of the necessity of maintaining a distinction between ordinary and constitutional jurisdiction. First of all, the fact that Article 6 may apply to constitutional court proceedings, does not necessarily imply that individuals have a right to access that remedy, quite the contrary: the ECtHR has constantly denied that the refusal by the ordinary judge to raise a question of constitutionality on the request of a party constitutes a violation of the right to access to a judge.[101] More generally, the ECtHR stressing the "special role and status of a Constitutional Court"[102] within domestic legal systems, clarified the necessity of leaving to constitutional courts a wider margin of appreciation concerning the requirements of the right to a fair trial,[103] as the guarantees of the right to a fair trial "cannot be construed in the same way for a constitutional court as for an ordinary court".[104] Just to provide an example, in *Süssmann* it held reasonable a delay of 3 years and 5 months to declare the inadmissibility of an appeal in light of the "unique political context of German reunification" entitling the German

[97] See, for instance, *Meznaric v. Croatia* (71615/01), 15/07/2005; *Liga Portoguesa de Futebol Profissional c. Portugal*, (4687/11), 17/05/2016.

[98] See for example, *Pauger v. Austria* (16717/90), 208/05/1997; *Selmani and Others v. The Former Yugoslav Republic of Macedonia* (67259/14), 09/02/2017.

[99] Amongst many see, *Krčmar and Others v. The Czech Republic* (35,376/97), 03/03/2000; *Feliciano Bichao c. Portugal*, (40225/04), 20/11/2007.

[100] See, *Stavebna Spolocnost Tatry Poprad, S.R.O. v. Slovakia* (7261/06), 03/05/2011; *Zvolsky and Zvolska c. République tchèque* (46129/99), 12/11/2002.

[101] *Coeme and Others v. Austria* (32492/96), (32547/96), (32548/96), 22/06/2000, par. 114; *Wynen and Centre Hospitalier Interrégional Edith-Cavell v. Belgium* (32576/96), 05/11/2002.

[102] Ibidem, para. 37.

[103] Cohen Jonathan (1994).

[104] *Pammel v.* Germany (17820/91), 01/07/1997. para. 68.

Constitutional Tribunal to prioritise some cases above others.[105] This deference—which can be explained by the above-mentioned institutional necessity of relying on cooperative constitutional courts-[106] produces as a consequence that the geometry of the right to a fair constitutional trial is variable, and may have a different, more limited, perimeter compared to the right to a fair trial before ordinary tribunals.

It is also worth mentioning that the expansion of the applicability of Article 6 to constitutional proceedings is not confined to individual constitutional appeals. Soon after the ruling in *Ruiz Mateos*, the ECtHR indeed realised that Article 6 ECHR could be a tool capable of influencing the functioning of all aspects of constitutional justice.[107] The Court progressively expanded the applicability of Article 6 to a vast array of constitutional courts' ancillary powers,[108] ranging from the power to dissolve political parties,[109] to the conflict of attributions between the powers of the State,[110] and disciplinary proceedings.[111] Nevertheless, in the ECtHR case law, there are still some shadow cones concerning the applicability of Article 6, first and foremost electoral justice and constitutional proceedings for the removal of elected officials.[112] As regards electoral justice, since the landmark judgment in *Pierre Bloch v. France*,[113] the ECtHR excluded the applicability of Article 6 to electoral proceedings before constitutional courts, since they are not aimed at determining the applicant's civil rights and obligations but rights of a political nature, e.g. the right to stand for parliamentary elections. At the same time, it must be noted that the ECtHR revised, and censored, a judgment of the Bulgarian Constitutional Court annulling an election for irregularities in the voting procedure, through the prism of Article 3 of Protocol 1, thus subjecting also this competence of constitutional courts to its scrutiny.[114] In essence, inasmuch as the controversy before the constitutional court concerns a right protected by the Convention, the proceedings are susceptible to fall

---

[105] Ibidem, para. 60.

[106] See, above para. 1.1.3.

[107] This extension of the reach of Article 6 ECHR has been considered as an attempt by the ECtHR to promote a unique integrated European system for the protection of fundamental rights, of which the Strasbourg Court was going to be the supreme guardian Burgorgue Larsen (2008), pp. 265–266.

[108] By ancillary powers, we mean all the competences attributed to constitutional courts different from judicial review of legislation. The definition is taken from: Ginsburg and Elkins (2008).

[109] In this ambit, the first judgment has been delivered in the landmark case *United Communist Party of Turkey and Others v. Turkey* (9392/92), 30/01/1998, but can also be mentioned the case, *United Macedonian Organization Ilinden - Pirin and Others v. Bulgaria* (59489/00), 20/11/2005.

[110] On this point the abundant case law against Italy must be mentioned: *Cordova (no. 1) v. Italy* (40877/98), 30/01/2003; *Cordova (no. 2) v. Italy* (45649/99), 30/01/2003; *C.G.I.L. and Cofferati v. Italy* (46967/07) 24/02/2009; *Onorato v. Italy* (26218/06), 24/05/2011; *Belpietro v. Italy* (43612/10), 24/09/2013.

[111] *Harabin v. Slovakia* (58688/11), 20/11/2012.

[112] *Paksas v. Lithuania* (34932/04), 06/01/2001

[113] *Pierre Bloch c. France* (24194/94), 21/11/ 1997.

[114] *Riza and Others v. Bulgaria* (48555/10), (48377/10), 13/10/ 2015; *Petkov and Others v. Bulgaria* (7568/01), (178/02), (505/02), 11/06/ 2009.

under the scrutiny of the ECtHR by virtue of the procedural obligation that accompanies every ECHR right according to *Kudla*.

In conclusion, through an extensive interpretation of Article 6, the ECtHR had shaped the very organisation of constitutional courts, reviewing different aspects of constitutional justice systems, from the right of parties of constitutional proceedings to the deliberative procedures of constitutional courts.[115] This gradual expansion of the material scope of Article 6 has resulted in an almost complete subjection of national constitutional justice systems to the exigencies of the right to a fair trial and nowadays it can be safely affirmed that the aspects of constitutional justice that are exempt from the ECtHR scrutiny constitute the exception rather than the rule. Yet, the eminently casuistic approach of the Strasbourg Court, the limited effects of its judgments, as well as the diversity existing between the European systems of constitutional justice, generate uncertainties as to what extent it is possible to speak of a rationalisation of constitutional justice systems.[116] Against this backdrop, analysing the applicability of Article 6 to constitutional jurisdiction, allows to clarifying whether is possible to define the contours of the right to a fair constitutional trial as resulting from the Strasbourg case law and also to assess how the application of Article 6 is shaping the organization and functioning of constitutional justice systems.

2.4 The Relationship in Figures

Having provided a general overlook of the different forms of interactions between constitutional courts and the ECtHR, it is now time to present the most relevant quantitative aspects of the relationship. By looking at its quantitative dimension, it will also be possible to draw some preliminary conclusions about the relationship that that are helpful to orientate the qualitative analysis of the judgements.

As a first point, the research for the citations of constitutional courts in the ECtHR case law resulted in a pool of 3024 judgments pronounced against 29 Respondent States, covering a time span of more than 50 years.[117] In the same period, up to the 1st January 2023, the ECtHR delivered a total of 12,233 judgments against the States included in the pool, meaning that constitutional courts are cited in approximately 24% of the cases. This very rough data thus seems to *prima facie* confirm the criticism of scholars affirming that the role of constitutional courts in the Strasbourg Court jurisprudence is rather marginal.[118]

---

[115] See, for instance, *Marini v. Albania* (738/02), 18/12/2007.

[116] This conclusion was reached already at the beginning of the century by Burgorgue Larsen (2001), p. 32.

[117] A more detailed explanation of the parameters is contained in the Introduction to this book. See, above.

[118] Favoreu (2004); Berger (2011). However, considering only the judgements delivered by the Grand Chamber that, as a rule of thumb, have a greater political significance and a stronger impact on the national level, we obtain a different picture: on a total of 228 judgments, constitutional courts

However, it is interesting to note that, if we zero in on the last 5 years of jurisprudence, from 2018 to 2022, this ratio doubles, as on a total of 1107 judgements delivered, citations of constitutional courts occur in 539 (48.69%). In absolute terms, the most frequently cited constitutional court is the Croatian, which appeared in 359 judgments. However, this figure is scarcely relevant if not related to the total number of judgments pronounced against the Respondent State to which the constitutional court belongs.

As illustrated by the below figure (Fig. 2.1), significant discrepancies are observable concerning the percentage of citations of the different constitutional courts: if the French Constitutional Council is cited in roughly 10% of all the judgments pronounced against France, the percentage of cases in which the German Constitutional Court is cited is 85.5%.

At a closer analysis, it is easy to identify the cause of this difference in the organisation of the national system of constitutional justice, more precisely in the presence of judicial avenues for individuals to access the constitutional court. In countries where the constitutional justice system provides individual direct access to the constitutional court to complain about the misapplication of law by ordinary courts or lament a fundamental right violation caused by the public administration, as in the case of Albania, Croatia, Germany, the Czech Republic, Slovakia, Slovenia, and Spain, the percentage of citations varies between 80 and 90 per cent, since the constitutional appeal constitutes, at least in general, an effective remedy under Article 35 ECHR and thus has to be exhausted by the applicant before going to Strasbourg.

In a slightly lower percentage are cited the constitutional courts to which individual access to constitutional justice is limited to the possibility of challenging the unconstitutionality of a legislative or regulatory provision, such as the constitutional courts of Austria, Latvia, Lithuania, Poland, and Portugal. The lowest percentages of citation, finally, are those of constitutional courts for which individual direct access is excluded, such as the French Constitutional Council, and the constitutional courts of Bulgaria, Italy, Romania. The percentage of citations from these courts out of the total number of judgments rendered against the Respondent state is less than 20% for all of them. A special mention must be made for the Bosnian Constitutional Court, which probably because three judges appointed by the President of the Strasbourg Court sit there, is cited in all judgments against Bosnia.

Those differences seem to indicate that the presence of a constitutional court in ECHR case law is not influenced by political considerations relating to the authority of the constitutional judge[119] but appears rather to be determined primarily by the

---

are cited in 122, a proportion corresponding to 53% of the total. This difference may indicate that in cases where the political and legal stakes are higher, the ECtHR pays more attention to constitutional courts' decisions.

[119]This seems to *prima facie* contradict the hypothesis that constitutional courts with established authority on the domestic level have more chance of having a close partnership with Strasbourg. See: Petrov (2018), p. 526. However, the validity of this assumption needs to be tested with a qualitative analysis of the ECtHR case law.

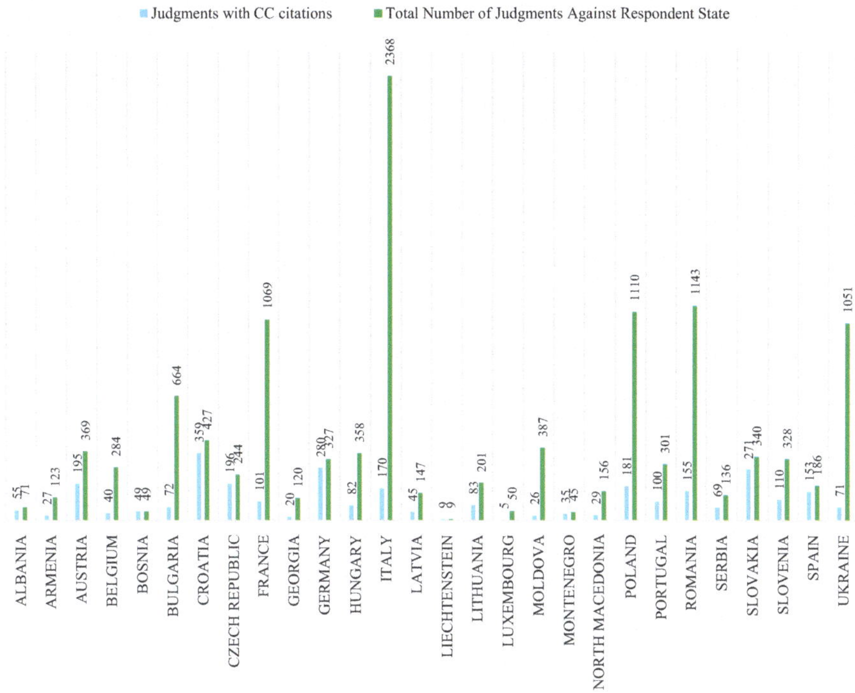

Fig. 2.1 Total number of judgments with CC citations (1960–2017)

width of the avenues for individual access to constitutional justice: as this narrows down, the percentage of judgments in which the constitutional court is cited decreases. To test the soundness of this claim, we can combine these percentages with that on the average number of citations per judgment of each constitutional court.

As illustrated by the graph below (Fig. 2.2), the average number of recurrences per judgment also seems to corroborate the decisive influence of the structure of the domestic constitutional justice system on the citations' pattern. In fact, the constitutional courts with the highest citation rates are also those with the highest average number of recurrences per judgment. Conversely, the constitutional courts with the lowest citation percentages are those with the lowest average number of recurrences per judgment. What those data ultimately seem to indicate is that constitutional courts' citations depend to a large extent on the procedural path followed by the applicant before reaching Strasbourg and that when the constitutional has somehow been involved in the domestic procedure the number of citations is on average higher.

If we zoom in again on the period between 2018 and 2022, the picture varies significantly. As illustrated by the Figure above (Fig. 2.3), in the period considered, the average number of citations increased for almost all the constitutional courts included in our research, the main exceptions being the French Constitutional

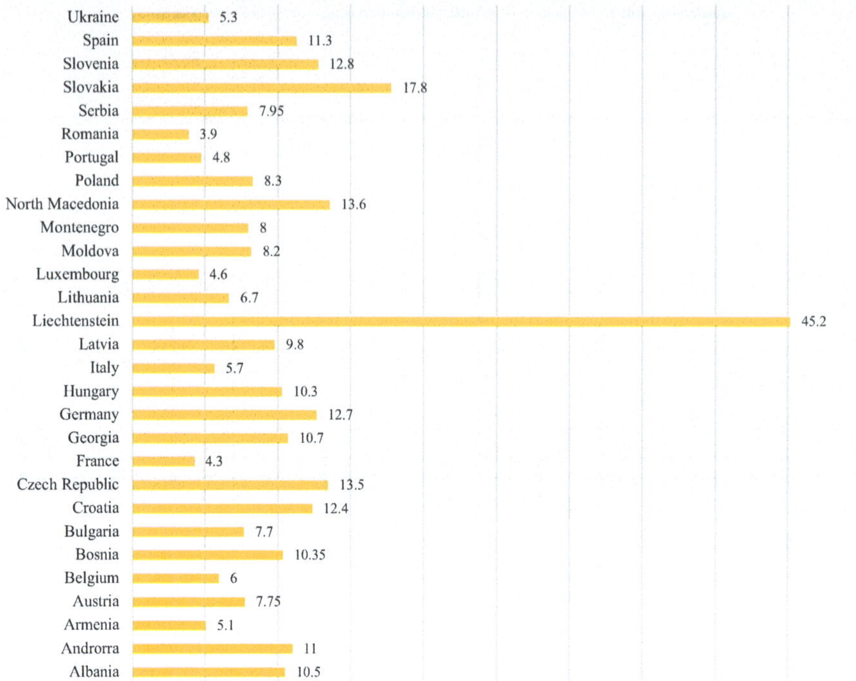

Fig. 2.2 Average number of CC citations per judgment (1960–2017)

Council and the German Constitutional Court, whose average number of citations remained stable.

In some cases, like the Italian, Polish and Portuguese ones, the magnitude of the growth is exponential, compelling us to search for possible causes. At least in the Italian and Polish cases, the cause is readily found. Both the Italian and the Polish Constitutional Tribunal have been protagonists of open confrontations with the ECtHR, it appears hence reasonable to interpret this increase as an answer to those rebellions; the validity of this hypothesis will be tested during the qualitative analysis. The existence of a trend towards an intensification of the dialogue with constitutional courts is also certified by considering the number of ECtHR judgments delivered in the period 2018–2022 in which constitutional courts are cited. The above figure (Fig. 2.4), in fact, points in the same direction as the preceding one, evidencing for instance that, in the period considered, the French Constitutional Council was cited in 37.5% of all judgments delivered in the period against France, whilst the overall percentage for the preceding period is just of 10%. Similar increases can be observed for the Italian (from 12% to 39%) and the Romanian (from 13.5% to 27.5%) constitutional courts, and to a smaller extent for all the other constitutional courts that can only be reached by individuals through incidental procedures.

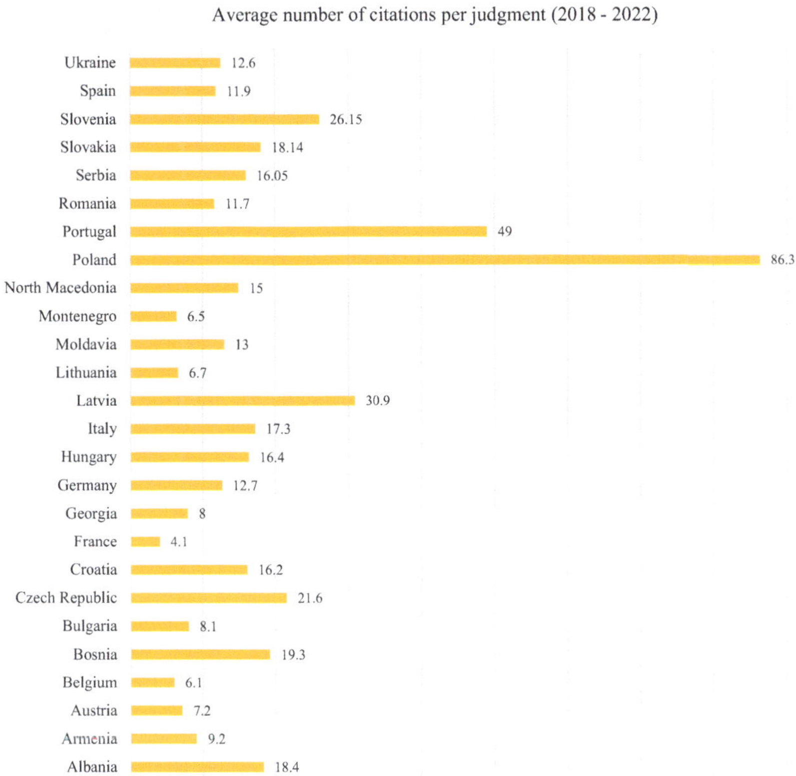

Fig. 2.3 Average number of CC citations per judgment (2018–2022)

It is also interesting to mention the limited usage by the ECtHR of constitutional judgments as comparative materials. As the figure below shows (Fig. 2.5), the ECtHR resorted to constitutional courts' jurisprudence to carry out its comparative analysis only in a handful of cases, thus essentially ignoring the transnational law of liberties composed of the constitutional jurisprudence of CoE Member States.[120]

This also means that the role of constitutional jurisprudence in the establishment of consensus is rather limited, something that should not surprise as soft law is normally considered the main source from which the ECtHR derives the existence of a consensus.[121] Besides, in the few ECtHR judgments where is possible to find a comparative analysis finalised at the establishment of a consensus,[122] the constitutional case law is often introduced either by a party of the proceeding, an *amicus*

[120] See, Favoreu (2004), p. 17.

[121] For an illustration of the role of soft law in the case law of the ECtHR see the Dissenting Opinion of Pinto de Albuquerque in *Muršić v. Croatia* [GC] (7334/13), 20/10/2016.

[122] See: Dzehtsiarou (2015), p. 86.

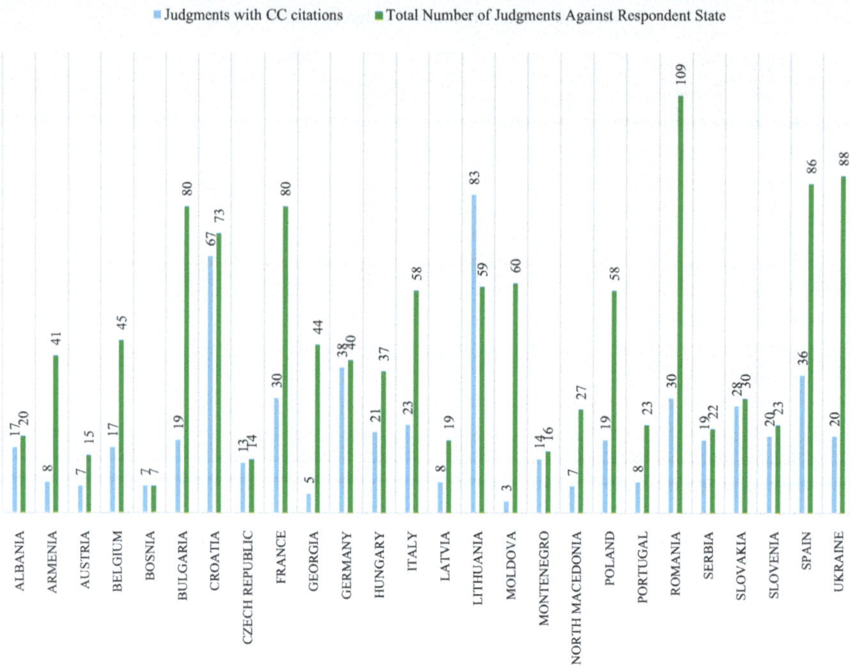

Fig. 2.4 Total number of judgments with CC citations (2018–2022)

curiae,[123] or in a separate opinion.[124] In this sense, this data seems to indicate that the trend toward a more intense recourse by the ECtHR to comparative law observed in the literature,[125] does not seem to concern constitutional case law.

The only partial exception in this regard is the German Federal Constitutional Tribunal, cited in 26 judgments rendered against Respondent States other than Germany. To this regard, it is worth noting that 11 of these judgments have been delivered in the last 10 years, thus confirming a general trend of increased use of constitutional case law by the Strasbourg Court.[126] Finally, it should be noted how the only two extra-systemic constitutional courts of which we retrieved citations are the South African and Ugandan constitutional courts.[127]

[123]The introduction of comparative material is a typical function of amicus curiae before the ECtHR. See Eynde van den (2013).

[124]For an analysis of the role of separate opinions in the ECtHR case law see: White and Bossiakou (2009).

[125]Mahoney and Kondak (2015) p. 119.

[126]See: Dzehtsiarou (2015), p. 86.

[127]It is worth emphasising that since all the keywords used contained the term ‘constitutional’, the results do not include, for example, the Canadian Supreme Court, a usual reference for the Strasbourg Court. See: Garlicki (2017).

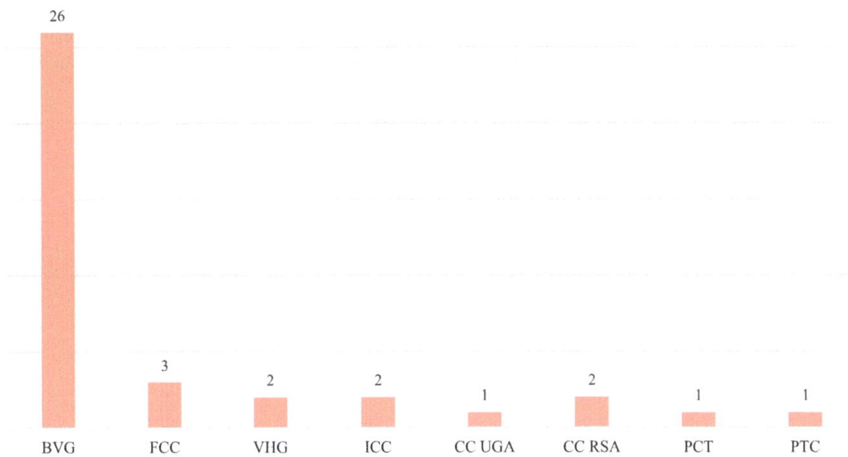

Fig. 2.5 Number of citations of CC as comparative material

All in all, from the data collected it is possible to draw a couple of preliminary conclusions. The first element that emerged is the decisive influence of the system of constitutional justice on the relationship between the two courts. This seems to entail that the constitutional justice systems that offer the widest access to individuals are, for this very reason, the most prone to be subjected to ECtHR scrutiny. Conversely, courts to which individual access is excluded for instance the French and Italian constitutional jurisdictions, more easily evade the Strasbourg review.[128] Second, the data collected have shown that in recent years the ECtHR seems to have adopted a more dialogic posture towards constitutional courts, whose presence in the ECtHR case law, significantly increased in the last decade. The validity of these preliminary indications coming from the quantitative analysis will be tested in the following pages.

References

Abashidze AK, Ilyashevich MV, Solntsev AM (2017) Anchugov & Gladkov v. Russia. Am J Int Law 111:461–468

Alvarez Rodriguez I (2021) El Convenio Europeo de Derechos Humanos desde la perspectiva constitucional. Revista Española de Derecho Constitucional 41:409–423

Arato (2019) Populism, constitutional courts, and civil society. In: Landfried C (ed) Judicial power. How constitutional courts affect political transformations. Cambridge University Press, Cambridge, pp 318–341

[128] On the paradoxical nature of this conclusion see: Favoreu (2004), pp. 9–16.

Arcari M, Ninatti S (2017) Narratives of constitutionalization in the European Union court of justice and in the European court of human rights' case law. Vienna J Int Const Law 11:11–41
Arnardóttir OJ (2017) Res Interpretata, Erga Omnes effect and the role of the margin of appreciation in giving domestic effect to the judgments of the European court of human rights. Eur J Int Law 28:819–843
Beernaert MA (2004) Protocol 14 and new Strasbourg procedures: towards greater efficiency? And at what price? Eur Human Rights Law Rev 9:544–557
Berger V (2011) Les Cours constitutionnelles et la Cour européenne des droits de l'homme. Les Nouveaux Cahiers du Conseil constitutionnel 32:7–17
Bernhardt R (1995) Reform of the control machinery under the European convention on human rights: protocol no. 11. Am J Int Law 89:145–154
Biondi Dal Monte F, Fontanelli F (2008) The decisions no. 348 and 349/2007 of the Italian constitutional court: the efficacy of the European convention in the Italian legal system. Germ Law J 9:889–932
Bowring B (2000) Russia's accession to the Council of Europe and Human Rights: four years on. Hels Monit 53:53–72
Brems E (2011) Transitional justice in the case law of the European court of human rights. Int J Transl Just 5:282–303
Bugarič B, Ginsburg T (2016) The assault on Postcommunist courts. J Democr 27:69–82
Burgorgue Larsen L (2001) L' "Autonomie constitutionnelle" aux prises avec la Convention européenne des droits de l'homme. Revue belge de droit constitutionnel 1:31–64
Burgorgue Larsen L (2008) L'Influence de la Convention Européenne sur le Fonctionnement des Cours Constitutionnelles. Revue internationale de droit comparé 60:265–282
Castro-Rial Garron F (1994) El derecho a un juicio equitativo (Comentario a la Sentencia del Tribunal Europeo de Derechos Humanos de 23 de junio de 1993, en el asunto «Ruiz Mateos c. España»). Revista de instituciones europeas 21:157–170
Chueca Sancho G (1994) La sentencia dictada por el Tribunal Europeo de Derechos Humanos en el caso Ruiz Mateos. Derechos y Libertades: revista del Instituto Bartolomé de las Casas 2:553–570
Cohen Jonathan G (1994) Justice constitutionnelle et Convention européenne des droits de l'homme. L'arrêt Ruiz Mateos c. Espagne. Revue française de Droit constitutionnel 17:175–183
Cortes A, Violante T (2011) Concrete control of constitutionality in Portugal: a means towards effective protection of fundamental rights. Penn State Int Law Rev 29:759–776
Drzemczewski A (2000) The European human rights convention: protocol no.11- entry into force and first year of application. Human Rights Law J 21:357–379
Dzehtsiarou FK, O'Meara N (2014) Advisory jurisdiction and the European court of human rights: a magic bullet for dialogue and docket-control? J Leg Stud 34:444–468
Dzehtsiarou K (2015) European consensus and the legitimacy of the European court of human rights. Cambridge University Press, Cambridge
Dzehtsiarou K, Fontanelli F (2018) Unprincipled disobedience to international decisions: a primer from the Russian constitutional court. Eur Yearb Human Rights 10:319–341
Eynde van den L (2013) An empirical look at amicus curiae practice of human rights NGOs before the European court of human rights. Neth Q Human Rights 31:271–313
Favoreu L (2004) Corti costituzionali nazionali e Corte europea dei diritti dell'uomo. Rivista di Diritto Costituzionale 1:3–24
Flauss JF (2003) Faut-il transformer la Cour européenne des droits de l'homme en juridiction constitutionnelle? Recueil Dalloz 25:1638–1645
Gamper A (2016) Austria: endorsing the convention system, endorsing the constitution. In: Popelier et al (eds) Criticism of the European Court of Human Rights. Shifting the convention system: counter-dynamics at the national and EU level. Intersentia, Cambridge, pp 75–101
Garlicki L (2017) The European court of human rights and the Canadian case-law. In: Albert R, Cameron D (eds) Canada in the world. Cambridge University Press, Cambridge, pp 348–370
Ginsburg T, Elkins Z (2008) Ancillary powers of constitutional courts. Tex Law Rev 87:1431–1461

Glas LR (2016) The functioning of the pilot-judgment procedure of the European court of human rights in practice. Neth Q Human Rights 34:41–70

Grabenwarter C (2013) European fundamental human rights in the case law of the Austrian constitutional court. In: Weitzel L (ed) L'Europe des droits fondamentaux. Mélanges en hommage à Albert Weitzel. Pedone, Paris, pp 71–90

Granat M (2022) On the experiences of a constitutional court in an illiberal democracy. Incapacitated but necessary. In: Castellà JM, Simonelli MA (eds) Populism and contemporary democracy. Old problems and new challenges. Palgrave Macmillan, Cham, pp 137–156

Greer S, Wildhaber L (2012) Revisiting the debate about "constitutionalising" the European court of human rights. Hum Rights Law Rev 12:655–687

Groppi T (2016) La jurisprudence de Strasbourg dans les décisions de la Cour constitutionnelle italienne. Une recherche empirique. In: Burgorgue-Larsen L (ed) Les défis de l'interprétation et de l'application des droits. De l'ouverture au dialogue. Pedone, Paris, pp 323–361

Halmai G (2019) Dismantling constitutional review in Hungary. Rivista di Diritti Comparati 1:31–47

Harmsen R (2007) The European court of human rights as a 'constitutional court': definitional debates and the dynamics of reform. In: Morison J et al (eds) Judges, transition, and human rights. Oxford University Press, Oxford, pp 33–53

Ibrido R (2016) Intorno all'equo processo costituzionale: il problema dell'operatività dell'art. 6 CEDU nei giudizi dinanzi ai tribunali costituzionali. Rivista AIC 1:1–32

Keller H, Stone Sweet A (2008) A Europe of rights: the impact of the ECHR on national legal systems. Oxford University Press, Oxford

Kosar D (2018) The Strasbourg court meets abusive constitutionalism: Baka v. Hungary and the rule of law. Hague J Rule Law 10:83–110

Kosar D, Petrov J (2017) The architecture of the Strasbourg system of human rights: the crucial role of the domestic level and the constitutional courts in particular. Zeitschrift für ausländisches öfentliches Recht und Völkerrecht 77:585–621

Lemmens K (2019) Protocol no 16 to the ECHR: managing backlog through complex judicial dialogue? Eur Const Law Rev 15:691–713

Mahoney P, Kondak R (2015) Common ground: a starting point or destination for comparative-law analysis by the European court of human rights? In: Andenas M, Fairgrieve D (eds) Courts and comparative law. Oxford University Press, Oxford, pp 119–140

Malinverni G (1994) Droit à un procès équitable et cours constitutionnelles. Revue universelle des droits de l'homme 6:389–395

Mancano L, Martinico G (2016) An Italian tale of two courts. Judgment no 49/2015 of the Italian constitutional court and its relationship with Strasbourg. Revista española de derecho europeo 58:199–214

Martinico G (2012) Is the European convention going to be 'supreme? Comparative-constitutional overview of ECHR and EU law before National Courts. Eur J Int Law 23:401–424

Martinico G (2020) Functional disobedience, National Courts and the ECtHR. In: Sajó A, Uitz R (eds) Critical essays on human rights criticism. Eleven Publishing International, The Hague, pp 247–268

Motoc I, Ziemele I (2016) The impact of the ECHR on democratic change in central and Eastern Europe. Judicial perspectives. Cambridge University Press, Cambridge

Paraskeva C (2003) Human rights protection begins and ends at home: the 'pilot judgment procedure' developed by the European court of human rights. Human Rights Law Commentary 3:1–16

Paris D (2017) Allies and counterbalances constitutional courts and the European court of human rights: a comparative perspective. Zeitschrift für ausländisches öfentliches Recht und Völkerrecht 77:623–649

Pech L, Platon S (2018) Judicial independence under threat: the court of justice to the rescue in the ASJP case. Common Mark Law Rev 55:1827–1854

Petrov J (2018) Unpacking the partnership: typology of constitutional courts' roles in implementation of the European court of human rights' case law. Eur Const Law Rev 14:499–531
Piqani D (2007) Constitutional courts in central and Eastern Europe and their attitude towards European integration. Eur J Legal Stud 1:1–22
Ploszka A (2022) It never rains but it pours. The polish constitutional tribunal declares the European convention on human rights unconstitutional. Hague J Rule Law 15:51–74
Ripol Carulla S (2014) Un Nuevo Marco de Relacción entre el Tribunal Constitucional y el Tribunal Europeo de Derechos Humanos. Revista Española de Derecho Internacional 66:11–53
Sadurski W (2009) Partnering with Strasbourg: constitutionalization of the European court of human rights, the accession of central and east European states to the Council of Europe, and the idea of pilot judgments. Hum Rights Law Rev 9:397–453
Sadurski W (2019) Poland's constitutional breakdown. Oxford University Press, Oxford
Sadurski W (2021) Quasi-constitutional court of human rights for Europe? Comments on Geir Ulfstein. Glob Const 10:175–181
Schwartz H (2000) The struggle for constitutional justice in post-communist Europe. Chicago University Press, Chicago
Simonelli MA (2019) Towards a theory of unconventional constitutional amendments. Some lessons from the Baka case. DPCE Online 39:1561–1577
Stone Sweet A (2009) On the Constitutionalisation of the convention: the European court of human rights as a constitutional court. Revue Trimestrielle des Droits de l'Homme 80:923–944
Szymczak D (2007) Ła Convention Européenne des droits de l'homme et le juge constitutionnel national. Bruylant, Bruxelles
Tello Mendoza JA (2023) Control de convencionalidad y Estado Constitucional de Derecho. Tirant Lo Blanch, Mexico City
Tulkens (2004) Les prisons en Europe: Les développements récents de la jurisprudence de la Cour européenne des droits de l'homme. Déviance et Société 38:425–448
Turnbull L (1995) A victim of its own success: the reform of the European court of human rights. Eur Public Law 1:215–225
Ulfstein G (2021) Transnational constitutional aspects of the European court of human rights. Glob Const 10:151–185
van de Heyning C (2013) Constitutional courts as guardians of fundamental rights: the constitutionalization of the convention through domestic constitutional adjudication. In: Popelier et al (eds) The role of constitutional courts in multilevel governance. Intersentia, Cambridge, pp 21–48
Voland T, Schiebel B (2017) Advisory opinions of the European court of human rights: unbalancing the system of human rights protection in Europe? Hum Rights Law Rev 17:73–95
White RCA, Bossiakou I (2009) Separate opinions in the European court of human rights. Hum Rights Law Rev 9:37–60
Zwaak LF, Cachia T (2004) The European court of human rights: a success story? The European court of human rights: a success story? Human Rights Brief 11:32–54

Chapter 3
The ECtHR and the Constitutional Courts of Consolidated Western Democracies

This Chapter is dedicated to the individual analysis of the relationship between the Strasbourg Court and each of the national constitutional courts of the consolidated democracies of the Council of Europe. To maintain a coherent structure throughout this analysis, the same framework has been employed for all constitutional jurisdictions. Each section begins with a concise overview highlighting key aspects of the respective constitutional justice system, focused on the avenues for individual access to constitutional court. Then, the most significant statistical data on the relationship dynamics between these national courts and the ECtHR are presented. Subsequently, the analysis delves into specific judgments where the interaction between the Strasbourg Court and the constitutional jurisdiction is more visible. The focus of this scrutiny lies first of all on ECtHR judgments where the Court declares the non-conformity of national constitutional decisions with the ECHR. Second, cases where the ECtHR overturns a previous assessment of conventionality made at the national level. Third, situations where the ECtHR, by condemning the respondent state, effectively enforce a constitutional judgment. Brief concluding remarks at the end of each paragraph highlight the defining traits of the relationship between the ECtHR and the constitutional jurisdiction under consideration.

Supplementary Information The online version contains supplementary material available at https://doi.org/10.1007/978-3-031-71268-5_3.

M. A. Simonelli, *The European Court of Human Rights and Constitutional Courts*, Ius Gentium: Comparative Perspectives on Law and Justice 120,
https://doi.org/10.1007/978-3-031-71268-5_3

3.1 The ECtHR and the Austrian Constitutional Court. Converging Standards

Due to its special political and geographical situation in the immediate post-war period,[1] Austria did not become a member of the Council of Europe until 1956.[2] However, the Austrian Constitutional Court (*Verfassungsgerichthof*, hereafter simply the 'VGH') in addition to being the paradigm for almost all constitutional courts established after World War II, was also the first active constitutional court in the post-war European landscape, as in 1946 had already resumed its work with the powers granted to it by the 1920 Constitution.[3]

For what is most relevant here, it must be emphasised that Austria represents a peculiarity among the Member States of the Council of Europe, as the ECHR, following a constitutional amendment adopted in 1964,[4] enjoys constitutional rank in the Austrian legal system. This incorporation of the ECHR at the constitutional level has led to the creation of a high level of awareness within Austrian civil society of the rights arising from the Convention,[5] which explains, rather satisfactorily, the high number of appeals that are brought against the Austrian state annually. As of 1 January 2023, 371 judgments had been pronounced against Austria, of those, a citation of the VGH can be found in 196, a percentage of roughly 52.8%. For a better understanding of this jurisprudential material, it is opportune to briefly presents the characteristics of the Austrian constitutional justice system. In a gradual departure from the model outlined in the 1920 Constitution, the competences of the VGH have progressively expanded, as a consequence of the major changes to the structure of the 1920 Constitution, which has been subject to more than one hundred revision.[6] Concerning judicial review of normative acts, the VGH can check the legitimacy of acts of parliament (art. 140 Const.), the legality of administrative regulations (art. 139 Const.) as well as the decisions of the administrative court for breaches of fundamental rights (Art. 144 Const.).[7]

As far as access routes are concerned, the VGH can rule on a preliminary question raised by any court that has doubts about the constitutionality of a rule (Art. 89 Const.), as well as on two types of individual appeal. The first (the

---

[1] As it is well-known, due to its geographical position along the Iron Curtain, remained under military occupation until 1955, when Austrian State Treaty was signed, and as a compromise to ensure the departure of Soviet forces from Austria, it declared the neutral status of Austria. Further see: Schmidl (2016).

[2] For an overview of Austria's participation in the European integration process see: Gehler and Kaiser (1997).

[3] Öhlinger (2003), p. 208.

[4] Bundesverfassungsgesetz [BVG], Bundesgesetzblatt [BGBl], Nr. 59/1964, Art. II.

[5] See Rechberger (2012), pp. 232–233.

[6] Lachmayer (2017), pp. 76–85.

[7] For a comprehensive illustration of the competences of the Austrian Constitutional Court, including the so-called 'other functions', see: Faber (2008); Gamper, and Palermo (2008).

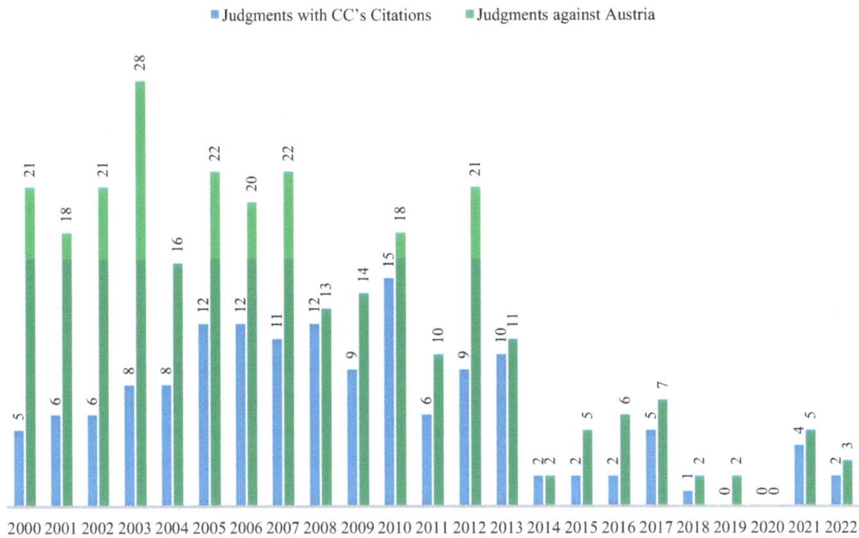

Fig. 3.1 Judgments with VGH citations per year (2000–2022)

Bescheidbeschwerde) is outlined in Article 144 of the Constitution; in order for this remedy to be validly exercised, it requires that all appeals against the administrative decision have been exhausted beforehand. The second (the *Individual beschwerde*) was introduced in 1975 by constitutional amendment,[8] and allows any individual to challenge the constitutionality of a legislative before the VGH if he has suffered direct and actual personal injury and considers that the applied provision itself infringes his or her constitutional rights. The strict interpretation of these requirements by the VGH makes them residual instruments, the question of constitutionality remaining the main route to the VGH.[9]

Before turning to the analysis of the Strasbourg case-law, we shall to first dwell on some interesting statistical evidence. As the chart below shows (Fig. 3.1), in the last decade it is observable a marked decrease in the number of citations of the VGH in conventional case law, with only 17 judgments citing the VGH in the period 2014–2023. In the same period, the European Court of Human Rights delivered a total of 39 judgments against Austria, which means that against an overall average of 52.8%, this percentage has fallen to around 43.5% in recent years. The circumstance that against an average number of recurrences of VGH per judgment of 7.75 in the period under review, the average falls to 4.14 may be indicative of a change of attitude on the part of the Strasbourg Court. At the same time, the fact that during the

[8] Bundesverfassungsgesetz [BVG], Bundesgesetzblatt [BGBl], Nr. 302/1975.

[9] See Gentili (2011).

period under review, the ECtHR decided minor cases is undoubtedly a contributing factor to this trend.[10]

Turning to the analysis of the ECtHR case law, the first aspect on which it is necessary to focus is the consideration of the two individual constitutional complaints in the ECtHR case law. As regards the *Bescheidbeschwerde*, the ECtHR, in the *Zumtobel* case,[11] held that when deciding on such appeals the VGH is not a "tribunal with full jurisdiction" within the meaning of Art. 6 ECHR, as it is only competent to review whether the decision of the administrative judge conforms with the Constitution, without having the possibility of re-examining the facts of the case.[12] As a consequence, the right to access the VGH through this procedure is not guaranteed by Article 6 ECHR.[13] However, this does not automatically mean that it does not constitute an effective remedy whose exhaustion is required under Article 35 ECHR, as the effectiveness of the *Bescheidbeschwerde* ultimately depends on the specific circumstances of the case. Since the complaint shall be based on the illegality of a norm applied in the course of a proceeding, and cannot be used to challenge its misapplication, in principle applicants will be required to use it when the fundamental rights' violation is provoked by a provision is *per se* illegal (or unconstitutional).[14] The same applies to the individual constitutional complaint of Article 140 of the Austrian Constitution. In the most recent authority on the point, the 2021 judgment in *Liebscher*, the government pleaded the inadmissibility of the application because the applicant did not make use of the *Individual Beschwerde*. The ECtHR, while recalling that applicants are required to avail themselves of the individual constitutional complaint to the VGH if they are challenging a provision of a statute as being in itself contrary to the ECHR, rejected the objection because

[10] In the period considered, the European Court of Human Rights handed down thirteen judgments that were assigned relevance 3; twenty that were assigned relevance 2; and only six decisions classified as key cases.

[11] *Zumtobel v. Austria* 1 (2235/86), 21/09/1993.

[12] Ibidem, paras. 29–30. This principle was subsequently reiterated in the following judgments: *Ortenberg v. Austria*, (12884/87), 25/11/1994, para. 32; *Stojakovic v. Austria* (30003/02), 09/11/2006, para. 45; *Ohneberg v. Austria* (10781/08), 18/09/2012, para. 31.

[13] See: *Zumtobel v. Austria*, para. 30. However, in a series of subsequent cases, the Strasbourg Court held that the right of access to a judge was violated precisely because the VGH, when ruling on appeals under Article 144 Const. does not constitute a court with full jurisdiction. See: *Schmautzer v. Austria* (15523/89), 23/10/1995; *Gradinger v. Austria* (15963/90), 23/10/1995, paras 43–45; *Farfmeier v. Austria* (16841/90), 23/10/1995; *Palaoro v. Austria* (16718/90), 23/10/1995; *Pramstaller v. Austria* (16713/90), 23/10/1995; *Umlauft v. Austria* (15527/89), 23/10/1995. However, in these cases, the Strasbourg judges did not affirm the existence of a right of access to a constitutional court, since the European Court of Human Rights held that the penalty imposed on the appellant was criminal in nature and therefore, for this purpose, not even the administrative court could be considered a court with full jurisdiction. See, for example: *Schmautzer v. Austria*, para. 36.

[14] Concerning specifically the *Bescheid Beschwerde*, the issue was never dealt with it in a judgment. The last decision on this issue is: *Siebenhandl v. Austria* (dec.) (31778/96),16/05/2000.

> the applicant did not *primarily* allege that the relevant provisions [...] should be considered as unconstitutional, but focussed on his allegation that the violation of his right [...] originated in their wrong interpretation by the domestic courts.[15]

As we shall see also in the following Chapter, in the ECtHR case law there are some uncertainties concerning the effectiveness under Article 35 ECHR of the s.c. "normative constitutional complaints",[16] as it is not always easy to draw a distinction between when is the interpretation of ordinary court to be unconstitutional, and when instead is the norm itself.

Concerning the application of Article 6 ECHR, it is worth noting that, when ratifying the Convention, Austria made a reservation, pursuant to Art. 64 ECHR, to the application of Art. 6(1) ECHR. The reservation reads "[t]he provisions of Article 6 of the Convention shall be so applied that there shall be no prejudice to the principles governing public court hearings laid down in Article 90 of the 1929 version of the Federal Constitutional Law".[17] In 1997, the ECtHR held that since the fourth paragraph of Art. 19 of the Constitutional Court Act, introducing public hearing in constitutional proceedings was introduced in 1984, i.e. after the reservation, since according to Article 64 ECHR reservations only apply to "the legislation then in force", the reservation could not be considered to be operative.[18] In the case the Strasbourg judges concluded that there was no violation of Article 6, as the applicant—a university professor of public law—had not explicitly requested a hearing before the VGH.[19] Conversely, in *Kugler*, decided in October 2010, where the applicant had explicitly requested a public hearing, which was denied by the VGH, the Strasbourg Court finds a breach of Article 6.[20]

As far as the dialogue between the two jurisdictions is concerned, the VGH's traditional openness to supranational courts,[21] as well as the constitutional status of the ECHR, are two decisive factors that have determined the success of this relationship. In particular, it has to be mentioned that the VGH affirmed that if the execution of an ECtHR judgment so requires, it will depart from the principles established in its own case law.[22] Evidence of the interpenetration of the Convention

---

[15] *Liebscher v. Austria* (5434/17), 06/04/2021, paras 42–43.

[16] By normative constitutional complaints we refer to complaints which can be directed only against an unconstitutional legislative or regulatory provision. See: Dürr (2014), p. 79. Individual Access to Constitutional Courts as an Effective Remedy against Human Rights Violations in Europe - The Contribution of the Venice Commission. Journal of Law and Politics 258, 88 (67–89).

[17] In Strasbourg case law see, *ex multis*: *Fischer v. Austria* (16922/90), 26/04/1995, para. 36.

[18] *Pauger v. Austria* (16717/90), 28/05/1997, paras. 53–55. Three years later, the ECtHR declared the reservation inoperative in its *entirety* due to its excessive generality. See *Eisenstecken v. Austria* (29477/95), 03/10/2000, para. 29.

[19] *Pauger v. Austria*, paras. 60–61. More generally on the value of the implied waiver of public hearing in *Pauger* and its framing in conventional jurisprudence see: Vidal Zapatero (2012), pp. 211–214.

[20] *Kugler v. Austria* (65631/01), 14/10/2010, para. 52.

[21] Lachmayer (2017), pp. 80–81.

[22] Gamper (2016), p. 95.

into the Austrian legal system can also be found in the Strasbourg case law. In the *Tele 1 Privatfernseh* case, we learn how the VGH, when ruling on the case of the applicant, recognised that given the constitutional status of the contested provision, the only court competent to review its compatibility with the ECHR was the Strasbourg court,[23] implicitly admitting the possibility that a constitutional provision may be incompatible with the Convention.

Concerning the fundamental rights' dialogue between the two jurisdictions, we have identified just five major cases of conflicts, whereas we retrieved at least twelve judgments in which the two courts agreed on the interpretation to be given to the ECHR provisions, i.e. where the ECtHR confirmed the conventionality review carried out by the VGH.[24] Focusing our attention on the former cases, the 2004 judgment in the *Weh* case must be mentioned first,[25] as the ECtHR adopted an interpretation of Article 6 ECHR more restrictive than that of the VGH. The judgment essentially consists of an assessment of the conventionality of Section 103(2) of the Austrian Motor Vehicle Act, obliging the owner of a car to provide the driver's data in the event of a remote detection of a criminal offence. The VGH had twice declared the rule in question unconstitutional because it violated the principle of *nemo tenetur se detegere*. On a third occasion, the Austrian Constitutional Court reaffirmed that Article 103(2) of the Motor Vehicle Act was unconstitutional but, since the Austrian legislator amended the rule introducing a norm of constitutional rank declaring that the right of the authority to request information should prevail over the right of the individual to refuse, it could not declare the rule unconstitutional as it deemed that there rule in question was not contrary to the guiding principles of the Constitution.[26] Despite the fact that the unconstitutionality of the norm had been reaffirmed three times by the VGH, the European Court of Human Rights, by a majority of 4 to 3, affirmed the non-violation of Article 6 ECHR, holding that State authorities have the power to compel individuals to provide information outside of criminal proceedings, without this being in breach of Article 6 ECHR.[27] What is striking about the case is that the Strasbourg Court provides an interpretation of Article 6 ECHR which is more restrictive than that

[23] *Tele 1 Privatfernseh v. Austria* (32240/96), 21/09/2000, para. 13.

[24] See: *Prötsch v. Austria* (15508/89), 15/11/1996; *Stallinger and Kuso v. Austria* (14696/89), (14697/89), 23/04/1997; *Petrovic v. Austria* (20458/92), 27/03/1998; *Franz Fischer v. Austria* (37950/97), 29/05/2001; *W. F. v. Austria* (38275/97), 30/05/2002; *Sailer v. Austria* (38237/97), 06/06/2002; *Müller-Hartburg v. Austria* (47195/06), 19/02/2013; *P.B. and J.S. v. Austria* (18984/02), 22/07/2010; *Klug v. Austria* (33928/05), 15/01/2009; *Schmidt v. Austria* (513/05), 17/07/2008; *S.H. and Others v. Austria* [GC] (57813/00), 03/11/2011.

[25] *Weh v. Austria* (38544/97), 08/04/2004.

[26] Ibidem, para. 26.

[27] Some authors have emphasised the 'hypocrisy' of this interpretation, arguing that it would have been preferable to state that the restriction was justified by the need to promote road safety, rather than to deny outright the violation of the right not to self-incriminate. See: Asworth (2008), pp. 764–765.

provided by the Austrian Constitutional Court, preferring to side with the government.

Another contrast regarding the interpretation of the guarantees of due process is that resulting from the jurisprudential strand that began with the *Asan Rushiti* case.[28] Here, the applicant complained to the Strasbourg Court about the violation of the principle of the presumption of innocence guaranteed by Article 6(2) ECHR because although he had been acquitted—with a dubitative formula—the domestic courts denied him compensation for the period spent in pre-trial detention in prison. The VGH, ruling on the case, proposes a restrictive reading of the ECtHR relevant precedent,[29] stating that the denial of the right to compensation does not in itself constitute a violation of Art. 6(2) ECHR, as the judge called upon to decide on the claim for compensation is prevented from carrying out an autonomous assessment of the evidence. However, turning to the legislature, the VGH also calls for the rule on which the lower courts have based their refusal to be amended. The ECtHR, on the other hand, merely reaffirms its consolidated case law which requires Member States to compensate for pre-trial detention to any individual who is found innocent at the end of his or her trial, independently of the formula used for the acquittal.[30]

A similar dynamic is observable in the *Frodl* case,[31] concerning the deprivation of the right to vote for prisoners. The VGH making a distinction with the leading case *Hirst v. United Kingdom*,[32] considers that in the case pending before it there was no violation of Art. 3 Prot. 1 ECHR since the disqualification was only triggered by a final conviction with a prison sentence of more than one year and in any case the national court had the power to order its suspension.[33] Here again, the Strasbourg judges consider the interpretation made by the VGH to be excessively restrictive and reaffirmed the consolidated principle according to which for a restriction on the right to vote to be justified it must be ordered individually by reasoned decision of the judicial authority.[34]

In all the cases outlined above, the ECtHR sanctions the unconventionality of the VGH's interpretation of ECHR standards, by reaffirming the right interpretation of its own precedents, in face of an attempt of the VGH to partially revise them, in this sense therefore they can be considered instances of principled dialogue.

A different situation is instead the one in the ECtHR judgment in *Öllinger*.[35] Here, the Strasbourg judges simply substituted their own balancing act for that

[28] *Asan Rushiti v. Austria* (28389/95), 21/03/2000.

[29] *Sekanina v. Austria* (13126/87), 25/08/1993.

[30] More extensively on the extension of the presumption of innocence in conventional jurisprudence, see Stumer (2010), p. 89.

[31] *Frodl v. Austria* (20201/04), 08/04/2010.

[32] *Hirst v. United Kingdom* (74025/01), 06/10/2005. For a commentary on the case and its framing in the Strasbourg Court's jurisprudence on the right of prisoners to vote see: Powers (2006).

[33] *Frodl v. Austria*, para. 15.

[34] Ibidem, para. 35.

[35] *Öllinger v. Austria* (6900/01), 29/06/2006.

carried out by the VGH, even though the latter judgment explicitly took into account the ECHR.[36] In this case, the Austrian authorities had banned a counter-manifestation organised by an Austrian MP to protest against a commemoration for the death of nazi soldiers, with the Austrian Constitutional Court confirming the administrative decision. The VGH had held that the prohibition of the counter-manifestation was justified by the necessity of protecting the public who traditionally flock to cemeteries on All Saints' Day, as the pro-Nazi commemoration would take place in a cemetery. The ECtHR, in carrying out its balancing, emphasises the unconditional prohibition of a counter-demonstration and the small number of participants to the counter manifestation in order to conclude that "too little weight" was given to the interest of the applicant in manifesting its dissent towards the SS comrades' meeting and thus declared a breach of Article 11 ECHR.[37] It is interesting to note that the judgment declares the breach "notwithstanding the margin of appreciation afforded to the State in this area",[38] seemingly recognising to have gone beyond what the principle of subsidiarity would—normally impose. In this sense, the outcome of this case seems to be dictated mainly by the specific circumstances of the case, where the Austrian authorities essentially restricted the right of the applicants, in order to guarantee the undisturbed celebration of a SS commemoration.[39]

Quite a different 'sensitivity' was shown by the Grand Chamber of the Court in the widely discussed 2011 judgment in *S.H. and Others v. Austria*.[40] The case concerned the restrictions, then in force in Austria, on the use of artificial assisted procreation techniques. The Grand Chamber, overturning the judgment of the First Chamber, recognised—in view of the particular ethical sensitivity of the matter—a very wide margin of appreciation for the Austrian State, confirming the balancing exercise carried out by the VGH, even if dating from 1999.[41]

Finally, it has to be mentioned a series of cases in which the Strasbourg Court *de facto* enforced a VGH's judgment. In a judgment of 21 June 2002, the VGH declared Article 209 of the Austrian Criminal Code unconstitutional on the grounds that under that article a legal homosexual relationship—such as that between two persons aged 16 and 18—became punishable under criminal law when the older person turned 19. The VGH found the provision unconstitutional for being unreasonable, and it was thus repealed.[42]

---

[36] See also: Ambrus (2009), pp. 367–368.

[37] *Öllinger v. Austria,* para. 49.

[38] Ibidem, para. 50.

[39] In its dissenting opinion, Judge Loucaides instead considers the reference to the margin of appreciation to not be pertinent, as the majority basically denied its existence. Ibidem, *Loucaides Dissenting*, para. (f).

[40] *S.H. and Others v. Austria* (57813/00), 03/11/2011.

[41] It is worth noting that the Austrian judge who had voted in favour of the violation of Art. 14 in conjunction with Art. 8 ECHR as regards two of the four applicants in the Chamber's judgment, in the Grand Chamber's judgment sided with the majority that affirmed the non-violation of Art. 8.

[42] *Verfassungsgerichtshof*, 21.06.2002 (G602 - 15565).

The European Court of Human Rights, ruling six months after the VGH decision, condemns Austria for discriminating against the applicants on the basis of their sexual orientation, the cause of discrimination being Article 209 of the Austrian Criminal Code, meanwhile repealed by the VGH.[43] The Court, in fact, states that "the Constitutional Court's judgment, which is based on other grounds than those relied on in the present application, has not acknowledged let alone afforded redress for the alleged breach of the Convention, and proceed to declare the violation of Article 8.[44] Similarly, in a series of subsequent cases,[45] the ECtHR provided economic compensation to homosexual couples who suffered discrimination caused by Article 209 of the Austrian Criminal Code. In this sense, all these judgments of the ECtHR can be considered an enforcement of the VGH judgment, as they essentially provide compensation for the damages suffered as a consequence of the application of a provision which the VGH had declared unconstitutional.

In conclusion, an overall analysis of the Strasbourg jurisprudence citing the VGH allows to appreciate the existence of a dialogue between the two jurisdictions characterised by a substantial convergence of interpretative standards. The frequency with which the VGH engages with the interpretation of ECtHR case law turns out to be a decisive factor in ensuring jurisprudential harmony. As we have seen, in cases of conflicts concerning the breadth of a ECHR right—in particular the *Frodl* and *Asan Rushiti* cases—the ECtHR had the opportunity to clarify the meaning of its own precedents to the VGH, ensuring a more uniform application of conventional law. The Austrian case also seems to indicate that a widespread review of conventionality could have an important deflationary effect on the workload of the Strasbourg Court. As we noted a the beginning of this paragraph, especially since 2014, in face of a constant number of registered applications,[46] there has been a steady decrease in the number of judgments pronounced against Austria. Our analysis offers a convincing explanation of this trend: the ECtHR is starting to accept the progressive decentralisation the conventionality review.

---

[43] *S.L. v. Austria* (45330/99), 09/01/2003; L. *and V. v. Austria* (39392/98), (39829/98), 09/01/2003.

[44] *S.L. v. Austria*, para. 35.

[45] In addition to those mentioned above see: *Woditschka and Wilfling v. Austria* (69756/01), (6306/02), 21/10/2004; *Ladner v. Austria* (18297/03), 03/02/2005; *R.H. v. Austria*, (7336/03), 19/01/2006; *H.G. and G.B. v. Austria* (11084/02) (15306/02), 02/06/2005. For an overview of those cases see: Tretter H, Liegl B, Buchinger K, Steinkellner A (2007) State of the Art Report Strasbourg Court Jurisprudence and Human Rights in Austria: An overview of Litigation, Implementation and Domestic Reform. Ludwig Boltzmann Institute of Human Rights, available at https://www.echr.coe.int/LibraryDocs/JURISTRAS-2007-EN-Austria.pdf. All the links were last accessed on the 30 of June 2024.

[46] The data have been obtained by consulting the ECtHR Annual Reports from 2001 to 2021. Considering only these two extremes, in 2001 the number of applications registered was 229 whilst in 2021 was 222.

3.2 The End of a Long Absence? The Belgian Cour Constitutionnelle in the ECtHR Case Law

As its original name (*Cour d'arbitrage*) suggests, the Belgian Constitutional Court (in the following pages also 'the BCC') was established in 1980 to act solely as an arbiter of the distribution of competences between the various federal entities of the Belgian state.[47] Initially limited to the verification of compliance with the constitutional rules concerning the vertical separation of powers, the competences of the *Cour d'Arbitrage* were increased as early as 1989,[48] just four years after the *Cour d'Arbitrage*'s first ruling in 1985, allowing it to scrutiny legislation for compliance with the principles of equality, non-discrimination, freedom of association and freedom of education.[49] Later, in 2003, incorporating a well-established jurisprudential orientation developed by the same *Cour d'Arbitrage*, the legislator attributed to the latter the competence to review legislation for compatibility with the fundamental rights guaranteed by the Belgian Constitution.[50] Finally, in 2007, the constitutional legislator completed the transformation into a fully-fledged constitutional jurisdiction, and consequently the name of the body was changed to 'Cour constitutionnelle'.

As far as individual access is concerned, there are two distinct procedures for bringing a case before the Belgian Constitutional Court. Directly, by means of an action for annulment (*recours en annulation*) that may be brought by any individual who can show an interest in obtaining a declaration of the unconstitutionality of the challenged legislative act.[51] Only the acts specified in Article 142 of the Constitution, i.e. federal laws, laws of regional parliaments and acts having the force of law, may be challenged. The availability of such an appeal is, however, subject to a strict time limit of six months from the date of publication of the act. The second avenue is the incidental one.[52] The question may be raised by the judge of its own motion or by one of the parties; in the latter case, the court is in principle obliged to raise the question unless it considers that the BCC lacks jurisdiction to rule on the matter or that it has already ruled on an identical question.[53]

Considering the period spanning from 1985—the year of the first pronouncement of the *Cour d'arbitrage*—to 1 January 2023, the BCC is mentioned in only 40 judgments of the Strasbourg Court out of a total of 284 pronounced against the Belgian

[47] Rosoux (2013), p. 201.

[48] Loi speciale du 6 janvier 1989 '*sur la Cour d'arbitrage*', [*Moniteur belge* du 7 janvier 1989].

[49] Rosoux (2013), p. 204.

[50] Loi speciale du 9 mars 2003, *modifiant la loi speciale du 6 janvier 1989 sur la Cour d'arbitrage.*

[51] Loi speciale du 6 janvier 1989, art. 2.

[52] Loi speciale du 6 janvier 1989, articles 26–30.

[53] It must be also noted that legislative acts transposing into the Belgian Legal systems the ECHR and its protocols, as well as act implement EU law, are excluded from the Constitutional Court's scrutiny through an incidental review and can only be challenged through an action for annulment. See: Behrendt (2020), pp. 88–89.

State during the same period, a percentage of roughly 14%.[54] The average number of recurrences per judgment is 3.[55] As we shall see in the following Section, these data are comparable to that obtained for the *Conseil Constituttionnel,* despite the avenue for accessing the French constitutional jurisdictions being much narrower than that to Belgian Constitutional Court. However, if we zero in on the last five years, it seems that the ECtHR is now giving more space to Belgian constitutional case law in its judgments, as the BCC is cited in 30 out of 97 judgments delivered against Belgium in the period 2018–2022 (a percentage of roughly 36%), with 6 citations per judgement as an average. In this sense, also the Belgian case seems to confirm an overall tendency by the Strasbourg Court to paying more attention to constitutional case law in its judgements.

As regards the application of due process guarantees to constitutional proceedings, the BCC has so far remained immune to Article 6 ECHR. The only aspect on which the ECtHR has ruled is the interpretation of Article 26-1 of the Constitutional Court Act; in particular, on the extent of the obligation of the court *a quo* to raise the question of constitutionality if requested by one of the parties.[56]

The issue was addressed by the Strasbourg judges in the judgment in *Coeme* where, rejecting the applicant's complaints on this point, the ECtHR clarified that "the Convention does not guarantee, as such, any right to have a case referred by a domestic court to another national or international authority for a preliminary ruling" while at the same time reminding that *it is not completely impossible* that in certain circumstances, refusal by a domestic court trying a case at final instance might infringe the principle of a fair trial".[57] To this regard, it should be noted that, according to the results of our research, the Belgian Government has never attempted

[54] The search was carried out with the following keywords: 'cour constitutionnelle' and 'constitutional court'. Using the keyword 'cour d'arbitrage' produced no results, so we had to use the term 'arbitrage' alone and filter out the relevant judgments. Instead, the English term used by the ECtHR to refer to the *Cour d'arbitrage* is 'Administrative Jurisdiction and Procedure Court', used in 6 judgments.

[55] Further, the two judgments containing the most citations are judgments in which constitutional jurisprudence is never actually taken into account, as the conventionality of the Belgian Court of Cassation's refusal to raise a preliminary ruling to the Court of Justice question is analysed. See: *Coeme and Others v. Belgium* (32492/96), (32547/96), (32548/96), 22/06/2000; *Wynen and Centre Hospitalier Interrégional Edith-Cavell v. Belgium* (32576/96), 05/11/2002.

[56] The issue was addressed by the Court in two judgments issued two years apart: *Coeme and Others v. Belgium* (32492/96), (32547/96), (32548/96), 22/06/2000; *Wynen and Centre Hospitalier Interrégional Edith-Cavell v. Belgium*, (32576/96), 05/11/2002.

[57] *Coeme et Autres v. Belgium*, para. 114. It is not without significance to point out that the two precedents cited by the judgment to support this passage are two inadmissibility decisions stating that Article 6-1 ECHR is not violated in the event of a reasoned refusal by the national court to refer the case to the Court of Justice of the European Union. See: *Dotta v. Italy* (dec.) (38399/97), 07/09/1999; *Predil Anstalt S.A. v. Italy* (dec.) (31993/96), 08/06/1999. With specific reference to preliminary rulings under Art. 267 TFEU, in another judgment against Belgium, the Strasbourg Court, while reaffirming its jurisdiction to review, through the lens of Art. 6 ECHR, the possible arbitrariness of a refusal to refer, declares that the refusal by the Council of State and the Court of Cassation did not violate the claimants' right of access to a court.

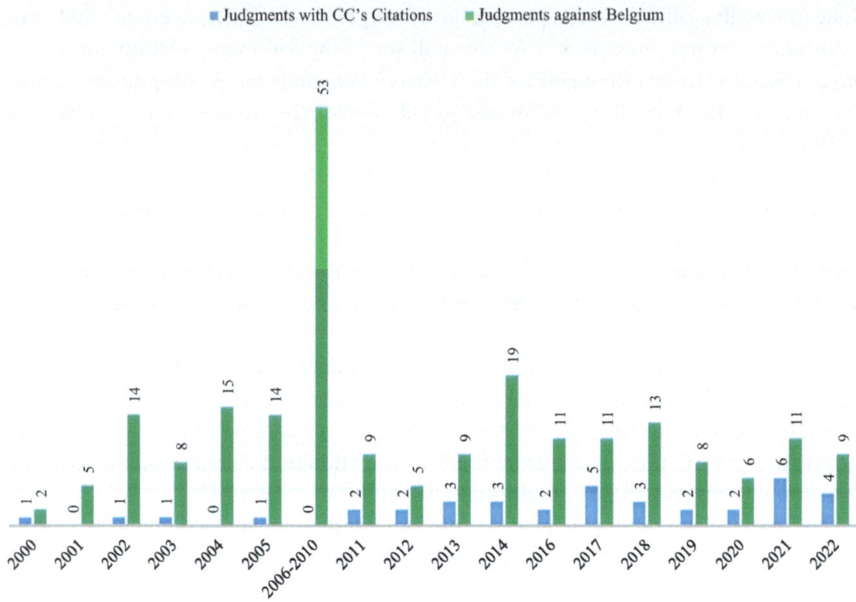

Fig. 3.2 Judgments with BCC citations per year (2000–2022)

to plead the inadmissibility of an application under Article 35 ECHR for failure to exhaust domestic remedies, alleging that the applicant did not bring the case before the BCC.

Concerning the dialogue between the two jurisdictions, it is worth noting that the Belgian *Cour constitutionnelle* considers itself to be bound by the ECHR as interpreted by Strasbourg Court, and albeit not being formally competent to review the conventionality of national law it makes an extensive use of this power,[58] so that its same President, Luc Lavrysen, defined the body is presiding a 'satellite of the ECtHR'.[59] In recent years, the Strasbourg Court has shown increased attention to BCC judgments, citing the conclusions reached by the BCC when they are in line with the outcome of the case;[60] as already mentioned this has resulted in a slight increase in the number of BCC judgments cited each year by the Strasbourg Court (see Fig. 3.2). In spite of this, it has not been possible to find in the Strasbourg's case law, many instances of engagement with the Belgian constitutional jurisprudence: as the low number of citations per judgment indicated, the

[58] L. Lavrysen, J. Theunis et al, *Developments in Belgian Constitutional Law: The Year 2016 in Review*, available at: https://www.researchgate.net/publication/319976766_Developments_in_Belgian_Constitutional_Law.

[59] See, Lavrysen and Theunis (2013), pp. 331–354.

[60] See: *Mortier v. Belgium*, (78017/17), 04/10/2022, para. 154; *Venken and Others v. Belgium*, (46130/14), 76251/14, 42969/16), 06/04/2021, para. 204; *Rooman v. Belgium*, (18052/11), 31/01/2019, para. 80.

ECtHR in fact rarely engaged in an analysis of BCC case law. The most significant example is provided by two "twin judgments" of 2017 on the ban on the full-face veil in public places.[61] As both judgments followed the unanimous Grand Chamber judgment in *S.a.s. v. France*[62]—which concerned the similar French ban—the outcome of the judgment was somewhat predetermined.[63] However, the ECtHR did not shy away from verifying the legitimacy of the different legitimate interests advanced by the Belgian government, namely the protection of women (whereas the French state had invoked public security).[64] Similar to the French case, where the law had been judged compliant by the *Conseil Constitutionnel*, the BCC rejected an action for annulment brought against the law.[65] The Court emphasised this judgment to reach the conclusion that the domestic authorities, following a procedure that lasted for years, had struck a correct balance between the conflicting rights. In this sense the judgment confirms that in matters of religious pluralism the ECtHR leaves a wide margin of appreciation to the Member States, it can also be interpreted as a 'pilatesque' decision.

A second pair of judgments paying close attention to Belgian constitutional case law, is composed of the Grand Chamber and Third Section judgments in the *Vegotex International* case.[66] The case concerned a law enacted by the Belgian parliament, which was given retrospective effects, in order to avoid a significant number of tax-recovery proceedings becoming time-barred. Both formations of the ECtHR declared that the retrospective application of the law did not violate the applicant's right to a fair trial. And in order to do that, both judgments rely extensively on the BCC's judgment affirming the constitutionality of the legislative intervention since it was justified by a 'compelling public interest'.[67]

All in all, this brief analysis of the ECtHR has highlighted that the Court is switching its attitude towards the Belgian *Cour Constitutionelle*, now welcoming the fact that it operates a decentralised review of conventionality. More generally, it seems to also confirms that in highly sensitive issues, for instance the financial

---

[61] *Dakir v. Belgium* (4619/12), 11/07/2017; *Belcacemi et Oussar v. Belgium* (37798/13), 11/07/2017. For a critical commentary on the two judgments see: M. Ferri, *Belkacemi and Oussar v Belgium and Dakir v Belgium: the Court again addresses the full-face veil, but it does not move away from its restrictive approach*; on the differences between French and Belgian law, it is instead interesting to see the comment of one of the third parties intervening before the Court in *Dakir*: E. Brems, *Face veils in Strasbourg (bis): the Belgian cases.* Both in *Strasbourg Observers*, available at: https://strasbourgobservers.com/category/cases/dakir-v-belgium/ (last visited 1 March 2018).

[62] See: above, Sect. 3.3.

[63] Despite the extreme sensitivity of the topic, as evidenced by the interventions in the case by the NGO Liberty and the Centre for Human Rights at the University of Ghent, the relevance assigned to the case is 2.

[64] See *Dakir v. Belgium*, para. 39.

[65] *Ibid*, paras. 18–22.

[66] *Vegotex International S.A. v. Belgium* (49812/09), 03/11/2022.

[67] Ibidem, paras 100–119.

interests of the State, the ECtHR seems to be more deferent to the judicial review carried out by national constitutional courts, which enjoy a wider margin of appreciation in those areas.[68]

3.3 The Conseil Constitutionnel and the Strasbourg Court: A Still "Immature" Relationship

Although the French *Conseil Constitutionnel* (hereafter also 'the FCC') issued its first decision some three years before the Strasbourg Court became operational, it is only relatively recently that the French Constitutional Court can be regarded, despite its peculiarities, as a constitutional court belonging to the European model,[69] i.e. since the 2008 constitutional reform introduced the *Question Prioritaire de Constitutionnalité* ('the QPC').[70] In fact the FCC, as a product of a legal culture traditionally adverse to judicial review of legislation,[71] could only verify the constitutionality of laws on a preventive basis, and any possibility of individual, even indirect, access to constitutional jurisdiction was excluded. It is therefore legitimate to expect, following the introduction of the QPC, an increase in the presence of French constitutional jurisprudence in Strasbourg *case-law*. As the graph below shows (Fig. 3.3) that is indeed the case. If one considers the last decade, the *Conseil Constitutionnel* is cited in 53 out 193 (36.5%) judgments delivered against France, whereas the average percentage of judgment with citations considering the whole period covered by the research (1960–2022) is of 10.58%.

However, while there has been a significant increase in the frequency of judgment with FCC's citations, this does not seem to correspond to an intensification of the dialogue between the two levels of jurisdiction. In fact, if one considers that the average number of citations of the FCC in each Strasbourg judgment the figure does not vary significantly in the last decade, remaining stable at an average of 4 citations per judgment, amongst the lowest figure obtained. This data is easily explained. First of all, in order for a question of constitutionality to reach the FCC, it has to pass two scrutinies, the first carried out by the judge before whom the question is raised and the second, more in-depth, carried out by the Court of Cassation or the Council of State, the only jurisdictions that are legitimated to submit the question of

[68] Besides the cases analysed above, it shall be mentioned the judgment in *Mortier v. Belgium*, concerning the Belgian legislation on eutanasia. The Belgian Constitutional Court affirmed that on the subject of euthanasia, national authorities enjoy a wide margin of appreciation, and thus declared the legislation compatible with Article 2 ECHR. The ECtHR confirmed the findings of the constitutional court. See: *Mortier v. Belgium*, cit., paras 65, 137, 154.

[69] See Badinter (2009), pp. 2–3.

[70] To be more precise, the QPC was introduced by Article 29 of the *Loi constitutionnelle n° 2008-724 du 23 juillet 2008 de modernisation des institutions de la Ve République*.

[71] Stone Sweet (1992), in particular Ch. 1.

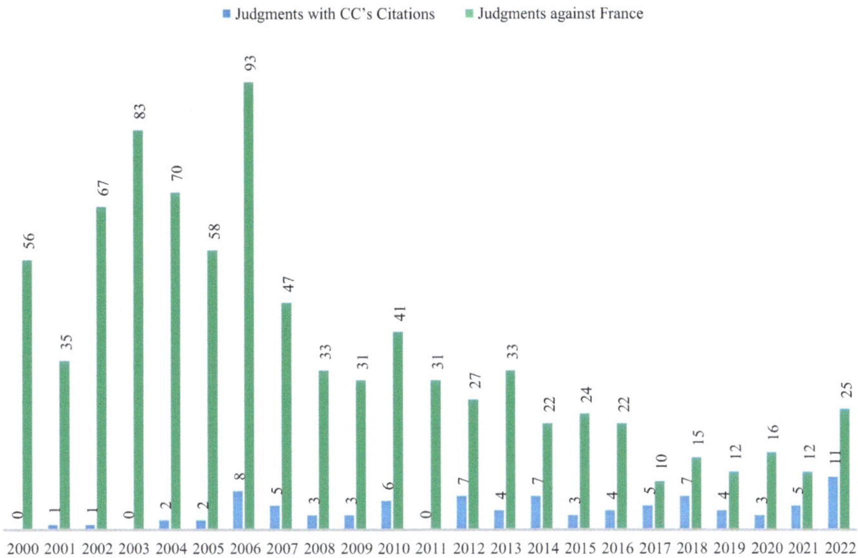

Fig. 3.3 Judgments with FCC citations per year (2000–2022)

constitutionality.[72] This articulated procedure has an obvious deflationary effect on the body's workload: since its introduction in 2009 the FCC had decided just over 1000 questions of constitutionality, [73]when, for example, the Italian Constitutional Court had settled around the same number of questions in the period 2018–2022.[74] Furthermore, it must be considered that, in the French legal system, the main actor in the dialogue with the European Court is the *Cour de Cassation*,[75] as only the latter is competent to judge the conformity of laws with international treaties.[76] The same

[72]More on the functioning of the French incidental-appeal, see: Carcassonne et al. (2015); Rousseau (2012).

[73]See: *Rapport annuel 2022 du Conseil constitutionnel*, 5. Available at: https://www.conseil-constitutionnel.fr/rapport-activite-2022-numerique/pdf/rapport-conseil-constit-2022-web.pdf.

[74]See: Corte Costituzionale, *Giurisprudenza Costituzionale dell'anno 2022. Dati Quantitativi ed* Analisi, 17. Available at: https://www.cortecostituzionale.it/annuario2022/pdf/Dati_quantitativi_e_di_analisi_2022.pdf.

[75]See: *Discours prononcé par M. Guy Canivet, premier président de la Cour de cassation lors du séminaire organisé à la Cour européenne des droits de l' homme le 21 janvier 2005*, available at url: https://www.courdecassation.fr/publications_26/discours_entretiens_2039/archives_2201/nationales_convention_8451.html.

[76]This is possible thanks to the strong, if not insuperable, presumption of constitutionality that assists international treaties. This is moreover due to the fact that before they can be ratified by the President, treaties must necessarily pass the constitutionality review carried out by the *Conseil constitutionnel* itself.

FCC in the so-called *Arret IVG*, on the subject of the voluntary interruption of pregnancy, ruled out being able to review the conformity of laws with international treaties.[77]

If we finally add to this picture the fact that the FCC never cites the Strasbourg judgments in its decisions—even though it shows knowledge of the conventional jurisprudence—one can understand why the one between these two jurisdictions has been effectively called a "dialogue sans paroles".[78] In light of the narrowness of the avenues for individual access, and the objective nature of its review, the *Conseil Constitutionnel* essentially benefit of a conventional immunity,[79] as the guarantees of a fair trial have never been applied to proceedings before it.[80] The only partial exception is constituted by the Constitutional Council's jurisdiction in electoral disputes, however, the ECtHR, upon receiving the application, excluded the applicability of Article 6 ECHR in this ambit. The principle was affirmed in the famous case of *Pierre-Bloch v. France*,[81] in which although the applicant claimed that the litigation before the FCC was of a mixed nature, the Court affirmed the exclusively political nature of the judgment and consequently declared Article 6 ECHR inapplicable.[82] Silent though it may be, in the dialogue between these two courts it is nevertheless possible to identify some issues which were object of debate. The main one was undoubtedly that of the retroactive application of laws, measures known in French law as '*lois de validation*'.[83]

---

[77] The Constitutional Council affirmed that "il n'appartient pas au Conseil constitutionnel, lorsqu'il est saisi en application de l'article 61 de la Constitution, d'examiner la conformité d'une loi aux stipulations d'un traité ou d'un accord international". See: C.C., Décision N° 74-54 du 15 janvier 1075, *Considerant* 7.

[78] See O. Dutheillet de Lamothe, *Conseil Constitutionnel et Cour européenne des droits de l'homme: un dialogue sans paroles*, in *Le Dialogue des juges. Mélanges en l'honneur du président Bruno Genevois*, Paris, Dalloz, 2009, 403 ff. cited in F. Tulkens, *Convention européenne des droits de l'homme et Cours suprêmes*, available at url: http://www.conseil-constitutionnel.fr/conseil-constitutionnel/root/bank_mm/cedh_13fev2009/cedh_ftulkens_130209.pdf.

[79] Burgorgue Larsen (2008), p. 266.

[80] Moreover, it should be noted how this principle, according to our empirical research, supplemented for this purpose also with the admissibility decisions, has never been explicitly affirmed by the Court edu in relation to the QPC, one can however easily come to this conclusion by analogically applying the case law against Italy, for which please refer to: *supra*, footnote 64. However, the EDU Court affirmed the conventional legitimacy of the QPC in a 2015 admissibility decision (*Renard et autres v. France* (3569/12), 17/07/2015. For a commentary on the decision see: Sudre (2015).

[81] *Pierre-Bloch v. France* (24194/94), 21/10/1997.

[82] J. F. Flauss, *L'applicabilité de la Convention européenne des droits de l'homme au contentieux des élections parlementaires: les enseignements de l'arrêt Pierre Bloch*, in *Cahiers du Conseil constitutionnel*, no. 4/1998, available at: https://www.conseil-constitutionnel.fr/nouveaux-cahiers-du-conseil-constitutionnel/l-applicabilite-de-la-convention-europeenne-des-droits-de-l-homme-au-contentieux-des-elections.

[83] In French law, validation law is a law approved by the parliament to retroactively validate an act that has been or may be recognized as illegal by a judge. On the point see: Massot (2009).

The leading case *Zielniski et Pradal* of 1999 made manifest a latent contrast between the position of the *Conseil constitutionnel* and that of the Strasbourg Court.[84] In particular, the latter court held that the risk of a financial loss for the State was insufficient as a justification for the retroactivity of the law:

> [t]he Court considers that the financial risk adverted to by the Government (see paragraph 53 above) *and expressly noted by the Constitutional Council in the reasons it gave for its decision* cannot in itself warrant the legislature's substituting itself both for the parties to the collective agreement and for the courts in order to settle the dispute[85]

and therefore, condemned the French State for violation of Art. 6(1) ECHR. It is evident from the above passage that the ECtHR openly censures the decision of the *Conseil Constitutionnel,* which had held that financial stability alone could suffice to justify the retroaction of a rule.[86] In a series of subsequent judgments,[87] the ECtHR acknowledges a rapprochement between the two jurisprudences, noting that the FCC started to require a sufficient general interest.[88] Nevertheless, the ECtHR continued to condemn France on the grounds that it was not established that the risk to the stability of the banking system, the interest that the retroactive rule was intended to protect, was sufficiently serious and real.[89] A last condemnation concerning the *lois de validation* arrived in *Lilly France (no. 2),*[90] which is however the last, due to the fact that the Constitutional Council ultimately adopted the criteria established by Strasbourg, requiring that the retroactive law be justified not by a sufficient general interest, but by "un motif impérieux d'intérêt général",[91] in line with what required by the ECtHR in *Zielinski et Pradal.*[92]

An issue on which the Strasbourg Court has shown itself in agreement with French constitutional jurisprudence is the principle of secularism. The case to which reference must necessarily be made is the Grand Chamber's ruling in *S.A. S. v. France.*[93] As is well known, the applicant in *S.A.S.* had lamented before the Strasbourg Court that the absolute ban of wearing of niqabs and burqas throughout

[84] *Zielinski et Pradal & Gonzalez et autres v. France* (24846/94), (34165/96 to 34173/96), 28/10/1999.

[85] Ibidem, para. 59 (emphasis added).

[86] See CC, Décision n° 93-329 DC du 13 janvier 1994.

[87] See. *Lecarpentier et autre v. France* (67847/01), 14/02/06; *Cabourdin v. France* (60796/00), 11/04/2006; Vezon v. France (66018/01), 18/04/2006; *Saint-Adam et Millot v. France* (72038/01), 02/05/2006; *Ducret v. France* (40191/02), 12/06/2007; and *Achache v. France* (16043/03), 03/10/2006, where the Edu Court explicitly states that it is merely making an analogical application of the principle contained in *Carpentier.*

[88] *Ibid,* para. 46 (emphasis added); and with identical wording, *Cabourdin v. France,* para. 36; *Vezon v. France, para.* 36; *Saint-Adam et Millot v. France*, para. 26.

[89] See amongst others, Le *Carpentier et autre v. France*, para. 47.

[90] *Lilly France (no. 2) v. France* (20429/07), 25/11/2010.

[91] See, most recently, CC, dec. nn° 2013-366 QPC du 14 février 2014, *Recital* 3.

[92] See, *Zielkinski et Pradal & Gonzalez et autres v. France*, para. 57.

[93] *S.A.S. v. France* (43835/11), 01/07/2014.

French territory violated her freedom of religion guaranteed by Article 9 ECHR.[94] The norm in question, prior to its entry into force, had been submitted to the Conseil Constitutionnel for scrutiny at the request of the presidents of the two branches of parliament. The judges of the Rue de Montpensier had concluded that the rule was constitutional in as much as it did not prevent the wearing of the burqa or niqab in places of worship open to the public, i.e. mosques.[95] Despite the substantive absoluteness of the prohibition, the Strasbourg judges did not depart from the proportionality test carried out at national level essentially affirming the conventionality of the contested law.[96] In the *Ebrahimian* case the Strasbourg Court maintained the same attitude.[97] The case concerned a French citizen of Muslim faith whose contract as a social worker at a psychiatric hospital had not been renewed because of her refusal to work with the uncovered head.[98] The ECtHR found that the measure was proportionate to the interest pursued, namely the neutrality of the public service. In this respect, it should be noted that the ECtHR proportionality test, rather than being conducted with regard to the existence of a 'less restrictive means' is focused on the importance of the principle of secularity in the French legal system as elaborated by the domestic courts.[99] Considering that the Strasbourg Court's mission is the protection of human rights in individual cases, the omission of the proportionality test with regard to the specific circumstances of the case, preferring instead to abstractly analyse the compatibility of the measure, and of the entire French legal system, in the light of ECHR law, seems nonetheless censurable,[100] as it may have precluded a virtuous dialogue between the two levels of jurisdiction aimed at achieving the best balance between the principle of secularism and freedom of religion. At the same time, one may also consider that this deference towards the principle of secularism as articulated by the FCC appears entirely legitimate, as the secular nature of the French state is affirmed in Article 1 of the 1958 Constitution.

Finally, it is worth considering two cases in which the ECtHR applied the *dicta* of the FCC to cases pending before it, thus enforcing its rulings. The first is the judgment in *N.M. v France*.[101] Here, the Strasbourg Court, underlining that the

---

[94] Loi n° 2010-1192 du 11 octobre 2010, *interdisant la dissimulation du visage dans l'espace public*. For a more detailed exposition of the circumstances of the case, see instead: Ruet (2016).

[95] C.C., Décision No° 2010-613 DC du 7 octobre 2010, *Considerant* 5.

[96] On this point see: *S.A.S. v. France as a problematic precedent*, in *Strasbourg Observers*, available at: https://strasbourgobservers.com/2014/07/09/s-a-s-v-france-as-a-problematic-precedent/ (last visited 30 November 2017).

[97] *Ebrahimian v. France* (64846/11), 26/11/2015.

[98] Ibidem, paras. 5–9.

[99] Judge O'Leary's dissenting opinion criticises precisely the excessive abstractness of the proportionality test, complaining how the majority failed to consider the possible repercussions of non-renewal on the applicant. See, Ibid, *Opinion en partie concordante et en partie discordante de la juge O'Leary*, V.

[100] Similar criticisms have been raised by: Ruet (2016), pp. 5–9. Available at:https://journals.openedition.org/revdh/2516.

[101] *N.M. v France* (66328/14), 03/02/2022.

FCC had abrogated the transitory disposition of a law allowing for its retroactive application,[102] concluded that the interpretation by Council of the State of the FCC's judgment as allowing the retroactive application of the same law to cases pending at the date of delivery of the judgment even if referring to facts precedent to the same date, violated the applicant's right to peaceful enjoyment of possession.[103] In the 2021 judgment in *Jarrand v. France*, instead, the Court affirmed that the applicant's detention was not legal according to the criteria established by the FCC, requiring that a person's suspect of having committed a crime can be interrogated only after having being informed of the date and nature of the offence they are suspected of having committed, and of his right to leave the police premises at any time.[104] In both cases then, the ECtHR not only repaired a breach of ECHR right, but seemingly framed its ruling as an implementation of the principles established by the FCC.

At the end of this brief analysis of the Strasbourg case law in which the FCC is cited, a few reflections are in order. First of all, the narrowness of the avenues of access to the FCC, as well as the fact that is the Cour de Cassation which is competent to review the conventionality of domestic law, has considerably limited the impact of Strasbourg jurisprudence on the functioning of the French constitutional justice system. For the same reason, until now, the role of the Constitutional Council's jurisprudence as a formant of conventional law has been extremely limited, as evidenced by the small number of citations of the latter body in Strasbourg judgments. In conclusion, such a relationship can be said to be unripe as it does not yet seem to have borne significant fruit. Yet, in light of the peculiarities of the French legal system repeatedly stressed, it is not possible to say with certainty whether this fruit will ever ripen.

3.4 A Relationship Based on Mutual Respect. The ECtHR and the Bundesverfassungsgericht

When the European Court pronounced its first judgement in the *Lawless* case in 1960,[105] the Federal Constitutional Court was the one of the two active constitutional courts in Europe—the other was the Italian Constitutional Court—having already been in operation for nine years, and had already developed a considerable reputation as a constitutional court committed to the protection of human rights.[106]

[102] It must be noted that the ECtHR pays close attention to the Constitutional Council judgment, even citing in its decision a passage of a commentary to the judgement by the secretariat of Constitutional Council. See, ibidem, para. 29.

[103] Ibidem, paras 60–62.

[104] *Jarrand v. France* (56138/16), 09/12/2021, in particular paras 65–66.

[105] *Lawless v. Ireland* (332/57), 14/11/1960.

[106] Quint (2006), p. 152.

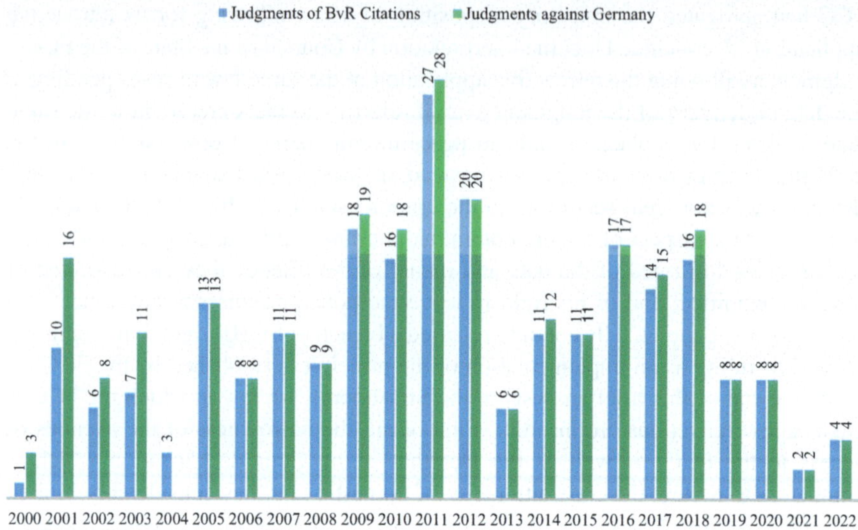

Fig. 3.4 Judgments with BVG citations per year (2000–2022)

The relationship between the two courts has been facilitated by the ease with which it is possible to appeal to the Constitutional Tribunal,[107] it is difficult for the ECtHR to rule on a case that has not been analysed beforehand by the German Constitutional Court. The numerical data concerning the judgments against the German State in which the *Bundesverfassungsgericht* (hereafter 'the BVG') is cited is clear in this respect: (Fig. 3.4) out of a total of 327 judgments with Germany as Respondent State,[108] the BVG is cited in 311, a percentage of approximately 95,1%. Another data confirms that the European Court pays particular attention to German constitutional jurisprudence: in each of these judgments, the average number of citations of the BVG is approximately 12.7—one of the highest figures among those obtained.

As regards the applicability of Article 6 to the proceedings before the BVG, it has been confirmed both in relation to the *Verfassungsbeschwerde* of Article 93(4a) of the German Basic Law—i.e. the individual direct appeal—and to the *Konkrete Normenkontrolle* of Article 100 of the German Constitution, i.e. the incidental procedure.[109] However, only the individual direct complaint (*Verfassungsbeschwerde*) governed by Article 93(4a) Grundgesetz (GG) is generally

---

[107] For doctrinal works on the powers and competences of the Federal Constitutional Court, see first of all: Kommers (2012).

[108] Please note that the judgments counted here are those identified in the previous chapter. See *supra*, Part I, Ch. 2, para. 1.

[109] See *Probmeister v. Germany*, paras. 47–48.

considered by the Strasbourg Court an effective remedy to potentially prevent a violation of any of the rights guaranteed by the ECHR.[110] Nonetheless, it has to be noted that this appeal has very low success rates: in 2022, out of a total of 4645 decisions adopted by the two BVG Senates, only 57 were successful, a percentage of approximately 1.22%.[111] Moreover, in 3357 cases, the complaint was rejected without the appellant being given any reasons (77% of the total). This practice of the BVG to not giving reasons for the rejection, whilst has never been deemed a violation of the right to access a court by the ECtHR, is not without consequences from a conventional perspective. On several occasions, the ECtHR has indeed held an application admissible even if the applicant did not respect the mandatory formal requirements to lodge a complaint before the BVG, emphasising that "the Court cannot speculate as to why the Federal Constitutional Court decided not to admit the complaint for adjudication and whether or not it examined the substance of the complaint".[112]

Moving to consider how the ECtHR affected the functioning of the German constitutional justice system, the most significant profile is undoubtedly the application of the notion of due process to the BVG. On this issue, it is necessary to briefly review the historical development of Strasbourg case law. The starting point is the *Buchholz* case from 1981,[113] where the Strasbourg Court was called upon to decide whether the duration of the domestic proceedings had been unreasonable. In establishing the period to be taken into account for the assessment under Article 6, the ECtHR stated that "the Constitutional Court was not called on to determine the dispute ("contestation") between Mr. Buchholz and his employers which had been before the labour courts [...] [t]he proceedings subsequent to the judgment by the Federal Labour Court thus fall outside the ambit of Article 6 par. 1 (art. 6(1)). *There is no need to decide whether it might be otherwise in different circumstances*".[114] While holding that Article 6(1) ECHR does not apply to constitutional proceedings,

[110] Lastly see: *Hanan v. Germany* [GC] (4871/16), 16/02/2021. Here the ECtHR declared that the constitutional complaint constituted an effective remedy to challenge a decision to discontinue an investigation, in as much as the German Constitutional Court had the power to annul the decision.

[111] All these data were obtained from reading the statistics of the *Bundesverfassungsgericht* made available by the court itself on its website at: http://www.bundesverfassungsgericht.de/EN/Verfahren/Jahresstatistiken/2016/statistik_2016_node.html.

[112] Lastly see: *P.N. v. Germany* (74440/17), 11/06/2020 para. 29. Similarly also see: *Affaire Epple v. Germany* (77909/01), 24/03/2005; *Annen v. Germany* (3690/10), 26/11/2015; *Marc Brauer v. Germany* (24062/13), 01/09/2016. It is perhaps not superfluous to remind that a well-established principle of the ECtHR case law is that for the purposes of admissibility under Article 35 ECHR, the last domestic action brought must have been brought in compliance with the procedural requirements of domestic law. See *ex multis, Guzzardi v. Italy*, Plenary (7367/76), 06/11/1980; *Cardot v. France* (11069/84), 19/03/1991, para. 34.

[113] *Buccholz v. Germany* (7759/77), 06/05/81. A commentary on the case can be found in: D'Orazio (1991), pp. 105-106.

[114] Ibidem, para. 48 (italics added).

the last sentence seems to suggest that under different circumstances constitutional jurisdiction might fall within the scope of that provision. This is exactly what occurs five years later with the *Deumeland* judgment.[115] Although, in reality, no significant differentiation from *Buchholz* can be found, here the ECHR considers that in order to assess the reasonable duration of the trial *under* Article 6(1) ECHR, the proceedings before the BVG must also be taken into account. The Court omits to give reasons for the *revirement* from the previous case-law,[116] merely stating that, with regard to the determination of the overall duration of the proceedings "[t]he Federal Constitutional Court is to be taken into account in this respect [. . .], in that, although it had no jurisdiction to rule on the merits, its decision was capable of affecting the outcome of the claim".[117] The principle contained in *Deumeland* is of absolute relevance as it affirms for the first time the applicability of Article 6 ECHR also to constitutional proceedings, albeit limited to the reasonable duration of proceedings. A few years after this judgment, in 1989, the ECHR, in the *Bock* case,[118] however, refuses to reiterate what was stated in *Deumeland.* Avoiding ruling directly on the question of whether constitutional proceedings are subject to the application of Article 6(1) ECHR, the Court states that "the question whether those proceedings come within the purview of Article 6 para. 1 (Art. 6(1)) does not need to be resolved in order to decide the main issue".[119] The Court, on the other hand, in *Süssmann,*[120] which followed the landmark ruling in *Ruiz Mateos v. Spain,*[121] takes up the dictum of *Deumeland* confirming that Article 6(1) ECHR is applicable to constitutional proceedings subject to the condition that the latter are capable of influencing the outcome of the proceedings before the domestic courts.[122]

This condition turns out to be little more than a formal clause, as it can only exclude those constitutional proceedings on a different subject matter from the main proceedings in which the applicant participates, or other proceedings on a similar subject matter but whose decision is not considered by the Strasbourg Court to be prejudicial to the resolution of the dispute. In fact, in subsequent judgments on the subject, the Court will omit to repeat it.[123] After having definitively affirmed the applicability of Article 6(1) ECHR to constitutional jurisdiction, the European Court

[115] *Deumeland v. Germany* (9384/81), 29/05/1986.

[116] The same observation has also been made by: Ibrido (2016), p. 14.

[117] *Deumeland v. Germany*, para. 77.

[118] *Bock v. Germany* (11118/84), 29/03/1989.

[119] Ibidem, para. 37.

[120] *Süssmann v. Germany* [GC] (20024/92), 16/09/1996.

[121] *Ruiz-Mateos v. Spain* (12952/87), 23/06/1993.

[122] Ibidem, para. 39.

[123] It is indeed repeated in the *Probstmeister* judgment (20950/92), 01/07/1997, para. 48) and in *Pammel* (17820/91, 01/07/1997), but traces of it are lost in the jurisprudence of the so-called *nouvelle Cour*, in which the applicability of Art. 6(1) ECHR to constitutional proceedings is no longer considered to be at issue, although the German Government continues to contest it. See *Klein v. Germany* (33379/96), 27/07/2000; *Affaire Becker v. Germany* (45448/99), 26/09/2002; *Affaire Hesse Anger v. Germany* (45835/99), 06/02/2003.

of Human Rights (ECHR) then sought to define what is the maximum duration of a constitutional trial that can be called reasonable.

This definitional work was mostly carried out through decisions of inadmissibility in the early 2000s,[124] and one has to wait until 2007 to find a trace of it in the case-law on the merits, when with the judgment in the *Kirsten* case,[125] the Strasbourg Court, recalling these decisions, states that, in principle, the duration of a constitutional trial is reasonable if it falls within a range of three years and six months up to four years and eight months, taking into account, in particular, the "unique context of the German reunification".[126] Consequently, four years later, when the BVG had already cleared the backlog caused by the German re-unification, the ECtHR, in the *Kuhlen-Rafsandjani* case,[127] declared a duration of approximately four years unreasonable. In this judgment, the ECtHR, emphasising the peculiar nature of the case before the BVG—the applicant had asked for the annulment of the decision depriveing him the right to visit to his children—stated that the need to adopt a decision within a short time, regardless of the complexity of the case, must be taken into account in affect the assessment of whether the duration of the proceedings was reasonable.[128]

This principle was confirmed in a judgment delivered twenty days later, in which the Strasbourg Court criticised the fact that the BVG had rendered its decision one year and seven months after the introduction of the constitutional appeal in which the applicant had also requested the annulment of the decision a denying him access rights to his son, as the proceedings before the lower courts had already lasted more than four years.[129] On the contrary, in *Gast and Popp* it was held that a duration of constitutional proceedings of approximately three years was to be considered reasonable also in light of the celerity of ordinary proceedings.[130] In essence, from an overall reading of the abode illustrated case law, it is difficult to derive generally applicable rules, as the ECtHR is oriented towards a decidedly casuistic approach which also takes into account the global duration of the proceedings in which the applicant participated. The only benchmark consistently applied by the ECtHR seems, ultimately, to be the one according to which a constitutional trial lasting more than five years violates Article 6(1) ECHR.[131]

---

[124] See in particular the decisions: *Schwengel v. Germany* [dec] (52442/99), 02/03/2000; *Goretzki v. Germany* [dec.] (52447/99), 24/01/2002.

[125] *Kirsten v. Germany* (19124/02), 15/02/2007.

[126] *Ibid*, para. 46.

[127] *Kuhlen-Rafsandjani v. Germany* (21980/06), (26944/07), (36948/08), 20/01/2011.

[128] Ibidem, para. 83.

[129] See *Tsikakis v. Germany* (1521/06), 10/02/2011, para. 67.

[130] *Gast and Popp v. Germany* (29357/95), 25/02/2000.

[131] This limit can be deduced from an overall reading of the jurisprudence as no contingent circumstance, not even reunification, is considered to justify a duration of proceedings longer than this threshold. In this sense, see the following judgments: *Klasen v. Germany* (75204/01), 05/10/2006; *Kirsten v. Germany*; *Leela Forderkreis E.V. and Others v. Germany* (58911/00), 06/11/2008; *Kaemena and Thonebohn v. Germany* (45749/06), (51115/06), 22/01/2009; *Hoffer*

The topic of the reasonable length of trial also comes into consideration when looking at the German constitutional justice system through the lens of Article 35 ECHR. The effectiveness for conventional purposes of the German individual constitutional complaint has known, for a considerable period of time, a significant exception concerning the unreasonable duration of proceedings in civil matters. Indeed, since the BVG does not have the power to award pecuniary compensation to individuals who complain about the excessive length of a civil case, the European Court of Human Rights, starting with the *leading-case Sürmeli,*[132] declared the ineffectiveness of the complaint to the BVG to challenge the violation of the right to a reasonable duration of civil proceedings.

The Grand Chamber's pronouncement, as has often happens, was followed by an avalanche of appeals in which German citizens sought redress for the violation of their right to a trial of reasonable duration.[133] From 6 June 2006—the date of the ruling in *Sürmeli*—until 2 September 2010—the date of the pilot judgment in the *Rumpf* case[134]—we counted 26 judgments in which claimants complained about the unreasonable length of proceedings.[135] It is relevant to point out that in some of these judgments the Strasbourg Court notes that the BVG itself recognised the violation of Article 6 ECHR, although it did not have the means to remedy it.[136] This repetitive jurisprudence culminated in the adoption by the ECHR of a pilot judgment ordering the German legislature to provide "without delay, and at the latest within one year of the date on which the judgment becomes final in accordance with Article 44 § 1 of the Convention, an effective domestic remedy or combination of such remedies capable of securing adequate and sufficient redress for excessively long proceedings, in line with the Convention principles as established in the Court's case-law".[137] A year later, the German Parliament implemented this judgment by providing for a system of compensation for the excessive duration of civil proceedings, constitutional proceedings and the investigation phase of criminal pro-

and Annen v. Germany (397/07), (2322/07), 13/01/2011. In contrast, a duration of 4 years and 6 months, in the *Peter* case, was considered reasonable in light of the fact that the BVG had prioritised the decision of a case of greater public interest that could also have had a direct effect on the applicant's case. See *Peter v. Germany* (68919/10), 04/09/2014.

[132] *Sürmeli v. Germany* [GC] (75529/01), 08/06/2006.

[133] From 2007 until 2010, approximately 80% of the sentences pronounced by Strasbourg against Germany concerned the excessive length of proceedings. See Braasch (2010), p. 1007.

[134] *Rumpf v. Germany* (46344/06), 02/09/2010.

[135] It must also be emphasised that in many of these judgments, the ECHR acknowledges that the procedure before the Constitutional Court was swift and efficient. See *Bayer v. Germany* (8453/04), 16/07/2009; *D. E. v. Germany* (1126/05), 16/07/2009; *Wildgruber (No. 2) v. Germany* (42402/05), (42423/05), 21/01/2010; *Gromzig v. Germany* (13791/06), 04/02/2010.

[136] See in particular: *Ballhausen v. Germany* (1479/08), 23/04/2009, para. 66.

[137] *Rumpf v. Germany,* Device no. 5.

ceedings.[138] It is worth stressing that the law did not take into account the trial phase of criminal proceedings, as the ECthR itself has clarified in *Ommer,*[139] in those cases the constitutional complaint is an effective remedy as the BVG can grant relief to the defendant by declaring the offence inadmissible or by requiring the prosecuting court to take into account the excessive duration of the proceedings as a mitigating factor of the sentence.[140]

As a last note concerning the ECtHR scrutiny on the duration of constitutional proceedings, it is worth mentioning that that it can also be conducted under Article 5(4) ECHR, guaranteeing the right to detained to a speedy review of the legality of their detention. Under this provision, as it appears from the 2018 judgment in *Ilnseher v Germany,* the maximum legitimate duration of constitutional proceedings is, as for ordinary courts, far shorter than under Article 6 ECHR.[141] In this judgment the ECtHR held that a 8-month duration was a relatively long period, ultimately considering it compatible with ECHR requirements in light of the “special features” of the proceedings before a constitutional court and the fact that the Constitutional Court did not remain inactive during that time, having adopted an interim decision denying the applicant’s request for a suspension of the detention measure.[142]

As regards the dialogue between the two jurisdictions, the first element to be pointed out is how the BVG frames the position of the ECtHR judgments in the German legal system. According to Art. 59(2) GG, the ECHR enjoys the same rank of all international treaties, i.e. that of ordinary federal laws. The Federal Constitutional Court, with a landmark decision of 2004, in the *Görgülu* case,[143] specified that, whilst the ECHR as interpreted by the Strasbourg Court is an interpretative tool for constitutional provisions concerning fundamental rights, the judgments of the ECtHR are not directly applicable and ordinary judges shall only give execution to an ECtHR judgment to the extent that it is compatible with the national constitutional framework. Read alone this affirmation may seems to encourage disobedience from ordinary judges,[144] and indeed even the then president of the ECtHR Luzius Wildhaber feared that it could be misinterpreted and abused by judges in

[138]The regulation in question is the: *Gesetz über den Rechtsschutz bei überlangen Gerichtsverfahren und strafrechtlichen Ermittlungsverfahren*, Vom 24. November 2011. For a content analysis of the standard, see: Arnaud (2015), pp. 119–120.

[139]*Ommer v. Germany (No. 2)* (26073/03), 13/11/2008.

[140]Ibidem, para. 61.

[141]See: *Ilnseher v Germany* [GC] (10211/12), (27505/14), 04/12/2018.

[142]Ibidem, paras 266–270.

[143]*Bundesverfassungsgericht* decision of October 14, 2004, 2 BVG 1481/04, *Görgülü.*

[144]Indeed, in doctrine the pronouncement has been the subject of differing interpretations as to its real significance: some see it as a sign of “rebellion”, see Hartwig (2005), p. 870; others glimpse behind an apparent harshness, an attitude of openness: see F. Palermo, *Il Tribunale costituzionale federale e la teoria selettiva" dei controimiti*, in *Forum costituzionale*, available at url: http://www.forumcostituzionale.it/wordpress/wp-content/uploads/pre_2006/107.pdf (last visited 30 November 2017); still others emphasise that the pronouncement definitively affirmed the fact that ordinary judges are generally bound to execute Strasbourg judgments.

authoritarian countries.[145] Yet, in the same judgment the BVG also affirms that the ECHR system of fundamental rights protection is a concretion of Article 1(2)GG, which establishes human rights as a the basis of society—and that

> [t]he binding effect of a decision of the ECHR extends to all state bodies and in principle imposes on these an obligation, within their jurisdiction and without violating the binding effect of statute and law, to end a continuing violation of the Convention and to create a situation that complies with the Convention." [...] A complainant may challenge the disregard of this duty of consideration as a violation of the fundamental right whose area of protection is affected in conjunction with the principle of the rule of law.

De facto, then, the BVG has enhanced the ECHR rank within the German legal system, declaring the observance of the ECHR as interpreted by the Strasbourg Court an element of the "rule of law principle" which is an "eternal principle" of the German Basic Law.[146]

As regards jurisprudential conflict, the first arose in the famous *Von Hannover* saga.[147] Ruling on the appeal by Princess Caroline of Monaco, who complained that the publication of some photos depicting her while skiing had violated her right to privacy, the Strasbourg Court censured the previous decision in the case by the BVG, which had found the publication to be lawful in as much the photos were taken in places open to public.[148] In its judgment, the Strasbourg Court replaces its own balancing criteria with those developed by German constitutional jurisprudence. In particular, the judgment criticises the spatial criterion adopted the BVG, affirming that the decisive criterion for evaluating the legitimacy of a publication is whether it contributes to the debate in a democratic society,[149] consequently declaring the publication in violation of the Princess's right to privacy. Eight years later, the Grand Chamber of the Court was again called upon to rule on the extension of the right to privacy at the request of the same applicant.[150] The judgment in *Von Hannover (No. 2),* is characterised first and foremost by its extensive examination of the Federal Constitutional Court's second decision on the case,[151] which lead the European judges to confirming the balancing carried out by their German colleagues. The ECtHR in light of the concession from the BVG, which abandoned the spatial criterion harshly criticised in the judgment four years before, accepts the decidedly broad interpretation of the concept of "capacity to contribute to the public debate" of Karlsruhe, accepting that a photo of the Princess of Monaco portrayed skiing can contribute to the public debate because it shows how the princess behaves during her

---

[145] See Hoffmeister (2006), p. 729.

[146] Of particular interest is the commentary on the judgment offered by German constitutional judge Lübbe-Wolff, which constitutes a kind of 'authentic interpretation' of the judgment. See: Lübbe-Wolff (2006).

[147] *Von Hannover v. Germany* (59320//00), 24/6/2004.

[148] BVerfG, 15/12/09, 1 BVG 653/96.

[149] *Von Hannover v. Germany*, para. 63.

[150] *Von Hannover v. Germany (No. 2)* (40660/08), (60641/08), 07/02/2012.

[151] Ibidem, paras 40–53.

father's illness.[152] The case as a whole can be taken as an instance of principled dialogue between courts, in which the content of the fundamental rights is determined through an exchange of views between European and national judges and in which the Strasbourg Court, once established the principle, leaves its application to the national constitutional court

Another subject on which there has been a particularly intense—and tense—dialogue between the two Courts is that of preventive custodial measures (*Sicherungsverwahrung*) provided for by German law.[153] The problems with the compatibility of these measures with the Convention have their roots in 2004, the year in which the so-called 'posthumous security custody' was introduced, i.e. a custodial measure, in prison or in a psychiatric hospital, which can be disposed after the execution of a criminal sentence regardless of any indication to that extent in the conviction decision, if elements arise that highlight a high social dangerousness of the offender. This rule also provided for a transitional regime during which the new legislation was to be applicable to persons already sentenced. The first case concerning the *Sicherungsverwahrung* arrived to Strasbourg in 2009.[154] The applicant complained that his pre-trial detention had been extended beyond the statutory limit of ten years pursuant to a law that was not in force at the time of the commission of the offence. The conventional parameters invoked were therefore Article 5(1) ECHR, which protects personal liberty, and Article 7(1) ECHR, which establishes the principle of non-retroactivity of unfavourable criminal law. The BVG decision on the applicant's case found the applicant's complaint manifestly ill-founded,[155] declaring that the *Sicherungsverwahrung,* not being a criminal penalty, was not subject to the prohibition of retrospective application. Contrarywise, the ECtHR concludes that the German security custody constitute a criminal sanction under Article 7 ECHR and therefore that its retrospective application violated the ECHR. Similarly to what happened after the pilot judgment in *Rumpf*—and also thanks to the fact that the government did not try to appeal the judgment before the Grand Chamber—the Strasbourg Court was faced with a series of appeals by individuals who had seen the duration of their security custody extended retroactively. On 13 January 2011, the Fifth Chamber, with four different judgments, definitively reaffirmed the conventional incompatibility of

[152] *Von Hannover v. Germany (No. 2),* paras. 117–118. Reading these paragraphs, one cannot help but notice how the negative form of the statements suggests a skeptical position of the European judges regarding the conclusions reached by the domestic courts.

[153] These measures, due to their partial analogy with those provided for in Law no. 1423 of 27 December 1956, later transposed, with certain amendments, into the 'Anti-Mafia Laws Code', Legislative Decree no. 159 of 6 Sep. 2001 No. 159, have attracted the attention of Italian criminal doctrine. See for example: S. Porro, *La custodia di sicurezza nell'ordinamento penale tedesco. Alcune riflessioni alla luce di Bundesverfassungsgericht, II Senato, 4 maggio 2011, 2 BVG 2365/09 et al.*, in Diritto penale contemporaneo, 18 Nov. 2011, available at: https://www.penalecontemporaneo.it/osservatori/5-diritto-penale-e-processuale-comparato?page=5.

[154] *M. v. Germany* (19359/04), 17/12/2009.

[155] See Ibidem, para. 27.

Sicherungsverwahrung.[156] With a decision of 4 May 2011,[157] the Federal Constitutional Court declared the retroactive application of the extension of security custody beyond ten years to be unconstitutional, but only as long as the legislation did not sufficiently distinguish between preventive detention and sentences of imprisonment, and extended its validity until the intervention of the legislature.[158] The ECtHR, while taking note of the BVG judgment,[159] continued to condemn the German State in similar cases.[160] In December 2012 the German Parliament, amended the legislation governing the security custody in order to comply with the BVG indications,[161] but not with that of the ECtHR, as the retrospective application of the *Sicherungsverwahrung* was maintained. Nonetheless, in subsequent cases where it had the opportunity to review the new regime, the ECtHR, emphasising that the precondition for the retrospective application of the custodial measure is a mental disorder and that its objective is treating it, concluded that it was no longer to be classified as a penalty and was thus compatible with Article 7 ECHR.[162]

One can appreciate a similar attitude of deference on the part of the European Court of Human Rights in cases concerning freedom of conscience and religion, guaranteed by Article 9 ECHR, where the European judges show a decisive deference to the rulings of the German constitutional court. A significant example is provided by two cases in which applicants complained to the Strasbourg Court that they had been dismissed for reasons of 'moral unfitness' by their employers, two religious organisations.[163] Despite the different parameters invoked, Art. 8 and Art. 9 ECHR respectively, the Strasbourg Court, in both cases, shows itself to be respectful of a constitutional jurisprudence, indeed a rather long-standing one,[164] according to which labour judges are called upon to assess the legitimacy of a

---

[156] See *Schummer v. Germany* (No. 1) (27360/04), (42225/07), 13/01/2011; *Mautes v. Germany* (20008/07), 13/01/2011; *Kallweit v. Germany* (17792/07), 13/01/2011; *Haidn v. Germany* (6587/04), 13/01/2011.

[157] 2 BVerfGE 2365/09, 2 BVerfGE 740/10, 2 BVerfGE 2333/08, 2 BVerfGE 1152/10, 2 BVerfGE 571/10.

[158] The German Constitutional Court maintained that its conception of the penalty was different from that of Strasbourg and that the ECtHR concepts are characterised by flexibility and lack of precision. See: Mariniello (2021), p. 284.

[159] See *ex multis*, *O.H. v. Germany* (4646/08), 24/11/2011, paras. 54–55.

[160] In addition to the above-mentioned judgment see: *Schönbrod v. Germany* (48038/06), 24/11/2011; *Kronfeldner v. Germany* (21906/09), 19/01/2012; *Glien v. Germany* (7345/12), 28/11/2013.

[161] *Gesetz zur bundesrechtlichen Umsetzung des Abstandsgebots im Recht der Sicherungsverwahrung*, of 5 December 2012.

[162] Lastly see: *Ilnseher v. Germany* [GC] (10211/12), (27505/14), 04/12/2018. In a similar vein but concerning the retrospective application of the custodial measure beyond statutory limits see: *Bergmann v. Germany* (23279/14), 07/01/2016.

[163] The cases in question are: *Obst v. Germany* (425/03), 23/09/2010 and *Siebenhaar v. Germany* (18136/02), 03/02/2011.

[164] The judgment of the BVG—referred to in both cases cited in the previous footnote—is in fact from 1985. See 2 BVerGe 1703/83, 1718/83 et 856/84.

dismissal only in the light of the rules of ecclesiastical law; thus an adulterous relationship or membership of another confession may well be considered as a serious breach of trust justifying dismissal.[165]

On the opposite side of the spectrum, is worth considering two cases in which the ECtHR censure the interpretation of its judgements given by the BVG. In the 2011 judgment in *Herrmann v. Germany*,[166] the First Chamber of the Strasbourg Court held that the fact that owners of land exceeding 75 hectares were *de jure* members of a hunting association did not violate the applicant's right to property (Article 1 of Protocol 1 ECHR). Considering the margin of appreciation awarded to the State in this ambit the judgment held that the German authorities struck a fair balance between the competing interests.[167] Following a request in that sense by the applicant, the case was referred to the Grand Chamber pursuant to Article 43 ECHR. In the Grand Chamber judgment, extensive reference is made to the judgment of the Federal Constitutional Court, which declared that compulsory membership did not breach the applicant right to property as the restriction was justified by objectives recognised as legitimate by the same ECtHR in *Chassagnou v. France,*[168] namely regulating hunting and rationally managing game stocks.[169] Nonetheless, the Grand Chamber once again substituted its own balancing to that of the BVG and partially overturned the verdict of the First Section, affirming the violation of Article 1 Protocol 1 ECHR. Despite the strong public criticism generated by the judgment, and also a more academic one concerning the *de facto* denial of the existence of the state margin of appreciation in the area,[170] the German legislator promptly intervened to amend the legislation allowing the landowners interests to be taken into account by authorities delimitating hunting areas,[171] thus avoiding a potential conflict.

In conclusion, the relationship between the ECtHR and the BVG can be said to be of substantially loyal cooperation. On the one hand the BVG demonstrates that it takes the case law of the Convention into account, on the other in more politically

[165] However, it must be emphasised that, regardless of the role of the BVG, the European Court of Human Rights to the date has never condemned Germany for a violation of Article 9 ECHR.

[166] *Herrmann v. Germany* (9300/07), 20/01/2011.

[167] Ibidem, para. 56.

[168] *Chassagnou v. France* (25088/94), (28331/95), (28443/95), 29/04/1999.

[169] *Herrmann v. Germany* [GC] (9300/07), 26/06/2012., paras 16–23.

[170] For both see: I. Leijten, "Herrmann v. Germany (GC): The Importance of Precedent and Strasbourg Micromanagament", *Strasbourg Observer*, 12 July 2012, available at: https://strasbourgobservers.com/2012/07/12/herrmann-v-germany-gc-the-importance-of-precedent-and-strasbourg-micromanagement/.

[171] Shields (2022), pp. 36–37. Available at: https://www.gov.scot/binaries/content/documents/govscot/publications/research-and-analysis/2022/12/review-evidence-land-acquisition-powers-land-ownership-restrictions-european-countries/documents/review-evidence-land-acquisition-powers-land-ownership-restrictions-european-countries/review-evidence-land-acquisition-powers-land-ownership-restrictions-european-countries/govscot%3Adocument/review-evidence-land-acquisition-powers-land-ownership-restrictions-european-countries.pdf.

sensitive areas, such as freedom of religion and criminal law, the Strasbourg Court has shown deference for the BVG case law. It is also worth noting the fundamental contribution of the German parliament to the success of this dialogue, often intervening to mediate between the *dicta* of Strasbourg and the indications coming from Karlsruhe.

3.5 The Anomalies of the Italian Case. From Indifference to Dialogue?

Any attempt to analyse the relationship between the Italian Constitutional Court (hereafter also 'the ICC') and the European Court of Human Rights must necessarily start from the consideration that individuals do not have direct access to the ICC. The only way an individual may reach the constitutional court is in the course of a judicial proceeding, by asking the judge to submit a question of constitutionality to the Constitutional Court, with the decision to submit the question lying entirely in the hands of the referring judge. Unsurprisingly then, according to the Strasbourg Court, the Italian *giudizio in via incidentale* does not constitute an effective remedy *under* Article 35 ECHR and therefore a person who intends to turn to Strasbourg to obtain relief for the violation of one of his rights is not obliged to turn first to the Constitutional Court. Starting with the *Brozicek* judgment, the Strasbourg Court has in fact repeatedly affirmed that "in the Italian legal system an individual is not entitled to apply directly to the Constitutional Court for a review of the constitutionality of a law. Only a court which is hearing the merits of a case has the possibility of making a reference to the Constitutional Court, at the request of a party or of its own motion. Accordingly, such an application cannot be a remedy whose exhaustion is required".[172]

From an ECHR perspective, the narrowness of the avenues of access to the ICC has produced two main consequences. The first is that Italian constitutional judges rarely have the opportunity to rule on a case before it reaches Strasbourg. As a consequence, it is not surprising that, as of 1 January 2023, the Constitutional Court is cited only in 335 out of 2368 (14.4%) judgments pronounced against Italy; a ratio of citations about seven times lower than that of the German Constitutional Court in judgments against Germany. As the graph below shows (Fig. 3.5), from a quantitative point of view the relationship between the ICC and the ECHR appears to be in flux.

---

[172] See *Brozicek v. Italy* (10964/84), 19/12/1989, para. 34. This statement has been reiterated several times, most recently in: *Cordella v. Italy* (54414/13), (54264/15), 24/01/2019. This conclusion is fully supported by the Italian doctrine, that emphasised how, in light of the obligation of ordinary judges to try to give to legislative dispositions a constitutionally compliant interpretation before raising the question to the Constitutional Court, the raising of the question of constitutionality is considered as an *ultima ratio*. See: Lamarque (2012), pp. 88–91; Passaglia (2012) pp. 323–324.

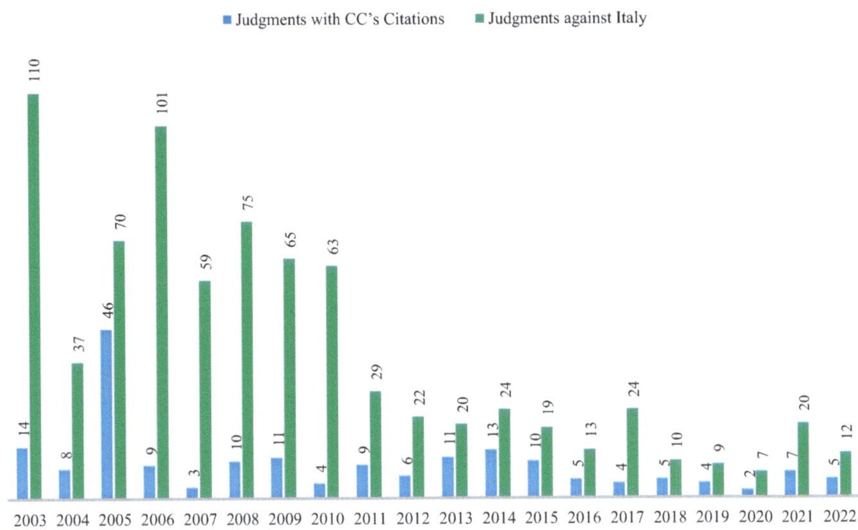

Fig. 3.5 Judgments with ICC citations per year (2003–2022)

Generally speaking, it is impossible not to note how in the last decade there has been a drastic reduction in the number of judgments pronounced each year against Italy. Also, it is observable a trend consisting of an increased number of citations of the ICC. Considering the five-year period 2018–2022, the ratio of ICC's citations out of the total number of judgments delivered each year against Italy is of 39%, almost thrice the overall figure. That the ECtHR is engaging in a more intense dialogue appears to be confirmed also by the data concerning the average number of ICC's citations in each judgement of the Strasbourg Court. The anomaly in 2018 evidence in the graph above (Fig. 3.6) is essentially due to the Grand Chamber judgment in *G. I.E.M.*[173]—which constituted the ECtHR answer to judgment 49/2015 of the Italian Constitutional Court—whose content will be presented in the following pages. Apart from this deviance, the chart evidence that in the last decade also the average number of citations significantly increased, being 16.7 for the period 2013–2023 against roughly 5.7 for the previous decade. Faced with can be described as an episode of 'rebellion', judgment 49/2014 indeed essentially challenged the binding nature of ECtHR rulings, the Strasbourg Court's response seems to have been to consider more attentively the Italian constitutional case law in its decisions.[174]

The second consequence flowing from the limited avenues for individual access to the Constitutional Court is that the ICC's has so far been largely exempt from the applicability of the fair trial guarantees. The only partial exception is represented by the ECtHR scrutiny of the reasonable duration of constitutional proceedings.

[173] *G.I.E.M. S.R.L. and Others v. Italy* [GC], (1828/06), (34163/07), (19029/11), 28/06/2018.

[174] A similar effect has been observed, following Sentence 49/2015, in Italian constitutional jurisprudence. See: Groppi (2016).

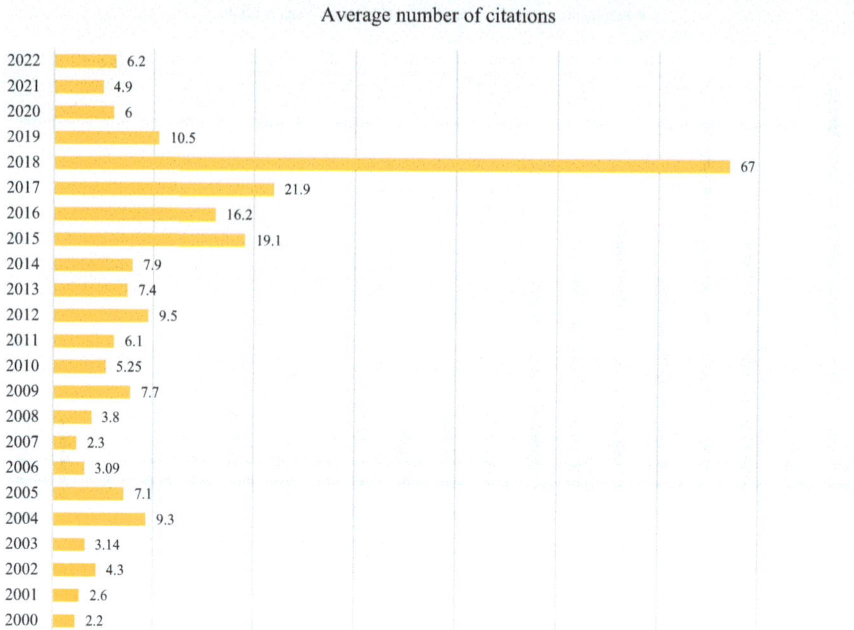

Fig. 3.6 Yearly average number of ICC citations per judgment (2000–2022)

Consistently with its previous case-law, the ECtHR held that proceedings before the ICC shall be taken into account for the purposes of assessing the reasonableness of the duration of the proceedings, in as much as they cause the suspension of the main proceeding.[175] However, it should be noted that insofar the Strasbourg Court never censored the ICC procedural performance—in none of the cases analysed constitutional proceedings lasted than four years.[176] It thus seems that it can still be said that, at least with regard to the timing of proceedings, the ICC is "absolutely sovereign of its own trial".[177]

Considering the limited possibilities of individual access, it may thus be surprising that in a series of cases the Italian State has been condemned for denying access to the ICC. These judgments concerned the competence of the ICC as judge in conflicts of attributions between State powers under Article 134 of the Italian

[175] See *Giancarlo Lombardo v. Italy* (12490/86), 26/11/1992; *Terranova v. Italy* (17156/90), 04/12/1995; *Di Donato and Others v. Italy* (41513/98), 26/04/2001; *V.P. et F.D.R. v. Italy* (44333/98), 12/02/2002.

[176] Indeed, the decision of the Constitutional Court, in the cases mentioned in the previous footnote, appears to have come rather quickly. It took 7 months in the *Di Donato case*, 11 months in the *V.P. and F.D.R. cases*, 1 year and 8 months in the *Terranova* case, and a total of 4 years to decide two questions of constitutionality in the *Giancarlo Lombardo* case.

[177] See. Groppi (1997), p. 214.

Constitution.[178] More specifically, the Constitutional Court has been called upon to establish the extent of parliamentary immunity for opinions expressed under Article 68 of the Italian Constitution.

With the two judgments on the *Cordova* case,[179] the ECtHR affirmed that, taking into account the ICC jurisprudence requiring a substantial connection between the opinions expressed and a prior parliamentary activity for the activation of parliamentary immunity,[180] the refusal of the district court to raise a conflict of State powers before the Constitutional Court, deprived the applicant of his right of access to a court guaranteed by Article 6 ECHR.

The ECtHR returned to rule on parliamentary immunity five years later, with the *Cofferati* judgment.[181] Here, the applicant complained that he had been defamed by two Italian MPs and that he had not been able to take legal action against them due to the refusal of authorisation to proceed by Parliament. On both occasions the ICC,[182] seized by the Tribunal of Rome asking for a declaration that it was not for the Parliament to state that the parliamentarian's statements were covered by parliamentary immunity, had found the appeals inadmissible for the lack of observance of procedural requirements—the MP's statement were not reproduced verbatim, impeding the Constitutional Court to evaluate the existence of a functional link. The European judges therefore once again condemned Italy for violation of the applicant's right of access to a court. Similarly, in the *Onorato* judgment,[183] the ECtHR found a violation of Article 6 caused by the application of parliamentary to opinions that, according to the ICC criteria, should not be covered by the immunity. In the case, the Constitutional Court had to declare the appeal inadmissible because it was lodged out of time according to the Constitutional Court procedural rules.[184]

It has to be noted that, in all these cases the ECtHR does not censure the procedural rules governing proceedings before the Constitutional Court or their interpretation, rather it seems that the Strasbourg Court frames its role as substitute of the ICC, applying the latter court's case law on the extension of parliamentary immunity, when the Italian constitutional judges were prevented to do so for

[178] Under Article 134 of the Italian Constitution the conflicts of attribution over which the Constitutional Court adjudicates are of two different types: conflicts between the powers of the State, and those between the State and the Regions, or between the Regions themselves.

[179] *Cordova (no. 1) v. Italy* (40877/98), 30/01/2003; *Cordova (no. 2) v. Italy* (45649/99), 30/01/2003.

[180] See *Cordova (no. 1)*, para. 27. Similarly see also: *De Jorio v. Italy* (73936/01), 03/06/2004, para. 56; *Ielo v. Italy*, 23053/02, 06/12/2005, para. 54.

[181] *C.G.I.L. et Cofferati v. Italy* (46967/07), 24/02/2009.

[182] See Constitutional Court, Sentence No. 305/2007.

[183] *Onorato v. Italy* (26218/06), 24/05/2011; *Belpietro v. Italy* (43612/10), 24/09/2013.

[184] According to Article 26 of the Constitutional Court procedural rules, the appeal must be lodged with the Court Registry within 20 days of the last notification in: Article 26(4), *Norme integrative per i giudizi davanti alla Corte costituzionale (Approvate con delibera della Corte in sede non giurisdizionale del 22 luglio 2021 e successive modificazioni)*. Available at: https://www.cortecostituzionale.it/documenti/download/pdf/Norme_integrative_2021.pdf.

procedural reasons. As a last remark, it has to be noted that in all those cases the ECtHR consistently affirms that, given the impossibility for an individual to bring the conflict of attributions directly before the ICC, the latter is not configurable as an effective remedy under Article 35 ECHR.[185] In a nutshell, it can be said that the impact of conventional case law on the proceedings before the ICC, due to narrowness of the avenues for accessing the ICC, has been very small, if any.[186]

It is now appropriate to switch our attention to how the Strasbourg Court deals with the decisions of the ICC interpreting fundamental rights. To this regard, of particular interest are the judgments delivered by Strasbourg after the ICC's Judgment 49/2015. With this judgement the ICC redefined the effects of ECtHR judgments into the Italian legal system, establishing a set of criteria for helping ordinary judges to identify which ECtHR judgments are binding for them.[187]

Delivered just four months after this decision, the judgment in *Parrillo* concerned the conventionality of the prohibition on donating unfertilised embryos to scientific research laid down in Article 13 of Law No 40 of 2004.[188] The judgment contains an extensive review of the Constitutional Court's rulings concerning various aspects of Law 40/2004,[189] and the ECHR rank in the Italian legal system,[190] also mentioning

---

[185] More extensively on the relationship between parliamentary immunity and the European Convention with specific reference to the issue of the exhaustion of domestic remedies, see: Malfatti (2009, 2012).

[186] For an opposite opinion see: Ibrido (2016), p.15. The author states that *the impact of Strasbourg jurisprudence on the evolution of the Italian constitutional justice system cannot therefore be underestimated* even though it must be admitted that at present it is a *factor potentially capable of* producing changes. In any case, one cannot help but note that to date there has not yet been a ruling of the European Court that has recognised a violation of Article 6 ECHR in the rules governing the constitutional process. Nor can be traced attempts to adapt to the ECtHR case law on Article 6 by the ICC, as the author himself points out. On another note, Cartabia points out the significant influence of the ECtHR on themes discussed by the Italian Constitutional Court and its style of adjudication. See: Cartabia (2016), pp. 49–50.

[187] More extensively see: Mancano and Martinico (2016).

[188] *Parrillo v. Italy* [GC] (46470/11), 27/08/2015).

[189] In particular, reference is made to the following judgments: Constitutional Court, Sentence No. 151/2009; Sentence No. 1612/2014 and Ordinances No. 396/2006; 97/2010 and 150/2012 as well as the twin Judgments No. 348, 349 of 2007. the issues analysed by the Court in the cited judgments concern other aspects of the law, including the prohibition on heterologous fertilisation and the prohibition on pre-implantation diagnosis.

[190] As the ECtHR itself states, the purpose of this review is basically to show how, in adjudicating the questions submitted to it, the Constitutional Court has never taken the ECHR into account and therefore an appeal before it could not be judged effective under Article 35 ECHR. See *Parrillo v. Italy*, para. 94. The Government had in fact asked the Court, in the light of the reconstruction of the relationship between the ECHR and domestic law contained in the so-called twin judgments (judgment 348/2007 and 349/2007 of the Italian Constitutional Court), to declare the appeal inadmissible because the applicant had not first brought the case before the domestic courts. See: Ibidem, paras 79-83. The Court, recalling the existence of a well-established European case-law affirming the ineffectiveness of the incidental procedure for Article 35 ECHR purposes, willfully decided to ignore the fact that no domestic authority had ruled on the applicant's case.

en passant judgment 49/2015.[191] Such an extensive, and not fully relevant, analysis of the Italian constitutional case law, seems ultimately to be due to already mentioned judgment 49/2015 of the ICC.

It is worth noting that that the Italian Constitutional Court's decided the suspension of a constitutional proceedings concerning the same provision of Law 40/2004, pending the Strasbourg Court's verdict in the case. The ECtHR, considering that the prohibition was contained in a norm of legislative rank, that in the Italian constitutional justice system cannot be challenged by individuals, rejected the Government's submission concerning the non-exhaustion of domestic remedies, and admitted the application even though the applicant never submitted its case to the attention of any domestic judge. Such a relaxed interpretation of admissibility requirements under Article 35 ECHR seems to imply that the Court would declare admissible applications lamenting a fundamental right's breach directly provoke by a legislative norm, if individuals do not have in their national legal system, a remedy to directly challenge the validity of the act. However, rather than establishing a general principle, the reason that prompted the ECtHR to admit the application, is evidently the suspension of the constitutional proceedings concerning the same Article 13 of Law 40/2004, ordered by decree of the President of the Constitutional Court on 19 March 2014, pending the Court's verdict in the *Parrillo* case.[192] In this sense, one may argue that the ECtHR interpreted the suspension of constitutional proceedings as equivalent to a request for an advisory opinion, which was hoverer not possible as Protocol 16 ECHR was not in force at the time.

Radically different is the situation in the *Oliari* case,[193] where the European Court had to deal with two specific precedents of the Italian Constitutional Court. The first is judgment 138/2010, pronounced in the context of the same case pending before Strasbourg, where the Constitutional Court refused to introduce gender-neutral marriage through a judical decision, and instated the legislator to intervene to regulate the legal status of same-sex couples. The second is judgment 170/2014, on the subject of compulsory divorce resulting from the rectification of the sex attribution of one of the couple's members. The judgment in *Oliari* seeks to frame itself as a logical consequence of these two pronouncements, seeking to highlight how in both occasions the constitutional judges called on the legislature to intervene to give some form of legal recognition to same-sex unions. In particular, the Strasbourg Court notes that the President of the Constitutional Court himself censured the inertia of the legislature in regulating the matter of same-sex unions.[194] The

[191] Ibidem, para. 100.

[192] It is almost paradoxical that the Constitutional Court, adjudicating on a new and highly sensitive issue such as the donation of embryos to scientific research, essentially admitted that it had to interpret the Constitution in the light of the ECtHR judgments, only to declare a year later that common judges are not bound to respect ECtHR case law when it is not consolidated.

[193] *Oliari and others v. Italy* (36030/11), 21/07/2015.

[194] See *Oliari and others v. Italy*, paras. 43 and 184. In particular, it is cited an excerpt from the 2012 Annual Report by President Gallo, in which he invited—admittedly in a general manner—the legislature not to ignore the warnings coming from the Constitutional Court. See *Relazione annuale*

European judges' also emphasise how the ICC has clearly affirmed the need to give legal recognition to such unions,[195] conversely leaving aside the many aspects of dissonance that exist: above all, the fact that for the ECtHR homosexual unions are to be considered a family within the meaning of Article 8 ECHR.[196] A similar approach is followed by the Court in the *Marcello Viola (no. 2)* and in the *Scalzo* judgments.[197] Despite in both cases the Strasbourg judges found a breach of a fundamental right guaranteed by the ECHR where the ICC found none, the two judgements seek to present themselves in harmony with the constitutional case law. In *Marcello Viola* (no. 2), where it was declared the unconventionality of sentences of life imprisonment without parole for mafia-condemned prisoners not collaborating with the authorities, the ECtHR emphasised that

> at the domestic level, there appears to be a recent trend in favour of questioning the irrebuttable presumption of social dangerousness, as evidenced by Constitutional Court judgment no. 149 of 11 July 2018, the referral order from the Court of Cassation to the Constitutional Court regarding the constitutionality of Article 4 bis, as well as two recent government-initiated plans to reform Article 4 bis.[198]

Similarly, in *Scalzo*, the ECtHR whilst it condemns Italy for not guaranteeing the applicant's right to have his biological father determined, it notes that the ICC invited the legislature to intervene to regulate matters relating to the establishment of biological truth, agreeing with the latter court that the balancing of interests is a complicated one.[199]

Even when the conflict with the constitutional Court is evident, the European judges seem to spare any criticism to their Italian colleagues, consider to this regard the judgments in *Nasr and Ghali* and *De Tommaso*.[200] In *Nasr et Ghali*, the Strasbourg judges were confronted with kidnapping of the imam of Milan, known as Abu Omar, by US agents on the Italian soil.[201] With two judgments delivered in two conflicts of attributions between State powers promoted by Italian judges seeking to prosecute the suspected persons despite the Government imposition of the State's secret, the ICC affirmed the pre-eminence of state secrecy[202] over the

del Presidente Gallo, 8; available at: https://www.cortecostituzionale.it/jsp/consulta/documentazione/relazioni_annuali.do.

[195] See *Oliari and others v. Italy*, paras. 179–184.

[196] See *Vallianatos v. Greece* (29381/09), (2684/09), 07/11/2013; *Hamalainen v. Finland*, (37359/09), 16/07/2014; *Gas and Dubois v. France* (25951/07), 15/03/12. On this point see: Simonelli (2017), pp. 437–438.

[197] *Marcello Viola v. Italy (no. 2)* (77633/16), 13/06/2019; *Scalzo v. Italy* (8790/21), 06/12/2022.

[198] Ibidem, para. 132.

[199] *Scalzo v. Italy*, paras 67–69.

[200] *Nasr et Ghali v. Italy* (44883/09), 23/02/2016; *De Tommaso v. Italy* (43395/09), 23/02/2017.

[201] Among the numerous comments on the judgment can be seen: Selvaggi (2016) available at: https://www.penalecontemporaneo.it/d/4670-il-caso-abu-omar-davanti-alla-corte-europea-qualche-opportuna-precisazione; Valentino (2016) available at the url: http://www.astrid-online.it/static/upload/vale/valentino-definitivo_aic_novembre2016.pdf.

[202] Judgment of the Italian Constitutional Court of 13 February 2014, nr. 24/2014.

applicant right to an effective investigation.[203] In a situation where the Constitutional Court had openly sided with the Government against the judiciary, the Strasbourg Court avoided an open conflict with the judges of the *Palazzo della Consulta:* after an extensive report of the constitutional jurisprudence contained in the facts, the ECHR omits to make any reference to this case law in the reasoning,[204] and condemns Italy for violating Articles 3, 5, 8 and 13—read in conjunction with the three previous ones—of the Convention. With regard to the violation of the procedural facet of Article 3 ECHR, i.e. the State's obligation to conduct an official and effective investigation into the allegations of the person claiming to have been tortured, the judgment does not censure the ICC decision to aval the government's decision to impose the secret, putting the blame exclusively on the "attitude of the executive, which exercised its power to invoke state secrecy, and of the President of the Republic".[205] With the ruling in *De Tommaso*, the Strasbourg Court instead declared the outright compatibility with the ECHR of *ante poenam* prevention measures provided for by Italian legislation due to the insufficient level of precision of the so-called cases of generic dangerousness.[206] In the ECtHR judgment the reconstruction of the development of constitutional jurisprudence is particularly accurate: 11 pronouncements of the ICC are quoted and analysed in detail, starting with the second judgment in the history of the ICC, dating from 1956.[207] The citation of Judgment 177/1980 is particularly extensive. The ruling, in fact, had declared the unconstitutionality of the generic dangerousness case represented by those who 'by the events to which they have given rise, give well-founded reason to believe that they are likely to commit a crime' for violation of Article 25 of the Constitution. This 'category', not being defined in a sufficiently precise manner, was declared illegitimate because the rule allowed 'the adoption of restrictive measures of personal freedom without the identification of either the prerequisites or the specific purposes justifying them'.[208] Reading the reasoning of the *De Tommaso* judgment, it appears that the ECtHR intended to "appropriate" the principle affirmed by judgment 177/1980, extending its application to all the categories of Article 1 of Law 1423/1956: "the Court notes that the Italian Constitutional Court annulled the law in respect of a category of persons which it considered were not defined in sufficient detail" while being obliged to conclude, with regard to the other cases that: "notwithstanding the fact that the Constitutional Court has intervened on several occasions to clarify the criteria to be used for assessing whether preventive measures are

[203] For an accurate examination of the scope of the state secret in particular in relation to the two aforementioned rulings see: Giupponi (2014).

[204] Out of a total of 58 citations, only seven are found in the 'Law' part, of which, however, five are contained in the parties' submissions.

[205] *Nasr and Ghali v. Italy*, para. 272.

[206] Exhaustively on this point, see: Menditto (2017), pp. 127–131.

[207] The other rulings cited are: Constitutional Court Judgments Nos. 27/1959; 45/1960; 126/1962; 23/1964; 32/1969; 76/1970; 93/2010; 282/2010; 80/2011.

[208] Italian Constitutional Court, Judgment nr. 177/1980.

necessary",[209] the legislation still lacked of a sufficient level of determinacy and was thus incompatible with Article 5 ECHR. The wording of the passages cited seems to praise rather than criticise the previous constitutional jurisprudence, although the latter is in clear contrast with the ECtHR findings.

As a final point, is now necessary to briefly review the *G.I.E.M.* saga, concluded by the eponymous judgment. To a better understanding of the context is worth underscoring that limitations on the right to private property have constituted one the main points of friction between the two courts,[210] in particular the ECtHR has criticised the excessive discretion of the legislator to limit the right to property in view of the pursuit of a public interest according to Article 42 of the Italian Constitution.[211] In doing that, the ECtHR often disregarded the ICC jurisprudence, in *Carbonara and Ventura, Belvedere Alberghiera* and *Scordino (no. 1)*,[212] for example, despite a consolidated constitutional jurisprudence on the subject—expropriation procedures for public utility—this is not even taken into consideration by the Strasbourg Court when affirming a violation of Article 1 Protocol 1 ECHR.[213]

The issue in *G.I.E.M.* was different and it essentially concerned the possibility for judges in the Italian legal system to dispose a confiscation without the necessity of a criminal conviction. The position of the ECtHR, expressed in *Varvara v. Italy*, was that confiscation was a measure of criminal nature, and therefore its imposition in a sentence declaring the extinction of the process for being the continuation of the proceedings time-barred, violated Article 1 Protocol 1 ECHR and Article 7 ECHR.[214] Asked by the *Corte di Cassazione* to interpret how the ruling in *Varvara* should be interpreted in accordance with the Italian Constitution, the ICC answered that the judgment in *Varvara* was not expression of a consolidated case law of the ECtHR, and therefore the ECHR interpretation thereby contained was not binding.[215] Also, the

[209] *De Tommaso v. Italy*, paras 116–117.

[210] No less than 103 judgments, out of the 335 in which references to the Italian Constitutional Court are found, concern an alleged violation of Article 1 Prot. 1 ECHR.

[211] Conti (2006), p. 247.

[212] See *Belvedere Alberghiera v. Italy* (31524/96), 30/05/2000; *Carbonara and Ventura v. Italy* (24638/94), 30/05/2000; *Scordino v. Italy (No. 1)* (36813/97), 29/03/2006.

[213] A partial exception is the *Scordino* judgment, in which the Court refers to two judgments of the Constitutional Court. See *Scordino v. Italy (No. 1)*, para. 127. All the three judgments found a violation of Article 1 Protocol 1 ECHR, as the amount of the compensation was deemed excessively lower than the market value of the property.

[214] *Varvara v. Italy*, para. 72.

[215] This reaction of the Italian Constitutional Court needs to be seen in the broader picture. Limitations on the right to property have constituted one the main point of friction between the two Court—no less than 103 judgments, out of the 335 in which references to the Italian Constitutional Court are found, concern an alleged violation of Article 1 Prot. 1 ECHR. In particular the ECtHR has criticised the excessive discretion of the legislator to limit the right to property in view of the pursuit of a public interest according to Article 42 of the Italian Constitution, often disregarding the Italian Constitutional Court position. Taking as example the rulings of the Strasbourg Court in *Carbonara and Ventura* ((24638/94, 30/05/2000), *Belvedere Alberghiera* ((31524/96), 30/05/2000) and *Scordino (no. 1)* ((36813/97), 29/03/2006), despite the fact that there were a vast amount of constitutional jurisprudence on the subject - expropriation procedures for public utility - this is not taken into consideration by the Strasbourg Court. All the three judgments found a violation of Article 1 Protocol 1 ECHR, as the amount of the compensation

ICC affirms that the confiscation may well be contained in a criminal judgment which, while not having convicted the defendant, has nevertheless adequately demonstrated the personal responsibility of the person subjected to the measure. Answering to the ICC, the ECtHR first of all unequivocally reaffirmed that all "its judgments all have the same legal value. Their binding nature and interpretative authority cannot therefore depend on the formation by which they were rendered."[216] However, interpreting Article 7 ECHR, the judgments affirms that personal liability can be established even in the absence of a formal criminal conviction.[217] In this sense the ECtHR seems thus to have avoided to enter into a confrontation with the ICC, even if this implied contradicting its precedent in *Varvara*, clearly stating that Article 7 ECHR requires the confiscation to be disposed in a formal criminal conviction.[218]

All in all, an analysis of the cases above gives the impression that the Strasbourg Court, regardless of the Constitutional Court's position on the issue, now always gives adequate space to constitutional case law, thus proving to the constitutional judges that they have not dropped a decision from above but have adequately taken into consideration the specificities of the Italian legal system and tried to propose a solution that is in accordance with the Italian Constitution. The rebellion of the Constitutional Court, which can well be qualified as functional disobedience,[219] has therefore stimulated a reaction on the part of the European Court of Human Rights consisting of a more attentive posture towards the constitutional case law.

3.6 A Substantial Lack of Consideration. The ECtHR and the Portuguese Constitutional Tribunal

When, on 9 November 1978, Portugal ratified the ECHR—and thus accepted the jurisdiction of the Strasbourg Court—its Constitution did not yet provide for a an *ad-hoc* constitutional justice body.[220] It was only in 1982, with the first revision of the 1976 Constitution, that the *Tribunal constitucional* of Portugal (hereinafter also

was deemed excessively lower than the market value of the property. All the three judgments found a violation of Article 1 Protocol 1 ECHR, as the amount of the compensation was deemed excessively lower than the market value of the property. For an analysis of these rulings see: Conti (2006), p. 247.

216 *G.I.E.M. s.r.l. v. Italy*, para. 252.

217 Ibidem, paras 253–262.

218 Indeed, this is the main point of criticism of the dissenting opinion of Judges Sajó, Karakaş, Pinto De Albuquerque, Keller, Vehabović, Kūris and Grozev. See: Ibidem, *Joint Partly Dissenting Opinion of Judges Sajó, Karakaş, Pinto De Albuquerque, Keller, Vehabović, Kūris and Grozev*, para. 2.

219 See, Mancano and Martinico (2016).

220 The Portuguese constitutional system from 1976 to 1982 can be defined as the fact that a concrete and diffuse jurisdictional control on the US model was flanked by one that was abstract and centralised in character but carried out by a non-jurisdictional body, namely the Council of the Revolution, flanked by the Constitutional Commission. More extensively on the evolution and early years of constitutional justice in Portugal: Bon (1989).

'the PTC') was introduced (Articles 221–224), with a physiognomy that has remained more or less unchanged until today.[221] In its current set-up, the modalities through which the PTC exercises its jurisdiction are four: the preventive control (Art. 278 Const.), the abstract concentrated control (Art. 281 Const.), the control on unconstitutionality by omission (Art. 283 Const.) and, finally, the concrete concentrated control (Art. 280 Const.) The cases in the ECtHR case law only concerning this latter procedure, hence it is not necessary to dwell further on the others.

The concrete concentrated control represents the most peculiar element of the Portuguese system, making it a *unicum* in the European panorama of constitutional justice systems. The procedure start at the initiative of a party of proceeding raising an objection of constitutionality before the trial judge, if the judge considers the objection to be well founded, it shall *not* refer the matter back to the Constitutional Tribunal, as it would do for instance in the Italian system, but is required to rule on the objection with *inter partes* effect. Such a decision is appealable by the parties before the PCT, which will first rule on the admissibility of appeal in a single judge formation whose decisions can be challenged before a three-judges committee.[222] It must be emphasised that this procedure is not comparable to the others individual complaints analysed insofar, such as the German *Verfassungsbeschwerde* or the Spanish *amparo*,[223] since the object of the appeal can only be a norm deemed unconstitutional. Neither it can be assimilated to the incidental procedures of the French and Italian systems, as in the Portuguese system are the individual parties, and not the judge, who can bring the matter before the PCT.

The peculiarities of the concentrated concrete control outlined above seem to have produced uncertainties also in the case law of the European Court of Human Rights, especially concerning its effectiveness for the purposes of Article 35 ECHR. Noting that the appeal can only concern the unconstitutionality of a norm, the ECtHR, starting from 2010, has consistently declared that applicants are not required to use it in order to comply with the rule of prior exhaustion of domestic remedies.[224]

However, already in 2007, the Strasbourg Court, ruling on a plea of inadmissibility raised by the Portuguese Government, had used the PTC judgment as the date for the calculation of the six-months under Article 35 ECHR, arguing that "l'on ne saurait reprocher aux requérants d'avoir essayé d'utiliser un moyen de recours qui semblait, au moins à l'époque, pouvoir porter remède à leurs griefs".[225] More recently, in 2020, with the judgment in *Dos Santos Calado*, the ECtHR,

[221] See: Moreira (2001), p. 2.

[222] On the point see: Cortes and Violante (2011), pp. 764–765.

[223] The necessity of a distinguishing is perceived also by the Strasbourg Court. See: *Dos Santos Calado and Others v. Portugal* (55997/14), (68143/16), (78841/16), 31/03/2020, paras 78–79.

[224] See*: Publico - Comunicacao Social, S.A. and Others v. Portugal* (39324/07), 07/12/2010, para. 31; *Gouveia Gomes Fernandes et Freitas e Costa v. Portugal* (1529/08), 29/03/2011, para. 31; *Rolim Comercial, S.A. v. Portugal* (16153/09), 16/04/2013, para. 46; *Sérvulo & Associados - Sociedade de Advogados, RL et autres v. Portugal* (27013/10), 03/09/2015, para. 69; *Soares de Melo v. Portugal* (72850/14), 16/02/2016, para. 72.

[225] See *Campos Costa and Others v. Portugal* (10172/04), 30/10/2007 para. 24.

summarising its case-law, essentially affirmed that the effectiveness of the concentrated control procedure for the purposes of Article 35 ECHR shall be evaluated on a case-by-case basis. In particular, the ECtHR established a rule according to which in any case brought against Portugal raising an issue of normative unconstitutionality or normative interpretation, the applicant must lodge an appeal with the Constitutional Tribunal in order to satisfy the obligation to exhaust domestic remedies laid down in Article 35(1) ECHR. Conversely, since a constitutional appeal against a judicial decision will be doomed to fail it shall not be proposed.[226] Such a rule, however, is deeply problematic, since the PTC adopts a wide interpretation of the notion of 'norm', which cause that "it may sometimes be very difficult to draw the line between what is a normative control or a control of the decision itself".[227]

From a quantitative point of view, the dialogue between the PTC and ECtHR does not appear an intense one. As of 1 January 2023, out of a total of 302 judgments delivered against Portugal, the TC is cited in 95 of them, a percentage of approximately 31%.[228] This figure, taken in conjunction with the average number of recurrences per judgment—which is around 4.8—is a sure indicator of the Strasbourg Court's scarce attention to Portuguese constitutional jurisprudence. To put this number in comparison with that of other constitutional courts, the average number of citations per judgment is comparable to that of the *Conseil Constitutionnel*, and significantly lower than that of the Italian Constitutional Court, despite the fact that individual do not have direct access to those two jurisdictions. Actually, since 2016, it is observable a trend in the direction of a greater focus on constitutional precedents. As shown in the graph below (Fig. 3.7), in 2016, 2017, 2018, 2020, and 2021 the average number of citations is significantly higher than in the previous years, even if the limited number of judgments with PCT's citations in those years, renders the statistic less meaningful. Nonetheless, considering that, prior to 31 December 2015, there were only 5 judgments with more than 10 TC citations, this figure deserves to be emphasised.[229]

Another significant trend that has to be underscored is that in the last 5 years considered (2018–2022), the percentage of judgments delivered against Portugal with PTC's citations is significantly lower than the overall average, attesting at a mere 25% (8 out of 32). This reduction seems to indicate a consolidation of the case law in admissibility decisions, in the sense of no longer requiring to appeal to the constitutional court with the procedure of Article 280 of the Constitution. As regards the application of Article 6 ECHR to the PTC there is a handful of judgments which

[226] *Dos Santos Calado and Others v. Portugal,* para. 85.

[227] See: Cortes and Violante (2011), p. 766.

[228] These 95 judgments were found using the following search strings: 86 with 'tribunal constitutionnel', 7 with 'constitutional court'; 2 'cour constitutionnelle'. The keyword 'Constitutional Tribunal' produced no results.

[229] Incidentally, it should also be noted that this increase coincided with an internal transfer of jurisdiction within the Strasbourg Court: as of 1 December 2015, all judgments with Portugal as the respondent State were in fact decided by the Fourth Chamber whereas previously they were assigned alternatively to the First or Second Chamber.

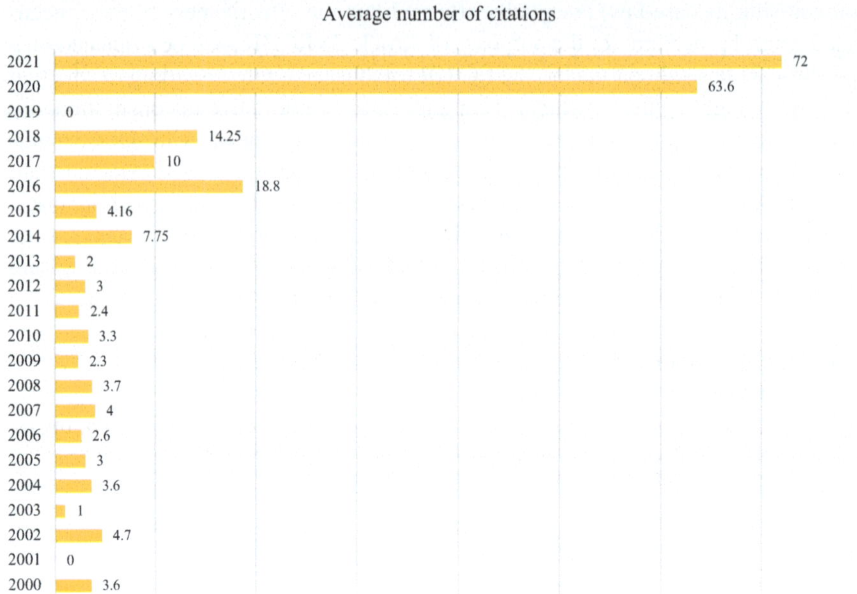

Fig. 3.7 Yearly average number of PCT citations per judgment (2000–2021)

are worth considering. The first is the one in the *Rosa Marquez* case, where the ECtHR held that a duration of 3 years and 1 month for a proceeding concluded with a decision of inadmissibility, was unreasonable.[230] In *Liga Portoguesa*, instead, the Strasbourg Court applied the principle of impartiality to the PTC, affirming that the formation of the PCT that ruled on the applicant's appeal was not impartial because the judge-rapporteur, before being elected constitutional judge, had presided over the panel of the Supreme Court that had held a hearing in the same case.[231]

More attention should be paid to the ruling in the *Gramaxo Rozeira* case, where the ECtHR extended the principle of equality of arms to the concentrated control procedure before the PCT.[232] Here, the applicant complained of a violation of his right to a fair trial caused by a request for information to the Government by the PTC, of which he had not been informed. According to the ECtHR, the circumstance that the PTC subsequently referred to the content of the letter in the text of the judgment does not sufficient guarantee the principle of parity of arms, and that the applicant

[230] *Rosa Marques et autres v. Portugal* (48187/99), 25/07/2002, para. 29.

[231] *Liga Portoguesa de Futebol Profissional v. Portugal* (4687/11), 17/05/2016.

[232] *Gramaxo Rozeira v. Portugal* (21976/09), 21/01/2014. Also, the *Feliciano Bichao* judgement, delivered 7 years before, concerned the principle of parity of arms. The ECtHR condemned the Portuguese State because the submissions filed by the prosecution before the Coimbra Court of Appeal and the Constitutional Tribunal were not notified to the appellant. From a reading of the judgment, it is however impossible to distinguishing if the Strasbourg Court intended to censure the conduct of the PCT. See: *Feliciano Bichao v. Portugal* (40225/04), 20/11/2007, paras 37–38.

should have been informed immediately of the letter requesting information and should have had the possibility to make comments on it.[233] The judgment reaches its conclusions rather straightforwardly,[234] by means of a simple analogical application, something which may give rise to more than one perplexity, especially considering the eminently objective nature of the concentrated control procedure before the PTC. Also, in the present case—as noted in Judge Popović's dissenting opinion—the applicant suffered no prejudice from the non-disclosure of the information, as it concerned the respect of a procedural requirement in the elaboration of the impugned norm.[235]

Concerning the fundamental rights dialogue between the two Courts, it may be worth signalling that that Article 16 of the Portuguese Constitution affirms that "the provisions of this Constitution and of laws concerning fundamental rights shall be interpreted and construed in accordance with the Universal Declaration of Human Rights." However, since the provision only refers to the Universal Declaration of Human Rights, the position of the ECHR is less clear.[236] In any case, the Portuguese Constitutional Tribunal frequently employs the ECHR as an interpretative tool,[237] an attitude which is not corresponded by the Strasbourg Court. The only right around which a dialogue between the two jurisdictions can be traced is freedom of expression,[238] on this right the interpretation proposed by the PCT appears to be consistently more restrictive than that put forward by the ECtHR. A paradigmatic example is the judgment in the *Pinto Coelho* case,[239] where the ECtHR explicitly declares that it is re-evaluating the balancing act carried out by the TC—which had considered proportional the obligation to request authorisation to record and broadcast the contents of court hearings—and then concludes by condemning Portugal for violation of Article 10 ECHR. Although on two separate occasions the PCT had positively assessed the compatibility of the disputed rule with the Convention, the Court

[233] *Gramaxo Rozeira v. Portugal,* para. 37.

[234] The reasoning only occupies 6 paragraphs: See: Ibidem, paras 31–36.

[235] More specifically, the PTC sought to ascertain whether the trade unions had participated in the drafting of labour law legislation, as required by Article 56(2) of the Portuguese Constitution. Moreover, the Government had replied to the PCT that it could not provide the requested information as the dossier was lost.

[236] During the 1982 revision, there were proposals for the inclusion of a reference to the European Convention, but these were unsuccessful. See Martinico (2012), p. 408.

[237] See: Pereira Coutinho (2010).

[238] Of the 95 judgments analysed, 10 are on the subject of Article 10 ECHR, and all are convictions. See: *Lopes Gomes Da Silva v. Portugal* (37698/97), 28/09/2000; *Roseiro Bento v. Portugal* (29288/02), 18/04/2006; *Laranjeira Marques Da Silva v. Portugal* (16983/06), 19/01/2010; *Publico - Comunicacao Social, S.A. et autres v. Portugal*; *Gouveia Gomes Fernandes et Freitas e Costa v. Portugal*; *Conceicao Letria v. Portugal* (4049/08), 12/04/2011; *Pinto Coelho v. Portugal* (28439/08), 28/06/2011; *Almeida Leitão Bento Fernandes v. Portugal* (25790/11), 12/03/2015; *Pinto Coelho v. Portugal (No. 2)* (48718/11), 22/03/2016; *Tavares De Almeida Fernandes and Almeida Fernandes v. Portugal* (31566/13), 17/01/2017.

[239] *Pinto Coelho v. Portugal (No. 2) (*8439/08), 28/06/2011.

nevertheless handed down a conviction, moreover without pointing out the reasons to depart from the verdict of the constitutional judges.[240]

The analysis of the Strasbourg case law in which the PCT is cited, ultimately, confirms the evidence resulting from the quantitative data, indicating that the ECtHR pays scarce attention to the Portuguese constitutional jurisprudence. This would seem to suggest that, in addition to the specific features of the constitutional justice system, and in particular the presence of a direct appeal, the authoritativeness of the constitutional court as well as the political weight of the Respondent State may also be relevant factors capable of influencing the relationship between constitutional jurisdiction and the Strasbourg Court.

3.7 Affinities and Divergences between the Strasbourg Court and the Spanish Constitutional Tribunal

Unlike most of the constitutional jurisdictions discussed so far, when the *Tribunal constitucional* issued its first ruling in 1981, Spain had already ratified the ECHR and was thus subject to the jurisdiction of the Strasbourg Court, (even though the first ruling against Spain only arrived in 1988).[241] This circumstance, combined with the presence in the Spanish Constitution of a clause (Article 10(2) CE) obliging to interpret fundamental rights in harmony with international human rights treaties,[242] explains rather satisfactorily the great deal of attention reserved by Spanish judges and scholarship to the influence of Strasbourg rulings on the jurisprudence of the *Tribunal constitucional* (hereinafter also 'the SCT).[243]

Concerning the STC case law some statistical studies have highlighted the high frequency of ECtHR citations —reaching up to 75 per cent in *amparo* appeals—[244] which have been considered symptom of a 'fascination' of the Spanish constitutional judge towards the Strasbourg jurisprudence, seen as an authoritative minimum standard of human rights protection.[245] Below, we will instead examine whether the SCT rulings have had a similar effect in the case law of the ECtHR. Before beginning this analysis, a brief introduction to the Spanish system of constitutional justice is necessary. Its distinguishing feature, which has informed the relationship with the Strasbourg Court, is undoubtedly the *recurso de amparo*, established by Articles 161(1b) of the Spanish Constitution. Through this instrument, in fact, any

[240] Ibidem, paras 31–41; *Lopes Gomes Da Silva v. Portugal*, paras 31–37.

[241] *Barberà, Messegué and Jabardo v. Spain* (10590/83), 06/12/1988.

[242] For more details on how this provision has been interpreted by the Spanish Constitutional Tribunal see: above, Ch.1, fn 96.

[243] See for example: Sospedra (1987); Carrillo Salcedo (2003); Queralt Jiménez (2008) and more recently, Alvarez Rodriguez (2021).

[244] Tur Ausina (2010) fn 29.

[245] Retortillo Baquer (1995), p. 11.

citizen can access the SCT to complain about the violation of one of the fundamental rights listed in Articles 14 to 30 of the Spanish Constitution, the so-called 'derechos amparables', which roughly correspond to those guaranteed by the ECHR.[246]

In its first twenty years of operation, this instrument came to be configured as a kind of fourth jurisdictional instance, since one of the amparable rights is precisely the right to effective judicial protection. This ultimately provoked what has been called an *amparo* crisis,[247] i.e. an uncontrolled increase in the number of appeals reaching the SCT each year.[248] Faced with a situation where individual direct actions accounted for about 99% of the STC's workload, the Spanish legislator intervened with Organic Law 6/2007 by introducing the requirement of special constitutional relevance (*especial transcendencia constitucional*) as a condition for the admissibility of *amparo*.[249]

In the *Arribas Anton* case,[250] the Strasbourg Court was called to review the conventionality of this reform, and in particular of the requirement of *especial transcendencia constitucional*. The applicant complained about the excessive formalism of the SCT in assessing the special constitutional relevance of his appeal and the consequent decision of inadmissibility allegedly depriving him of the right of access to a court. The Strasbourg Court, after referring to the most relevant constitutional case-law on the subject—although without offering any comment—concluded that "le but poursuivi par le changement législatif de 2007 est légitime"[251] and that a court of last instance may adopt its rulings of inadmissibility by giving reasons only by referring to the legislative provisions on the basis of which the decision is pronounced, without this violating Article 6 ECHR.[252] Even though in 2022 only 12 individual constitutional complaints were admitted for consideration against a total of 6953 that were declared inadmissible,[253] to the date the Strasbourg Court continues to require applicant to exhaust that remedy for complying with Article 35 ECHR. Both findings seem perfect in line with the case law concerning the individual constitutional complaint in the German system, where the Court

[246]For a detailed analysis of the rights that can be protected by the *amparo*, see Carrasco Durán (2002).

[247]See Groppi (1997).

[248]In 2007 alone, the year the reform came into force, 9850 *amparo* appeals were filed with the *Tribunal Constitucional*.

[249]Article 50(1b) of Ley Organica 2/1979, as amended by the 2007 amendment, provides for the requirement of *especial trascendencia constitucional*. The recurrence of this condition must be assessed by the TC having regard to three elements: the importance of the case for the interpretation of the Constitution; for its application; or for the determination of the content of fundamental rights.

[250]*Arribas Anton v. Spain*, 16563/11, Court (Third Section), 20/01/2015.

[251]Ibidem, para. 49.

[252]Ibidem, para. 47.

[253]Of these, around 4500 were declared inadmissible for lacking, or not being sufficiently justified, the special constitutional importance. See: Tribunal Constitutional, *Memoria 2022*, 53–54. Available at: https://www.tribunalconstitucional.es/en/memorias/Documents/Memoria%202022.pdf.

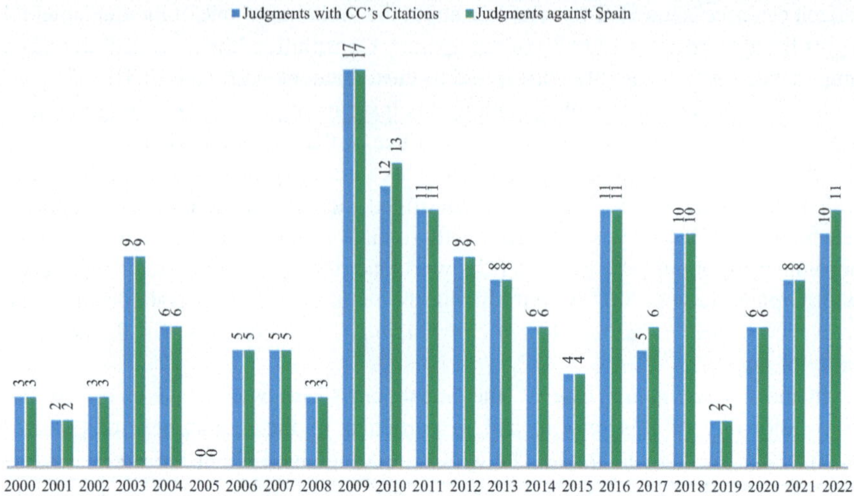

Fig. 3.8 Judgments with SCT citations per year (2003–2022)

consistently held that its unmotivated rejection does not per se violates the right of access to a court and that the extremely low rate of success does not *per se* deprive the constitutional appeal of its effectiveness.

As the graph above shows (Fig. 3.8), although the 2007 reform significantly restricted the possibilities of access to the SCT, this had no impact on the number of constitutional case law citations in Strasbourg jurisprudence. In fact, the SCT continues to be cited in almost every judgment of the ECHR: as of 1 January 2023, out of a total of 186 judgments delivered against Spain, the SCT appears in no less than 177 of them (approximately 95%).

Any analysis of the relationship between the SCT and the European Court of Human Rights can only take as its starting point the *Ruiz Mateos* judgment,[254] in which for the first time the Strasbourg judges affirmed *tout court* the applicability of Article 6 ECHR to constitutional proceedings.[255] In addition to reaffirming what is called a 'well-established case law',[256] i.e. that, if capable of influencing the outcome of the dispute, the constitutional process shall be taken into account to determining the duration of the proceedings under Article 6(1) ECHR, the ECtHR also states for the first time that substantive due process guarantees, such as the principle of

[254]The ruling immediately attracted the attention—and criticism—of Spanish doctrine See in particular: Chueca Sancho (1994); Castro-Rial Garron (1994).

[255]The reference is to the case of *Deumeland v. Germany, in which* the ECHR had stated, rather unpredictably, that the constitutional trial had to be included in the calculation of the duration of proceedings for the purpose of assessing their reasonableness under Article 6 ECHR. This precedent, however, remained isolated until the judgment in *Ruiz Mateos,* where the Court, with a greater abundance of arguments, definitively made the constitutional principle subject to respect for due process guarantees. For an analysis of *Deumeland* see: *supra*, Ch. II para. 1.

[256]*Ruiz Mateos v. Spain*, para. 35.

equality of arms, are also applicable to constitutional proceedings.[257] One of the main criticisms addressed to the judgment is that it affirmed this principle in the context of an incidental proceeding—the SCT had been seized by the *Audiencia Provincial* de Madrid—[258] hence conferring on the applicants the status of parties to the proceedings before the SCT, although Spanish law did not recognise them as such.[259] Had the same principle been affirmed in the context of an *amparo* judgment, it would have been decidedly less controversial, given the prevalence in the latter procedure, at least in its structure prior to the 2007 reform, of the subjective component—the claimant's alleged infringement of a right—over the objective one, namely the need to ensure a uniform interpretation of the Constitution.

Moreover, as Judge Pettiti's dissenting opinion notes, having affirmed the applicability of Article 6 ECHR on the basis of the fact that the constitutionality judgment concerned "a law which directly concerns a restricted circle of persons "appears a decidedly vague criterion.[260] Ten years later the judgement in *Ruiz Mateos*, ECtHR to rule on the applicability of Article 6-1 ECHR to incidental proceedings for the review of constitutionality in the *Gorraiz Lizarraga* case.[261] The Spanish Government had in fact asked the Strasbourg Court to make a distinguishing with respect to *Ruiz Mateos* and thus to declare Article 6(1) ECHR inapplicable to constitutional proceedings, since the law challenged before the SCT was of general application.[262] The ECtHR, while emphasising the eminently publicist character of the *cuestión de inconstitucionalidad*, states definitively that the only criterion on the basis of which to assess the applicability of Article 6 ECHR to constitutional proceedings is that of assessing its capacity to affect the applicant's right.[263] Nevertheless, the Strasbourg Court ended up stating that the fact that the applicants did not participate in the proceedings before the SCT did not violate their right to a fair trial because "nothing in the case files to suggest that the applicants applied to the Constitutional

[257] Ibidem, paras. 63–64.

[258] Ibidem, paras. 14–15.

[259] This interpretation of Article 6(1) ECHR has been criticised for being too broad. Indeed, stating that a preliminary question of constitutionality is a procedure aimed at ascertaining the civil rights and duties of the applicant is tantamount to giving an almost all-encompassing meaning to the notion of a dispute on civil rights and duties. See: Chueca Sancho (1994), p. 570. As suggested in Judge Pettiti's dissenting opinion, the decision to deem the guarantees of due process applicable to constitutional proceedings of a prednominant objective nature may have been determined by the desire to sanction the expropriation without just compensation of the *Rumasa group*, despite the fact that Spain at the time had not yet ratified the First Additional Protocol to the Convention. See *Ruiz Mateos v. Spain, Partly dissenting opinion of judge Pettit, approved by judges Lopes Rocha and Ruiz-Jarabo Colomer.* This suggestion is certainly reflected in the aforementioned *Süssmann* judgment, where the European Court of Human Rights states that "the applicants were using the sole - and indirect - means available to them of complaining of an interference with their right to property". See *Süssmann v. Germany*, para. 39.

[260] *Ruiz Mateos v. Spain*, para. 63.

[261] *Gorraiz Lizarraga v. Spain* (62543/00), 27/04/2004.

[262] Ibidem, para. 41.

[263] Ibidem, para. 47.

Court any time for leave to take part in the proceedings".[264] The apparent contrast between these two judgments, which appears fully justified in the light of the manifest differences in the factual circumstances of the two cases, can be easily resolved if one identifies as the crucial element to trigger a violation of Article 6, the denial of an explicit request by the applicant to be admitted as a party to the constitutional proceeding. ECtHR.

Although the judgment in *Ruiz Mateos* is without doubt among the Strasbourg Court's historic decisions, its application in subsequent rulings against Spain has been rather limited. For another ruling applying Article 6 to constitutional proceedings one has to wait until 2011, when the Strasbourg Court decided the *Diaz Aparicio* case.[265] Here, the applicant complained about the unreasonable length of proceedings that had lasted approximately ten years in total—the proceedings before the SCT had lasted 3 years and 22 days. The ECtHR, although without stating it explicitly, seems to consider the processing time of the *amparo* unreasonable;[266] the violation of Article 6-1 ECHR is, however, affirmed with regard to the duration of the entire procedure. Conversely, in cases in which the proceedings before the SCT lasted less than a year—and therefore in the light of the ECtHR criteria was in principle not excessive—the ECtHR does not directly affirm, as it did in some judgments against Germany,[267] the reasonableness of the duration of the constitutional trial.[268]

The ECtHR judgment in the *Soto Sanchez* case is one of the keys to understanding the relationship between SCT and the Strasbourg Court.[269] The judgment states that the *recurso de amparo* allows in general "to remedy an alleged violation of the right to have one's case heard by the Spanish courts within a "reasonable time" and thus constitutes an effective remedy within the meaning of Article 35 ECHR".[270] From the point of view of substantive law, this means that, with regard to the reasonable duration of the trial, in Spain there is a duplication of forms of protection—conventional and constitutional—due to the fact that Article 24(2) of the Spanish Constitution explicitly recognises the right to a trial *sin dilaciones indebidas,* and therefore this right falls within the group of 'amparable rights'. As a matter of fact, the same holds true for all the preceptive content of Article 24 of the Spanish Constitution, as its content essentially reflects that of Article 6 ECHR. Given this overlap, it is therefore necessary for the SCT to be seised in *amparo* before the applicant being able to appeal to Strasbourg to complain of a violation of

---

[264] Ibidem, para. 60.

[265] *Diaz Aparicio v. Spain* (49468/99), 11/10/2001.

[266] Ibidem, paras. 21–22.

[267] See *D.E. v. Germany* (1126/05), 16/07/2009, para. 69; *Bayer v. Germany* (8453/04), 16/07/2009, para. 52.

[268] See in this sense: *Gonzalez Doria Duran de Quiroga v. Spain* (59072/00), 28/10/2003; *Lopez Sole y Martin de Vargas v. Spain* (61133/00), 28/10/03.

[269] *Soto Sanchez v. Spain* (66990/01) 25/11/2003.

[270] Ibidem, para. 30.

the right to effective judicial protection. This situation has not failed to produce contrasts between the jurisprudences of the two courts in relation to the interpretation of due process guarantees, in particular concerning the different weight attached by the two courts to the respect of formal procedural requirements. With specific regard to the *amparo*, reference should first be made to the *Rodriguez Valin* judgment.[271] The applicant argued that the rejection of his *amparo* for having been submitted out of time, had violated his right to access to a court. The ECtHR while noting that a longstanding practice of the SCT considers that, in the case of appeals dispatched by post, the date of dispatch shown on the postmark is considered as the day of submission of the appeal, concluding that Article 6 ECHR was not violated, invites the SCT to give formal recognition to this interpretation.[272]

The judgment in *Ferré Gisbert* also concerns an inadmissibility decision by the STC of an amparo for the lack of respect of procedural requirements.[273] The SCT had affirmed that since the lamented fundamental right's violation found its cause in an interlocutory order of the court of first instance, which given the lack of appeal by the public prosecutor became final, the time limit of 20 days to submit an amparo shall be calculated form the date of delivery of that order and not from the final judgment of the same court. The Strasbourg Court observed that applicant had been placed under a disproportionate burden which disrupted the fair balance between, on the one hand, the legitimate concern to ensure compliance with the formal requirements for bringing a case before the constitutional court and, on the other hand, the right of access to constitutional jurisdiction, and thus concluded that the applicant's right to access to a court had been violated.[274] It is also worth signalling to be noted that the applicant made an explicit request to the ECtHR to declare its *amparo* admissible, to which the ECtHR, quite obviously, replied that it was not within its competence to declare the *amparo* admissible.[275] The last ECtHR judgment concerning the admissibility rules of *amparo* has been delivered in December 2022 in the *Olivares Zuniga* case.[276] In 2017 the SCT, ruling on the applicant's *amparo*, declared its inadmissibility on the grounds that the applicant did not exhaust all the prior domestic remedies, in particular for having failed to bring an action for annulment of proceedings, an extraordinary procedural remedy which can only be activated if there exists no other ordinary appeal against a decision that is considered to have violated a fundamental right.[277] However, before declaring the violation of the applicant's right to access to a court, the judgment notes that in 2019 the SCT changed its case law and no longer requires the prior exhaustion of the action for

[271] *Rodriguez Valin v. Spain* (47792/99), 11/10/2001.

[272] Ibidem, para. 26.

[273] *Ferré Gisbert v. Spain* (39590/05), 13/10/2009.

[274] Ibidem, paras 33–35.

[275] Ibidem, para. 46.

[276] *Olivares Zuniga v. Spain* (11/18), 15/12/2022.

[277] See: Gómez de José (2023).

annulment for lodging an amparo. To this regard, the judgment in *Olivares Zuniga* can be considered a retroactive application of the SCT ruling of 2019.

Broadening the spectrum of analysis, the *Pérez de Rada Cavanilles* case is emblematic of the different approach of the two Courts on the issue of the conditions of admissibility of appeals.[278] In this case, the applicant had filed an appeal which was sent by mail to the registry of the appellate court. The appeal arrived there three days late and was therefore declared inadmissible. The applicant then appealed to the SCT, which declared the *amparo* inadmissible, ruling that the decision of the ordinary court to declare the appeal inadmissible was legitimate, recalling its previous case law on the point.[279] Instead, the ECtHR came to an opposite conclusion, and substituting its appreciation of the facts to that of the Constitutional Tribunal, censured the strict adherence of constitutional judges to the principle of formal legality, stating that the "l'application particulièrement rigoureuse faite par les juridictions internes d'une règle de procédure a privé la requérante du droit d'accès à un tribunal".[280]

Again on the subject of the calculation of time limits for bringing an appeal is the judgment of the Fourth Chamber of the Court in the *Miragall Escolano* case.[281] In a nutshell, the applicants complained that the decision of the *Tribunal supremo*—upheld by the SCT—to set the *dies a quo* for the calculation of time limits at the date of delivery of the judgment and not from the date of its publication, had violated their right to effective judicial protection.[282] The ECtHR points out that both the Advocate General of the State and three judges of the TC, supported the applicants' arguments, finding the decision of the *Tribunal Supremo* unlawful, especially in view of the fact that the applicants were not parties to the main proceedings and that the grounds of the judgment were only made available to the applicants upon publication. Relying on the existence of a dissent within the SCT,[283] the ECtHR thus censures the interpretation of national norms by the *Tribunal Supremo* and the SCT, clarifying that an excessively rigid interpretation of procedural requirement shall not preclude the actual delivery of justice.

With regard to the dialogue between the two jurisdictions on the subject of substantive rights, although, as noted at the outset, the SCT often makes use of ECtHR precedents in its judgments, there has been no shortage of cases in which the jurisprudence of the Strasbourg Court has met with resistance from the SCT, as happened concerning the extension of the notion of inviolability of the domicile.[284] The dialogue can be said to have begun in 1994, with the judgment delivered by the

---

[278] *Pérez de Rada Cavanilles v. Spain* (28090/95), 28/10/1998.

[279] TC Sentencia 287/1994, de 27 de octubre (BOE núm. 285, de 29 de novembre de 1994).

[280] *Pérez de Rada Cavanilles v. Spain*, para. 49.

[281] *Miragall Escolano and Others v. Spain* (38366/97), (38688/97), (40777/98) et al. 25/01/2000.

[282] For a detailed exposition of the facts of the case, see: *Miragall Escolano and Others v. Spain*, in *Human Rights Case Digest*, vol. 11, no. 1-2/2000, 29 ff.

[283] *Miragall Escolano and Others v. Spain*, para. 37.

[284] Tur Ausina (2005).

ECtHR in the *López Ostra* case.[285] Before domestic courts, the applicant had complained about the inaction of the municipal authorities with respect to her complaint concerning fumes entering into her house from a waste treatment plant. After unsuccessfully exhausting all ordinary remedies, the applicant turned to the SCT, which, however, declared the appeal manifestly unfounded. In particular, the SCT stated that the mere presence of fumes and noise was not sufficient to cause a violation of the right to inviolability of the domicile under Article 18.2 of the Spanish Constitution, and that the applicant's right to freely decide her place of residence was not violated as she did not receive any order to leave her home from the authorities.[286] The European Court of Human Rights instead takes a radically different approach: the judgment clearly states that

> des atteintes graves à l'environnement peuvent affecter le bien-être d'une personne et la priver de la jouissance de son domicile de manière à nuire à sa vie privée et familiale, sans pour autant mettre en grave danger la santé de l'intéressée.[287]

After clarifying that immissions of fumes and noise can cause interference with the right enshrined in Article 8 ECHR, the Court proceed to find a violation of Article 8 ECHR in the applicant's case. Ten years later, the ECtHR had the occasion to clarify the breadth of this statement in the *Moreno Gomez* case.[288] In the proceedings before domestic courts, Ms Moreno Gomez had complained of a violation of her right to inviolability of domicile, guaranteed by Article 18(2) of the Spanish Constitution. It is worth emphasising how, in her *amparo* appeal before the SCT, she specifically referred to the ECtHR judgment in *López Ostra*.[289]

The SCT, while declaring the appeal admissible, affirmed that the breach the right complained of by the applicant was not sufficiently substantiated, under the criteria established by the ECtHR.[290] The judgment of the European Court of Human Rights is noteworthy in at least two respects. First, as already seen in *Miragall Escolano* in the ECtHR judgment, ample space is devoted to the two separate opinions annotated to the SCT judgment.[291] Second, in condemning the Spanish authorities for failing to protect the applicant's right, the ECtHR disregarded the conventionality judgement

---

[285] *López Ostra v. Spain* (16798/90), 09/12/1994.

[286] Ibidem, paras. 15–16.

[287] Ibidem, para. 51.

[288] *Moreno Gomez v. Spain*, 4143/02, 16/11/2004.

[289] Ibidem, paras. 24–30.

[290] Ibidem, paras. 34–36.

[291] In particular, in the opinion annotated by Judge Jimenez de Parga, it is pointed out that Ms. Moreno Gomez in order to assert her right guaranteed by Article 18(2) Const. would in fact have had to prove the infringement of three different fundamental rights: the right to physical integrity, the right to a healthy environment and the right to privacy of the domicile. See: STC, Sentencia 119/2001 de 24 de mayo (ECLI:ES:TC:2001:119). For a commentary see: Canosa Usera (2002–2003), pp. 704–705.

carried by the SCT, without even motivating why the SCT interpretation was not tenable.[292]

Called upon to adjudicate a factual situation identical to that of Ms *Moreno Gomez*, the SCT incorporates the criteria listed in the ECtHR judgment, while maintaining that the burden of proof of the injury remains with the plaintiff.[293] The ECtHR, in the *Martinez-Martinez* case,[294] demonstrates to have accepted the SCT position. Indeed, the judgment dwells at length on the evidence adduced by the applicant to prove the infringement of his right.[295] The Spanish doctrine, however, criticised the European ruling for ignoring the fact that the property had been built illegally in a non-residential area.[296] A circumstance which becomes decisive in a judgment shortly afterwards, where the ECtHR, although in essence recognising the violation of Article 8 ECHR caused by noise from a motor racing track, did not condemn the Spanish State on the grounds that the property had been built illegally.[297] An analysis of the case law of the Convention on the subject of noise immissions thus allows us to appreciate how the European Court of Human Rights, in the context of a constructive dialogue, has been ready to take on board the observations of the TC, although without explicitly saying it.

Another issue on which it is interesting to analyse how the ECtHR interacts with the SCT is that of telephone tapping. The first judgment to be analysed is the one in *Valenzuela Contreras.*[298] The peculiarity of this judgment is that the ECtHR essentially carries out an *in abstracto* analysis of the Spanish legislation—no longer in force at the date of delivery of the judgment, concluding that Article 8 ECHR had been violated. The ECtHR came to the same conclusion in *Prado Bugallo*,[299] which declared that Article 579 of the Spanish Criminal Code was *per se* incompatible with Article 8 ECHR,[300] whereas the SCT, also ruling on the applicant's *amparo*, had not found any violation of Article 18(3) of the Spanish Constitution, guaranteeing the right to secrecy of communications. With judgment 184/2003, the TC accepted the findings of the ECtHR on the national legislation, finding Article 579 of the Criminal Code unconstitutional in the light of Art. 18(3) interpreted in the light of Art. 8 ECHR.[301] However, the SCT concluded that the unconsitutionality could not be

---

[292] See *Moreno Gomez v. Spain,* paras. 56–63.

[293] Auto n° 37/2005 de TC, Sección 4ª, 31 de Enero de 2005 (RTC 2005/37). For a commentary on the decision, see: García Gestoso (2012), pp. 120–122.

[294] *Martinez-Martinez* (21532/08), Court (Third Section), 18/10/2011.

[295] Ibidem,paras. 48–51.

[296] García Gestoso (2012), pp. 126–127.

[297] *Martínez Martínez et Pino Manzano* (61654/08), 03/07/2012.

[298] *Valenzuela Contreras v. Spain* (27671/95), 30/07/1998.

[299] *Prado Bugallo v. Spain* (58496/00), 18/02/2003.

[300] *Prado Bugallo v. Spain* (58496/00), 18/02/2003. On this point more extensively see: Catalá i Bas (2010), p. 287.

[301] TC Sentencia 184/2003, de 23 de octubre.

declared as it would generate a legislative vacuum, which cannot be remedied by judicial means.[302] With a decision of inadmissibility,[303] pronounced in the declared hope that the Spanish legislature would comply with the judgment of the SCT,[304] the Strasbourg Court essentially endorsed the interpretation of right to secrecy of communication provided by the 184/2003 judgment.

Finally, we have to conclude our analysis by briefly reviewing the dialogue between the two courts on what currently represents the main reason of dissonance between them, i.e. the limits and content of freedom of expression. The first case to be mentioned is the 2011 judgment in *Otegi Mondragon.*[305] The applicant was a Spanish MP who had been condemned by the Spanish Supreme Court to one year of prison for having called the monarch "king of torturers". The SCT declared inadmissible the appeal considering that insults are not an exercise of freedom of expression. The ECtHR, instead, emphasising that the applicant was a politician, that the sentence was pronounced in a conference press and thus had to be considered linked to his political activity, that prison-sentences should be in principle avoided in the domain of political discourse,[306] concluded that the applicant's right to freedom of expression guaranteed by Article 10 ECHR had been violated. Seven years later, in the judgment in *Stern Taulats and Roura Capellera*, the ECtHR once again contradicted the SCT, affirming that the applicants' gesture of burning a real size photo of the King was covered by freedom of expression,[307] whereas the *Tribunal Constitucional* held that it was an act inciting to violence, hence excluded from constitutional protection. Following this judgment, the Strasbourg Court condemned Spain another 6 times for an excessively broad notion of what constitutes insult, and by reading the last act of this series, the 2023 judgment in *Fragoso Dacosta,*[308] it emerges that the Spanish Constitutional Tribunal is not following well-consolidated ECtHR standards, by way of elaborating a distinction between the specific case pending before it and the cases previously decided by the Court.[309] Despite the several condemnation pronounced by Strasbourg and more generally a widespread international pressure,[310] to the date neither the Spanish Parliament nor

[302]In this sense see: Catalá i Bas (2010), p. 288.

[303]*Coban v. Spain* (dec.) (17060/02), 25/09/2006.

[304]Català i Bas (2002).

[305]*Otegi Mondragon v. Spain* (2034/07), 15/03/2011.

[306]Ibidem, paras 51–61.

[307]*Stern Taulats and Roura Capellera v. Spain* (51168/15), (51186/15), 13/03/2018.

[308]*Fragoso Dacosta v. Spain, (27926/21), 08/06/2023.*

[309]See: Ibidem, para. 16; where is reported extensively an extract of the Constitutional Tribunal decision on the applicant's case.

[310]See, for instance, the 2020 Spain Periodic Review by the UN Human Rights Council, inviting Spain to "[g]uarantee freedom of expression and opinion by revising the Criminal Code to ensure that its crimes are in line with internationally recognized definitions" or the 2022 Freedom House report on Spain, where it is affirmed that" aggressive enforcement of laws banning the glorification of terrorism has begun to threaten free speech". See: United Nations Human Rights Council, *2020 Universal Periodic Review - Spain (Third Cycle)*, available at: https://www.ohchr.org/en/hr-bodies/upr/es-index; Freedom House, *Freedom in the World 2022 - Spain*, available at: https://freedomhouse.org/country/spain/freedom-world/2022.

the Constitutional Tribunal have taken formal steps to bring national legislation in line with European standards.

In conclusion, observed by Strasbourg, the dialogue between the ECtHR and the *Tribunal constitucional* seems to be a dialogue that, although not without frictions, is nevertheless oriented towards cooperation, within which the Strasbourg Court in the face of loyal cooperation on the part of the SCT in the implementation of conventional law—which has often made up for the failures of the legislature—[311] has responded either by recognising a wider margin of appreciation for the SCT, as seen on the issue of telephone tapping, or by incorporating the jurisprudential criteria developed by the constitutional case law and incorporating them into its own case law, as happened in the *Martinez Martinez* case. Also, it must be noted that in the dialogue with the Spanish Constitutional Tribunal, the separate opinions attached to constitutional judgments seems to play a prominent role, in particular when those opinions are aligned with the ECtHR's position on a given case.[312] In this sense, the possibility of annotating a separate opinion appears to be another element capable of influencing the dialogue between Strasbourg and national constitutional courts, as the ECtHR can facilitate the domestic acceptance of its rulings by pointing out that its reasoning is shared also by some national constitutional judges.

3.8 The Constitutional Courts of the s.c. Micro-States

The definition of what constitutes a micro-State is still the subject of debate among international law scholars.[313] However, for the purposes of this work, it was arbitrarily decided to consider the Principalities of Andorra and Liechtenstein and the Grand Duchy of Luxembourg as micro-States.[314] One circumstance unites the

[311] Lopéz Guerra (2013), p. 142.

[312] See: *Garrido Herrero v. Spain* (61019/19), 11/10/2022, para. 40; *Ghailan and Others v. Spain*, (36366/14) 23/03/2021, paras 35, 73; *Benitez Moriana and Iñigo Fernandez v. Spain* (36537/15, 36539/15), 09/03/2021, para. 25; *Gil Sanjuan v. Spain* (48297/15), 26/05/2020, para. 12; *Otegi Mondragon and others v. Spain* (4184/15), (4317/15), (4323/15) et al., 06/11/2018, para. 20; *Arrozpide Sarasola and Others v. Spain* (65101/16), (73789/16), (73902/16), 23/10/2018, para. 85; *Cuenca Zarzoso v. Spain* (23383/12), 16/01/2018, para. 24; *Fernández Martínez v. Spain* (56030/07), 12.6.2014, para. 29; *Del Río Prada v. Spain* (42750/09), 21/10/2013, para. 53; *García Mateos v. Spain* (38285/09), 19/02/2013, para. 15; *Muñoz Díaz v. Spain* (49151/07), 08/12/2009, paras 17–20. It has to be emphasised that in the case law citing the German Constitutional Court, only two judgments were found in which dissenting opinions are cited. See: *Stubing v. Germany* (43547/08), 12/04/2012, para. 23, *Haidn v. Germany* (6587/04), 13/01/2011, paras 26–29. The fact that as a rule of thumb Spanish Constitutional judges are more prone to annotate dissenting opinions than their German colleagues only partially explains such a striking difference. See: Kelemen (2013), p. 1439.

[313] See: Minaissan (2007).

[314] The Republic of San Marino, although endowed with constitutional jurisdiction, is not dealt with in this section, as no judgments citing its constitutional jurisdiction were found.

three constitutional jurisdictions of these countries: the fact that they are almost entirely absent from the jurisprudence of the European Court of Human Rights.

Therefore, it is possible to dwell only briefly on each of these courts.

(A) Andorra

The *Tribunal Constitucional* of Andorra—established by the 1993 Constitution—can be appealed directly by any individual lamenting a violation of his/her fundamental right through a '*recurs d'empara*'.[315] It is worth noting that until 1999 access to the Constitutional Tribunal was subject to the Andorran General Prosecutor's approval. After the Strasbourg Court's admissibility decision in the case *Millan i Tornes*,[316] the Constitutional Court Act was amended to allow applicants to lodge an appeal with the *Tribunal Constitucional* without prior approval.[317] In total, against the Principality of Andorra, which has been a Member State of the Council of Europe since November 1994, a total of 7 judgments have been handed down by the Strasbourg Court.[318] The *Tribunal Constitucional* is cited in each of these judgments, with an average of 10,4 citations per judgment. Although the statistical sample is obviously not significant, the quantitative data obtained are more or less in line with those of other countries with an individual direct appeal to the constitutional court such as Germany and Spain.

Among these judgments, the *Vidal Escoll et Guillan Gonzalez* case is particularly worth mentioning,[319] as the European Court of Human Rights condemned the respondent state for failing to execute the judgment of the *Tribunal Constitucional,* thus requiring the execution of the constitutional judgement. In particular, the ECtHR notes that the Andorran Constitutional Court had recognised the applicants' right to receive compensation for the damages suffered as a consequence of an expropriation procedure, in addition to the payment of the expropriation of the value, and that the applicant did not receive such compensation. As a consequence, it awards a particular conspicuous compensation for non pecuniary damages under Article 41 ECHR, € 41,000, which is roughly 10 times higher than the average amount awarded by the ECtHR.[320]

[315] Powers and competences of the *Tribunal Constitucional* are defined by a special law coeval with the Constitution. See: BOPA, Any 5 Núm. 51 (28 de setembre de 1993) *Llei qualificada de la Justícia*, de 3-9-93. For a more detailed overview of the functioning of this jurisdiction, see: Garoupa (2018), pp. 184–186.

[316] *Millan i Tornes v. Andorra* [dec.] (35052/97), 17/11/1998.

[317] In light of this, a friendly settlement was reached and the application was struck out of the list by judgment of 6 July 1999. See *Millan i Tornes v. Andorra* (35052/97), 06/07/1999 paras 19–23.

[318] The most interesting judgment, however, is the one rendered by the Court in the *Millan i Tornes* case (35052/97, 06/07/1999). The case, which ended with a decision to remove the case from the register due to an amicable settlement of the dispute, concerned the need for the Attorney General's approval in order to bring an individual direct action, a requirement that is clearly incompatible with conventional law. For a commentary on the decision see: Burgorgue Larsen (2008), pp. 268–269.

[319] *Vidal Escoll et Guillan Gonzalez v. Andorre* (38196/05), 29/07/2008.

[320] Altwicker-Hámori et al. (2016), p. 50.

(B) Liechtenstein

Similar to the *Tribunal Constitucional* of the Principality of Andorra, the Constitutional Court of Liechtenstein is also cited in all the nine judgments rendered against the Alpine micro-state. This is not surprising since according to Section 15(1), (2) (a) of the Constitutional Court Act, the Constitutional Court can be seized by any individual who complains about the violation, caused by a decision of a court of last instance but also by the decisions of an administrative authority, of one of his rights guaranteed by the Constitution or the ECHR. Quite extraordinary, especially when compared to the data obtained for the other constitutional courts, is the average number of citations per judgment, which is 41. Those data seems to suggests that there will be element worth analysing in the judgments against Liechtenstein, and indeed that is the case.

Proceeding in chronological order, the first judgment on which it is necessary to dwell is *Steck-Risch and Others.*[321] Here, the ECtHR was called upon to decide whether the fact that one of the judges of the Constitutional Court was partner of the same law firm of the judge who adopted the decision challenged before the Constitutional Court, had undermined the impartiality of the judge of law. The Strasbourg judges, making a close *distinction* with their own precedents on the impartiality of the judiciary, stated that the absence of a bond of dependence and the lack of evidence concerning the existence of a friendly relationship between the two judges, lead to exclude that the mere fact that the two judges shared the same office could have affected the impartiality of the Constitutional Court.[322]

In the *A.K.* case, on which the ECtHR has ruled on two occasions,[323] the applicant challenged the impartiality of all five judges of the Constitutional Court on various grounds. The ECtHR essentially declared that the manner in which the Constitutional Court dealt with the requests for recusal, i.e. having the other four judges decide each individual request to the exclusion of the one to whom the specific request was addressed, violated the applicant's right to a fair trial.[324] In particular, the Strasbourg judges considered that the Constitutional Court should have appointed five substitute judges to decide on the five requests for recusal, thus not paralysing the work of the body.[325] In the subsequent judgment, it simply reiterates that the procedure used for dealing with requests for recusal is in breach of Article 6(1) ECHR.[326]

---

321 *Steck-Risch and Others v. Liechtenstein* (63151/00), 19/05/2005.

322 *Ibid*, paras. 46 50.

323 *A.K. v. Liechtenstein* (38191/12), 09/07/2015; A.*K. v. Liechtenstein (no. 2)* (10722/13), 18/02/2016.

324 *A.K. v. Liechtenstein (no. 1)*, para. 72.

325 Ibidem, para. 83.

326 On a more positive note, in the same judgment the Strasbourg Court also praises the Constitutional Court as "in its more recent case-law [. . .]no longer restricted itself to a finding of a breach of Article 6 § 1 of the Convention where the proceedings before the lower courts and/or those before itself, having regard to the criteria developed in this Court's case-law, had lasted unreasonably long. Filling a gap in Liechtenstein law [. . .] the Constitutional Courtdeveloped a right for the complainant to be exempted from, or be reimbursed, certain costs of the proceedings, in particular lawyer's fees and court costs, as redress for such damage". See: *A.K. v. Liechtenstein (no. 2)*, para. 91.

In conclusion, the ECtHR case law against Liechtenstein is interesting especially because it elaborates on the notion of impartiality of the constitutional judge. To this regard, it must be emphasised that in the judgments just analysed, the ECtHR's respect for constitutional judges. Even if in *Steck-Risch and Others* the Strasbourg judges deny *tout court* the violation of the principle of impartiality of the judge; and in the two judgments on the A.K. declares the violation of the applicant's right to an impartial tribunal "on account of the procedure the Constitutional Court had chosen in order to reject the applicant's complaints of bias",[327] the Strasbourg carefully avoids to cast doubts as to the actual impartiality of constitutional judges.

(C) Luxembourg

The jurisprudence concerning the Luxembourg Constitutional Court is certainly the one that offers the least insights among the three courts considered in this work. First of all because although the Strasbourg Court has delivered 47 judgments against the Grand Duchy of Luxembourg, the Constitutional Court is cited in only 3 (4.2%). From a quantitative point of view, therefore, this figure is even lower than that of other constitutional courts which, like the Luxembourg Constitutional Court, can only be reached by individuals through a question of constitutionality. The extreme smallness of the statistical sample, combined with the fact that quotations appear only in the factual part of the judgments, makes a qualitative analysis unnecessary.

3.9 The ECtHR and Western Constitutional Courts. Preliminary Conclusions

After the comparative analysis, it can be affirmed that, as a rule of thumb, constitutional courts of Western consolidated democracies are friends rather than foes of the ECtHR. The majority of the constitutional courts of the region, indeed, never had significant episodes of confrontations with the Strasbourg Court. In particular, the relationship of the Strasbourg Court with the Austrian, Belgian, and Portuguese courts appears substantially frictionless. Quite unsurprisingly, the attitude of those national courts is of maximum openness towards the ECHR system. In the case of Austria, since the ECHR enjoys constitutional rank, enforcing the Convention means enforcing the Constitution, and as a consequence the Austrian Constitutional Court routinely interprets and applies the Convention.[328] In Belgium, the constitutional court, according to one of its former Presidents, is ready to overrule its precedents to comply with ECtHR judgments "without even the slightest indications to resist",[329]

[327] Ibidem, *Operative Part,* §4.

[328] Gamper (2016), p. 90.

[329] Popelier (2016), p. 118.

and since 2004 the ECHR has enjoyed supra-constitutional status. The Portuguese Constitutional Tribunal for its part maintains an attitude of general receptiveness towards international law, and in particular towards the ECHR,[330] which is frequently used as an interpretative canon for fundamental rights guaranteed in the constitution. Besides a friendly posture towards the ECHR, another common feature amongst those courts is that they all offer limited possibilities for individuals to access the constitutional court. In the case of the Austrian and Portuguese Court, individual direct access is essentially limited to challenge the objective unconstitutionality of a normative provision applied in the course of a proceeding, but not its misapplication, whereas in Belgium direct individual access is limited both objectively, being limited to legislative acts, and temporally, as it can proposed within six months from the publication of the act. From the ECtHR perspective, this obviously means that there are few cases in which the Strasbourg Court and the constitutional courts deliver a judgment in the same individual case. Conversely, in constitutional justice systems with a "full" individual constitutional complaint,[331] this happens on a routinary basis, the opposite being the exception.[332] In fact, where such an individual mechanism is present, applicants shall first bring the case to the attention of the constitutional court via an individual constitutional complaint, as long as this constitutes an effective remedy to be exhausted under Article 35 ECHR. This is the case, for instance of the German *Verfassungsbeschwerde* and the Spanish *recurso de amparo*. In this regard, it should be noted that the effective success rate of both these remedies is extremely low—the two constitutional courts declare inadmissible roughly 99% of individual appeals received without providing any substantial reasons.[333] From the Strasbourg perspective, once again, this means a reduction of the potential for open conflicts, which appears beneficial for the relationship between the two levels of jurisdictions. Yet, this does not mean that

[330] Amaral and Pereira (2020), p. 715.

[331] The Venice Commission adopts the expression 'full constitutional complaint' to refer to appeal mechanisms in which individuals are allowed to "challenge a general act if it is directly applicable on them, or challenge an individual act addressed to them." See: CDL-AD (2010), Study on Individual Access to Constitutional Justice, Adopted by the Venice Commission at its 85th Plenary Session (Venice, 17–18 December 2010), para. 5.

[332] Although the figures are different for each Respondent State, constitutional courts that do have a full individual constitutional complaint, are cited in at least 80% of the case. See, above, Ch. 1.3.

[333] The rate of success of the German *Verfassungsbeschwerde* is 1,69%. In the case of the *recurso de amparo*, the percentage is even lower, in 2022 for instance the SCT only admitted for consideration 12 out of 6953 complaints received see respectively: Bundesverfassungsgeritch, 2022 Annual Report, p. 54, available at:https://www.bundesverfassungsgericht.de/SharedDocs/Downloads/EN/Jahresbericht/jahresbericht_2022.pdf?__blob=publicationFile&v=3; Tribunal Constitutional, *Memoria 2022*, 53–54. Available at: https://www.tribunalconstitucional.es/en/memorias/Documents/Memoria%202022.pdf.

the German Federal Constitutional Tribunal and its Spanish homologue did not have their disagreements with the Strasbourg Court.

As to the latter, despite an overall friendly attitude of the SCT towards the ECHR system, in the Strasbourg Court case law is possible to find several episodes in which the two courts had irreconcilable views concerning fundamental rights' content. In the most recent, the ECtHR engaged in a close dialogue with the SCT, concerning the compatibility of the reinforced criminal protection awarded to state's symbols, like the Crown or the national flag, against insults. Despite a constant jurisprudence of the SCT affirming the constitutionality of the imposition of criminal penalties for excesses in the exercise of freedom of expression, as this right does not include a supposed 'right to insult', the Strasbourg Court had insofar repeated that the imposition of criminal penalties for crimes of opinions, is in principle incompatible with the spirit of the Convention, especially when the opinions are political in nature. Even if it is possible to define the attitude of the SCT as functional disobedience, as it engages with the ECHR case law proposing an alternative reading in line with the established Spanish constitutional jurisprudence,[334] as the Strasbourg case law on the point is well-consolidated and crystal clear, its lack of implementation constitutes a challenge to the ECtHR interpretative authority over fundamental rights issues. In light of these apparently irreconcilable differences, the only way out of this judicial clash seems to be an intervention of the Spanish legislator repealing the relevant provisions of the Criminal Code.[335] The divergences between the ECtHR and the German Constitutional Court instead all find a solution. In the *Hannover* and *Sicherungsverwahrung* sagas, the BVG has indeed been capable of defending its interpretation of fundamental rights, ultimately inducing the ECtHR to accept them, even if that meant a departure from its case law.[336] Overall, the BVG may well be a "strong promoter" of the ECHR,[337] but is one that makes sure its voice is heard in Strasbourg.

A similar definition could apply, *mutatis mutandis*, to the Italian Constitutional Court. Especially starting from the s.c. twin judgements of 2007, the ICC essentially acted as a proxy agent of the Strasbourg Court, even annulling legislative norms

[334] See, for instance: Judgment of the Spanish Constitutional Tribunal of 15 December 2020, (STC 190/2020), in particular FJ 3,4. There, the SCT engages in a distinguishing between the case under its consideration and the cases previously decided by the ECtHR. It is also worth noting that four judges annotated a dissenting opinion to the judgment, criticising the majority for failing to comply with the ECtHR judgment in *Stern Taulats and Roura Capellera*.

[335] See, above Ch. 2.7, fn 314. Further, it must be noted that is the whole Spanish notion of freedom of expression which is at odds with European standards. The EU European Economic and Social Committee considered that the Organic Law 4/15 on Citizens Security violated international standards concerning freedom of expression, that the provisions of the Criminal Code concerning free speech were excessively vague. See: European Economic and Social Committee, *Fundamental rights and the rule of law – Report on the visit to Spain*, p.3. Available at: https://www.eesc.europa.eu/sites/default/files/files/qe-03-22-211-en-n_0.pdf.

[336] See, above Sect. 3.3.

[337] Pabel (2016), p. 175.

exclusively on the grounds of their incompatibility with the ECHR.[338] However, as it has been observed, this openness ultimately generated disagreements between the two courts.[339] These disagreements reached their apex during the *Varvara* saga, concerning the compatibility with Article 7 ECHR of 'confiscation without conviction'. Faced with an ECtHR ruling affirming that confiscation could only be imposed in a formal criminal conviction,[340] in its judgment 49/2015 the ICC maintained its substantive notion of 'criminal conviction', requiring only the commission of the offence to be adequately ascertained, independently of the formal vest of the judicial decision.[341] Even though also this resistance can be qualified as a functional one,[342] it was accompanied by a challenge to the binding nature of the Strasbourg case law, which induced the Strasbourg Court to concede to the ICC demands.[343] Moreover, as a reaction to the ICC's 'disobedience', the Strasbourg Court seems to have started to pay more attention to Italian constitutional jurisprudence, which is now cited in roughly one-third of judgments against Italy. In contrast, before 2015 the percentage of citations was below 10%, showing that the warning did not go unnoticed. Finally, concerning the French Constitutional Council, although the introduction of the preliminary question of constitutionality in 2009 resulted in a slightly increased visibility of its jurisprudence in the Strasbourg case law, the main French interlocutor of the Strasbourg Court continues to be the *Cour de cassation*.[344] At the same time, in the few dialogues between the ECtHR and the FCC, both courts have demonstrated a careful consideration of the other's case law. For instance, when called to assess the conventionality of restrictions on freedom of religion, such as the ban on the use of headscarves for workers of the public sector,[345] the Strasbourg Court attached decisive weight to the principle of secularism as elaborated by the FCC in order to exclude a breach of Article 9 ECHR.[346]

---

[338] For the reasons behind the adoption of the twin judgments and an overall assessment of the ICC posture vis-à -vis the ECtHR see, Martinico (2016), p. 184.

[339] Mancano and Martinico (2016), pp. 199–214.

[340] *Varvara v. Italy* (17475/09), 29/10/2013.

[341] Judgment of the Italian Constitutional Court of 14 January 2015, nr. 49/2015.

[342] Martinico (2020).

[343] See, above, Sect. 2.5.

[344] This observation finds full confirmation in the number of ECtHR judgments in which the *Cour de Cassation* is cited, namely 716 out of a total of 1069, a percentage of approximately 67%.

[345] See: *Ebrahimian v. France* (64846/11), 26/11/2015. Such an excessive reliance on the FCC jurisprudence generated strong criticism, as the ECtHR did not assess the legitimacy of the restriction in the applicant's case but limited itself to reviewing the legitimacy of the objective pursued by the ban. The judgment was even voted by the users of the specialised blog *The Strasbourg Observers*, as the worst judgment delivered by the Court in 2015. See: https://strasbourgobservers.com/2016/02/18/the-winners-poll-on-best-and-worst-ecthr-judgment-of-2015/.

[346] See, above, Ch. 2.3.

References

Altwicker-Hámori S, Altwicker T, Peters A (2016) Measuring violations of human rights: an empirical analysis of awards in respect of non-pecuniary damage under the european convention on human rights. Zeitschrift für ausländisches öffentliches Recht und Völkerrecht 76:1–51

Alvarez Rodriguez I (2021) El Convenio Europeo de Derechos Humanos desde la perspectiva constitucional. Revista Española de Derecho Constitucional 41:409–423

Amaral ML, Pereira RA (2020) The Portuguese Constitutional Court. In: Bogdandy von A et al (eds) The Max Planck Handbooks in European Public Law: Volume III: Constitutional Adjudication: Institutions, pp 673–718

Ambrus M (2009) Comparative law method in the jurisprudence of the European Court of Human Rights in the light of the rule of law. Erasmus Law Rev 2:353–371

Arnaud von A (2015) Damages for the infringement of human rights in Germany. In: Bagińska E (ed) Damages for violations of human rights: a comparative study of domestic legal systems. Springer, Heidelberg, pp 101–120

Asworth A (2008) Self-incrimination in European human rights law-a pregnant pragmatism? Cardozo Law Rev 30:751–774

Badinter R (2009) Une longue marche "Du Conseil à la Cour constitutionnelle". Cahiers du Conseil constitutionnel 25:9 pp

Behrendt C (2020) The Belgian constitutional court. In: Bogdandy von A et al (eds) The Max Planck handbooks in European public law: volume III: constitutional adjudication: institutions. Oxford University Press, Oxford, pp 72–117

Bon A (1989) La justice constitutionnelle au Portugal. Economica, Paris

Braasch P (2010) Follow up: the European Court of Human Rights' pilot judgment on excessive length of proceedings before German courts. German Yearb Int Law 53:1007–1012

Burgorgue Larsen L (2001) L'"Autonomie constitutionnelle" aux prises avec la Convention européenne des droits de l'homme. Revue belge de droit constitutionnel 1:31–64

Burgorgue Larsen L (2008) L'Influence de la Convention Européenne sur le Fonctionnement des Cours Constitutionnelles. Revue internationale de droit comparé 60:265–282

Canosa Usera R (2002–2003) Pretensiones ambientales en amparo constitucional. Comentario a la STC 119/2011 de 24 de mayo. Teoría y realidad constitucional 10–11:697–716

Carcassonne G, Duhamel O, Dufy A (2015) QPC. La question prioritaire de constitutionnalité. Dalloz, Paris

Carrasco Durán M (2002) Los procesos para la tutela judicial de los derechos fundamentales. Centro de Estudios Políticos y Constitucionales, Madrid

Carrillo Salcedo JA (2003) El Convenio Europeo de Derechos Humanos. Tecnos, Madrid

Cartabia M (2016) Of bridges and walls: the 'Italian Style' of constitutional adjudication. Ital J Public Law 8:37–55

Castro-Rial Garron F (1994) El derecho a un juicio equitativo (Comentario a la Sentencia del Tribunal Europeo de Derechos Humanos de 23 de junio de 1993, en el asunto "Ruiz Mateos v. España"). Revista de instituciones europeas 21:157–170

Català i Bas AH (2002) La problemática adecuación de la legislación española sobre escuchas telefónicas a las exigencias del convenio europeo de derechos Humanos y sus consecuencias. Revista del Poder Judicial 66:13–71

Català i Bas AH (2010) Escuchas telefónicas: un encuentro con el Tribunal constitucional y un desencuentro con el legislator español. Revista Europea de Derechos Fundamentales 15:279–294

Chueca Sancho GA (1994) La sentencia dictada por el Tribunal Europeo de Derechos Humanos en el caso Ruiz Mateos. Derechos y Libertades: revista del Instituto Bartolomé de las Casas 2:553–570

Conti R (2006) L'occupazione acquisitiva. Tutela della proprietà e diritti umani. Giuffrè, Milan

Cortes A, Violante T (2011) Concrete control of constitutionality in Portugal: a means towards effective protection of fundamental rights. Penn State Int Law Rev 29:764–765

D'Orazio G (1991) Il giudizio delle leggi ed i "nuovi" tempi del suo svolgimento (profili processuali ed istituzionali. In Romboli R (cur.) La giustizia costituzionale a una svolta. Giappichelli, Turin, pp 105–121
Dürr SR (2014) Individual access to constitutional courts as an effective remedy against human rights violations in Europe - the contribution of the Venice commission. J Law Polit 258:67–89
Faber R (2008) The Austrian constitutional court. An overview. Int J Const Law 1:49–53
Gamper A (2016) Austria: endorsing the convention system, endorsing the constitution. In: Popelier P et al (eds) Criticism of the European Court of Human Rights. Intersentia, Cambridge, pp 75–101
Gamper A, Palermo F (2008) The constitutional Court of Austria: modern profiles of an archetype of constitutional review. J Comp Law 3:64–79
García Gestoso N (2012) Contaminacion acústica y derechos fundamentales. Protección y discrepancias in su tutela judicial. Foro, Nueva época 15:109–134
Garoupa N (2018) Does being a foreigner shape judicial behaviour? Evidence from the Constitutional Court of Andorra, 1993-2016. J Inst Econ 14:181–195
Gehler M, Kaiser W (1997) A study in ambivalence: Austria and European integration 1945-95. Contemp Eur Hist 6:75–99
Gentili G (2011) Una prospettiva comparata sui sistemi europei di ricorso al giudice costituzionale: suggestioni e spunti per la Corte costituzionale italiana. Revista de estudios jurídicos 11:207–248
Giupponi TF (2014) La Corte e il segreto: Abu Omar, ultimo atto. Quaderni costituzionali 2:386–388
Gómez de José C (2023) Presentación del incidente de nulidad de actuaciones como cauce de admisión del recurso de amparo a la vista de la reciente sentencia del TEDH (15 de diciembre de 2022, asunto Olivares Zúñiga c. España). Revista de derecho UNED 31:225–242
Groppi T (1997) I poteri istruttori della Corte costituzionale nel giudizio sulle leggi. Giuffrè, Milan
Groppi T (2016) La jurisprudence de Strasbourg dans les décisions de la Cour constitutionnelle italienne. Federalismi 2:2–46
Hartwig M (2005) Much Ado about human rights: the federal constitutional court confronts the European Court of Human Rights. German Law J 6:869–894
Hoffmeister F (2006) Germany: status of European convention on human rights in domestic law. Int J Const Law 5:722–731
Ibrido R (2016) Intorno all'equo processo costituzionale: il problema dell'operatività dell'art. 6 CEDU nei giudizi dinanzi ai tribunali costituzionali. Rivista AIC 1:1–32
Kelemen K (2013) Dissenting opinion in constitutional courts. Germ Law J 14:1345–1371
Kommers D (2012) The constitutional jurisprudence of the Federal Republic of Germany. Duke University Press, Durham
Lachmayer K (2017) The Austrian constitutional court. In: Jakab A, Dyevre A, Itzcovich G (eds) Comparative constitutional reasoning. Cambridge University Press, Cambridge, pp 75–114
Lamarque E (2012) Corte costituzionale e giudici nell'Italia repubblicana. Laterza, Roma-Bari
Lavrysen L, Theunis J (2013) The Belgian constitutional court: a satellite of the ECtHR? In: Liberae Cogitationes. Liber amicorum Marc Bossuyt. Intersentia, Cambridge
Lopéz Guerra L (2013) El diálogo entre el Tribunal Europeo de Derechos Humanos y los tribunales españoles. Coincidencias y divergencias, Teoría y Realidad Constitucional 32:139–158
Lübbe-Wolff G (2006) ECHR and national jurisdiction - the Görgülü case. Humboldt Forum Recht 1:138–146
Malfatti E (2009) Immunità parlamentari e terzi "offesi": "l'accerchiamento" del modello di giudizio della Corte italiana è davvero completo? Quaderni costituzionali 4:966–972
Malfatti E (2012) L'insindacabilità parlamentare e i diritti dei terzi "offesi" ancora tra Roma e Strasburgo. Quaderni Costituzionali 1:121–124
Mancano L, Martinico G (2016) An Italian Tale of Two Courts. Judgment 49/2015 of the Italian Constitutional Court an its Relationship with Strasbourg. Revista Española de Derecho Europeo 58:213–214

Mariniello T (2021) Judge Pinto de Albuquerque and the progressive development of international human rights law. Brill Nijhoff, Leiden

Martinico G (2012) Is the European convention going to be 'Supreme?. Comparative-constitutional overview of ECHR and EU law before national courts. Eur J Int Law 23:401–424

Martinico G (2016) Italy: Between Constitutional Openness and Resistance. In: Popelier P et al. Criticism of the European Court of Human Rights. Shifting the Convention System: Counter-Dynamics at the National and EU level. Intersentia, Cambridge, pp 177–198

Massot J (2009) Les juges et les validations legislatives: un chœur à cinq voix non sans dissonances. In: Badinter R et al (eds) Le Dialogue des juges. Mélanges en l'honneur du président Bruno Genevois. Dalloz, Paris, pp 709–723

Menditto F (2017) La sentenza De Tommaso: verso la piena equiparazione e compatibilità convenzionale del sistema della prevenzione. Diritto penale contemporaneo 4:127–174

Minaissan G (2007) 'Micro-etat', 'Mini-etat'. Essai de classification. Annuaire Français de relations internationales 8:329–338

Moreira V (2001) Le Tribunal constitutionnel portugais: le "contrôle concret" dans le cadre d'un système mixte de justice constitutionnelle. Nouveaux Cahiers du Conseil 10:2–52

Öhlinger T (2003) The genesis of the Austrian model of constitutional review of legislation. Ratio Juris 16:206–222

Pabel K (2016) Germany: the long way of integrating the Strasburg perspective into the protection of fundamental rights. In: Popelier P et al (eds) Criticism of the European Court of Human Rights. Shifting the convention system: counter-dynamics at the national and EU level. Intersentia, Cambridge, pp 155–176

Passaglia (2012) Sull'inopportunità di introdurre il ricorso diretto individuale. (Qualche riflessione ed una provocazione). In: Tarchi R (ed) Patrimonio costituzionale europeo e tutela dei diritti fondamentali. Il ricorso individuale diretto, Giappichelli, Torino, pp 323–349

Pereira Coutinho F (2010) Report on Portugal. In: Martinico G, Pollicino O (eds) The national judicial treatment of the ECHR and EU laws. A comparative constitutional perspective. Europa Law Publishing, Groningen, pp 351–368

Popelier P (2016) Belgium: faithful, obedient and just a little irritated. In: Popelier P et al (eds) Criticism of the European Court of Human Rights. Shifting the convention system: counter-dynamics at the national and EU level. Intersentia, Cambridge, pp 103–130

Powers WA (2006) Hirst v. United Kingdom (No. 2): a first look at prisoner disenfranchisement by the European Court of Human Rights. Connecticut J Int Law 21:243–295

Queralt Jiménez A (2008) La interpretación de los derechos: del Tribunal de Estrasburgo al Tribunal Constitucional. Centro de Estudios Políticos y Constitucionales, Madrid

Quint PE (2006) The most extraordinarily powerful Court of Law the world has ever known? Judicial review in the United States and Germany. Maryl Law Rev 65:152–170

Rechberger W (2012) The impact of the ECHR Jurisprudence on Austrian practice in the field of judicial independence. In: Shetreet S, Forsyth C (eds) The culture of judicial independence. Conceptual foundations and practical challenges. Martinus Nijhoff, Leiden, pp 231–242

Retortillo Baquer LM (1995) La recepción por el Tribunal Constitucional de la jurisprudencia del Tribunal Europeo de Derechos Humanos. Revista de administración pública 137:7–24

Rocchi F (2012) L'istituto tedesco della Sicherungsverwahrung. Il dialogo tra la Corte di Strasburgo e la Corte costituzionale. In: Gaboardi A et al (eds) Libertà dal carcere libertà nel carcere. Affermazione e tradimento della legalità nella restrizione della libertà personale. Giappichelli, Torino, pp 327–381

Rosoux G (2013) La Cour constitutionnelle de. Les Nouveaux Cahiers du Conseil Constitutionnel 41:201–214

Rousseau D (2012) Question Prioritaire de Constitutionnalité. Lextenso, Paris

Ruet C (2016) Interdiction du port de signes religieux par les agents du service public: La combinatoire subtile de l'arrêt Ebrahimian. Revue des droits de l'homme. Actualités Droits-Libertés:1–15

Schmidl EA (2016) Lukewarm neutrality in a cold war? J Cold War Stud 18:36–50

Selvaggi E (2016) Il caso Abu Omar davanti alla Corte europea: qualche opportuna precisazione. Diritto penale contemporaneo

Shields K (2022) A review of evidence on land acquisition powers and land ownership restrictions in European countries. APS Group, Glasgow

Simonelli MA (2017) Towards a gender-neutral marriage? Il riconoscimento giuridico delle unioni omosessuali in Europa e in Italia. Diritto pubblico comparato ed europeo 2:421–454

Sospedra MM (1987) El convenio de Roma y la jurisprudencia del Tribunal europeo de derechos humanos en el derecho español. Revista General de Derecho Constitucional 510:891–907

Stone Sweet A (1992) The birth of judicial politics in France: The constitutional council in comparative perspective. Oxford University Press, Oxford

Stumer A (2010) The presumption of innocence. Evidential and human rights perspectives. Hart, Oxford

Sudre F (2015) La compatibilité avec l'article 6, § 1 de la Convention EDH du refus de renvoi d'une QPC au Conseil constitutionnel. La Semaine Juridique -Edition Générale 46–47:2104–2107

Tur Ausina R (2005) Contaminación acústica, derechos fundamentales y calidad de vida medioambiental. STEDH Moreno Gómez v. España, de 16 de noviembre de 2004. Revista europea de derechos fundamentales 4:157–176

Tur Ausina R (2010) L'utilizzazione da parte del Tribunal supremo e del Tribunal Constitucional spagnolo della giurisprudenza comunitaria e della Corte europea dei diritti dell'uomo in materia di diritti. In: Rolla G (ed) Il sistema europeo di protezione dei diritti fondamentali e i rapporti tra le giurisdizioni. Giuffrè, Milano, pp 119–146

Valentino A (2016) The Strasbourg Court's ruling on the Abu Omar case: the protection of fundamental rights in the relationship between the powers of the State. Osservatorio costituzionale 3:1–28

Vidal Zapatero JM (2012) The right to a public hearing: a guarantee downplayed by the Strasbourg court. In: García Roca J, Santolaya P (eds) Europe of rights: a compendium on the European Convention of Human Rights. Martinus Nijhoff, Leiden, pp 197–218

Chapter 4
The Constitutional Courts of New Democracies

The present Chapter analyses the relationship of the Strasbourg Court with the constitutional courts of 'new democracies',[1] i.e. constitutional courts emerged during the transition to democracy in the countries of Eastern and Central Eastern Europe, and the Balkans, following the USSR collapse in 1991. During these democratic transitions national actors were generally eager to follow the recommendations coming from EU Institutions and the Council of Europe bodies,[2] to bring their legal systems in line with European Standards both concerning institutional design and in the fundamental rights domain. In particular, the states of those areas were prompted to establish a specialised constitutional jurisdiction, in most cases adopting the German Federal Constitutional Court as a blueprint.[3] Those newly-created constitutional courts played a decisive role in the reception process of European standards in their respective legal systems,[4] and are still generally considered faithful allies of the Strasbourg Court.[5] Despite the unavoidable difficulties

Supplementary Information The online version contains supplementary material available at https://doi.org/10.1007/978-3-031-71268-5_4.

[1] Albeit never formally adopted, the distinction between established and new democracies is commonly used in its opinions and reports by the Venice Commission. See for instance: CDL-AD(2019)015, *Parameters on the Relationship between the Parliamentary Majority and the Opposition in a Democracy: A Checklist*, Adopted by the Venice Commission at its 119th Plenary Session (Venice, 21–22 June 2019), para. 9.

[2] Unlike most of the systems reviewed so far, the vast majority of them indeed adopt a monistic approach to international law, as for the nations with little to no democratic traditions. See: Keller and Stone Sweet (2008), p. 679.

[3] Elster (1991), p. 469.

[4] Arato (2016), pp. 79–80.

[5] Ziemele (2016); Sadurski (2009), p. 402. Scholarship also refers to those courts as the constitutional courts of the fourth wave. This classification arose in French doctrine following the expansion of constitutional justice in Central and Eastern Europe due to the fall of the Soviet Union. See in

M. A. Simonelli, *The European Court of Human Rights and Constitutional Courts*,
Ius Gentium: Comparative Perspectives on Law and Justice 120,
https://doi.org/10.1007/978-3-031-71268-5_4

involved in the passage to democracy, thanks also to the European supervisory and advisory mechanisms, the overall balance of these transitions is positive and the countries of this European region continues to be the European "epicentre of democratic growth".[6]

Yet, one cannot avoid noting the serious problems that have affected, and that are affecting, many of the legal systems in which those courts operate. Notwithstanding a general trend of democratic growth in the region, many of its states, such as Albania, Montenegro, North Macedonia, and Serbia are still not considerable as fully-fledged democracies,[7] and have, amongst other issues, serious problems in the implementation of ECtHR judgments and standards. Others are even experiencing democratic regression. This is notoriously the case of Hungary where, during his prolonged rule, Prime Minster Orbán has progressively captured and neutralised all the institutions for the protection of constitutional democracy, including the constitutional court.

Inevitably, those differences in the nature and magnitude of the problems affecting those legal systems also affect the functioning and the role of the national constitutional court and its relationship with Strasbourg. On this latter aspect, the case of Poland is emblematic, where following the capture by the PiS-led ruling majority, the constitutional court started to develop a more challenging posture *vis-á-vis* the Strasbourg Court.[8] Considered from this standpoint, the constitutional courts hereafter considered constitute a less homogenous group compared to that of established western democracies. With this *caveat* in mind, it is possible to proceed to analyse the ECtHR case law citing the constitutional courts of the new democracies of Central and Eastern Europe, which will follow the same structure adopted in the preceding chapter.

---

particular: Favoreu and Mastour (1996); Fromont (1996). For an overview of the different waves of constitutional courts see: Olivetti and Groppi (2003), p. 1 ff.

[6]The 2023 Report of the International Institute for Democracy and Democratic Assistance (IDEA), seems to contradict the common perception of a generalise regression of the rule of law in the region, as it affirms that Central Europe was amongst the top-performing sub-regions concerning rule of law improvements. See: IDEA, *The Global State of Democracy 2023 The New Checks and Balances*, pp. 102–103. Available at: https://www.idea.int/sites/default/files/2023-11/the-global-state-of-democracy-2023-the-new-checks-and-balances.pdf. All the websites were last accessed on the 30 of June 2024.

[7]According to the 2023 Report of Freedom House, all these countries are only partly free, whilst the Economist EIU's global democracy index classify them as flawed democracies. See, respectively: Freedom House, 2023 Freedom in the World Report, available at: https://freedomhouse.org/explore-the-map?type=fiw&year=2023; and EIU, Democracy Index 2022, available at: https://www.economist.com/graphic-detail/2023/02/01/the-worlds-most-and-least-democratic-countries-in-2022.

[8]It was already mentioned that in 2021 the Polish Constitutional Tribunal (judgement K 6/21) even declared the unconstitutionality of Article 6 ECHR, inasmuch as it applies to constitutional courts.

4.1 Business As Usual? The ECtHR and the Albanian Constitutional Court

Considering that the Hoxha's regime was probably the most illiberal of all former communist countries, Albania completed its transition to democracy relatively rapidly. As early as 1992, albeit in the absence of a formal constitution, the Constitutional Court (hereafter 'the ACC') was established to verify the compatibility of laws and other regulatory acts with constitutional norms.[9] After its accession to the Council of Europe and the subsequent ratification of the ECHR in 1996, the Albanian state finally succeeded in adopting a Constitution in 1998. For the first judgment of the Strasbourg Court against Albania, we have to wait until the end of 2004.[10] Significantly, in this judgment, the Strasbourg Court directed a recommendation to the ACC to include the right to have judgments executed in its notion of fair trial.[11] As the same Strasbourg Court noted in a subsequent judgment, the ACC immediately changed its practice in the sense suggested by the Strasbourg judges. This example is well illustrative of the attitude of the ACC, which is generally considered an ally of the Strasbourg Court in the promotion of ECHR standards in Albania.[12]

As to 1 January 2023, the Strasbourg Court had delivered a total of 71 judgments against Albania, the ACC being cited in 55 of them (77.5%), with no significant variance in their temporal distribution (see Fig. 4.1). The average number of citations per judgment is of roughly 14.[13] Those data reflect the width of the avenues of individual access to the ACC. With regard to individual access, Article 134 of the Albanian Constitution allows every individual to appeal to the ACC. Regarding the possible contents of the constitutional complaint, in 2016 the Constitutional Court Act was amended to allow the submission of a constitutional appeal for all the rights guaranteed in the Albanian Constitution, whereas before was limited to the right to a fair trial[14]At the same time, the ACC's jurisprudence has made it clear that the appeal must be constitutional in nature, i.e. in principle it cannot concern the interpretation of a rule made by the judge on the merits or the way in which the

---

[9]More on the evolution of the Albanian constitutional system until the adoption of the 1998 Constitution, see: Alimehmeti (2011).

[10]*Qufaj Co. Sh.p.k. v. Albania* (54268/00), 18/11/2004.

[11]See *Qufaj Co. Sh.p.k. v. Albania*, para. 42.

[12]Dedja (2018) available at: chrome-extension://efaidnbmnnnibpcajpcglclefindmkaj/https://dergipark.org.tr/en/download/article-file/939070.

[13]All the judgments were retrieved by using the keyword 'constitutional court'.

[14]See: Law No. 8577 of 10 February 2000 *on the Organisation and Functioning of the Constitutional Court of the Republic of Albania*, Article 71(1) of The English text of the Law on the Albanian Constitutional Court can be found on the CODICES database of the Venice Commission at the url: https://codices.coe.int/codices/documents/law/5C90C5DC-9586-46E9-8448-08DC0D38DFC5#a5c90c5dc-9586-46e9-8448-08dc0d38dfc5.

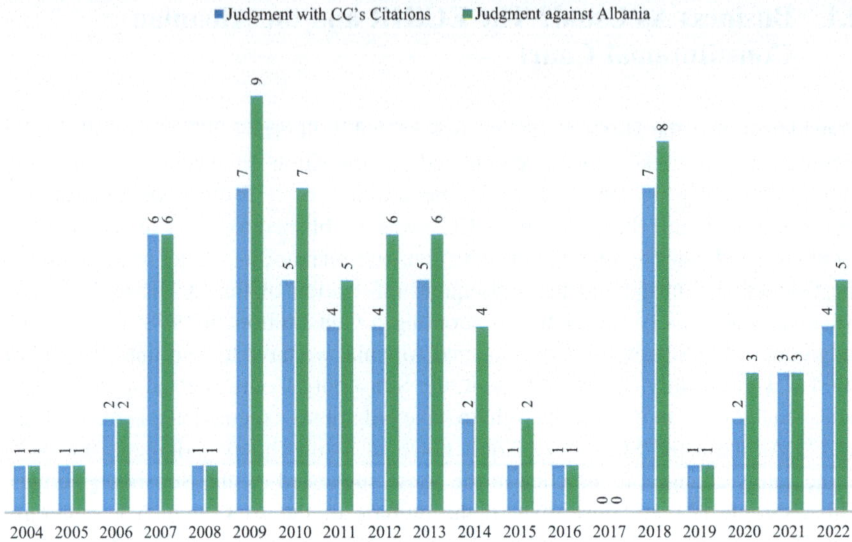

Fig. 4.1 Judgments with ACC citations per year (2004—2022)

evidence is assessed. However, this restrictive rule has been the subject of numerous exceptions.[15]

Although according to the same Strasbourg Court criteria, the judgments against Albania are largely applications of consolidated case law,[16] for the purposes of our research they present some noteworthy aspects, first of all as regards the effectiveness under Article 35 ECHR of individual constitutional complaint. Initially, the 2004 judgment in *Vrioni and Others* stated that a compliant to the ACC "could be considered an effective remedy which had to be used for the purposes of Article 35 of the Convention where fair-trial issues arose".[17] In a series of judgments delivered afterwards, the Strasbourg Court repeatedly found a violation of Article 13 ECHR on the grounds that the judgments of the ACC were declaratory in nature as they did not provide compensation to applicants.[18] Finally, in *Luli and Others*, the Strasbourg Court changed its posture and held that a constitutional complaint is not a remedy whose exhaustion is mandatory for Article 6 ECHR applications.[19] In 2016

[15] See Mercuri and Anastasi (2017), pp. 50–52.

[16] In the HUDOC database, of the 71 judgments delivered against Albania, only 4 are classified as 'Key cases' and 4 as Relevance 1 cases. The rest of the judgments 'does not make a significant contribution' to the Court's case law.

[17] See for example: *Vrioni and Others v. Albania* (2141/03), 24/03/2009, para. 43; and the case law cited therein.

[18] *Gjonbocari and Others v. Albania* (10508/02), 23/10/2007; *Gjyli v. Albania* (32907/07), 29/09/2009; *Mishgjoni v. Albania* (18381/05), 07/12/2010.

[19] See: *Luli and Others v. Albania* (64480/09), (64482/09), (12874/10) 01/04/2014, para. 80; and most recently, *Topallaj v. Albania* (32913/03), 21/04/2016, para. 71.

the Albanian legislator passed an amendment to the Constitutional Court Act, allowing the ACC to award compensation in cases of proceedings of unreasonable length and to annul decisions of ordinary courts breaching fundamental rights.[20] Starting from the entry into force of these amendments (1 January 2017), a constitutional complaint for breach of the right to a fair trial, and more general for breaches of all rights guaranteed by the Albanian constitution, is to be considered once again an effective remedy under Article 35.[21] What this saga seems to suggest is that in absence of specific legislative provisions concerning the constitutional courts remedial powers, individual constitutional complaints benefit from a presumption of effectiveness under Article 35 ECHR, which is deactivated once the jurisprudential practice of the constitutional court, or the legislature, fills the legal vacuum.

As to the application of fair trial guarantees to constitutional proceedings, there are only two judgments both finding a breach of Article 6 provoked by a procedural rule. In the *Marini* case,[22] the applicant complained that his right of access to a court had been violated because the ACC had been unable to reach a majority on the decision to be taken on his case and decided to reject the complaint without ruling on the merits. The Strasbourg Judgment first notes that since the panel was composed of seven judges, the rejection of the appeal could not have been the consequence of a tie, given the impossibility of the judges to abstain.[23] Therefore, the ECHR affirms the violation of the right of access to a court insofar as this right includes "the right to have a final determination on a matter submitted to a court including, in the applicant's case, a decision on the admissibility and/or merits of his constitutional complaint".[24] The judgment, however, does not stop here. After an abstract examination, it affirms that Article 74 of the Constitutional Court Act is capable of depriving applicants of their rights under Article 6 ECHR, in as much as it allows the ACC to pronounce a *non liquet* decision.[25] This *obiter dictum* led the Albanian legislature to repeal, in 2016, Article 74 of the Constitutional Court Act.

In *Çela,* instead, the question concerned the legislative reduction of the time to introduce a constitutional complaint from 2 years to 4 months, calculated from the last judicial decisions. In particular, the applicant complained that the previous time limit should have been applied to its case, as the last ordinary judgment in his case was delivered before the date in which the amendment entered into force. The ECtHR judgment, while noting that the shortening of time limits for constitutional complaints reinforces legal certainty and that it "is a generally recognised principle

[20] Law No. 8577 of 10 February 2000 *on the Organisation and Functioning of the Constitutional Court of the Republic of Albania*, Article 71/ç(1), and Article 76(6).

[21] The Strasbourg held the same applies for all ECHR rights in the 2022 inadmissibility decision in *Fullani*. This statement has not yet been repeated in a judgment. See: *Fullani v. Albania* (dec.) (4586/18), 20/09/2022, para. 79.

[22] *Marini v. Albania* (3738/02), 18/12/2007.

[23] Ibidem, para. 119.

[24] Ibidem, para. 120.

[25] Ibidem, para. 123.

that procedural rules apply immediately to pending proceedings", finds a violation of the applicant's right to access to court on the grounds that, despite establishing a date of entry into force of the new time-limit, the new law was not sufficiently clear as to whether it applied to proceedings concluded before its entry into force.[26] It is worth noting that the applicant's only complaint was the denial of access to the constitutional court and that the ECtHR awarded no compensation. However pursuant to Article 71(c) of the Constitutional Court Act, the ACC has an obligation to reopen the judicial process if so requested by an applicant who has obtained a favourable decision from the Strasbourg Court.

As already said, the substantive aspects of the judgments against Albania are scarcely relevant and numerically reduced, as the vast majority of the judgments against Albania concern procedural violations of Article 6 ECHR. The conclusion that is possible to infer from the previous analysis is that both the ACC and the Legislature are willing to abide by the indications coming from Strasbourg. In this sense, the Strasbourg Court must preserve this capital of legitimacy, aware of the fact that in Albania, some scholars and politicians are already voicing their opposition to the hypertrophy of ECtHR case law.[27] In this sense, the judgment in *Çela* probably does not go in the right direction.

4.2 The Bosnian Constitutional Court as a Satellite of the Strasbourg Court

If only due to the fact that the President of the Strasbourg Court appoints three of the nine judges of the Bosnian Constitutional Court (*Ustavni sud Bosne i Hercegovine*, hereafter, sometimes, 'the CCBH'),[28] the relationship between the latter and the ECtHR deserves to be be analysed with particular attention. First of all, given the peculiarities of the Bosnian Constitution—which, as it is well known, is contained in an international treaty—[29] it can be safely affirmed that the Bosnian constitutional order is *unique* among the member states of the Council of Europe. Another peculiarity is undoubtedly that, under Article I/2 of the Constitution, the ECHR is to be considered hierarchically superordinate to the internal legal order, including the

[26] *Çela v. Albania* (73274/17), 29/11/2022.

[27] In this sense see: Bianku (2016), p. 38.

[28] See Art. VI(1)(a) of the Bosnian Constitution. As it is known, the text of the Constitution is contained in the Fourth Annex of the *General Framework* Agreement for Peace (the so-called Dayton Agreement), therefore the English version, according to Art. XI of the *General Framework Agreement for* Peace, must be considered as official as those drafted in Bosnian, Serbian and Croatian. Indeed, since the Bosnian Parliamentary Assembly never translated the English text, the latter must be considered the only authentic one. See Vehabović (2016), p. 90.

More extensively on the drafting process of the Bosnian Constitution see: Morrison (1996).

[29] In this sense it has been said that the Bosnian Constitution represents the archetype of a transitional constitution. See Morrison (1996), p. 145; Vehabović (2016), p. 84.

Constitution, making the ECHR *the supreme law of the land* in Bosnia and Herzegovina.[30]

As regards specifically the CCBH is widely considered one of the few successful institutions established by the 1995 Dayton Agreement, essentially because there are no veto mechanisms allowing ethnic groups to block its functioning.[31] Concerning individual access to constitutional justice, Article VI(3)(b) of the Constitution states that "[t]he Constitutional Court shall also have appellate jurisdiction over issues under this Constitution arising out of a judgment of any other court in Bosnia and Herzegovina." It is thus unsurprising that the CCBH is cited in all 49 judgments handed down by the European Court of Human Rights with Bosnia and Herzegovina as the respondent state.[32] The average number of citations is also particularly high at 10.35 occurrences per judgment. The quantitative analysis regarding the temporal distribution of citations does not offer significant insights, so it is possible to go straight to analysing the content of the case law. Preliminarily, it shall be noted that in 23 judgments (out of a total of 49, i.e. roughly 47%),[33] explicit reference is made to the fact that the constitutional court carried out a conventionality review, which, if one bears in mind the fact that the ECHR is a *supra-constitutional* norm in Bosnia and Herzegovina, once again cannot be surprising. In spite of this fact, there are few cases in which the ECtHR proceeds to assess the correctness of the review of conventionality carried out domestically.

It should first be noted that, from a substantive point of view, the jurisprudence of the ECtHR, especially in the first years after Bosnia and Herzegovina's accession to the ECHR, has mainly focused on typical *post-conflict issues.*[34] Moreover, in these cases, the role of the CCBH is marginal, as the European Court of Human Rights has repeatedly declared appeals by Bosnian citizens admissible without them having first approached the national constitutional jurisdiction—[35] although the ECHR has always stated that, as a general rule, a complaint before the CCBH is an effective remedy under Article 35 ECHR.[36]

For the purposes of this book, there are only a few cases which are worth considering. First, on the subject of the application of due process guarantees to constitutional jurisdiction, the ruling in the *Avdić and Others* case, finding a

[30] Morrison (1996), p. 152.

[31] See, Išeric H and Sahadzic M (2023) Perils from within and without. Verfassungsblog, 27 July 2023, available at: https://verfassungsblog.de/perils-from-within-and-without/.

[32] All 42 judgments were obtained using the keyword 'constitutional court', the working language so far used by the European Court of Human Rights in its judgments against the Bosnian state is in fact English. Only eight judgments were translated into French.

[33] Most recently see: *Pranjić and Lukić v. Bosnia and Herzegovina* (4938/16), 02/06/2020, paras 44–46; *Al Husin v. Bosnia and Herzegovina (No. 2)* (10112/16), 25/06/2019, paras 41–44.

[34] Vehabović (2016), pp. 92–93.

[35] See *Šobota-Gajić v. Bosnia and Herzegovina* (27966/06), 06/11/2007; *Karanovic v. Bosnia and Herzegovina* (39462/03), 20/11/2007; *Pralica v. Bosnia and Herzegovina* (38945/05), 27/01/2009.

[36] See *Al Husin v. Bosnia and Herzegovina* (3727/08), 07/02/2012, para. 56; and the admissibility decisions cited therein.

violation Article 6 ECHR caused by Rule 40(3) of the CCBH's Rules of Procedure, which stated that in the event that a constitutional panel could not deliberate in the presence of all its members (i.e. nine), the minimum majority for adopting a decision should be five judges.[37] In the applicant's case, the CCBH, sitting in a formation of eight judges, had not achieved such a majority and had therefore adopted a '*seriatim*' decision in which each judge set out the reasons for or against the applicant without, however, the judgment having any dispositive content regarding the merits of the constitutional appeal. The ECtHR limited itself to stating that "[w]hen there is no real "determination" of civil rights and obligations, the right of access to court remains illusory" and concluded that Article 6(1) ECHR was violated. Complementing the majority opinion is the concurring opinion of Judge De Gaetano, which points out the absurdity of a rule requiring a majority of five votes even when the panel consists of only six members.[38] As we learn from the *Čović* judgment, delivered less than 5 months after *Avdić and Others*, the CCBH amended its rules of procedure following the ECtHR's indications, and also established a mechanism for the reopening of constitutional trials for cases in which the ECtHR had condemned the Bosnian State for the violation of the right to access to a court caused by the Rule 40(3).[39] Another case revelatory of how the ECtHR interacts with the CCBH is the judgment in *Muslija.* Affirming a violation of the ECHR, the Strasbourg Court states that "[t]he Constitutional Court failed to apply the principles established in the *Zolotukhin* case and thus to correct the applicant's situation".[40] Such a statement appears particularly harsh, especially considering that in the case law we have analysed insofar the ECtHR carefully avoids open confrontations with national constitutional courts. Having said that, much more frequent are cases in which Strasbourg Court upheld the conventionality review carried out by the CCBH, even on rights, such as freedom of expression, where the Court's jurisprudence tends to be very restrictive in allowing restrictions.[41]

[37] *Avdić and Others v. Bosnia and Herzegovina* (28357/11), (31549/11), (39295/11), 19/11/2013, paras 34–38.

[38] Judge De Gaetano also points out that such a rule, contained in the CCBH's Rules of Procedure, is contrary to the Bosnian Constitution, which provides that only for the adoption of the Rules of Procedure must the CCBH deliberate by an absolute majority of its members. Ibidem, De *Geatano Concurring,* paras. 3–4.

[39] *Čović v. Bosnia and Herzegovina* (61287/12), 03/10/2017, paras 19–20.

[40] *Muslija v. Bosnia and Herzegovina* (32042/11), 14/01/2014, para. 38.

[41] For example, in the case of *Medžlis Islamske Zajednice Brčko and Others,* where four NGOs complained about the violation of their right to freedom of expression caused by a conviction for defamation, both the Fourth Chamber and the Grand Chamber rely on the judgment of the CCBH to confirm the proportionality of the restriction. See *Medžlis Islamske Zajednice Brčko v Bosnia and Herzegovina* (7224/11), 03/11/2015, para. 35; *Medžlis Islamske Zajednice Brčko v Bosnia and Herzegovina* (7224/11), 27/06/2017, para. 82. It has been observed that this outcome is not fully consistent with the ECHR case law on Article 10. See: S. Smet, *Medžlis Islamske Zajednice Brčko v Bosnia and Herzegovina: A Simple Speech Case Made Unbelievably Complex?*, in *Strasbourg Observers*, available at:https://strasbourgobservers.com/2017/08/09/medzlis-islamske-zajednice-brcko-v-bosnia-and-herzegovina-a-simple-speech-case-made-unbelievably-complex/.

In conclusion, the peculiarities in the composition of the CCBH, in particular the fact that the ECtHR president still appoints three judges of this court, and the ECHR status in the Bosnian legal system, renders the latter court a sort of appellate court against constitutional court's decisions, as evidenced by the high significant number of judgments in which the Strasbourg Court recommended to Bosnian authorities to implement a CCBH's judgment.[42] Hence, a convergence between the two jurisprudences is the least that can be expected.[43]

4.3 The Strasbourg Court and the Constitutional Court of Bulgaria. Between Politics and Jurisdiction

On 7 May 1992, Bulgaria became the 26th member state of the Council of Europe. Only four months later Bulgaria ratified the ECHR which, pursuant to Article 5(4) of the Bulgarian Constitution, is directly applicable in the domestic legal system and enjoys an infra-constitutional status. Concerning individual access to constitutional justice, despite a progressive widening of access routes, is still precluded.[44] Article 150(2) of the Bulgarian Constitution provides for the possibility, reserved to higher courts, to raise a question of constitutionality before the Bulgarian Constitutional Court (hereinafter simply the CCB), if they have doubts as to the constitutionality of a legislative provision that they are called to apply.

The narrowness of the avenues of access to constitutional jurisdiction, as well as the fact that the CCB pronounces only a handful of judgments each year—just twenty-one in 2023—is reflected in the low presence of CCB's citations in the Strasbourg jurisprudence: out of a total of 561 judgments pronounced against Bulgaria, the CCB is cited in only 96, a percentage of about 13.9%.[45] The average number of citations per judgment (7.7) also confirms how, quantitatively, the dialogue between the two courts is scarcely relevant.

As it is expectable, there are no judgments concerning the effectiveness of constitutional remedy under Article 35 ECHR. Nor the Strasbourg Court has ever applied Article 6 ECHR to constitutional proceedings before the CCB. However, in the case law against Bulgaria, one finds interesting elements concerning what the doctrine calls the ancillary competencies of constitutional courts. In particular, the

[42] See: *Baralija v. Bosnia and* Herzegovina, (30100/18), 29/10/2019; para. 62; *Spahić and Others v. Bosnia and Herzegovina*, (20514/15 20528/15 20774/15 et al.), 14/11/2017, para. 33; *Kunić and Others v. Bosnia and Herzegovina* [GC], 29/03/2006, para. 230.

[43] In this sense also: Vehabović (2016), pp. 108–109.

[44] For a brief reconstruction of the evolution of the Bulgarian constitutional justice system with regard to individual appeal, see: CDL-AD(2015)022, *Opinion on the Draft Act to Amend and Supplement the Constitution (in the Field of Judiciary) of the Republic of Bulgaria*, Adopted by the Venice Commission at its 104th Plenary Session (Venice, 24–25 October 2015).

[45] The 96 judgments were all obtained through the use of the keywords 'constitutional court' (69) and 'cour constitutionnelle' (27).

ECtHR reviewed the conventionality of the BCC's exercise of the power to dissolve political associations and parties and the control of the legality of parliamentary elections.

On the first issue, the first decision that needs to be analysed is the 2005 judgment *UMO Ilinden—Pirin and Others*.[46] The applicant, a separatist political party, had complained to the Strasbourg Court that the dissolution following the CCB's judgment had violated its right to freedom of association. The CCB, in its 2000 ruling, had dissolved the political party on the grounds that the separatist activities promoted by the party represented a danger to national security and the State's territorial integrity. The CCB also assessed the compatibility of the dissolution with the Convention, finding that it was justified for reasons of national security in terms of Article 11(2) ECHR.[47] The Strasbourg Court, on the contrary, holds that the fact that a party has separatist intentions is not sufficient to order its dissolution, and that "the Constitutional Court's holding that the applicant party's activity truly "imperil [ed] [Bulgaria's] national security" was not based on an acceptable assessment of the relevant facts", therefore declaring a breach of Article 11 ECHR.[48] In essence, with this judgment the Strasbourg Court is substituting its own evaluation of what constitutes a threat to national security to that of the CCB.

On the subject of electoral constitutional justice, the judgments in *Petkov and Others,*[49] and in *Riza and Others* should instead be analysed.[50] In the first case, the applicants alleged that their exclusion from the electoral lists decided by the Central Electoral Commission on the grounds that they had collaborated with the security services of the former Communist regime was in breach of their right under Article 3 Protocol 1 ECHR. Despite the fact that the Supreme Administrative Court annulled the decision to exclude the three applicants, they were unable to take part in the electoral competition, and therefore the CCB, on a request of 57 MPS, was asked to annul the elections.[51] The latter court, however, refuses to annul the election, considering that the non-enforcement of a final judgment can, at most, lead to an extra-contractual liability of the State but cannot provoke the annulment of elections. Ruling on the exclusion of the three applicants, the Strasbourg Court, in accordance with its previous case law, first of all confirms that Article 3 Prot. 1 ECHR also includes the right to stand for election. Subsequently, the ECtHR finds a violation of that provision on the basis that the Bulgarian State had not executed the decision declaring their exclusion from the electoral list null and void. The ECtHR judgment also declares a violation of Article 13 ECHR, criticising the fact that the applicants did not have the right to bring the case directly before the CCB in light of the restrictive rules on standing established in Article 150 of the Bulgarian

[46] *United Macedonian Organization Ilinden - Pirin and Others v. Bulgaria*, 59489/00, 20/10/2005.

[47] Ibidem, para. 27.

[48] Ibidem, paras 59–62.

[49] *Petkov and Others v. Bulgaria,* (77568/01), (178/02), (505/02), 11/06/2009.

[50] *Riza and Others v. Bulgaria* (48555/10), (48377/10), 13/10/2015.

[51] See *Petkov and Others v. Bulgaria*, paras. 6–32.

Constitution.[52] This seems to imply that even though States are not obliged to set up a system of appeal for electoral disputes—as Article 6 ECHR does not apply in the field of electoral justice—if they decide to do so, such system must comply with ECHR standards, i.e. it must be effective.

In the 2015 judgment in *Riza and Others,* the Strasbourg Court was called upon to rule, on an application presented by 101 Bulgarian citizens concerning the compatibility with the ECHR of the BCC decision to annul votes in 23 constituencies, but without ordering their repetition, given that the constituencies in question were on Turkish territory. The Strasbourg judges, in finding a violation of Article 3 Prot. 1 ECHR, stated that the decision of the CCB to annul the vote was in breach of the ECHR because it was based on purely formalistic arguments, and did not take into account the ECHR criteria.[53] As it is emphasised in Judge Kalaydjieva's separate opinion, the fact that the majority of the Court reviewed the manner in which the CCB exercised its electoral jurisdiction constitutes a "stealth application" of Article 6 guarantees, and an overstepping of the principle of subsidiarity, as there were no elements of arbitrariness or "flagrant malfunctioning" in the procedure before the CCB.[54]

In conclusion, the jurisprudence examined here shows how the Strasbourg Court exercises a particularly intense control of the conventionality of the decisions of the constitutional court in highly political cases. Rather than a review of the manner in which constitutional jurisdiction is exercised, this review also seems to be aimed at promoting the Court's vision of democracy, in which political rights, and in particular the right to vote and stand for election,[55] play a cardinal role. Such a deep involvement of the Strasbourg in political domestic affairs, should impose on the Strasbourg Court a higher standard of reasoning as to the compelling motives justifying its intervention, and in any case should be aimed at supporting, rather than disqualifying the national constitutional court.

4.4 Strasbourg and the Croatian Super-Constitutional Court

Together with Slovenia, Croatia was the first state to declare its independence from Yugoslavia, on 26 June 1991. However, the ratification of the ECHR and its protocols did not take place until 6 years later, at the end of the war of independence, on 22 October 1997. According to Art. 141 of the Croatian Constitution, the Convention enjoys *supra-legislative* status in Croatia. In addition, the Constitutional Court of the Croatian Republic (*Ustavni sud Republike Hrvatske,* hereafter simply

[52] *Petkov and Others v. Bulgaria*, para. 82.

[53] *Riza and Others v. Bulgaria*, paras. 178–179.

[54] See *Ibid, Partly Dissenting Opinion of Judge Kalaydjieva.*

[55] See Rainey et al. (2020), p. 390.

'the CCC') affirmed its competence to directly review the compatibility of a domestic rule with the Convention, in fact making the Croatian state a monist system, at least as regards the ECHR.[56]

Of all the constitutional courts in the countries of the former Yugoslavia, the Croatian court is undoubtedly the most active: in 2023 only it had delivered 7554 decisions. This figure becomes even more impressive when one considers that since its establishment in 1991, the CCC has handed down no less than 128.314 decisions.[57] Of these, the vast majority, around 110.000, are individual appeals. In fact, Article 62(1) of the Constitutional Law on the CCC allows any individual, after exhausting ordinary remedies, to appeal to the CCC (1)

> if he deems that the individual act of a state body, a body of local and regional self-government, or a legal person with public authority, which decided about his/her rights and obligations, or about suspicion or accusation for a criminal act, has violated his/her human rights or fundamental freedoms guaranteed by the Constitution, or his/her right to local and regional self-government guaranteed by the Constitution.[58]

In addition, the subsequent Article 63 gives the CCC a specific competence in the area of unreasonable length of trial. Paragraph (1) empowers the CCC to decide a constitutional appeal brought during the pendency of a trial if the proceedings have lasted for an unreasonable length of time; while the subsequent paragraphs also enable the CCC to: (1) set a time limit within which the court hearing the case on the merits must decide the pending case and (2) award compensation to the appellant.

As for the attitude of the CCC towards the ECHR jurisprudence, it must be emphasised that Strasbourg judgments are cited in more than 1000 judgments and decisions of the CCC, which, moreover, has explicitly stated that it interprets the norms of the Constitution in light of the ECHR.[59] The hyper-activity of the CCC, its specific competences, as well as the very manner in which it exercises its jurisdiction have obvious reflections in Strasbourg jurisprudence.

With 359 Strasbourg judgments that refer to it, the CCC is, in absolute terms, the most cited constitutional jurisdiction among those considered. In relation to the total number of judgments pronounced against Croatia, the CCC is cited in 84% of them, with an average of 12.5 occurrences in each judgment.[60] As illustrated by the graph below (Fig. 4.2), the pattern of citations appears rather uniform, at least in the last

[56] See CCRC, Decision no U-I-745/1999, 8/11/2000. On this point see more extensively the detailed work of the President of the Croatian Constitutional Court on the relationship between the constitutional court and the European system of protection of human rights: Omejec (2016), p. 349.

[57] These data, compiled by the statistical office of the Croatian Constitutional Court, are available at https://www.usud.hr/sites/default/files/dokumenti/Received_cases_in_period_from_1990_to_31_December_2023.pdf.

[58] The English text of the law can be found on the official website of the Constitutional Court at https://www.usud.hr/sites/default/files/dokumenti/The_Constitutional_Act_on_the_Constitutional_Court_of_the_Republic_of_Croatia_consolidated_text_Official_Gazette_No_49-02.pdf.

[59] Turkovič and Omejec (2016), pp. 120–121.

[60] The sample was obtained using 'constitutional court' as the only keyword; the judgments against Croatia are in fact written exclusively in English. Moreover, only a small percentage is subsequently

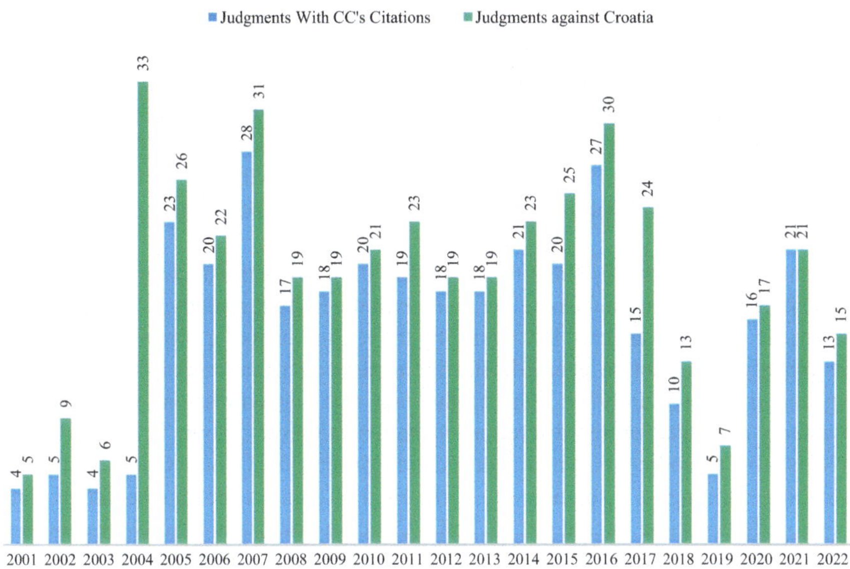

Fig. 4.2 Judgments with CCC citations per year (2001—2022)

20 years. Concerning the general trend we have identified in the quantitative analysis, consisting in an enhanced attention of the Strasbourg Court towards constitutional case law, it is only possible to observe a small increase in the average number of citations per judgment, which in the last 5 years (2018–2022) is of 15.

Moving on to the qualitative analysis of this jurisprudential material, it is first necessary to analyse the ECtHR case law concerning the application of Article 35 ECHR to CCC. In general, the ECHR repeatedly stated that

> before bringing complaints against Croatia to the Court, in order to comply with the principle of subsidiarity applicants are in principle required to afford the Croatian Constitutional Court, as the highest court in Croatia, the opportunity to remedy their situation.[61]

Nevertheless, the Strasbourg Court has continued to carry out a casuistic examination of the effectiveness of the Croatian constitutional appeal.[62] In fact, given the breadth of acts that can be challenged through Articles 62 of the Constitutional Court

translated into French (of the judgments in our sample, only 22 were translated into French, a percentage well below 10%).

[61] See *Pavlović and Others v. Croatia* (13274/11), 02/04/2015, para. 32; and the case law cited therein.

[62] For example, the Strasbourg Court has repeatedly held that given the system of calculating the duration of a trial used by the CCC—that excluded from the period to be considered segments of the proceedings before administrative authorities—a constitutional remedy could not be considered an effective remedy if part of the domestic proceedings took place before an administrative authority. See *Bozic v. Croatia*, para.34; *Pocuca v. Croatia*, para.37; *Vajagic v. Croatia*, para.30; *Smoje v. Croatia*, para.42.

Act, the ECtHR requires, in order for the constitutional appeal to be considered effective, that there be at least one judgment of the CCC that has dealt with similar case.[63] Given this casuistic-oriented case-law, to the date, the Croatian Government continues to argue, without success, in cases before the ECtHR that the individual constitutional complaint of Article 62 of the constitutional Court Act is not an effective remedy for the purposes of Article 35 ECHR, with the goal of obtaining a declaration of inadmissibility for having the applicants lodged the application out of time.[64]

Concerning specifically the effectiveness of the constitutional complaint of Article 63 of the Constitutional Court Act, in *Horvat* the ECtHR initially affirmed that, in the absence of domestic case law clarifying the requirements for bringing an appeal, this remedy could not be deemed effective to remedy violations of the right to an expedite trial, especially in light of the fact that the admission of the appeal ultimately depended on the discretion of the Constitutional Court.[65] After a series of legislative amendments, which reduced the Constitutional Court's workload at the same time limiting its discretionality,[66] the ECtHR comes to recognise, albeit with some oscillations due to changes in the CCC's case law,[67] the effectiveness of this remedy in relation to violations of the right to a trial of reasonable duration.[68] Still on the subject of admissibility, the Strasbourg Court censured the CCC for the insufficiency of the compensation awarded for violation of the rules of due process, in particular for violation of the right of access to a court and the right to a trial of reasonable duration, consequently declaring Art. 6-1 applications admissible despite the fact that reparation had, at least partially, taken place. Moreover, the fact that the

---

[63] See: *M.S. v. Croatia (no. 2)* (75450/12), 19/02/2015, paras. 122–123.

[64] See: *Trivkanović v. Croatia (no. 2)* (49083/18), 18/11/2021, paras 63–68; *Čolić v. Croatia* (49083/18), 18/11/2021, paras 26–31; *F.O. v. Croatia* (29555/13), 22/04/2021, paras 62–66; *Zustović v. Croatia* (27903/15), 22/04/2021, paras 58–64; *Smiljanić v. Croatia* (35983/14), 25/03/2021, paras 56–59; *Sabalić v. Croatia* (50231/13), 14/01/2021, paras 79–81.

[65] See, *Horvat v. Croatia* (51585/99), 26/07/2001, paras 41–45. Subsequently confirmed in: *Futterer v. Croatia* (52634/99), 20/12/2001, para. 22; *Mikulič v. Croatia* (53176/99), 07/02/02, para. 70; *Delic v. Croatia* (48771/99), 27/06/2002, para. 111; *Rados and Others v. Croatia* (45435/99), 07/11/2002, para. 79.

[66] See: Turkovič and Omejec (2016), pp. 123–125.

[67] Those changes and the legislative amendments concerning the remedies are fully described in: *Kirinčić and Others v. Croatia* (31386/17), 30/07/2020, paras 63–71; *Glavinić and Marković v. Croatia* (11388/15), (25605/15), 30/07/2020, paras 38–45.

[68] See *ex multis*: *Antonic-Tomasovic v. Croatia* (10/01/2005), para. 30; 5208/03, *Majski v. Croatia* (33593/03), 01/06/2006, para. 24; *Bozic v. Croatia* (22457/02), 29/06/2006, para. 30; *Pocuca v. Croatia* (38550/02), 29/06/2006, para. 34; *Vajagic v. Croatia* (30431/03), 20/07/2006, para. 29; *Muzevic v. Croatia* (39299/02), 16/11/2006, para. 74; *Macinkovic v. Croatia* (29759/03), 07/12/2006, para. 26; *Samija v. Croatia* (14898/04), 07/12/2006, para. 28; *Smoje v. Croatia* (28074/03), 11/01/2007, para. 41; *Mahmutovič v. Croatia* (9505/03), 15/02/2007, para. 21; *Sostaric v. Croatia* (39659/04), 12/04/2007, para. 25; *Lesnina D.D. v. Croatia,* (18421/05), 25/10/2007, para. 16; In any case, it must be underscored that the role of the Constitutional Court as instance of last resort in actions concerning the excessive duration of proceedings has gradually diminished to the point of becoming residual. See: Turkoviç and Omejec (2016), pp. 125–127.

amount of compensation is set by the highest court of the State does not seem to influence the Strasbourg Court in any way, which mechanically applies, and imposes, its own calculation criteria.[69]

Individual appeals under Articles 62 and 63 of the Constitutional Court Act are not the only ones to have come under the lens of Strasbourg jurisprudence. In fact, the same Act also provides, in Article 38, the institution of *actio popularis,* i.e. the possibility for any individual to appeal to the CCC to complain about the unconstitutionality of a legislative act or a governmental regulation irrespective of proof of concrete harm. The Strasbourg Court, confirming its consolidated case law, has clarified that its exercise is not necessary in order to be able to consider domestic remedies exhausted, since the *actio popularis* is not linked to the pendency of proceedings.[70]

Turning the attention to the application of Article 6 guarantees to constitutional proceedings, the ECtHR case law against Croatia embraces almost every aspect of the right to a fair trial. The 2011 judgment in *Juričic* shall be examined first for its multifaceted relevance.[71] The applicant in the case was a judge who has been considered as a candidate to the CCC. She was included in a shortlist of four candidates amongst which the Parliament would elect three constitutional judges but eventually she was not elected. She then decided to impugn the appointment of one of the elected candidates, on the ground that she lacked the fifteen years of experience in the legal professions required by Section 5(1) of the Constitutional Court Act. All national courts, including the CCC, dismissed her application, hence the case landed in Strasbourg, where the applicant alleged the violation of various aspects of Article 6 ECHR and in particular: (1)the right to an impartial tribunal, as the composition of the Constitutional Court which decided her complaint included two judges who were parties in the proceedings before administrative courts; (2) the lack of a public hearing before the constitutional court (3) the principle of equality of arms since various opinions and documents requested by the CCC were not communicated to her. First of all, the judgment, rejecting the objections of the Croatian government on the point, affirmed the applicability of Article 6 ECHR to proceedings concerning the validity of constitutional judges' appointment. The Strasbourg Court clarified that, according to the test developed in *Vilho Eskelinen*,[72] the

[69] On the insufficiency of damages for violation of the reasonable duration of the trial recognised by the Constitutional Court see: *Tomasic v. Croatia* (21753/02), 19/10/2006; *Popara v. Croatia* (11072/03), 15/03/2007; *Jacupovic v. Croatia* (12419/04), 31/07/2007; *Letica v. Croatia* (27846/05), 18/10/2007; *Rizman v. Croatia* (28704/06), 31/07/2008; *Sandra Jankovic v. Croatia* (38478/05), 05/03/2009; *Medic v. Croatia* (49916/07), 26/03/2009; *Parlov Tkalcic v. Croatia* (24810/06), 22/12/2009. For damages for violation of the right of access to a court see instead: *Novkovic v. Croatia* (43437/02), 05/04/207; *Radivoy Novakovic v. Croatia* (43446/02), 12/04/2007; *Hajdukovic v. Croatia* (38303/02), 12/04/2007; *Petrovic v. Croatia* (38292/02), 12/04/2007; *Terzin-Laub v. Croatia* (43362/02), 12/0472007.

[70] *Dragovic v. Croatia* (5705/02), 28/2004; *Dragicevic v. Croatia* (11814/02), 09/12/2004; *Zovanovic v. Croatia* 12877/02, (09/12/2004).

[71] *Juričić v. Croatia* (58222/09), 26/07/2011, paras. 76–78.

[72] For a detailed illustration of how this test works, see: Kloth (2010), pp. 9–12.

applicability of Article 6 ECHR is dependent on whether national law allows the act of appointment to be challenged before courts.[73] As it previously did for ordinary judges, the ECtHR affirmed that also constitutional judges are comparable to civil servants, therefore since the appointment was open to challenge before domestic courts, the ECtHR declared Article 6 applicable. The ECtHR instead declared the part of the application concerning the impartiality of the Constitutional Court inadmissible for failure to exhaust domestic remedies, since the applicant did not ask the recusation of the two judges.[74] Concerning the right to a public hearing, the ECtHR affirms the right to a public is not absolute and that in principle constitutional courts are not required to celebrate oral hearings.[75] Further elaborating on the point, the ECtHR judgment held that they cannot be required to hold a hearing when, as was the applicant's case, the "applicant waived her right to an oral and public hearing at first instance, Article 6 § 1 of the Convention does not require such a hearing to be held before the higher court where that court is called upon to examine the same questions of law as the first-instance court." Finally, as regards the right to an adversarial proceeding, the ECtHR rapidly concluded that since the experts' opinions and information obtained requested by the CCC were notified to the applicant only after the end of the proceedings, the applicant's right to an adversarial proceeding was violated.

The first judgment in which the right to a constitutional proceedign of reasonable duration was applied is the *Pitra* case, declaring excessive a duration of the constitutional proceeding of 3 years and 6 months, during which the CCC did not carry out any procedural activities.[76] In contrast, in a judgment rendered 5 months later, an identical duration of the constitutional trial is not sanctioned by the ECtHR in light of the fact that the overall duration of the proceedings was reasonable as the proceedings before lower courts were rather expedite.[77] By contrast, the same length is deemed excessive in *Butkovic*, despite the fact that the ECtHR itself recognises the complexity of the case, as the applicant was seeking to recover possession of his property.[78] A comparison between those rulings underlines, besides the ECtHR traditional casuistic approach, that the duration of constitutional proceedings is not evaluated in isolation, but always in the context of the overall duration of the applicant's proceedings.

Even more striking are the conclusions reached by the Strasbourg Court in *Prezec*, where an application alleging the unreasonable length of a constitutional proceeding lasted 2 years and 4 months was declared manifestly unfounded.[79] If one

[73] *Juričić v. Croatia*, para. 56.

[74] Ibidem, paras 61–64.

[75] Ibidem, para. 87.

[76] See *Pitra v. Croatia* (41075/02), 16/06/2005, para. 21.

[77] See *Posedel-Jelinovic v. Croatia* (35915/02), 24/11/2005, para. 26.

[78] See *Butkovic v. Croatia* (32264/03), 24/05/2007 para. 27.

[79] *Prezec v. Croatia* (48185/07), 15/10/2009, para. 42.

compares this ruling with the one made in 2001 by the ECtHR in *Tričković v. Slovenia,* which contains a detailed analysis of the conduct of the Constitutional Court despite the fact that the trial lasted only 2 years and 7 months, one cannot help but notice how in just 8 years the ECtHR has consolidated its jurisprudence on constitutional due process, seemingly introducing a presumption of reasonable duration for proceedings lasting less than 3 years. Conversely, following the 2010 Grand Chamber's judgment in *Oršuš and Others v. Croatia,* the fact that in the absence of exceptional circumstances, a duration of a constitutional trial of more than 4 years is incompatible with Article 6 ECHR seems to be established conventional law.[80] In fact, the Grand Chamber without any reasoning in support of the Croatian State's conviction, proceeded to a mechanical application of its own case law, and affirmed that a constitutional proceedings lasted 4 years, 1 month and 18 days violated Article 6(1) ECHR. In the ECtHR case law against Croatia, we also find indications concerning proceedings with a duration comprised in the interval from 3 years and 6 months to 4 years. In *Sikić*, where the applicant's proceedings before the CCC lasted 3 years, 9 months and 25 days, the ECtHR undertakes a more detailed examination of the circumstances of the case, assessing the conduct of the applicant, the complexity of the legal issues and the importance of the dispute, in order to conclude that that the duration was excessive.[81]

Another component of the right to a fair trial which has been applied by the Strasbourg Court to the CCC, is the right to an impartial judge. In the 2005 judgment in *Meznaric*, the ECtHR declared that the participation in the constitutional proceeding of a judge who had previously acted as a legal advisor—in a marginal role, as the judgment admits—for the applicant's opponent,[82] for only 2 months, and 9 years before the decision of the constitutional appeal violated the applicant's right to an impartial tribunal, considering that the judge advised the applicant's opponent in the framework of the same proceeding.[83] In 2020, coming back to the issue of the impartiality of the constitutional judge, the Strasbourg Court had to assess whether the fact that one of the three judges of the panel who decided the applicant's association complaint was the wife of a person against which the said association had instituted proceedings for the recovery of a debt, breached the applicant's right to an impartial tribunal.[84] The judgment first of all deals with the government's objection arguing that since the applicant did not ask the withdrawal of the judge from its case, its application should have been declared inadmissible. The judgment dismisses the objection affirming that the applicant could not be expected to know that the judge in question would have participated in the panel deciding its application, despite the information concerning the constitutional court's composition was publicly available on its website.[85] The ECtHR distinguished the situation from that

[80] *Oršuš and Others v. Croatia* [GC] (15766/03), 16/03/2010, paras. 108–110.

[81] *Sikic v. Croatia* (9143/08), 15/07/2010, paras. 35–38.

[82] *Meznaric v. Croatia* (71615/01), 15/07/2005.

[83] Ibidem, paras 34–35.

[84] *Croatian Golf Federation v. Croatia* (66994/14), 17/12/2020, para 132.

[85] Ibidem, para. 105.

in the *Juričić* case, affirming that since in the latter case the constitutional court had previously decided in plenary session, the applicant should have expected the participation of the two judges whose impartiality was in question.[86] As to the outcome, the judgment grounds its conclusions on the causal link between the two proceedings: since the proceeding before the Constitutional Court concerned the dissolution of the applicant's association, the decision of the CCC had an impact not only on the existence of the association but also on the debt of the judge's husband.[87] It is worth noting that in both the cases just analysed the ECtHR specifies that the personal impartiality of the judges is not in doubt,[88] yet appearances matter, and the legitimate doubts of an external observer are sufficient to find a breach of Article 6 ECHR.

Still another aspect on which the case law against Croatia offers interesting elements is the right to access to a constitutional court. In *Dragan Kovačević v. Croatia* the ECtHR clarified that, in principle, constitutional courts are not required to award the costs of the procedure to applicants, even if they rule in their favour; at the same time, however, affirming that this may constitute a restriction of the right to access a court.[89] Therefore, in order to assess the legitimacy of such a restriction in the applicant's case, the ECtHR carries out a proportionality test. Assessing the legitimate aim of the restriction, the Strasbourg Court accepts that protection of the State's budget and the necessity of avoiding to overburden the constitutional court constitute legitimate objectives for excluding reimbursement of legal expenses, also praising the fact that the Constitutional Court *may* decide to award the costs.[90] However, the ECtHR considered that in light of the specific circumstances of the case, denying compensation of costs constituted a violation of the right to access a court. In particular, the ECtHR criticised the Constitutional Court for not having motivated its decision to deny the costs.[91]

Moving on to analyse the techniques employed by the ECtHR to dialogue with the CCC, it should be first observed that the ECHR has been willing to grant a 'patent of conventionality' to judgments of the CCC in which the latter makes explicit use of Strasbourg precedents, emphasising the harmony between its jurisprudence and that of the Constitutional Court, inserting a passage in the reasoning in this regard.[92] Conversely, in case of dissonances, the ECtHR sometimes adopts the already seen strategy of finding support for its conclusions in dissenting opinions annotated by

---

[86] The distinction is not really compelling and seems to confirm that the Strasbourg judges in 2011 simply avoided to interfere in a highly sensitive domestic question.

[87] Ibidem, paras 130–131.

[88] *Meznaric v. Croatia,* para. 30; *Croatian Golf Federation v. Croatia,* para. 127.

[89] *Dragan Kovačević v. Croatia* (49281/15), 12/05/2022, paras 69–73.

[90] Ibidem, paras 75–78.

[91] Ibidem, paras 80–84.

[92] *Travaš v. Croatia* (75581/13), 04/10/2016, para. 113; *Milanković and Bošnjak v. Croatia* (37762/12), 23530/13, 26/04/2016, para. 157; *Muršič v. Croatia* [GC] (7334/13), 20/10/2016, para. 170. Incidentally, it should be noted, although it may be obvious, that all of these judgments denied the existence of a ECHR violation.

constitutional judges.[93] In any case, from a global reading of the case law, it is evident that the ECtHR tends to emphasise the harmony and play down the conflicts with the constitutional court.[94]

Finally, the ECtHR has also acted as an enforcer of constitutional rulings. In a series of cases the CCC, recognising the unreasonable length of proceedings, had unsuccessfully ordered the trial court to conclude them within a time limit set by it. Faced with the failure of the lower courts to comply with this time limit, the ECtHR held that the claimant's right to an effective remedy had been violated on the basis that the competent court 'has failed to implement the Constitutional Court's decision'.[95] Similarly, in *Zustović*, the ECtHR essentially gave retroactive effects to a constitutional court judgment that had declared the unconstitutionality of a norm which was applied before the declaration of unconstitutionality to the applicant's case.[96]

In conclusion, the relationship between the two jurisdictions is decidedly oriented towards loyal cooperation, which is primarily due, as mentioned in the opening paragraph, to the fact that the Croatian Constitutional Court maintains a friendly attitude towards the ECtHR jurisprudence. At the same time, the Strasbourg Court's significant contribution to the success of this dialogue cannot be denied, evidenced above all in a continuous enhancement of the elements of consonance with the CCC. The success of this dialogue is, moreover, decisively confirmed by the fact that the vast majority of the actions brought against the Croatian Republic concern procedural violations due to the malfunctioning of the judicial system, which testifies to the fact that the conventional *acquis on* substantive rights has been fully transposed in the domestic legal system by the CCC.[97]

[93] *Šeks v. Croatia* (39325/20), 03/02/2022, para. 17; *Baljak and Others v. Croatia* (41295/19), 25/11/2021, *Project Trade D.O.O. v. Croatia* (1920/14), 19/11/2020, para. 12; *M.H. and Others v. Croatia* (15670/18, 43115/18), 18/11/2021, para. 25.

[94] See for instance the *Ulemek* case, where the ECtHR despite the constitutional court found no violation of the ECHR in the applicant's case, in its reasoning instead mentioned another ruling of the same court expressing concerns for the conditions of detention in the prison where the applicant was detained in order to support its finding of a breach of Article 5 ECHR. See: *Ulemek v. Croatia* (21613/16), 31/10/2019, para. 129

[95] See *Kaic and Others v. Croatia* (22014/04), 17/07/2008, para. 43; *Vujcic v. Croatia* (33867/06), 25/06/2009, para. 40; *Lonza v. Croatia* (14062/07), 01/04/2010, para. 36.

[96] See: *Zustović v. Croatia*, in particular, paras 104–106.

[97] In this sense see: Turkovič and Omejec (2016), pp. 114–115.

4.5 Strasbourg and the Czech Constitutional Court. Between Formalism and Faithful Cooperation

Similarly to Slovakia, the Czech Republic did not ratify the Convention, as the Committee of Ministers of the Council of Europe considered the ratification made by the Federal Republic of Czechoslovakia on 18 March 1992 to be valid for the purpose of the Czech Republic's accession. The Constitution entered into force on 1 January, the first day of the Czech Republic's existence as an independent state; while the Czech Constitutional Court (henceforth also the 'CCCZ'), barely 6 months after the ECHR came into force, had already issued its first decision.[98] Initially adopting a timid deferential stance *vis-à-vis* political majorities, the CCCZ gradually consolidated its position within the national legal system, and nowadays it is considered the most powerful constitutional court in Central and Eastern Europe.[99] As regards individual access to the CCCZ, Article 87 of the Constitution provides that every individual may challenge before the CCCZ a decision or conduct of a public authority because it violates his or her fundamental right. The same provision, at Section 1(b), also specifies that the CCCZ can review and annul legislation adopting as a benchmark international human rights treaties, thus also the ECHR. This appeal, according to a constant constitutional jurisprudence can also be brought against omissive behaviour, thus also in cases of excessively long proceedings.[100]

The quantitative analysis of the case law under consideration here would seem to indicate an intense dialogue of the Strasbourg Court with the Czech constitutional court. Indeed, the CCCZ is cited in 82% of the judgments against the Czech Republic,[101] with an average number of citations per judgment of approximately 14.

Although the graph (Fig. 4.3) of the temporal distribution of citations shows a decrease in the absolute number of citations of the CCCZ, it must be noted that this decrease is simply the consequence of a decrease in the number of Chamber judgments against the Czech Republic. Actually, in the last 5 years (2018–2022), even considering the judgments of three-judges committee, the Czech Republic has only be condemned once by the Strasbourg Court, thus testifying the efficiency of the Czech machinery for fundamental rights protection works efficiently. Much of the merit for this must be ascribed too CCCZ, which is generally regarded as a close ally of the Strasbourg Court, extensively referring to ECHR judgments in its case law, and faithfully implementing them.[102] Emblematic of the CCCZ friendliness towards the ECHR system is its landmark judgement known as the 'Euroamendment

---

[98] See Pejchal (2016) p. 140.

[99] Kosař and Vyhnánek (2020), pp. 119–120

[100] Antos (2012), p. 121. Available at url: https://www.ajk.elte.hu/file/annales_2012_07_marek.pdf.

[101] To be more precise, the Constitutional Court is mentioned in 190 judgments out of a total of 231 rendered against the Czech Republic. The 178 judgments were derived as follows: 128 with the keyword 'cour constitutionnelle' and 50 with the keyword 'constitutional court'.

[102] Majerčík (2016); Vyhnánek (2017), p. 715.

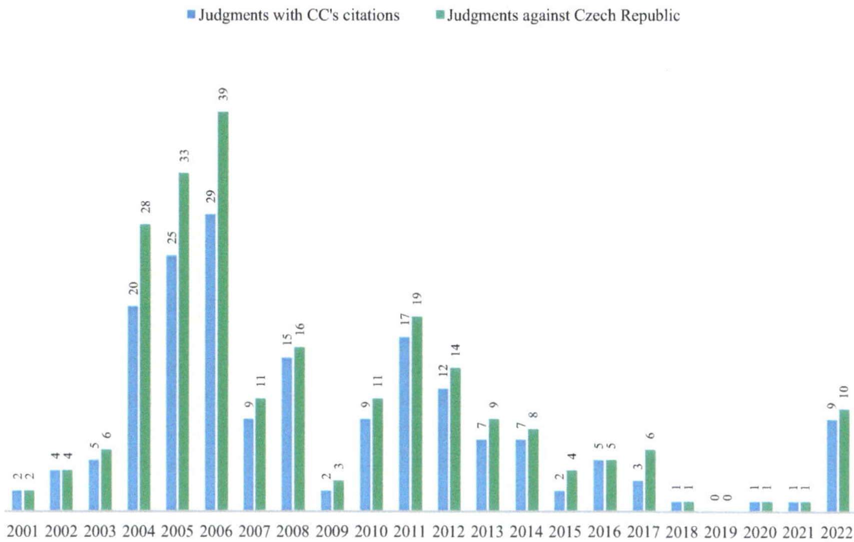

Fig. 4.3 Judgments with CCCZ citations per year (2001—2022)

judgment",[103] which conferred a de facto constitutional rank to the ECHR, despite Article 10 of the Czech Constitution only affirming its supralegislative status.[104]

In fact, reading the judgments against Czechia, it emerges how the CCCZ positively reacted even when Strasbourg judges censured its procedural rules and practice. Since its first judgments against the Czech Republic, the Strasbourg Court has highlighted two structural macro-problems in the functioning of the Czech constitutional justice system both concerning the admissibility rules of constitutional complaints. To give an idea of the magnitude of these problems, it is sufficient to mention that the Strasbourg Court, in no less than 37 judgments against the Czech Republic, has found a violation of Article 6 ECHR provoked by procedural and admissibility rules for individual constitutional complaints under Article 87 of the Czech Constitution.

The first judicial chain to be analysed is the one concerning the right of access to the constitutional court, the first judgment being the one rendered in the *Zvolsky et Zvolska* case.[105] The ECtHR finds a violation of Article 6 in the decision of the CCCZ to declare the application inadmissible because it was brought out of time, which was considered excessively strict.[106] In particular, the judgment criticises the

[103] Judgment n. Pl. ÚS 36/01 of 25.6.2002.

[104] The judgment was received with criticism by Czech scholars, lamenting that the CCC acted as the constitutional amendment modifying the text of Article 10 of the Constitution had never been enacted. For a reconstruction of the scholarly debate see: Kosar and Vyhnánek V (2020), p. 429.

[105] *Zvolsky and Zvolska v. Czech Republic*, (46129/99), 12/11/2002.

[106] Ibidem, para. 55.

fact that the CCCZ used as the *dies a quo* for calculating compliance with the time-limit for submitting the constitutional complaint, not the Supreme Court's judgment of inadmissibility, but the decision on the merits of the court of second instance. The excessive formalism of this interpretation is further aggravated by the fact that the CCCZ does not allow the simultaneous lodging of the constitutional appeal and the cassation appeal to the Supreme Court,[107] let alone the possibility of lodging the constitutional appeal without having first appealed to the Supreme Court.[108]

In a series of judgments rendered over the course of more than 5 years, the European Court of Human Rights notes 'with satisfaction' that the CCCZ has changed its practice to bring it line with ECHR standards, while still finding a violation of Article 6 ECHR because the appeals were all lodged prior to the change in the constitutional court's practice.[109] However, in the 2008 judgment in *Regálová* the ECHR had to note that the long-awaited change in case law did not bring the practice of the CCC into line with conventional law. According to the new orientation, the 60-day time limit can only be calculated from the decision of the Supreme Court if the latter has admitted the appeal for decision. Instead, if the appeal is declared inadmissible, the time limit is still counted from the last decision of the territorial court.[110] The ECtHR, taking into account that the Supreme Court enjoys wide discretion in deciding which appeals are to be admitted for decision, cannot but find that this interpretation is excessively rigid and deprives the applicants of their right of access to the constitutional court.[111] Since this ruling, the Strasbourg judges have continued to sanction this constitutional practice until 2011, after which no further rulings on the subject are to be found, which makes it possible to deduce with a reasonable degree of certainty that the CCCZ has modified once again its practice into line with ECtHR indications.[112]

The other critical issue in the Czech constitutional process is respect for the principle of adversarial and equality of arms. In this respect, the pivotal judgment is the first conviction handed down by the Strasbourg Court against Czechia, the one in

---

[107] Ibidem, para. 36.

[108] See *Beleš et autres v. Czech Republic* (47273/99), 12/11/2002, paras. 63–66.

[109] *Vodarenska Akciova Spolecnost A.S. v. Czech Republic* (73577/01), 24/02/2004, para. 35; *Soudek v. Czech Republic* (56526/00), 15/03/2005, para. 21; *Maríк v. Czech Republic* (73116/01), 12/04/2005, para. 16; *Turek v. Czech Republic*, 73403/01, 21/06/2005, para. 32; *Páleník v. Czech Republic* (64737/01), 21/06/2005, para. 28; *Pillmann v. Czech Republic* (15333/02), 27/09/2005, para. 21; *Šroub v Czech Republic*, (5424/03), 17/01/2006, para. 22; *Friedrich v. Czech Republic* (12108/03), 26/10/2006, para. 20; *Ješina v. Czech Republic* (18806/02), 26/07/2007, para. 26; *Glaser v. Czech Republic* (55179/00), 24/02/2008, para. 34; *Horení v. Czech Republic* (31806/02), 06/03/2008, para. 28; *Drahorad et Drahoradova v. Czech Republic* (10254/03), 20/03/2008, para. 25; *Mourek v. Czech Republic*, (17999/03), 03/04/2008, para. 19.

[110] See *Regálová v Czech Republic* (40593/05), 03/07/2008, paras. 32–34.

[111] *Ibid*, para. 35.

[112] *See Adamicek v. Czech Republic* (35836/05), 12/10/2010, para. 59; *Tieze et Semerakova v. Czech Republic* (26908/09), (30809/10), 13/10/2011, para. 41; *Šury v. Czech Republic* (16299/10), 13/10/2011, para. 30.

the *Krčmar and Others* case.[113] The principle affirmed therein is that the private party in a constitutional trial "must have the possibility to familiarise itself with the evidence before the court, as well as the possibility to comment on its existence, contents and authenticity in an appropriate form and within an appropriate time, if need be, in a written form and in advance".[114] This right, according to the judgment, extends to guaranteeing the applicant the opportunity to express their views "on every document in the file concerning their constitutional appeal".[115] In its subsequent case law, the ECtHR goes on to expand the scope of this principle, first of all clarifying that failure to respect the principle of the adversarial process generates a violation of the right to a constitutional fair trial even in the absence of concrete prejudice.[116] Moreover, the right to be informed of any document contained in the file of the constitutional appeal also extends to the observations made by the judge who delivered the judgment appealed against, in so far as they represent an additional reasoning to that contained in the judicial decision.[117] Similarly, observations concerning objective facts, such as for example the duration of the preliminary investigation, must also be communicated to the other party since they constitute elements capable of guiding the decision of the constitutional court.[118]

On the subject of the reasonable duration of constitutional proceedings, there are no judgments in which a violation of Article 6 ECHR is found. In *Pištorová* the Strasbourg Court seems to criticise the CCC for having taken 1 year and 4 months to determine the merits of a constitutional appeal. However, the violation of Article 6 ECHR is pronounced with regard to the overall duration of the procedure.[119] The only violation of the right to an expedite proceeding attributable to the CCCZ was pronounced in the context of a review of the legality of a detention, which is evidently characterised by the need for greater celerity. The judgment in question is *Fesar,* where the ECtHR rapidly reached the conclusion that a delay of 3 years, 9 months and 18 days for reviewing the legality of the applicant's detention amounted to a violation of the right to a speedy review guaranteed by Article 5(4) ECHR.[120]

Concerning the dialogic dimension of the relationship, the main judgment that comes to the fore is 2018 *Novotny*.[121] The judgment indeed openly criticises the

---

[113] *Krčmar and Others v. Czech Republic* (35376/97), 03/03/2000.

[114] Ibidem, para. 42.

[115] Ibidem, para. 43.

[116] *Milatová et autres v. Czech Republic* (61811/00), 21/06/2005, para. 65; *Mareš v. Czech Republic* (1414/03), 26/10/2006, para. 30; *Hubka v. Czech Republic* (500/06), 03/02/2011, para. 36; *Palšovič v. Czech Republic* (39278/04), 03/02/2011, para. 31.

[117] See *Vokoun v. Czech Republic* (20728/05), 03/07/2008, para. 27; *Kysilková and Kysilka v. Czech Republic* (17273/03), 10/02/2011, para. 39; *Janyr v. Czech Republic* (42937/08), 31/10/2013.

[118] See *Benet Praha Spol S.R.O. v. Czech Republic*, (33908/04), (7937/05), (25249/05), 24/02/2011, paras. 141–143.

[119] *Pištorová v. Czech* Republic (73578/01), 26/10/2004, para. 28.

[120] *Fesar v. Czech Republic* (76576/01), 13/11/2008, para. 69.

[121] *Novotny v. Czech Republic* (16314/13), 07/06/2018.

CCCZ for its failure to the apply the ECtHR relevant precedent—a judgment against Slovakia—to the applicant's case. Not only, the ECtHR even declared that

> the Czech Constitutional Court appears not to have to take into account [...]its own jurisprudence. [...] The Constitutional Court could have decided the case in line with the Court's case-law and on the basis of its own jurisprudence, even in the absence of legislative changes.[122]

As noted also in the Concurring Opinion of Judge Koskel and Eicke, this represents a clear overstepping of the ECtHR's role,[123] which surely does not include providing the right interpretation of domestic constitutional law. At the same time, is possible to read the statement using another key. The affirmation that the CCCZ could have decided the case according to the ECHR and "on the basis of its own jurisprudence", could indeed be interpreted as an indication to the CCCZ of which part of its case-law is ECHR-compliant, thus allowing it a smoother adaptation, not involving formal changes in legislation. In conclusion, the consistent presence of constitutional jurisprudence in Strasbourg judgments seems to be primarily due to the problems that have arisen with regard to the excessive rigidity of the constitutional process, as seems to be evidenced by the fact that the last conviction for violation of the right to constitutional due process dates back to 2013, the year from which a sharp decrease in the number of citations of the CCCZ, as well as constitutional judgments against the Czech Republic, began to be observed.

4.6 The European Court of Human Rights and the Hungarian Constitutional Court. A Necessary Collaboration?

Hungary was the first former Communist country to join the Council of Europe, having signed the ECHR in November 1990. Another distinguishing feature of the Magyar state is that it is the only nation in Central and Eastern Europe that did not adopt a new constitution during the democratic transition, initially retaining the communist constitution of 1949, albeit with the amendments necessary for accession to the Council of Europe. Following the landslide victory in the 2010 elections of Fidesz—the party led by PM Orbán — a new Constitution, called the 'Fundamental Law', entered into force in 2012, despite serious criticism expressed by international observers, in particular the Venice Commission, which indirectly participated in the drafting process.[124] The entry into force of the Fundamental Law can be considered

[122] Ibidem, para. 48.

[123] Ibidem, *Concurring Opinion of Judge Koskel and Eicke*, paras 3–4.

[124] See CDL-AD(2011)016, *Opinion on the New Constitution of Hungary*, Adopted by the Venice Commission at its 87th Plenary Session (Venice, 17–18 June 2011). There was also no lack of criticism in the academic literature. For an extensive commentary on the text of the Fundamental Law and the circumstances leading to its adoption see: Attila Tóth (2012).

the founding moment of what Viktor Orbán himself called an 'illiberal democracy'.[125] In fact, from this moment on, Hungary experienced a progressive and inexorable process of democratic erosion, which ultimately led the European Parliament, in September 2022, to define the Hungarian constitutional system as "a hybrid regime of electoral autocracy".[126] The CoE political bodies have insofar refrained from such bold statements, and only following the European Parliament resolution, in October 2022,[127] the Parliamentary Assembly of the Council of Europe finally placed Hungary under a full monitoring procedure.[128]

This progressive dismantlement of constitutional democracy inevitably affected also the Hungarian Constitutional Court (hereafter also 'the HCC'). The HCC started its operation in January 1990 and was immediately capable of affirming itself as the "guardian of the paradox of constitutional revolution" and the leader of the democratic transition.[129] Especially in its first decade of activity, marked by intense judicial activism, the HCC was generally regarded as one of the most authoritative constitutional courts of the region and a keen receptor of European standards.[130] The defining feature of the Hungarian constitutional justice system was the possibility for every citizen to apply to the HCC to review a piece of legislation without having any qualified interest or waiting for an implementing act, and with no time limits—the widest conception possible of *actio popularis*. The picture drastically changed from 2010 onwards. In the debates during the drafting of the Fundamental Law, it was even considered the possibility of suppressing the constitutional court as a constitutional organ. Ultimately, the HCC was maintained but with its counter-majoritarian function decisively curtailed. The Fundamental Law enlarged the HCC composition from 11 to 15 judges, allowing the ruling majority to appoint four-government friendly judges.[131] In parallel, the HCC saw its competencies significantly curtailed,

[125] In his famous Băile Tuşnad speech of July 2014, PM Orbán declared that he wished to establish Hungary as "an illiberal state, a non-liberal state [which] does not reject the fundamental principles of liberalism such as freedom [...] but it does not make this ideology the central element of state organisation, but instead includes a different, special, national approach." The text of speech is available in its English translation on the website of the Hungarian Government at: https://2015-2019.kormany.hu/en/the-prime-minister/the-prime-minister-s-speeches/prime-minister-viktor-orban-s-speech-at-the-25th-balvanyos-summer-free-university-and-student-camp.

[126] See: European Parliament resolution of 15 September 2022, *on the proposal for a Council decision determining, pursuant to Article 7(1) of the Treaty on European Union, the existence of a clear risk of a serious breach by Hungary of the values on which the Union is founded* (2018/0902R (NLE)).

[127] PACE, Resolution 2460 (2022)1, *The honouring of membership obligations to the Council of Europe by Hungary.*

[128] This procedure, carried out by the PACE Monitoring Committee, involves regular visits by PACE rapporteurs, ongoing dialogue with national authorities, and periodic assessments of how far a member State is honouring its Council of Europe obligations and commitments.

[129] Sólyom (2020), pp. 357–445.

[130] For a detailed account of the relationship between the two courts before the 2012 regime change see: Kovacs (2011).

[131] Sólyom (2020), p. 380.

as the *actio popularis* was abolished,[132] and its review on crucial pieces of legislation excluded.[133]

In this last regard, it is worthy of illustrating a couple of ECtHR judgments which allow a better understanding of the progressive neutralisation of the HCC. The first is the *N.K.M.* case, where the Strasbourg Court, for the first time, had to deal with the effects of the illiberal turn in the Magyar state. In July 2010, the Hungarian Parliament passed a law imposing a 98% tax on civil servants' severance pay for the portion exceeding 3.5 million Hungarian forints (roughly € 10.000 euros at the time of the judgment). The HCC, seized by an *actio popularis,* declared the law unconstitutional due to its unreasonableness. The Parliament reacted to the declaration of unconstitutionality by reintroducing the annulled rule and, at the same time, amending the Constitution by excluding the HCC's review of tax laws and allowing the introduction of new taxes retroactively for up to 5 years. Despite the constitutional amendment, the HCC declared the tax unconstitutional a second time. Once again, however, the Hungarian Parliament approved the same rule in May 2011, explicitly excluding its amenability to judicial review. The Strasbourg Court ruling in the judgement fall short of meeting the expectations.[134] Instead of declaring the interference to be illegitimate for lack of a proper legal basis, as the HCC annulled twice the legislation, the judgment undertakes a detailed proportionality test, which implicitly disavowed the two constitutional rulings,[135] before concluding that there was a breach of Article 1 Prot. 1. ECHR.[136]

---

[132] It has to be pointed out that the Venice Commission position on the presence of an *actio popularis* in the national constitutional justice system is at least skeptical. See for instance: CDL-AD(2014)020, *Opinion on the Draft Constitutional Law on Introduction Amendments and Additions to the Constitutional Law on the Constitutional Chamber of the Supreme Court of Kyrgyz Republic*, para. 10; CDL-AD(2014)026 *Opinion on the Seven Amendments to the Constitution of "The former Yugoslav Republic of Macedonia" concerning, in particular, the Judicial Council, the Competence of the Constitutional Court and Special Financial Zones*, para. 87.

[133] On this see: Sonnevend et al. (2015).

[134] The ruling was criticised also for failing to analyse the tax with regard to the principle of non-discrimination. Cf. I. Leijten, *N.K.M. v. Hungary: Heavy Tax Burden Makes Strasbourg Step In*, in *Strasbourg Observers*, 2013, available at url: https://strasbourgobservers.com/2013/06/10/n-k-m-v-hungary-heavy-tax-burden-makes-strasbourg-step-in/.

[135] The ECHR explicitly states that 'although the decisions of the Constitutional Court raise certain issues as to the constitutionality—and therefore the legality—of the impugned Act, it can nevertheless be accepted as providing a proper legal basis for the measure in question, taking into account the degree of additional deference and latitude afforded in this field'. See *N.K.M. v. Hungary*, para. 54. Overall, the impression one gets from a reading of the grounds is that the HCC did not receive adequate support from the judgment. In light of the delicacy of the domestic situation, at least an *obiter dictum* criticising the actions of the Hungarian legislature would have been desirable but is nonetheless absent.

[136] The 98% tax will also be declared incompatible with the ECHR in two subsequent judgments with identical operative content. See *Gáll v. Hungary* (49570/11), 25/06/2013; *RSz v. Hungary* (41838/11), 02/07/2013.

In the *Baka* case the Strasbourg Court instead could not avoid taking a stance against the ongoing democratic erosion.[137] The applicant in the case, a judge emeritus of the ECtHR, had, in fact, been removed from his post as president of the Supreme Court following statements he had made against the government. What is most relevant here is that the removal of the applicant was contained in a transitional rule of constitutional rank, thus depriving the applicant of the possibility of challenging it before the HCC.[138] In this case, the position of the Strasbourg Court, in particular that of the Grand Chamber, is much stronger. The Grand Chamber's ruling indeed affirms not only the violation of the applicant's right of access to a court, but also the dubious compatibility *per se* of the rule disposing the removal with the principles of the rule of law.[139] Ultimately, the ECtHR shows that it has become aware of the political situation in Hungary—especially with regard to the ostracisation of the HCC—without, however, going so far as to declare the unconstitutionality of a constitutional rule, as some of the Strasbourg judges supported,[140] as the HCC itself had refused to do that. An ever more pronounced deference was observed by the HCC in the *Erményi* case, concerning the removal of the Vice-President of the Supreme Court. Unlike Baka, his removal had been disposed by ordinary law, and he therefore had the possibility of appealing to the HCC to complain of its unconstitutionality. The HCC, however, rejected its appeal and therefore the case reached Strasbourg, where the applicant complained about the bias of two constitutional judges, because during their previous parliamentary tenure they had voted in favour of the law that had ordered his removal. The European Court of Human Rights held that the removal could not be considered justified and was thus in breach of the ECHR. However, the ruling omits to address the crucial question of the impartiality of the constitutional judge, thus avoiding further delegitimising a court already 'under siege'.[141] All in all, the radical shift in the political system in which it is called to operate and its consequent marginalisation from the political arena, as well as the fact that the judges currently sitting in the HCC have all been appointed by the ruling majority, ultimately had transformed the HCC into an instrument of legitimisation of the regime rather than a counter-majoritarian power.

---

[137] The European Court of Human Rights has ruled twice on the Baka case, both rulings condemned Hungary for violating Articles 6(1) and 10 ECHR. See: *Baka v. Hungary* (20261/12), 27/05/2014; *Baka v. Hungary* (20261/12), 23/06/2016.

[138] On the possibility for the ECHR to review the conventionality of constitutional amendments, let us refer to: Simonelli (2019).

[139] *Baka v. Hungary* [G.C.], para. 121.

[140] In the dissenting opinion of Judges Pinto de Albuquerque and Dedov, the very self-restraint of the Hungarian Constitutional Court is censured while claiming the role of a *European constitutional court* for the Strasbourg Court. See *Baka v. Hungary* [G.C.], *Joint Concurring Opinion of Judges Pinto de Albuquerque and Dedov*, paras. 9–23.

[141] See *Erményi v. Hungary: The European Court of Human Rights Expands the Notion of Privacy*, in *Quaderni Costituzionali*, No. 1/2017, 185–190.

However, for our purposes, it is relevant to underline that the Fundamental Law conferred to the HCC a more incisive competence, at least theoretically, in fundamental rights protection, as Art. 24(2)(d) of the Fundamental Law introduced an individual constitutional complaint for challenging the unconstitutionality of judicial decisions, giving the HCC the power to annul the judicial decisions in conflict with the Fundamental Law.[142] Section 27 of the Constitutional Court Act specifies that a constitutional complaint can be brought against judicial decisions terminating judicial proceedings violating a fundamental right.[143] Having lost its role of check on the majority power, the redress of individual injustices has now become the HCC's most significant competence.[144] Also, some scholars observed that in spite of the drastic change in the political environment, the HCC kept the "European outlook" that characterised the case law of its early years.[145] In this sense, analysing the ECtHR case law against Hungary, may also help to assess the validity of this claim.

First of all, in Strasbourg case law, the presence of the HCC is quantitatively reduced, being cited in roughly 22% of the judgments against Hungary.[146] On the other hand, the introduction of the individual direct constitutional appeal had produced a visible increase in the number of citations of the Strasbourg Court, as 61 of the 82 judgments with HCC's citations were delivered in the last decade (see Fig. 4.4). This is also true for the average number of citations per judgments: up to 2012 the average number of citations per judgment is of roughly 8.3, whilst in the decade 2013–2022 the figure is more than double: 17.2.

Given the differences in the Hungarian constitutional system before and after 2012, it is appropriate to follow a strict chronological order in the analysis of the ECtHR case law. Beginning with the effectiveness under Article 35 ECHR of constitutional remedies, in the ECtHR case law prior to the entry into force of the

[142] Under the previous constitutional framework, Section 48 of the Constitutional Court act allowed individuals could apply to the HCC after having exhausted all domestic remedies, however the HCC did not had the power to annul the judicial decision impugned, or to award compensation, but only the declare the unconstitutionality of the legislative norm applied. In this sense, the individual constitutional complaint was equivalent to an ex-post abstract control on legislation. Consequently, the ECtHR held that this remedy was not an effective one. See, *Csikos v. Hungary*, (37251/04), 05/12/2006, paras 16–19.

[143] Section 26(2b) of the Constitutional Court Act adds that "by way of derogation" a constitutional complaint may be submitted also without a judicial decision when the application of a legal provision violates directly a fundamental right and there are no judicial remedies available or these have been exhausted The English text of the Constitutional Court Act is available in the CODICEs database of the Venice Commission at: https://www.venice.coe.int/webforms/documents/default.aspx?pdffile=CDL-REF(2012)017-e.

[144] More extensively on the transformation of the HCC, and in particular on this new competence see: Gárdos-Orosz (2012).

[145] Sólyom (2020), p. 446.

[146] More precisely, as of 1 January 2023, we retrieved 82 judgments with HCC' citations out of a total of 358 delivered against Hungary. The rulings were all identified through the keyword 'constitutional court'.

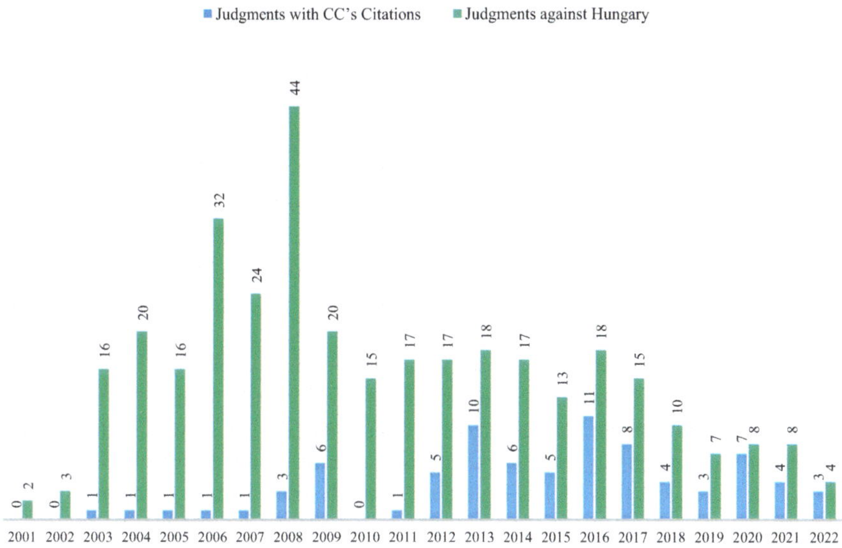

Fig. 4.4 Judgments with HCC citations per year (2001—2022)

Basic Law, there are no statements concerning the effectiveness under Article 35 ECHR of *actio popularis*.[147] There is, instead, an abundant jurisprudence on the effectiveness of the post-2012 individual constitutional complaint of Section 27 of the Constitutional Court Act, which, however, can hardly be called consistent. In its first judgment on the issue, in 2017 (*Király and Dömötör*),[148] the Strasbourg Court declared the application admissible although the applicant did not make use of the constitutional complaint. The ECtHR indeed held that since the Hungarian Government was not capable of indicating any HCC's decisions inferring from the right to privacy a positive obligation incumbent upon the State—and the applicant was claiming before the Strasbourg the existence of a right to seek for police protection against racist threats—the constitutional complaint could not be considered effective.[149] This conclusion *prima facie* contradicts the consolidated case law on Article 35 ECHR, imposing on the applicant the *onus* to test the effectiveness of all available remedies, and ultimately relies on the Court's autonomous interpretation not only of national procedural rules but also of substantive case law. However, read in the broader context of the dismantlement of constitutional democracy, it indicates that the ECtHR will not limit its review to the normative powers of the

[147] Yet, according to a consolidated case law, its exercise is not necessary in order to be able to consider domestic remedies exhausted, since it is not linked to the pendency of the applicant's proceeding.

[148] *Király and Dömötör v. Hungary* (10851/13), 17/01/2017.

[149] *Király and Dömötör v. Hungary*, paras 47–49.

HCC but will also assess whether the HCC case law actually protects the fundamental right invoked by the applicant.

In a judgment delivered 1 year later, the ECtHR indeed refused to dictate general principles on the effectiveness of Hungarian individual constitutional complaint, holding that it was not necessary to address "the question as to whether in general a constitutional complaint to the Hungarian Constitutional Court is an effective remedy for the purposes of Article 35 § 1 of the Convention".[150] A similar casuistic approach is followed in the 2021 judgment in *Sándor Varga*.[151] The case concerned four applicants alleging that their life sentences without parole were in breach of their rights under Article 3 ECHR. The ECtHR once again refrains from generalised statements simply noting that since Article IV of the Fundamental Law provides for the possibility of imposing life imprisonment without parole, the constitutional complaint could not be considered an effective remedy under Article 35 ECHR.[152] Four months later, with the judgment, in *Bancsók and László Magyar*,[153] the ECtHR affirmed that is a remedy whose exhaustion is required under Article 35 ECHR, subject to the caveat that ECHR rights are "equally protected by the Fundamental Law of Hungary".[154] This condition, in the case of Hungary, appears to be particularly relevant as the HCC's notion of fundamental rights appears to be significantly narrower than the Strasbourg Court's.[155]

As for the applicability of Article 6 to constitutional proceedings, the only judgment in which the ECtHR applies this provision, albeit indirectly, is *Merzey*.[156] In the domestic proceedings, the District Court of Pest had raised a question of constitutionality *ex officio*, suspending the proceedings accordingly. At the time of the Strasbourg Court's pronouncement, the HCC had not yet pronounced its decision, so the ECtHR declared the violation of the applicant's right to a trial of reasonable duration, stressing that it was "especially regrettable [...] that the Constitutional Court, a State body required to determine a preliminary legal question in the case, delayed the proceedings by failing to deliver its decision for over five

[150] *Könyv-Tár KFT and Others v. Hungary* (21623/13), 16/10/2018, para. 26.

[151] *Sándor Varga and Others v. Hungary* (39734/15), (35530/16), (26804/18), 17/06/2021.

[152] Ibidem, para. 34.

[153] *Bancsók and László Magyar v. Hungary (No. 2)* (52374/15), (53364/15), 28/10/2021. The case also concerned life imprisonment, as the applicants alleged that after serving 40 years of imprisonment his life-sentence remained *de facto* irreductible, this circumstance representing a violation of their rights under Article 3 ECHR.

[154] The Strasbourg Court however did not enter to assess whether the constitutional complaint was an effective remedy in respect of life imprisonment because, the constitutional complaint had been pending for 6 years before the HCC, thus rendering the protection it could eventually afford merely illusory. See: Ibidem, para. 24.

[155] Emblematic is the *Herbai* case, where the HCC held that freedom of expression under the Fundamental Law does not offer protection against termination of employment for the opinions expressed. See: *Herbai v. Hungary* (11608/15), 05/11/2019, para. 26.

[156] *Mezey v. Hungary* (7909/05), 14/10/2008.

years".[157] It must be emphasised that the fact that the stay was ordered ex officio seems to render irrelevant the verification of the requirement of the constitutional judgment's capacity to affect the outcome of the dispute.[158]

The only other instance in which the Strasbourg Court applied Article 6 ECHR to constitutional proceedings is the 2019 judgment in *Repcevirág Szövetkezet.*[159] For what is most relevant here, the HCC rejected the applicant's request to submit a preliminary reference to the Court of Justice affirming that this was a competence of ordinary courts and that it had no jurisdiction to review the refusal to do by ordinary courts.[160] For its part, the Strasbourg Court also excluded that it could review under Article 6 ECHR the decision of the HCC affirming that it lacked jurisdiction to submit a preliminary reference to the ECJ. In essence, the ECtHR refrained from declaring that, a denial of jurisdiction consisting in a refusal of submitting a preliminary reference - Article 267(4) TFEU affirms that courts "against whose decisions there is no judicial remedy under national law" are under an obligation to submit a preliminary reference if so requested—may amount to a violation of the right to access to a court under Article 6 ECHR.

The 2009 judgment in *Társásag a Szabadságjogokért* instead represents a rare case in which a constitutional performance is assessed under Article 10 ECHR. The ruling indeed censures the HCC for not granting access to the documents of a pending *actio popularis,* to the applicant, thus violating his freedom of information.[161] The judgment criticises the HCC with harsh terms, affirming that the denial to make available information concerning the constitutional procedure "amounted to a form of censorship",[162] which was not justified by any compelling public interest. The relevance of the judgment shall not be underestimated as it constitutes the first affirmation that constitutional courts are under an obligation to guarantee the transparency of their activities, not only *vis-à-vis* the parties of the proceeding, but also with respect to subjects wishing to gather information which may be of public interest.

As regards the substantive dialogue between the two courts, it is symptomatic that freedom of expression constitutes one of the main points of disagreement. In the last 10 years, on 15 occasions the Strasbourg Court found a violation of freedom of expression in cases where the HCC found none. Amongst those judgments, two adopted by the Grand Chamber must be singled out: the 2016 judgment in *Karacsony and Others*[163] and that in the *MKKP* case, delivered in 2020.[164] In *Karácsony and Others*, the applicants, two MPs of opposition parties, alleged that

[157] Ibidem, para. 21.

[158] See *Pammel v. Germany*, para. 53.

[159] *Repcevirág Szövetkezet v. Hungary* (70750/14),30/04/2019.

[160] Ibidem, para. 24.

[161] *Társásag a Szabadságjogokért v. Hungary* (37374/05), 14/04/2009, para. 28.

[162] Ibidem.

[163] *Karácsony and Others v. Hungary* [GC] (42461/13, 44357/13), 17/05/2016.

[164] See: *Magyar Kétfarkú Kutya Párt v. Hungary* [GC], (201/17), 20/01/2020.

the imposition of a fine by the plenary of the Parliament, for having displayed a placard accusing the government of corruption and robbery violated their freedom of expression. In a previous judgment, the HCC analysed the constitutionality of the law governing the disciplining of MPs, finding that the imposition of fines was a justified restriction to MPs' right to freedom of expression, in light of the necessity of guaranteeing the undistributed functioning of parliament. The Strasbourg Court held the opposite view, affirming that the imposition of a fine in the applicants' case, of € 430 and € 510, was not necessary in a democratic society and violated Article 10 ECHR.[165] The *MKKP* judgment instead concerned the MKKP, an opposition party that, on the occasion of the 2015 referendum on the mandatory quotas for the relocation of migrants, invited citizens to cast invalid ballots and created a mobile app allowing users to anonymously post photos of their ballots. The Hungarian National Election Commission found that the app breached the principles of voting secrecy and of fairness of elections and thus constituted unlawful campaigning, imposing on MKKP a fine of around € 2700,00. The MKKP sought judicial review of the decision, but both the Supreme Court (Curia) and the HCC held that its conduct was outside the perimeter of freedom of expression. The ECtHR instead affirms that the conduct is indeed protected by Article 10 ECHR and found the fine imposed by the National Elections Commission illegitimate. A similar pattern is also observable in the judgments in *Herbai* and *ATV ZRT*,[166] where the HCC denies that the applicants' conducts constitute an exercise of freedom of expression, whereas the ECtHR finds a violation of Article 10 ECHR. Such a difference in the interpretation of freedom of expression, ultimately makes it impossible a dialogue on the limits of freedom of expression, as the HCC denies *tout-court* that the applicants are actually exercising such fundamental right.

In conclusion, the attitude of the European Court of Human Rights following the illiberal turn in Hungary appears to be characterised by avoiding to openly delegitimise the HCC, as testified for instance by the recognition of the individual constitutional complaint as an effective remedy under Article 35 ECHR. At the same time, as we have seen, the HCC's deferential attitude towards the ruling majority had obliged the Strasbourg Court to intervene in the domestic political arena, assuming the counter-majoritarian function that the HCC is unable to perform. Whilst this approach undoubtedly benefits individual Hungarian citizens, it may become untenable in the long run as the Hungarian political bodies, unlike the HCC which has insofar carefully avoided open confrontations, does not shy away from challenging the ECtHR authority.[167]

---

[165] *Karácsony and Others v. Hungary*, paras 148–162.

[166] *ATV ZRT v. Hungary* (61178/14) 28/04/2020; *Herbai v. Hungary*, cit above, fn 156.

[167] In this sense see: Bárd (2016), p. 200.

4.7 A Harmonious Relationship. Strasbourg and the Latvian Constitutional Court

Latvia joined the Council of Europe in 1995, but only ratified the ECHR and its protocols 2 years later, on 4 June 1997. Since the Latvian Constitution of 1992 essentially re-instituted the 1922 Constitution, the status of international treaties in the legal system is not well defined and has been the focus of heated jurisprudential and doctrinal debate.[168] As far as the ECHR is concerned, following the 1998 constitutional reform, which introduced a *bill of rights* into the Latvian Constitution, the Constitutional Court of Latvia (hereafter 'the CCL') clarified that it enjoys infra-constitutional status.[169] As regards individual access, Article 19 of the Constitutional Court Law allows any individual to challenge before the CCL, after exhausting domestic remedies, a normative provision that violates one of his fundamental rights.[170] However, like in the Portuguese system, individuals cannot challenge the ordinary courts' interpretation of a legislative provision, the misapplication of a rule by an administrative authority, or the unconstitutionality of an omission, but only the unconstitutionality of the norm itself. This is why the Strasbourg Court has affirmed, despite constant Government's submissions arguing the contrary, that the constitutional complaint cannot be considered an effective remedy under Article 35 ECHR when the constitutionality of the norm itself is not at stake.[171] In this sense, in the 2020 judgment in *Zirnite*, the ECtHR admitted this criterion did not allow for a clear distinction as to under which circumstance a constitutional complaint could be considered an effective remedy, therefore it established a rebuttable presumption of effectiveness affirming that "where it is arguable that the individual decision, in respect of which the violation is alleged, was based on an unconstitutional legal provision, the Constitutional Court should be given an opportunity to address the matter",[172] and that this applies also to criminal procedures, because as a result of a finding of unconstitutionality by the CCL the applicant can obtain the reopening of the proceedings against him.[173]

Concerning its relationship with the Strasbourg Court, as of 1 January 2023, out of a total of 147 judgments rendered against Latvia, the CCL is cited in 57 of them

[168] Mits (2016), pp. 203–204.

[169] Mits (2016), p. 205.

[170] The English text of the Constitutional Court Act was consulted on the CODICES database maintained by the Venice Commission. Available at: https://codices.coe.int/codices/documents/law/55738E8D-7CEB-44EC-8472-08DC0D38DFC5#a55738e8d-7ceb-44ec-8472-08dc0d38dfc5.

[171] For contested cases in which the Government supported the inadmissible for failure to institute a constitutional complaint see: *Ēcis v. Latvia* (12879/09), 10/01/2019; *Savičs v. Latvia* (17892/03), 27/11/2012, para. 113; *Nagla v. Latvia*, 73469/10, 16/07/2013, para. 48.

[172] *Zirnite* v. *Latvia* (69019/11), 11/06/2020, para. 69.

[173] Ibidem, para. 72; *Markus v. Latvia* (17483/10), 11/06/2020, para. 48.

(38%) with an average number of citations per judgment of 11.5.[174] Concerning the temporal distribution of citations there is nothing particularly noteworthy, apart from the fact that in the last 5 years considered the average number of citations per judgment is significantly higher, being 30.85. Reading the judgments in question, an explication to this increase is readily found: it can be largely attributed to the ongoing discussions between the Latvian government and the Strasbourg Court concerning the effectiveness of the individual constitutional complaint.[175]

In relation to the application of the guarantees of Article 6 ECHR to constitutional proceedings, there is an ambiguity generated by the judgment in *Meimanis.*[176] Despite the government's objection that the constitutional proceedings of the applicant were not aimed at determining his civil or criminal obligations, the Strasburg Court held that 'it is unnecessary to reach a conclusion as to whether Article 6 § 1 applied to the constitutional proceedings in the present case.[177] Going on to read the reasoning, it becomes clear that the ultimate reason why the Court did not answer the exception of inapplicability is the fact that it did not find a violation of Article 6 ECHR, since despite the fact that the CCL did not hold a public hearing, the applicant had the opportunity to comment on all the material on which the CCL based its decision.[178] However, the fact that the Strasbourg judges did not deal with the exception solely because a ruling in favour of the government was adopted leaves one perplexed, also because one could have taken advantage of this opportunity to specify the exact content of the right to constitutional due process when it is predominantly objective in nature.

Turning instead to the role of constitutional judgments in Strasbourg jurisprudence, one must point out a few cases of enforcement of constitutional judgments. In general, the CCL albeit not particularly active, is considered the most trustworthy state institutions in Latvia, and its judgments are effectively executed.[179] In fact, the ECtHR judgments do not concern failures of the Latvian authorities to implement constitutional rulings, but the conferral by the Strasbourg Court of retroactive effects to the judgment of the CCL. In *Zaicevs,* this effect overturns the *res iudicata*;[180] whereas in *Raudevs,* the ECtHR retroactively applied a constitutional judgment to affirm that the applicant's detention was without legal basis and therefore in

---

[174] There are 49 judgments in which the Latvian Constitutional Court is mentioned, and they are identified as follows: 37 with the keyword 'constitutional court' and 12 with the term 'cour constitutionnelle'.

[175] In all judgments with more than one citation, i.e. 7 out 8, the Government submitted that the applications were inadmissible because applicant did not exhaust domestic remedies. In addition to the cases already cited above (ff nn 379–381) See: *Rimšēvičs v. Latvia* (56425/18), 10/11/2022, paras 74–78; *Bērzins and Otherrs v. Latvia* (73105/12), 21/09/2021, para. 74; *Savickis and Others v. Latvia* [GC], (49270/11), 09/06/2022, para. 141.

[176] *Meimanis v. Latvia* (70597/11), 21/07/2015.

[177] Ibidem, para. 44.

[178] Ibidem, paras. 51–54.

[179] Ziemele et al. (2020), p. 557.

[180] *Zaicevs v. Latvia* (65022/01), 31/07/2007, para. 56.

violation of Article 5(1) ECHR.[181] In *Zdanoka*, conversely, the ECtHR gives a patent of conventionality to the judgment of the CCL which, interpreting the Strasbourg case-law, had correctly deduced that a disqualification from standing for election contained in a legislative provision in order to be compatible with the ECHR must be of limited duration and subject to periodic review.[182] In *Ādamsons*, where the applicant complained about the absence of an individual examination of the reasons for his disqualification, the ECtHR, still referring to constitutional case law, seemed to condemn the Baltic State for not having adopted an individualised approach, as required by the constitutional case law, to the applicant's case.[183]

All in all, even if it is quantitatively limited, the conventional jurisprudence examined here shows that the relationship between the two Courts is devoid of significant frictions and that, on the contrary, the Strasbourg Court has often resorted to constitutional precedents to motivate and lend greater persuasiveness to its pronouncements.

4.8 The ECtHR and the Lithuanian Constitutional Court. Closer Than It Seems?

Together with Estonia, Lithuania was the first of the republics belonging to the former USSR to join the Council of Europe, on 14 May 1993. The Constitution, on the other hand, was adopted by popular referendum on 25 October 1992. According to Article 138(3) of the Lithuanian Constitution, all ratified international treaties become part of the legal system and have the same force as law. In 1999, the Lithuanian legislature also clarified that in the event of a conflict between a domestic law and a rule contained in an international treaty, the latter should prevail.[184] In addition, the Constitutional Court of Lithuania (hereinafter also 'the CCLT') made it explicit that the Constitution takes precedence over any rule applicable domestically, including the ECHR.[185] Until 2019, the CCLT was, together with the Romanian Constitutional Court, the only constitutional jurisdiction in the region that could not receive individual appeals. Following a legislative amendment approved that year, Article 65(2) of the Constitutional Court Act now provides that any person has the right to lodge an application before the CCLT asking it to examine whether, *inter alia*, primary or secondary law complies with the Constitution, provided that the following conditions are met: (1) a decision adopted on the basis of that legal instrument has violated that person's fundamental rights; (2) all legal remedies

[181] *Raudevs v. Latvia* (24086/03), 17/12/2013, para. 72.

[182] *Zdanoka v. Latvia* (58278/00), 17/06/2004, paras. 62 and 135.

[183] *Ādamsons v. Latvia* (3669/03), 14/06/2008, para. 131.

[184] Law on Treaties, Article 11(2). 1999, No. VIII-1248, *Valstybės žinios*, No. 60-1948, 1999. Quoted in: Jočienė (2016), p. 237.

[185] See Kūris (2004), p. 39.

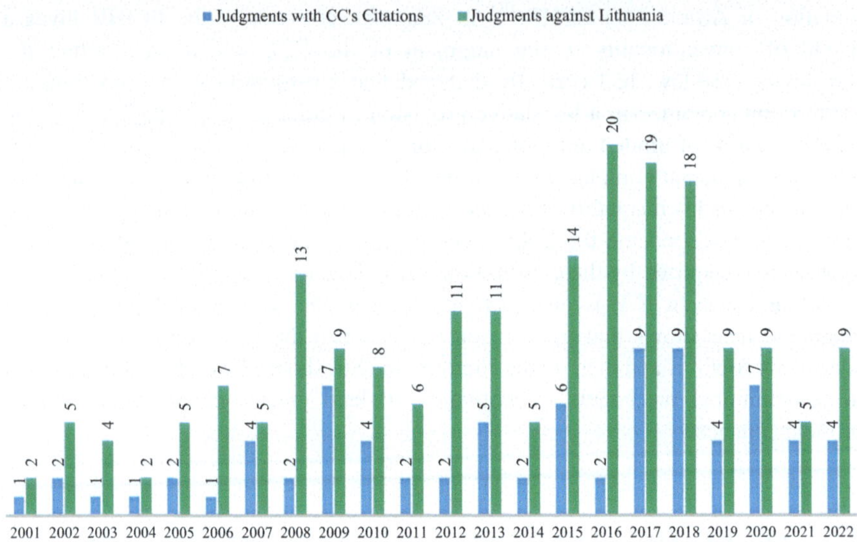

Fig. 4.5 Judgments with CCLT citations per year (2001—2022)

have been exhausted; (3) the application is lodged within 4 months of the final court decision. The Strasbourg Court did not have yet the opportunity to adjudicate on its effectiveness. Nonetheless, considering the characteristics of the Lithuanian individual constitutional complaint, it can be safely affirmed that the Strasbourg will require applicants to make use of it only when they complain about a fundamental rights' violation having its cause in a normative provision.

As of 1 January 2023, out of a total of 201 judgments delivered against Lithuania, the CCLT is cited in 83, a percentage of around 41%.[186] with an average number of 7,7 occurrences per judgment. The analysis of the temporal distribution of citations evidences a trend which is worth investigating. As the graph below (Fig. 4.5) shows, in the last 5 years considered, the CCLT has been cited in 28 out of 50 judgments delivered against Lithuania, with an average number of citations per judgment of 26.

Given its recent introduction—it became available to individuals only the 1 September 2019—this increase cannot be attributed to it. Nor during that period, the ECtHR had to deal with politically sensitive, or highly complex legal questions requiring closer attention to the CCLT jurisprudence. While it is true that this increase is part of the generalised trend of more frequent citations of constitutional courts' precedent, its magnitude, especially concerning the average number of citations in each judgment, invites to search for an additional explanation. In this sense, it is possible to speculate that the fact that the current Lithuanian Judge, Egidijus Kūris, was also President of the CCLT from 2002-2008, had an influence on this rediscovered interest in the CCLT jurisprudence by the Strasbourg Court.

[186] All the judgments were retrieved using the keyword 'constitutional court'.

Leaving aside speculations, it is absolutely certain that the signalled increase of CCLT citations cannot be attributed to systemic disfunction in fconstitutional proceedings, as Article 6 ECHR was never applied to the CCLT. A partial exception is the *Padalevicius* case, where the ECtHR, however, merely reaffirms a well-established conventional jurisprudence according to which the period of suspension of the main proceedings during the decision by the CCLT of the question of constitutionality must be taken into account for the assessment of the reasonable duration of the trial, without criticising the CCLT as it rendered its decision less than 14 months.[187]

The applicability of Article 6 ECHR was instead expressly excluded in what is probably the most significant ruling delivered by the ECtHR against Lithuania, the 2011 Grand Chamber's judgment on the *Paksas* case, that declared Article 6 ECHR inapplicable to the *impeachment* procedure of the President of the Republic before the CCLT.[188] The ECtHR held that, since the CCLT does not have the power to impose a sanction on the accused, the constitutional process cannot be construed as aimed at determining a criminal sanction within the meaning of Article 6 ECHR. More straightforwardly, the Strasbourg Court also held that since the purpose of the proceeding "was to determine whether, in discharging his duties as President, the applicant had committed gross violations of the Constitution or breached his constitutional oath",[189] the applicability of Article 6 under its civil head was also excluded. From the judgement, it is thus possible to infer that the impeachment procedure would not seem to fall *per se* outside the scope of Article 6 ECHR, as it could be applicable under its criminal head in cases where the constitutional court is empowered to adopt sanctions. Another aspect of the *Paksas* judgment that needs to be highlighted is the explicit *overruling* of a CCLT ruling. Indeed, in May 2004, the CCLT had ruled that dismissal from the office of president of the republic implies the permanent impossibility of being re-elected to any public office requiring an oath. The Strasbourg Court took a diametrically opposed view, affirming that this absolute and unlimited restriction to be a violation of Article 3 Prot. 1 ECHR. The Strasbourg Court's *overruling* appears to be poorly justified especially if one considers, as the Human Rights Committee pointed out in its decision on the *Paksas* case, that the vast majority of the world's constitutions provide for limits on the eligibility to stand for re-election to the office of President of the republic, and that therefore "[i]f presidents who have successfully completed one or more terms can be permanently ineligible for re-election for the sake of ensuring a healthy and competitive political system, then surely presidents who have been removed for abusing their office can also be permanently barred".[190]

---

[187] *Padalevicius v. Lithuania,* (12278/03), 07/07/2009, para. 44.

[188] *Paksas v. Lithuania* [GC] (34932/04), 06/01/2011.

[189] Ibidem, paras 65–66.

[190] UN Human Rights Committee, Communication No. 2155/2012, *Individual opinion by Committee member Mr. Gerald L. Neuman (partially dissenting),* 17.

Despite the quantitative data suggesting otherwise, in the last 5 years there are few judgments which are relevant for our purposes. There are two recent judgments, delivered in 2018 and 2021, assessing under Article 6 ECHR the refusal of ordinary courts to submit a question of constitutionality to the CCLT.[191] However, their content is hardly innovative, as they both exclude that this amounted to a violation of the right to access to a court. In the second judgment of the pair, *Šaltinytė* delivered in 2021, the Strasbourg Court, repeating the usual disclaimer that the ECHR does not guarantee, as such, a right to refer a question to the constitutional court, then adding that "the Court does not rule out the possibility that, where a preliminary reference mechanism exists, refusal by a domestic court to grant a request for such a referral may, in certain circumstances, infringe the fairness of proceedings—*inter alia*, where the refusal has not been duly reasoned". In the specific circumstances of the two cases, the ECtHR excluded that Article 6 ECHR was violated, as in both ordinary tribunasl gave reasons for rejecting the referral.[192] It is worth noting that in *Šaltinytė* only the Supreme Administrative Court considered the applicant's request for a referral, whilst the territorial court simply ignored it. Another case that can be signalled is the 2018 judgment in *Tumeliai*, where the Strasbourg Court's condemnation is essentially based on the national authorities' failure to execute a CCLT judgment.[193] In light of the introduction of the individual constitutional complaint, the relationship between two courts is destined to intensify, albeit one should not expect too much: as a matter of fact, the CCLT is not a very active court, in 2023 it adopted a total of just 13 rulings.[194]

4.9 The Montenegrin Constitutional Court as a Conventional Laboratory

Montenegro became the 47th Member State of the Council on 11 May 2007, i.e. less than one year after the celebration of the referendum approving the secession from Serbia, whilst the Strasbourg Court delivered its first judgment against this small Balkan state only on 28 April 2009.[195] Also because the short period of existence as an autonomous State, the Strasbourg Court only delivered 45 judgments against Montenegro, with 35 of them mentioning the Montenegrin Constitutional Court, a

[191] *Šaltinytė v. Lithuania* (32934/19), 26/10/2021.

[192] Ibidem, paras. 88–92.

[193] *Tumeliai v. Lithuania* (25545/14), 09/01/2018, paras 79–81.

[194] The data have been retrieved through the search tool of the CCLT's website, available at the url: https://lrkt.lt/en/court-acts/search/170.

[195] *Bjelic v. Montenegro and Serbia* (11890/05), 28/04/2009.

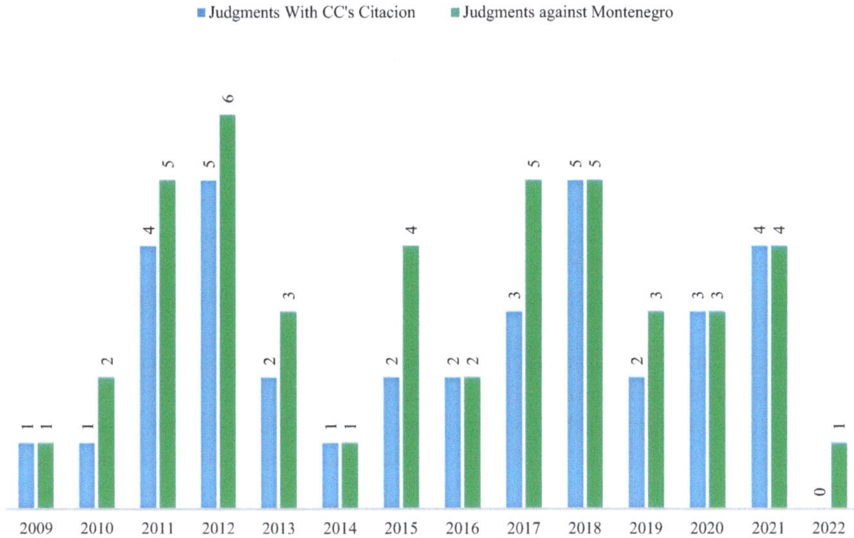

Fig. 4.6 Judgments with CCM citations per year (2009—2022)

ratio of approximately 77%.[196] Such a high percentage is due to presence in the Montenegrin constitutional justice system of an individual right to bring a constitutional complaint. This right is enshrined in Article 149 of the Constitution, which states that any individual may bring an action before the Constitutional Court only once all other remedies have been exhausted. Articles 68 of the Constitutional Court Act specifies the content of this right: an appeal may be brought by any person, natural or legal, who complains of the violation of one of his constitutional rights caused by the action, or omission, of a public authority.[197] The quantitative analysis of the data yielded scarcely significant results, and also the graph concerning the temporal distribution of citations does not show any statistical trend (see Fig. 4.6). However, the reading of the case law citing the Montenegrin Constitutional Court offers many interests insight, first of all concerning the effectiveness of the constitutional remedy.

Initially, in a series of judgments delivered between 2010 and 2012, the ECtHR considered the constitutional complaint ineffective in application concerning the

[196]All 35 judgments were obtained using the search string "constitutional court". By contrast, the keyword "cour constitutionnelle" produced no results.

[197]The English text of the rule can be found on the official website of the Montenegrin Constitutional Court at http://www.ustavnisud.me/dokumenti/LAW%20ON%20THE%20CONSTITUTIONAL%20COURT%20OF%20MONTENEGRO%20.pdf.

unreasonable duration of proceedings and,[198] more controversially, in cases of the failures to execute domestic judgments,[199] in as much as, in its original formulation, Article 68 of the Constitutional Court Act only allowed to challenge a judicial decision.[200] In essence, the Strasbourg Court autonomously interpreted Article 68 of the Constitutional Court Act in the sense of precluding the CCM to remedy to the no-execution of domestic judgments. As observed in the dissenting opinion of Judges Mijović and Hirvela in *Zivaljević,*[201] this finding however contradicts the consolidated approach of the ECHR according to which, in systems which provide constitutional protection for fundamental rights, freedoms it is incumbent on the aggrieved individual to test the extent of the protection afforded by a judicial remedy.[202]

In any case, it led the Montenegrin legislature to amend the rules on constitutional appeal, which in their current form no longer refer to the need to challenge an individual decision, on the contrary, they allow to challenge the unlawfulness of an omission, and grant the CCM the power to order compensation if it finds that an applicant's right has been violated. The ECtHR, 'signed a blank cheque' to the CCM by declaring that from the date of entry into force of the new law, i.e. 22 March 2015, the constitutional complaint constitutes an effective remedy within the meaning of Article 35 ECHR, consequently rendering mandatory its exhaustion from that date.[203] In light of this legislative innovation, it was foreseeable that the number of citations of the ECHR in case law increased in the coming years, yet as we have seen such an effect has not been observed.[204]

An interesting principle still concerning the exhaustion of domestic remedies is affirmed in *Asanović.*[205] Here, the Court held that since the CCM analysed the applicant's complaint in the merits, the governments objections alleging that the applicant should have instituted civil proceedings should be dismissed. In particular the ECtHR held that

> in a situation when the Constitutional Court already examined the merits of the complaint concerning the lawfulness of the applicant's deprivation of liberty, it cannot be said that the

[198] See: *Novović v. Montenegro* (13210/05), 23/10/2012, para. 45; *Stakić v. Montenegro* (49320/07), 02/10/2012, para. 41; *Zivaljević v. Montenegro* (17229/04), 08/03/2011, para. 68.

[199] See *Boucke v. Montenegro* (26945/06), 21/02/2012, paras 77–79; *Mijuskovic v. Montenegro* (49337/07), 21/09/2010.

[200] See, for all: *Mijuskovic v. Montenegro*, paras 73–74.

[201] See: *Zivaljević v. Montenegro, Mijović and Hirvela Dissenting*, in particular the last paragraph where the ECtHR jurisprudence on the applicant's obligation to test all available remedies is cited.

[202] See: *Vinčić and Others v. Serbia* (44698/06), 01/12/2009, para. 51.

[203] See *Siništaj and Others v. Montenegro* (1451/10, 7260/10, 7382/10), 24/11/2015, para. 123.

[204] This may be due to the fact that the effectiveness of a remedy is normally assessed by the European Court of Human Rights at the time the application to Strasbourg is lodged (see, *Baumann v. France* (33592/96), 22/05/2001, para. 47), and this may delay the effects on a legislative change in the Strasbourg's case law. Also, one should not forget that the limited number of judgments available precludes a meaningful speculation on statistical data.

[205] *Asanović v. Montenegro* (52415/18), 20/05/2021.

> national authorities have not been given the opportunity to put matters right through the national legal system. The fact that the civil proceedings are still pending cannot affect this conclusion.[206]

In other words, the judgement seems to introduce an absolute presumption of exhaustion of domestic remedies, according to which once the applicant's complaint is analysed in the merit by the national constitutional court, domestic remedies should be considered exhausted, independently of the pendency of a proceeding instituted by the same applicant. Even though the judgments did not specify that, it seems logical to deduce that this presumption may only operate when, as it is the case of the CCM; the constitutional complaint can be lodged only after all domestic remedies have been exhausted.

With regard to the role of the ECtHR as judge of constitutional decisions, the judgment in the *Mugoša* case deserves to be examined, particularly for the argumentative technique used.[207] Indeed, the ECtHR, while repeating the usual statement that it is primarily the task of domestic courts to interpret domestic legislation, exploits an apparent contradiction in constitutional jurisprudence in order to make its own interpretation of the domestic rule prevail. For a better understanding of the judgment, a brief reconstruction of the domestic proceedings is first necessary. Before the CCM, the applicant had argued the illegality of his detention on the grounds that the court competent to periodically examine the existence of the requirements for prolonging custody had ruled 4 days after the expiry of the 2-month deadline imposed by the Code of Criminal Procedure. The CCM, rejecting his appeal, had declared that a delay of 4 days had not violated the appellant's right to personal liberty.[208] The ECtHR referring to a precedent of the CCM decided a year earlier, noted instead that "the same Constitutional Court, in a similar situation, had found that non-compliance with the national legislation and the time-limits contained therein led to a violation of Article 5 of the Convention" and also pointed out that "when ruling on the applicant's constitutional appeal, the Constitutional Court provided no explanation whatsoever for this departure from its earlier reasoning".[209] In two judgments delivered 3 years later, the ECtHR follows the same argumentative strategy.[210] The main criticism that can be addressed to this line of argumentation is that none of those judgments omit to indicate the amount of the delay in the cited precedent, thus making its analogical application less compelling. Apart from that, the judgment seems to follow a consolidate strategy of the ECtHR, consisting in attempting to ground its rulings on domestic laws, even if this means exposing contradictions in the constitutional court case law, or dissent amongst its members.

---

[206] Ibidem, para. 55.

[207] *Mugoša v. Montenegro* (76522/12), 21/06/2016.

[208] Ibidem, para. 18.

[209] Ibidem, para. 53.

[210] *Bigović v. Montenegro* (48343/16), 19/03/2019; *Šaranović v. Montenegro* (31775/16), 05/03/2019.

Finally, the ECtHR also acted as enforcer of constitutional judgments. In *Baranin and Vukčeviç*,[211] the Strasbourg Court simply notes that the CCM's judgment ordering a "thorough, prompt and independent investigation" in the applicant's case was not executed, and thus went to find a breach of the procedural limb of Article 3 ECHR.[212] Even more straightforward is the judgment in *Barac and Others*,[213] where the ECtHR, with a substantive reasoning consisting of just two paragraphs, concluded that the application of a rule declared unconstitutional during the applicant's proceedings before domestic courts violated Article 6 ECHR. In their dissenting opinion Judges Kalaydjieva and De Gaetano, criticise the judgment for holding that a "decision of the Constitutional Court declaring a provision unconstitutional necessarily and automatically makes this provision inapplicable to the circumstances of the case before the national courts", further arguing that, even admitting that norm should not have been applied, this would merely constitute a misapplication of the law without any arbitrary element, thus not sufficient to trigger a violation of Article 6 ECHR.[214]

In conclusion, the case law just reviewed allows to formulate a couple of observations regarding the relationship between the two jurisdictions. First of all, it emerges that the Montenegrin Constitutional Court is routinely asked by appellants to rule on the compatibility of national law with the ECHR. This is a direct consequence of the ECHR status in the Montenegrin legal system which according to Article 9 of the Constitution is superior to that of ordinary law. On the other end of the relationship, the Strasbourg Court maintains a dialogic approach with the CCM, facilitated by the fact that both the constitutional court and national authorities have demonstrated a willingness to implement its judgments faithfully.[215] At the same time, however, the case law analysed evidences a particular intense application of the ECHR, leaving little margin of discretion to the CCM, who despite its constant engagement with ECtHR standards, often see its decisions overturned by the Strasbourg Court, sometimes clearly overstepping subsidiarity's boundaries.[216]

[211] *Baranin and Vukčeviç v. Montenegro* (24655/18, 24656/18), 11/03/2021.

[212] Ibidem, paras 142–149.

[213] *Barac and Others v. Montenegro* (47974/06), 13/12/2011.

[214] Ibidem, *Kalaydjieva and De Gaetano Dissenting*, paras 4–6.

[215] See: Vučinić (2016).

[216] Most recently see: *Špadijer v. Montenegro* (31549/18), 09/11/2021, para. 35; *Nešic v. Montenegro* (12131/18), 09/06/2020; para. 12; *Madzarovic and Others v. Montenegro* (54839/17), (71093/17), 05/05/2020, paras 21, 32. *Bigović v. Montenegro* (48343/16), 19/03/2019, para. 116; *Šaranović v. Montenegro*, para. 27; *Milićević v.* Montenegro (27821/16), 06/11/2018, para. 18; *Petrović and Others v.* Montenegro, (18116/15), 17/07/2018, para. 13. All those cases ended with the Strasbourg Court finding a breach of the ECHR where the Constitutional Court found none.

4.10 The ECtHR Relationship with the North Macedonian Constitutional Court. A Positive Outlook

The Republic of North Macedonia (before 2019 the Former Yugoslav Republic of Macedonia) joined the Council of Europe in 1995 and ratified the ECHR in April 1997. However, it took a good four years for the first judgement against the Republic of North Macedonia and another eight years for a judgement citing the North Macedonian Constitutional Court (hereafter only CCNM). Pursuant to Article 118 of the North Macedonian Constitution, the ECHR enjoys *infra-constitutional* status in the national legal system and is directly applicable to national courts.[217]

As for individual access to constitutional jurisdiction, Article 110 of the Constitution provides for two possibilities[218]: the *actio popularis* and the individual direct appeal, whose regulation is contained in the Constitutional Court's Rules of Procedure.[219] The latter may be brought by any individual against a decision or action of a public authority within 60 days from the adoption of the decision. However, the appeal may be brought only in the event of a violation of one of the rights listed in Article 110(4) of the Constitution. Those are precisely: freedom of conscience, thought and public expression of thought, political association and activity as well as the prohibition of discrimination among citizens on the grounds of sex, race, religion or national, social or political affiliation. To put it otherwise, the individual constitutional complaint is available only for possible breach of the rights corresponding to Articles 9, 10, 11 and 14 of the ECHR.

Given the narrowness of the avenues for fundamental rights' protection,[220] the CCNM appears cited in only 29 cases out of 156 judgments against North Macedonia,[221] a percentage of roughly 20%, and therefore similar to the percentages of citations of constitutional courts accessible only by way of incidental proceedings, such as the Italian one. On the other hand, the average number of CCNM's citations per judgment is 13.6, thus in line with the data obtained for constitutional jurisdictions with individual direct access. The temporal distribution of citations shows that, starting from 2016, an increased attention to the CCNM constitutional jurisprudence (see Fig. 4.7) is observable. This data is fully confirmed by the average number of citations per judgment in the years following 2016, which is roughly 20. This proved another confirmation of the existence of a trend towards increased attention to the constitutional case law of the Respondent State.

[217] See Trajkovska and Trajkovski (2016), p. 288.

[218] Available in English translation on the official website of the Macedonian Parliament at http://www.parliament.am/library/sahmanadrakan%20dataran/macedonia.pdf.

[219] See respectively Articles 11 and 51 of the Constitutional Court Rules of Procedure.

[220] See:. M. Risteska E. Shurkov, *The Transformative Role of the Macedonian Constitutional Court*, Centre for Research and Policy Making, 2016, 13; available at url: http://www.crpm.org.mk/wp-content/uploads/2017/01/Constitutional-Court-Macedonia.pdf.

[221] These judgments were all obtained using the keyword 'constitutional court'. Only three of the 20 listed judgments were translated into French.

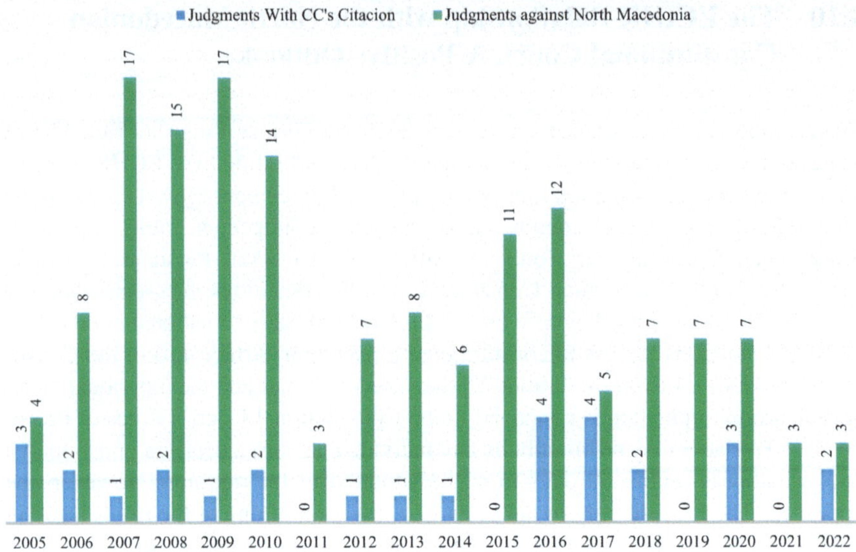

Fig. 4.7 Judgments with CCNM citations per year (2005—2022)

Turning to the qualitative analysis of the case law, there are no relevant judgments on the effectiveness of constitutional remedies, and on the application of Article 6 ECHR to constitutional proceeding, there is only relevant judgment, the one rendered in the *Selmani and Others* case.[222] Here the European Court of Human Rights sanctioned the CCNM for not holding a public hearing despite an explicit request by the appellant. Although the Strasbourg Court repeats that, in principle, a constitutional court is free to choose whether or not to hold a public hearing,[223] the fact that in the applicant's case the CCNM act as a single instance court triggers an obligation to hold a public and oral hearing, which can only be waived in exceptional circumstances.[224]

We must also briefly dwell on the *Ivanovski* case,[225] concerning the applicant's removal from its post as President of the Constitutional Court judge in the framework of a lustration proceedings.[226] The case deserves to be reported mainly because the fact that Article 6 ECHR is applicable in cases of removal from office of a

[222] *Selmani and Others v. The Former Yugoslav Republic of Macedonia* (67259/14), 09/02/2017.

[223] See, *Juričić v. Croatia*, para. 87.

[224] Ibidem, paras. 37–39.

[225] *Ivanovski v. The Former Yugoslav Republic of Macedonia* (29908/11), 21/01/2016.

[226] The term '*lustration proceedings*' refers to those processes, which took place in former communist countries, in which former members of the communist regimes were systematically removed from the public offices they occupied. On the significance of these proceedings and their historical significance, see: Ellis (2016).

constitutional judge is not challenged by the Macedonian Government,[227] and its application by the ECtHR consolidates its 2011 precedent in *Juričić v. Croatia*. Yet, since the Constitutional Court did not intervene in the proceedings, the relevance of the case for this book is limited to this aspect.

Turning instead to the ECtHR conventionality review on the decisions of the CCNM, the only judgment that comes to the fore is the one rendered in the *Association of Citizens Radko and Paunkowski* case. The CCNM had dissolved, under Article 112(2)(3) Const., the applicants' association on the grounds that it was aimed at denying the identity of the Macedonian people and at racial and religious incitement.[228] The ECtHR, on the other hand, disagreed with the decision of the CCNM, holding that the dissolution of the association, although legally valid and adopted for the protection of a general interest, was not necessary in a democratic society, i.e. it was not proportional *stricto sensu*.[229] The ECtHR, analogously to what we have seen in *Ollinger v. Austria*, offers a broad interpretation of the right to freedom of association, substituting its own balancing act for that of the national constitutional court in this case as well.

In conclusion the limited number of cases available makes it difficult to elaborate general observation as to the ECtHR's relationship with the North Macedonian Constitutional Court, which would be marked by provisional character. The general trend of the entire North Macedonian political system, which is that of a gradual adaptation to the ECHR jurisprudence,[230] only allows to predict a smooth relationship.

4.11 Strasbourg and the Polish Constitutional Tribunal. From Strict Alliance to Open War

The European Court of Human Rights delivered its first judgement against Poland in the same year that the new Polish Constitution came into force, 1997. Poland's accession to the Council of Europe had taken place 5 years earlier, in 1992. According to Article 91(1) of the Polish Constitution, international treaties, including the ECHR, once ratified are directly applicable within the Polish legal system and have vertical effects, i.e. any individual may invoke the violation of one of his rights guaranteed by an international treaty before any domestic court. Paragraph 2 of Article 91 also states that the rules contained in international treaties are hierarchically superior to parliamentary law. Although the Constitution does not

[227] The only question concerned whether Article 6 ECHR was applicable under its civil or criminal head, with the Government arguing for the applicability of the civil limb.

[228] See the passage of the CCNM judgment cited in: *Association of Citizens Radko and Paunkowski v. The Former Yugoslav Republic of Macedonia* (74651/01), 15/01/2009, para. 29.

[229] Ibidem, paras. 75–76.

[230] See Trajkovska and Trajkovski (2016), p. 288.

clarify how possible antinomies are to be resolved, a practice has been established whereby, in case of interpretative doubts, the common judge submits the question to the Constitutional Tribunal (hereafter only 'the PCT'), which may annul the conflicting domestic norm with *erga omnes* effects.[231] Although there is a substantial identity between the catalogue of rights of the Polish Constitution and that of the ECHR, and the applicants often invoke the articles of the Convention, the PCT in its judgments mainly refers to the norms of the Constitution,[232] without considering, at least explicitly, the ECHR as interpreted by the Strasbourg Court.[233]

This lack of attention is mirrored by the scarce presence of PCT precedents in the ECtHR case law. As of 1 January 2023, the PCT is cited in 213 out of a total of 1110 pronounced against Poland.[234] This data is primarily a result of the narrowness of the individual avenue for accessing the PCT. Similarly to the Portuguese *Tribunal constitucional*, according to Article 79 of the Polish Constitution, the PCT indeed does not have the power to review the constitutionality of a judgment, but only of the normative provision on which the trial judge based its decision.[235] Consequently, when called upon to review the effectiveness of this remedy under Article 35 ECHR, the Strasbourg held that 'a constitutional complaint is an effective remedy for the purposes of Article 35 § 1 of the Convention only in situations where the alleged violation of the Convention resulted from the direct application of a legal provision considered by the complainant to be unconstitutional'.[236] Another element which has reduced significantly the effectiveness of the Polish individual constitutional complaint is the consolidated practice of the PCT to postponing the effects of declarations of unconstitutionality, giving only in exceptional circumstances immediate effect to its judgments.[237]

Despite this apparent lack of communication, the Strasbourg Court had been an important ally for the PCT, which historically had to face serious problems in the execution of its judgments by national authorities, and in various occasions relied on the support of the Strasbourg Court. The Grand Chamber's ruling in the *Broniowski* case, which introduced the pilot judgment procedure in the Strasbourg's case law,[238]

---

[231] See Garlicki and Kondak (2016), pp. 308–309.

[232] Ibidem, 310.

[233] The PCT however admitted that it uses the ECHR "acquis humanitaire" as a canon when interpreting fundamental rights guaranteed by the Polish Constitution. See *Orchowski v. Poland* (17885/04), 22/10/2009, para. 85.

[234] The keywords used for the search were 'constitutional court', which produced 182 results, and 'cour constitutionelle', which produced 31 judgments in French only, for a total of 213 pronouncements.

[235] Szmulik and Poglodek (2016), pp. 32–33.

[236] See *Bugajny and Others v. Poland* (22531/05), 06/11/2007, para. 44; *R. R. v. Poland,* (27617/04), 26/05/2011, para. 116; *Sosinowska v. Poland* (10247/09), 18/10/2011, para. 54. On the ineffectiveness of the constitutional appeal as a means of complaining about a legislative omission, see instead: *Pietrzak v. Poland* (38185/02), 08/01/2008, para. 64.

[237] See *Orchowski v. Poland*, para. 110; *Kaperzynski v. Poland* (43206/07), 03/04/2012, para. 38.

[238] *Broniowski v. Poland* (31443/96), 22/06/2004.

was one these occasions. In a nutshell, the applicant complained before the ECtHR that the Polish authorities had denied him full compensation for the loss of family land property that had occurred in the execution of peace agreements at the end of World War II, whereby Poland had had to cede its eastern territories across the Bug River to the USSR.[239] In January 2002, the PCT had declared unconstitutional the rules restricting the right to compensation of the so-called 'Bug's river claimants', recognising them a right of claim. The judgment, when in 2004 the Strasbourg Court's delivered its decision, was still unexecuted. The ECtHR, after carrying out an extensive analysis of the PCT judgment, affirms the existence of a right capable of protection under Article 1 Protocol 1 ECHR as recognised by the PCT. In particular, the ECtHR, referring to the PCT judgment, affirmed that domestic authorities had rendered void of content the applicant's right to compensation, and concluded that it "sees no cause to depart from the Constitutional Court's findings, which were based on its direct knowledge of the national circumstances",[240] thus declaring a breach of Article 1 Protocol 1 ECHR. Subsequently, when justificating the necessity of general measures to remedy the violation, the ECtHR once again refers to the PCT which defined the "the Bug River legislative scheme [. . .] an inadmissible systemic dysfunction" once again fully endorsed the statement.[241]

A few months later, the Strasbourg Court handed down its second pilot judgment against Poland, in the *Hutten-Czapska* case.[242] In its essence, the case concerned Polish legislation that, for social benefit purposes, placed severe restrictions on landlords as to the maximum amount of rent they could demand from tenants as well as on the legal avenues for recovering possession of the property. The ECtHR intervened in the case after the PCT had already twice declared the unconstitutionality of the legislation in question, a first time on the original text and a second time on the reform approved following the first judgment. The ECtHR judgement, therefore, following the same structure of argumentation as *Broniowski*, merely repeats and endorses what was stated by PCT,[243] up to a point that one of the dissenting opinions complains about the excessive length of the citations of the judgments of the constitutional judge.[244] Following the ECtHR ruling, the PCT ruled on two other occasions on the subsequent reforms of the contested legislation, noting in both cases profiles of unconstitutionality and referring several times to the judgment in *Hutten-Czapska*. These constitutional judgments will in turn be

[239] For an extensive historical reconstruction of the dispute see: M. P. Carazo, *Broniowski Case*, in *Max Planck Encyclopedia of Public International Law*, available at: http://opil.ouplaw.com/view/10.1093/law:epil/9780199231690/law-9780199231690-e1797.

[240] *Broniowski v. Poland*, para. 173.

[241] Ibidem, para. 189.

[242] *Hutten-Czapska v. Poland* (35014/97), 22/02/2005.

[243] Ibidem, para. 187.

[244] In his separate opinion Judge Pavlovschi states that "I do not think that it was really necessary to reproduce all those very lengthy quotations from the Constitutional Court's judgments". See *Hutten Czapska v. Poland*, Partly concurring and partly dissenting opinion of judge Pavlovschi, para. 2.

extensively cited in the Grand Chamber's judgment confirming the adoption of a pilot judgment.[245]

Another issue on which the ECtHR found a systemic deficiency and suggested the adoption of general measures under Article 46 ECHR is the overcrowding of Polish prisons. In the judgments in *Orchowski* and *Norbert Sikorski*,[246] the ECtHR—after recalling a judgment of the TC that had declared that obliging detainees to live in a cell of less than 3 m^2 amounts to a degrading treatment—states that "the ruling of the Constitutional Court can constitute a basic criterion in the Court's assessment whether the overcrowding in Polish detention facilities breaches the requirements of Article 3 of the Convention. In consequence, all situations in which a detainee is deprived of the minimum of 3 m^2 of personal space inside his or her cell, will be regarded as creating a strong indication that Article 3 of the Convention has been violated".[247] However, despite the systemic nature of the problem, the ECtHR decided not to adopt a pilot judgment because the Polish state had begun to partially implement the judgment of the PCT.[248]

Even outside the context of pilot judgment procedures, it is possible to find cases in which the Strasbourg Court with its rulings essentially enforced constitutional judgments. An example of enforcement related to an individual case is *Kędzior*, where the applicant, who was partially deprived of legal capacity, alleged to have been deprived of access to a court, despite a PCT's judgment affirming that ordinary courts shall not restrict the access to legal remedies of incapacitated persons. The ECtHR's judgment underlines that "the Constitutional Court's judgment [. . .] was legally binding notwithstanding the unfinished legislative process and the domestic court's reluctance to apply directly that judgment", in order to conclude that "[oi]n these circumstances, the applicant was deprived of a clear, practical and effective opportunity to have access to court".[249] That the execution of the constitutional judgement has often been problematic in Poland is also evident from the judgement in *Joanna Szulc*, where the Strasbourg Court openly criticises the *Sejm* for its failure to execute three PCT judgments, which would have guaranteed the applicant's right and avoided a condemnation.[250] Ultimately, all these cases constitute a striking

---

[245] A systematic and detailed temporal reconstruction of the saga can be found in: Sadusrki (2008), pp. 17–21. Available at: https://cadmus.eui.eu/bitstream/handle/1814/9887/LAW_2008_33.pdf?sequence=1&isAllowed=y.

[246] *Orchowski v. Poland* (17885/04), 22/10/2009; *Norbert Sikorski v. Poland* (17599/05), 22/10/2009. It is curious to note that although the two judgments present an identical content, the first is written in English and the second in French.

[247] *Orchowski v. Poland*, para. 123; *Norbert Sikorski v. Poland*, para. 132. The same statement is also contained in: *Grzywaczewski v. Poland* (18364/06), 31/05/2012, para. 95.

[248] *Orchowski v. Poland*, paras. 150–152. Although it is clear from reading the grounds of the judgment and its operative part that the adoption of a pilot judgement is only considered by the ECHR (see paras. 147–154), in *Kurkowski* (36228/06, 24/06/2013), it is referred to as a 'pilot judgement' (para. 55).

[249] See *Kędzior v. Poland* (45026/07), 16/10/2012, para. 88–91.

[250] *Joanna Szulc v. Poland* (43932/08), 13/11/2012, para. 93.

demonstration of how a 'symbiotic' relationship ends up amplifying and mutually reinforcing the legitimacy and persuasiveness of the judgments of the two courts.[251] On the one hand, in fact, the obligations contained in the constitutional judgements are transformed into international obligations of the State, on the other hand, the Strasbourg Court—thanks to assessment made by the constitutional judge—can amplify the effects of its own ruling beyond the individual appeal pending before it.[252]

However, this alliance abruptly came to an end after 2015. As the reader is surely aware of, starting from 2015, Poland indeed entered into a constitutional crisis which had as its epicentre the Constitutional Tribunal. The origin of the crisis is the approval of a transitional provision of the Constitutional Court Act which allowed the seventh term of the *Sejm* to appoint five constitutional judges, even though two seats in the PCT would become vacant only in December 2015, after the parliamentary elections. Pursuant to this provision, in October 2015 the exiting parliamentary majority appointed those five 'midnight judges' to the PCT. The freshly elected President of the Republic, Andrzej Duda, however refused to receive the oaths of the five judges elected, thus preventing them from taking possession of the office. As was expected, the parliamentary elections turned to be a landslide victory for the opposition party, the conservative Law and Justice (*Prawo i Sprawiedliwość*, commonly abbreviated to PiS). After declaring null and void the election of the five judges, in December 2015 the new majority of the *Sejm* elected another five judges, who nevertheless could not take the possession of their office due to the opposition of the PCT president. The PCT itself was called upon to review the constitutionality of the actions of both the past and the incumbent majority, essentially affirming that the filling of two posts expiring in December 2015 was unconstitutional, and that the new appointments of the PiS-led majority were individual acts applying a legislative provision, hence unsusceptible of being subjected to its review.[253] During 2016, the PCT wrestled for its independence, but ultimately surrendered when a new law on the organisation of the TC entered into force, and a new President was appointed in December 2016 by the PiS majority.[254]

Subsequently, the PiS-led majority undertook a series of judicial 'reforms', affecting the independence, organisation, composition and functioning of the Judi-

[251] Ibidem, 20.

[252] In the same vein, see: Ibidem, 22–24.

[253] A full account of the various judgments of the PCT can be found in the ECtHR landmark judgment which will analysed in the following pages. See: *Xero Flor w Polsce sp. z o.o. v. Poland* (4907/18), 07/05/2021, paras 21–63.

[254] For an extensive examination of the content of the new law and its critical profiles, see the Opinion of the Venice Commission on the final text of the rule: CDL-AD(2016)026, *Opinion on the Act on the Constitutional Tribunal*, Adopted by the Venice Commission at its 108th Plenary Session (14–15 October 2016).

cial Council, the Supreme Court, and of the judiciary as a whole.[255] Initially, yet belatedly according to some authors,[256] it was the European Court of Justice that, together with the Commission, took action to protect the independence of Polish judges and safeguard the rule of law in Poland.[257]The Strasbourg Court remained a passive observer until 2021, when it delivered a disruptive judgement in the *Xero Flor* case,[258] which presented the Strasbourg Court with the opportunity of assessing the impact on the PCT of the 2015 constitutional crisis.

The core of the applicant's complaint before Strasbourg was in fact that the composition of the PCT panel that rejected his constitutional complaint, including one of the five judges, Mariusz Muszyński, appointed by the PiS-majority in December 2015, constituted a violation of his right to a tribunal established by law guaranteed by Article 6 ECHR.[259] The applicant also alleged a violation of Article 6 ECHR provoked by the refusal of ordinary courts to submit a question of constitutionality to the PCT. On this latter aspect, for the first time in the ECtHR case law, affirms that the refusal to submit a question of constitutionality violated Article 6 ECHR. This conclusion nonetheless is hardly consistent with its previous precedents, as the ECtHR finds a violation on the grounds that even though four level of ordinary courts provided reasons for the refusal, the ECtHR held them "insufficient",[260] thus significantly lowering the threshold to trigge a violation of Article 6 ECHR.[261] In this sense must be read also the passage of the judgment affirming that "a domestic court has to provide *specific* reasons justifying its refusal to refer the question",[262] as imposing higher standards of reasoning on ordinary judges for the refusal to refer.[263]

The ECtHR then moves on to analyse the lawfulness of the PCT's composition. First, the judgment confirms the applicability of Article 6 ECHR to constitutional proceedings as long as its outcome is capable of affecting the applicant's rights.[264] Having rejected the government's objection, the judgment clarifies that to assess possible violations of the right to a tribunal established by the relevant framework is the three-step test formulated law in *Guðmundur Andri Ástráðsson v. Iceland*.[265]

---

[255] For a full account see: Sadusrki (2019), p. 169.

[256] Pech et al. (2021).

[257] The milestone marking the entrance of the CJEU in the rule of law constitutional is the 2018 judgment in the s.c. "Portuguese Judges Case". See: Pech and Platon (2018).

[258] *Xero Flor w Polsce sp. z o.o. v. Poland* (4907/18), 07/05/2021.

[259] Ibidem, paras 211–212.

[260] Ibidem, para. 173.

[261] See *Coëme and Others v. Belgium* (32492/96), (32492/96),(32547/96),(32548/96),(33209/96), (33210/96), 22/06/2000 para. 114.

[262] Ibidem, para. 171 (italics added).

[263] Similar observations are formulated by judge Wojtyczek in his separate opinion. See: Ibidem, Partly Concurring Partly Disseting Opinion of Judge Wojtyczek, para. 10.

[264] Ibidem, para. 209.

[265] Ibidem, para. 254.

The Strasbourg Court heavily relies on the PCT's judgment of December 2015 in order to affirm that the composition of the panel that adjudicated the applicant's constitutional complaint was in manifest breach of domestic law, and thus impaired the very essence of the applicant's right. To put it otherwise, with this judgment the Strasbourg Court, is essentially affirming that the participation of the one five judges appointed in December 2015, automatically result in a violation of the right to a tribunal established by law under Article 6 ECHR. However, it is worth noting that, in its judgements, the PCT did not affirm that the appointment of all the five judges—including the one integrating the panel—by the PiS majority was unlawful.[266]

In a series of judgments delivered in the following months, the Strasbourg Court applied the *Guðmundur Andri Ástráðsson* test to the judicial institutions affected by the judicial reforms of the PiS ruling majority: the Disciplinary Chamber of the Supreme Court (*Reczkowicz*),[267] the Chamber of Extraordinary Review and Public Affairs of the Supreme Court (*Dolińska-Ficek*),[268] and the Civil Chamber of the Supreme Court (*Advance Pharma*),[269] concluding that the formations which examined the applicant's cases were in breach of Article 6 ECHR for not being established by law. All those cases ultimately have at their core an assessment of the amended system of appointment of the Polish National Council of the Judiciary ('the NCJ')—the constitutional organ selecting all the members of those bodies. For what is most relevant here, another salient feature of those judgments is their refusal to take into account the rulings of the PCT delivered from 2017 onwards, and in particular the rulings of 20 June 2017,[270] declaring the unconstitutionality of the old NCJ appointment system, and of 25 March 2019,[271] confirming the constitutionality of the newly introduced NCJ appointment system—according to which all the member of the judicial were to be elected by an absolute majority of the *Sejm*. *Reczkowicz* and *Dolińska-Ficek* infer far-reaching conclusions from *Xero Flor* when they affirm that the participation in the adoption of the above mentioned PCT judgements of the same Judge Muszyński is by itself "capable of compromising, if not vitiating, the legal force to be attached to the rulings."[272] In essence, the ECtHR judgments only consider as the relevant interpretation of domestic law the 18 July 2007 judgment of the PCT, in which it is affirmed that the judicial election of the NCJ is an indispensable guarantee of their independence. In particular, the ECtHR affirm that the departure, in the PCT judgment of 20 June 2017, from the principles established

[266] See: Szwed (2022), p. 141.

[267] *Reczkowicz v. Poland* (43447/19), 22/07/2021.

[268] *Dolińska-Ficek and Ozimek v. Poland* (49868/19), (57511/19), 08/11/2021.

[269] *Advance Pharma Sp. Z.O.O. v. Poland* (1469/20), 03/02/2022.

[270] Judgment of the Polish Constitutional Tribunal of 20 June 2017, No. K-5/17.

[271] Judgment of the Polish Constitutional Tribunal of 25 March 2019, No. K-12/18.

[272] *Dolińska-Ficek and Ozimek v. Poland* (49868/19), (57511/19), 08/11/2021, para. 319; similarly but in less straightforward terms: *Reczkowicz v. Poland* (43447/19), 22/07/2021, para. 263.

in the 2007 judgment was not legally justified and that the PCT appears to be "isolated in its perception and assessment of the necessity and legitimacy of the change in the procedure for election of the judicial members of the NCJ."[273]

In *Advance Pharma* instead, in addition to this argument, the Strasbourg Judges notes "in connection with the Constitutional Court's actions related to the application and interpretation of the Convention"[274] that the PCT, in a judgment of November 2021,[275] had declared Article 6 ECHR unconstitutional in as much as it applies to constitutional proceedings, implicitly affirming that the PCT interpretations of ECHR has to be considered abusive.[276] The 10 March 2022, PCT adopted another defiant judgement (K-7/21) declaring Article 6(1) ECHR unconstitutional essentially because it was the legal basis for the above-described judgments of the Strasbourg Court declaring that the various formations of the Supreme Court were not tribunals established by law.[277]

Just 5 days after this judgment, the Grand Chamber of the Court delivered its first decision in the Polish constitutional crisis, endorsed the above-illustrated approach, "nothing more but also nothing less".[278]And indeed, the far reaching consequences of such an approach, are already visible in the *M.L.* judgment,[279] assessing the compatibility with Article 8 ECHR of the restrictions on the right to abortion introduced in 2021 by a judgment of the PCT. Without even entering to assess the substantive content of those restrictions, the First Section of the ECtHR concluded that, since the bench that introduced the restrictions included Judge Muszyński and two other unlawfully appointed judges, the interference was not prescribed by law, and it was thus in breach of Article 8 ECHR.[280] In a nutshell, the judgment is saying that the PCT decisions, as long as are adopted by a bench with one of the three unlawfully appointed judges, are *per se* not compatible with rule of requirements and thus cannot be considered, under any circumstances, legitimate restrictions to fundamental rights.[281]

Ultimately this judgment seems to have made the very possibility of a relationship between the Strasbourg Court and the Polish Constitutional Tribunal dependent upon the presence of those three unlawfully appointed judges in the bench, as it should preclude to the Strasbourg Court to treat the PCT as a legitimate

[273] *Reczkowicz v. Poland*, para. 239; *Dolińska-Ficek and Ozimek v. Poland*, para. 295.

[274] *Advance Pharma Sp. Z.O.O. v. Poland*, para. 320.

[275] Judgment of the Polish Constitutional Tribunal of 24 November 2021, No. K 6/21.

[276] Such conclusion is supported by the harsh criticism of the PCT interpretation of Articles contained in..

[277] Judgment of the Polish Constitutional Tribunal of 10 March 2022, No. K-7/21.

[278] See: *Grzęda v. Poland* (43572/18), 15/03/2022, Concurring Opinion of Judge Lemmens, para. 2.

[279] *M.L. v. Poland* (40119/21), 14/12/2023.

[280] Ibidem, para. 175.

[281] In this sense the Strasbourg Court posture is much more rigid than that of the European Court of Justice, which adopts a contextual approach, taking into account the functioning of the legal system as a whole, to assess whether a body's composition is in breach of rule of law requirements. See: Leloup (2023).

interlocutor as long as the three judges are there. This interpretation of the *M.L.* judgment is probably excessive, as it appears likely that what the ECtHR wanted is avoid to entering into the highly contentious issue, especially in a catholic country like Poland, of the admissible restrictions on the right to abortion. Nevertheless, such bold statements are inevitably detrimental for the future relationship between the two courts and the consistency of the ECtHR case law as a whole.

4.12 The Silent 'Dialogue' with the Romanian Constitutional Court

The Romanian Constitution, approved by referendum on 8 December 1991, represents a peculiarity amongst Central Eastern European States, both for its form of government and its system of constitutional justice. On both aspects is indeed visible a strong influence of the French model,[282] as the same Romanian Constitutional Court (hereinafter only 'the CCR') admitted in 2012, the 1958 French Constitution was indeed a "source of inspiration" for the Romanian Constitution.[283] With specific regard to constitutional justice, the traces of such influence can be found in the competences of the CCR, above all in the preventive control of the constitutionality of the laws of the parliament (Art. 146(a) Constitution of Romania) as well as in the absence of an individual direct appeal to the constitutional judge. In fact, the CCR can examine the constitutionality of the interpretation of a legislative provision only in the context of an interlocutory proceeding (Art. 146(c) Constitution of Romania).

A far-reaching constitutional revision, approved in 2003, significantly increased the powers of the CCR, in particular by adding a fourth paragraph to Article 147 of the Constitution, which in its current version enshrines the *erga omnes* effect of CCR rulings, putting an end to a decade-long debate in the academic literature.[284] As for the ECHR status in the Romanian legal system, Article 11 Constitution confers supra-legislative status on all international treaties. Paragraph 3 of the same article, which was also added as part of the 2003 constitutional reform, would even seem to suggest a supra-constitutional status, as it provides for the obligation of the legislator

[282] This influence is above all visible in relation to the Romanian constitutional system, starting with the adoption of a semi-presidential form of government. See, on this point: Duculescu (2004), p. 195.

[283] Judgment of the Constitutional Court of Romania of 27 June 2012, N. 683.

[284] On this point, see the essay by the President Emeritus of the Romanian Constitutional Court on the powers of the constitutional justice body: A. Zegrean, T. Toader, *La Cour constitutionnelle de Roumanie*, in *Nouveaux Cahiers du Conseil constitutionnel*, No. 38/2013, available at url: http://www.conseil-constitutionnel.fr/conseil-constitutionnel/francais/nouveaux-cahiers-du-conseil/cahier-n-38/la-cour-constitutionnelle-de-roumanie.135711.html.

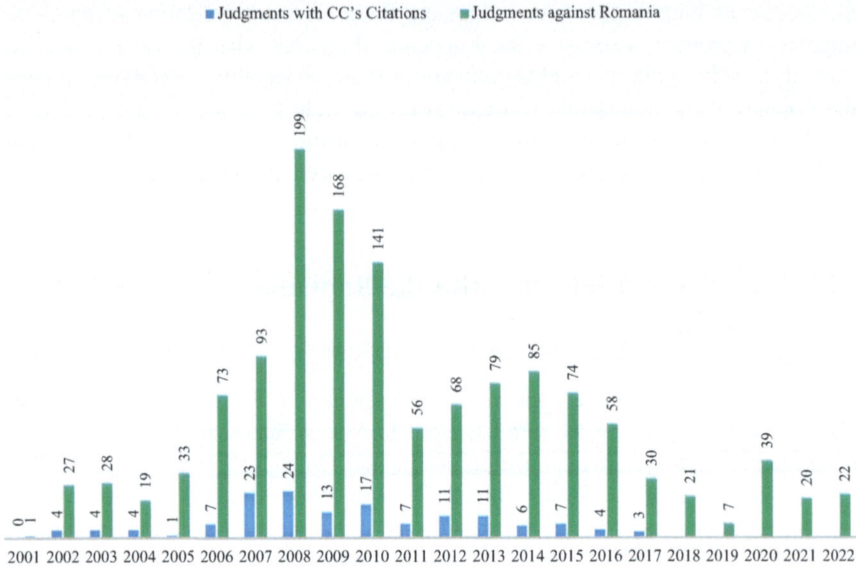

Fig. 4.8 Judgments with CCR citations per year (2001—2022)

to amend the Constitution if one of its articles contradicts a provision of an international treaty to which Romania is to become a party.[285]

Similar to the other constitutional jurisdictions that do not grant any form of individual access—namely Bulgaria, France and Italy—the presence of the CCR in the jurisprudence of the ECtHR is not significant. As of 1 January 2023, against 1252 judgments delivered against Romania, the CCR is cited in only 172,[286] i.e. a percentage of approximately 14.3%, very similar to the figure obtained for the Italian Constitutional Court. The number of citations, on the other hand, is the lowest of all those obtained, being an average 4 recurrences per judgment. These data are surprising especially in relation to other constitutional courts, such as the Constitutional Court of Bulgaria, fare less active than its Romanian counterpart. Whilst in 2022 the CCR delivered as many as 685 decisions, the Bulgarian Constitutional Court only delivered 21.[287]

[285] The constitutional reform was in fact primarily aimed at allowing Romanians to join the European Union. For an article-by-article commentary on the reform see: CDL-AD(2004)04, *Opinion on the Draft Revision of the Constitution of Romania (Unfinished texts by the Committee for the revision of the Constitution)*, adopted by the Venice Commission at its 54th Plenary Session (Venice, 14–15 March 2003).

[286] Judgments were obtained as follows: 125 by the keyword 'cour constitutionnelle' and 46 by the keyword 'constitutional court'.

[287] These data were found on the official website of the Romanian Constitutional Court. See *Situația dosarelor soluționate şi a deciziilor pronunțate în anul 2022*, available at url: https://www.ccr.ro/wp-content/uploads/2023/01/Statistica-site-2022.pdf.

In this sense, it must be emphasised that the quantitative data offer only partial confirmation of what some authors have observed about the increase in Strasbourg's dialogue with the CCR since 2007.[288] In fact, although, as the graph below (Fig. 4.8) illustrates, the number of citations in the four-year period 2007-2010 increased considerably—even though only in absolute terms —in this four-year period considered, the average number of citations per judgment is even lower than the overall number, being 3.5.[289]

Turning to the qualitative analysis of the ECtHR jurisprudence, given the lack of individual access to the CCR, there are no judgements in which the Strasbourg Court applies Article 6 ECHR to constitutional proceedings. Concerning the Romanian incidental procedure of judicial review of legislation, the Strasbourg Court has insofar refrained from assessing the conventionality of ordinary judges' refusal to raise a question of constitutionality.[290] Also, rejecting a Government objection in the *Sabou et Pircalab* case, the Strasbourg Court excluded that raising a question of constitutionality could constitute an effective remedy under Article 13 ECHR, as it is not directly available to individuals.[291]

As for the jurisprudential dialogue between the two courts, we must point out a series of judgments in which the ECHR, in order to assess the existence of the domestic legal basis to the decisions of the territorial courts, expressly states that it refers to the domestic rule as interpreted in the jurisprudence of the CCR, thus amplifying its effects in the domestic system.[292] Similarly, in a serie of cases in which the Strasbourg Court reviewed the extensive competences awarded to pre-trial judges in the Romanian legal system, the constitutional jurisprudence seems to have play a decisive role. The CCR in a 2011 judgment had indeed declared unconstitutional some provisions of the Code of Criminal Procedure governing the procedure before the pre-trial judge for not complying with Article 6 standards, while reminding the legislature that the ECHR only provides a minimum standard of

[288] Romania. J. Motoc, C. Kaufman, *Romania and the European Convention on Human Rights: A Dialogue of Judges* in J. Motoc, I. Ziemele (eds.), *The Impact of the ECHR on Democratic Change in Central and Eastern Europe,* cit., 344.

[289] In 21 of the 50 judgments, the reference to CCR case law is even limited to the citation of a case law precedent without further analysis. See ex *multis*, *Martin v. Romania* (14466/02), 10/03/2009, para. 13; *Abramiuc v. Romania*, 37411/02, 24/02/2009, para. 65.

[290] *See Hodos et autres v. Romania* (29968/96), 21/05/2002, para. 57; *Ciobanu v. Romania* (29053/95), 16/07/2002, para. 41; *Maatescu et autres v. Romania* (30698/96), 22/10/2002, para. 37; *Iosif et Autres v. Romania* (10443/03), 20/12/2007, para. 73.

[291] *Sabou et Pircalab v. Romania* (46572/99), 28/09/2004, paras. 55–56.

[292] See *Konolos v. Romania* (26600/02), 07/02/2008, para. 51; *Bujac v Romania* (37217/03), 02/11/2010, para. 58; *Avram v. Romania* (25339/03), 18/10/2011, para. 32.

protection.[293] The CCR judgment is explicitly endorsed in all the three cases of this serie,[294] and ultimately seems an implicit invitation to the Romanian legislature to follow the indications of the national constitutional court. Another instance of cooperation between the two courts is represented by the two judgments in *N. v. Romania*. In the first judgment of the pair, delivered in 2017, the Strasbourg Court found that the lack of legal remedies for obtaining the review of legality of the internment in psychiatric hospitals, as it was reserved to legal guardians for all incapacitated persons independently of their specific mental capacity, amounted to a violation of Article 5(4) ECHR.[295] With two decisions delivered in 2020, the CCR declared unconstitutional various provisions of the Romania Civil Code concerning legal incapacitation, in particular because they did no provide for a periodic and individualised assessment on the permanency of the incapacity.[296] In 2021, the Strasbourg Court adjudicating on the same applicant's case found a violation of Article 8 ECHR, essentially for the same reasons indicated by the CCR.[297] Moreover, in response to the applicant's request for general measures under Article 46 ECHR, which may have triggered a pilot judgment, the ECtHR simplify indicates that those general measures consist in the Romanian State amending its legislation to bring it into line with the findings of the Constitutional Court.[298]

In conclusion, although the presence of CCR precedents in the ECtHR jurisprudence certainly cannot be said to be massive, some interesting elements for reflection emerge. The first is the persistent denial of the Strasbourg Court to review the refusal of common courts to raise an issue of constitutionality at the request of the parties. The second is existence of a cooperation between the two courts which, especially in recent years, indicates that, despite the scarcity of the evidence of an ongoing dialogue, the Strasbourg Court now considers the CCR a reliable partner for the implementation of the ECHR.[299]

[293] A lengthy extract of the judgments is contained in the all the three judgments cited in the following footnote. See, for instance, *Alexandru-Radu Luca v. Romania* (20837/18), 14/06/2022, para. 37.

[294] *Alexandru-Radu Luca v. Romania*, para. 78; *Mihail Mihailhescu v. Romania* (3795/15), 12/01/2021, para. 90; *Victor Laurențiu v. Romania* (75614/14), 12/01/2021, para. 151.

[295] *N. v. Romania* (59152/08), 28/11/2017.

[296] The relevant passages of those judgments are reported in: *N. v. Romania (No. 2)* (38048/18), 16/11/2021, paras. 30–31.

[297] *N. v. Romania (No. 2)*, para. 64.

[298] Ibidem, para. 84.

[299] As signalled by Petrov (2018, p. 519) the CCR has also been an obstacle to implementation of ECHR standards. In 1999 the ECtHR held that the criminal conviction of a journalist for defamation violated Article 10 ECHR. (*Dalban v Romania,* (28114/95), 28/09/1999). Following this ruling and the ensuing debate, in 2006, the Romanian parliament passed a law fully decriminalising defamation. However, next year, the CCR annulled the new legislation on the grounds that it created a normative lacuna. Only in 2014, with the entry into force of the new Criminal Code, defamation was definitively depenalised.

4.13 The Serbian Constitutional Court and the ECtHR. Growing Rapprochement

The Republic of Serbia has never formally ratified the Convention, as it was recognised as the sole successor state to the State Union of Serbia and Montenegro—which had ratified the ECHR in April 2003—as regards its obligations under the Convention by the Committee of Ministers of the Council of Europe.[300] After Montenegro seceded, Serbia adopted a new Constitution, which was approved on 8 November 2006. For what is more relevant here, the Constitution gives the ECHR and international treaties infra-constitutional status, specifying at Article 194 that they may not conflict with the Constitution. However, as far as the ECHR and international human rights treaties are concerned, the Constitutional Court of Serbia (hereinafter simply CCSB) has clarified that the rights enshrined therein have the same value as those guaranteed by the Constitution and their violation may be complained of in the constitutional appeal of Article 170 of the Serbian Constitution.[301] This norm, introduced for the first time in the 2006 Constitution, allow individuals to appeal to the CCSB for challenging an action or decision of a state authority in violation of an individual fundamental right. The appeal may be brought after exhaustion of any other remedy available against the challenged act or directly, i.e. without having first exhausted all other remedies, if no remedy against the act or action in question exists in the system, such as in cases of proceedings of unreasonable duration (Article 82 of the Constitutional Court Act).[302]

Despite an individual remedy that represents a broad avenue of access to constitutional jurisdiction, the presence of the CCSB in ECtHR is not comparable to that of other constitutional courts with individual access. Indeed, out of 136 judgments delivered against Serbia, the Constitutional Court is cited roughly in half of them, 69.[303]

Looking at the graph above (Fig. 4.9), it is possible to see how in the last 5 years, the ratio of judgments with CCSB citations out of the total number of judgments delivered against Serbia is comparable to that of constitutional with individual direct access (roughly 86%), whereas in the first years following the Montenegro secession in 2006, the ratio is below 50%. This statistical evidence thus seems to confirm what was observed in constitutional scholarship concerning the marginal role of the

[300] See: *Declaration by the Committee of Ministers of the Council of Europe on Continuation by the Republic of Serbia of Membership of the State Union of Serbia and Montenegro*, Decl-14.06.2006/1E /14 June 2006, available at: https://rm.coe.int/16807215cd.

[301] See to that effect: *Opinions of the Constitutional Court regarding Proceedings on Consideration and Adjudicating on Constitutional Complaint*, nos. 1-8/11/09, 2 April 2009; cited in: Popović and Marinković (2016).

[302] The text of the law, translated into English, is available on the official website of the Serbian Constitutional Court: http://www.ustavni.sud.rs/page/view/en-GB/237-100030/law-on-the-constitutional-court.

[303] All 46 judgments were obtained using the keyword 'constitutional court'.

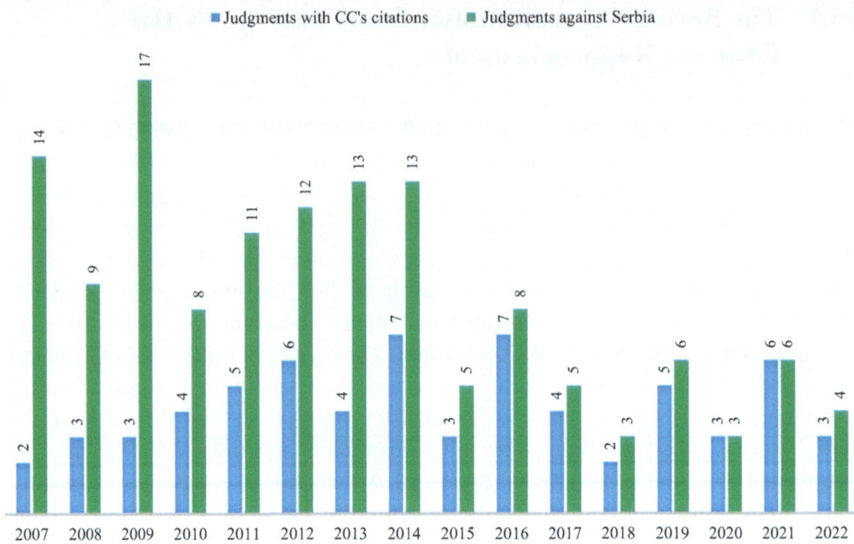

Fig. 4.9 Judgments with CCSB citations per year (2007—2022)

Serbian Constitutional Court during the transition to democracy and its consolidation, as well as the causal link between the possibility of individual access to the constitutional court and the latter presence in the ECtHR case law.[304] As for the average number of mentions of the word 'constitutional court' in each judgment, the overall average is roughly 8,5 whilst the average for the last 5 years is almost double that figure: 16. In this sense, the ECtHR case law against Serbia seems to confirm the overall trend of an increased attention towards constitutional case law.

Concerning the effectiveness of the individual constitutional appeal, it must be emphasised that the ECtHR, ever since the *Vinčić and Others* judgment, has considered the individual appeal of Article 170 of the Constitution to be an effective remedy that must be exhausted before an individual can turn to Strasbourg. Significantly, the date from which the ECtHR considers this remedy to be effective is the

[304]The main cause of this irrelevance is to be attributed to the Constitutional Court's traditional deference towards the political majorities. See: Papic and Djeric (2018), pp. 60–63.

date of the first substantive ruling of the CCSB, i.e. 7 August 2008.[305] The case law against Serbia is particularly interesting for analysing the effectiveness of constitutional complaints. A first aspect is the relevance under Article 35 ECHR of procedural requirements with a substantive dimension. To this regard, Article 85(2) of the Constitutional Court Act, according to which complaints raised before the Constitutional Court should be properly substantiated and corroborated with the proper evidence, came under the lens of the Strasbourg. In *Aktiva DOO*, the applicant's appeal was declared inadmissible by the CCSB for being incomplete, as it failed to specify the constitutional provisions whose breach was alleged.[306] Before the ECtHR, the Serbian Government asked the Court to declare the application inadmissible pursuant to the established principle obliging applicants to use domestic remedies observing the formal and procedural requirements established by national law.[307] The ECtHR however decided to dismiss the Government's objection, censuring the Constitutional Court's excessive formalism, and even affirming that "it appears that the applicant company's initial constitutional appeal fully complied with Article 85 § 1 of the Law on the Constitutional Court" thus essentially providing an autonomous interpretation of the admissibility rules of constitutional complaints which prevails over that of the CCSB.[308]

The judgment in *Popovic and Others* instead concerns situations in which applicants have a plurality of constitutional remedies at their disposal.[309] The Serbian Government submitted that since the violations alleged by applicants were caused by a provision of a legislative act, instead of using the constitutional complaint of Article 170 of the Serbian Constitution, they should have lodged an application for the assessment of the constitutionality of legislation under Article 168(2) of the Constitution, which is essentially an *actio popularis*, as any individual can submit the application to the Constitutional Court. The Strasbourg Court dismissed the Government's objection reaffirming that "where more than one potentially effective remedy is available, the applicant is only required to use one remedy of his or her own choosing" and since the individual constitutional complaint

[305] *Vinčić and Others v. Serbia* (44698/06, 44700/06, 44722/06) 01/12/2009, para. 51. The term applies also retroactively, meaning that before that date applicants were not required to lodge a constitutional complaint. This retrospective application, which is contrary to the principle according to which it is incumbent on the applicant to test the effectiveness of national remedies, also produces some paradoxical consequences. In the *Cupara* case indeed the Strasbourg Court declares admissible an appeal lodged on 4 July 2008, thus 1 month before the deadline from which a constitutional appeal is considered an effective remedy, even though the applicant did not lodged a constitutional complaint. The judgment then declared that the appellant's right to a fair trial was not violated because the "Constitutional Court was *at the relevant time* a part of the mechanism capable of remedying the case-law inconsistencies". Considering the casuistic approach of the ECHR to the admissibility of appeals, such a decision, the judgment's formalism, appears hardly comprehensible. See: *Cupara v. Serbia* (34683/08), 12/07/2016.

[306] *Aktiva DOO v. Serbia* (23079/11), 19/01/2021, paras 24–26.

[307] Ibidem, para. 61.

[308] Ibidem, para. 65.

[309] *Popovic and Others v. Serbia* (26944/13), (14616/16), (14619/16), 30/06/2020.

of Article 170 has to be considered an effective remedy, the judgment reaches the conclusion "the applicants could not have been required to pursue yet another avenue of potential redress before the very same court".[310] Noteworthy, the judgment does not enter into the issue of the effectiveness under Article 35 ECHR of the *actio popularis*, leaving unanswered the applicants' submission on the point.[311]

Regarding the applicability of due process guarantees to constitutional jurisdiction, only on two occasions did the ECtHR apply Article 6 ECHR to the CCSB. In the *Tešić* case, the Strasbourg judges considered the application, which complained about the excessive duration of the constitutional trial, to be manifestly unfounded as the trial had only lasted just under 3 years.[312] Apart from declaring the application unfounded—a practice already seen in some judgments against Croatia, and which confirms the existence of a presumption of non-unreasonableness for proceedings of such duration[313]— it is surprising that the ECtHR mentions as a circumstance susceptible of imposing stricter standards in the evaluation of the reasonabless of the duration, the advanced age of the applicant. Conversely in *Milovanovic*, the ECtHR declared unreasonable a constitutional proceedings with a duration of three years and nine months, considering that "what was at stake for the applicant in the proceedings before the Constitutional Court was of considerable importance", i.e. his child custody.[314] The reasonable duration of proceedings before the CCSB was assessed also through the prism of Article 5(4) ECHR in *Stevan Petrović*.[315] In this case, the applicant complained that the Constitutional Court failed to guarantee his right to a speedy review of the lawfulness of his detention, as the CCSB took two years and ten months to declare his appeal inadmissible.[316] Despite such a duration for an inadmissibility decisions would hardly comply with general requirements under Article 5(4) ECHR, the ECtHR emphasises that the guarantee of speedy review only applies when the applicant is in pretrial detention. Hence, since two months after the applicant lodged his appeal, he was sentenced to 5 years and 6 months of imprisonment, the ECtHR declared that the applicant's complaint under Article 5(4) ECHR was manifestly ill-founded.[317]

With regard to the review of the conventionality of constitutional decisions, the ECtHR's scrutiny of constitutional judgments seems to have become progressively more intense. In the *Milojević* case, for example, the ECtHR used a precedent of the

---

[310] Ibidem, paras 58, 62.

[311] Ibidem, para. 54.

[312] *Tešić v. Serbia* (4678/07), (50591/12), 11/02/2014, para. 77.

[313] See *supra*, footnote 21.

[314] Milovanovic v. Serbia (56065/10), 08/10/2019, para. 89.

[315] *Stevan Petrović v. Serbia* (6097/16, 28999/19), 20/04/2021.

[316] Ibidem, para. 79.

[317] Ibidem, paras 177–179.

CCSB rendered in a an "almost identical" case to declare the violation of Art. 6 ECHR. The terminology used by the ECtHR—"the Court sees no reason to depart from the reasoning of the Constitutional court" -[318] combined with the virtual absence of autonomous reasoning,[319] makes it clear that the Strasbourg judges merely applied the constitutional judgment to the case before them, grounding its conclusion in constitutional case law. Conversely, in *Milenković*, a judgment delivered two months later, the ECtHR sanctions the CCSB for its failure to correctly apply the principle of *ne bis in idem* as elaborated in *Zolotukhin v. Russia.*[320] It must be noted that the judgment of the CCSB was delivered outside the context of the applicant's proceedings.[321] Nonetheless, the Strasbourg Court censures the CCSB interpretation, implicitly inviting it to bring its case law in line with ECHR standards. In *Mitrović*, on the other hand, the ECtHR uses a 'softer' approach. Although it disagreed with the CCSB on the outcome of the case, it engaged in a detailed justification of the reasons of the divergence: it emphasises that whilst the CCSB correctly applied the proportionality, it overlooked to carry out a preliminary step, the analysis of the lawfulness of the measure.[322]

As a last case demonstrating the intensity of the ECtHR scrutiny, it must be briefly considered the 2019 judgment in *Jevtovic.*[323] Before the Strasbourg Court, the applicant affirmed having been ill-treated and tortured by prison guards. In the course of domestic proceedings, the CCSB, deciding his constitutional appeal, recognised both a substantive and procedural violations of Article 3 ECHR, ordered an official investigation and awarded to appellant a compensation of € 1.000.[324] The CCSB however discarded that the applicant was subjected to ill-treatments amounting to torture. In light of this, the Serbian Government asked the ECtHR to declare the application inadmissible for lack of victim status (Article 34 ECHR). The ECtHR rejected the objection affirming that the CCSB did not find that the applicant was subjected to torture, and that in any case the amount of compensation was significantly lower than the usually awarded by the ECtHR itself. Nevertheless, in the judgment the ECtHR confirms the CCSB's findings that the ill-treatment suffered by the applicant did not amount to the torture, that the authority's investigation even after the constitutional court's decision was not effective, and then award a compensation of € 4.000 for non-pecuniary damage. The ECtHR judgment is thus a mere repetition of the CCSB's one, and one is left to wonder the added value both for the

[318] *Milojević and Others v. Serbia* (43519/0, 43524/07, 45247/07), 12/01/2016, para. 84.

[319] The *Court's Assessment* consists of only two paragraphs; the first explains the case law on the duty to state reasons for court orders, the second refers to the judgments of the Serbian Constitutional Court as reported in the factual part. See: Ibidem, paras. 83–84.

[320] See *Milenković v. Serbia* (50124/13), 01/03/2016, para. 48.

[321] Ibidem, para. 23.

[322] *Mitrović v. Serbia* (52142/12), 21/03/2017, paras 42–43.

[323] *Jevtovic v. Serbia* (29896/14), 03/12/2019.

[324] Ibidem, paras 35–36.

applicant—especially considering that the ECtHR took more than 5 years to reach its decision—and for a more effective protection of fundamental rights in Serbia.

All in all, the case law just examined indicates a gradual increase in the Strasbourg Court's attention to Serbian constitutional jurisprudence fully confirming quantitative data. This gradual rapprochement must be read in conjunction with a similar trend that has been observed at the national level.[325] At the same time, the case law against Serbia also seems to confirm that the scrutiny of the ECtHR over constitutional courts of new democracies appears to be more intense respect to the level of scrutiny practiced on constitutional courts of Western consolidated democracies. This enhanced degree of scrutiny, in the case of the Serbian Constitutional Court regards both its procedural requirements, as evidence in *Aktiva DOO*, and the substantive interpretation of the ECHR carried out by the CCSB, as exemplified in the *Milenković* and in the *Jevtovic* judgments.

4.14 The Slovak Constitutional Court. A Paradigmatic Example of Conventional Adjudicator

The Federal Republic of Czechoslovakia ratified the ECHR and its Protocols on 18 March 1992, when the separation of its constituent entities was an issue already on table. The Slovak Republic indeed proclaimed its independence just 8 months later, on 25 November 1992. In January 1993, in an official statement to the Committee of Ministers, Slovakia affirmed that it considered itself bound by the ECHR. On 30 June of the same year, the Committee of Ministers admitted Slovakia as a Member State of the Council of Europe without the need for further ratification of the Convention and its Protocols.[326]

A defining feature in the relationship between the Strasbourg Court and the Constitutional Court of the Slovak Republic (hereafter sometimes 'the CCSK') is the ECHR status in the domestic legal system which, according to Article 7(5) of the Constitution, enjoy supra-legislative status.[327] Further, Article 125(1a) of the Slovak Constitution expressly empowers the Constitutional Court to judge the conformity of laws adopting ratified international treaties as a benchmark.[328] Another element which contributes to a close relationship between the two levels of jurisdiction is the possibility of individual access to the CCSK. According to Article 127 of the Constitution, the content of which is specified in Article 49 of the

[325] See Popović and Marinković (2016), pp. 399–400.

[326] More on Slovakia's accession process to the Council of Europe see: Kryzanowska-Mierzewska (2008), pp. 534–536.

[327] The provisions refers to all international human rights treaties: Blaško (2001a), pp. 755–759.

[328] Additionally, the Slovak Constitutional Court has also affirmed that the ECHR and its jurisprudence of the Strasbourg Court constitute binding interpretative criteria for all national courts. See Blaško (2001b), p. 404.

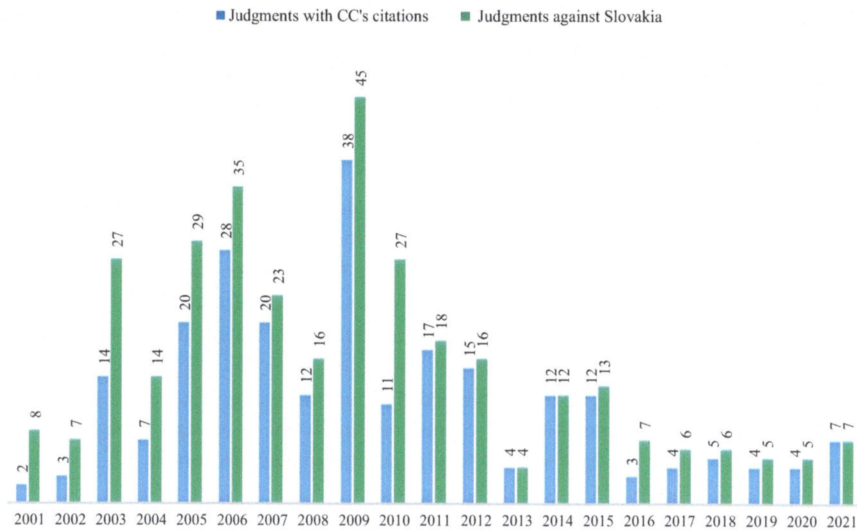

Fig. 4.10 Judgments with CCSK citations per year (2001—2022)

Constitutional Court Act,[329] individual can access to the CCSK to complain about the violation of a fundamental right, guaranteed by the Constitution or an international treaty, caused by an action or omission of a state authority. As a last preliminary remark, it must be emphasised that the CCSK—unlike the Constitutional Courts of Hungary and Poland—has insofar resisted the attacks and attempts of capture by political majorities, reaffirming its role as guardian of the national constitution.[330]

In the light of these brief introductory considerations, the robust presence of the CCSK in the conventional jurisprudence cannot come as a surprise: out of a total

[329] The English text of the Act was consulted on the CODICES database maintained by the Venice Commission. Available at: https://codices.coe.int/codices/documents/law/C3723E53-4F16-4D4D-848B-08DC0D38DFC5#ac3723e53-4f16-4d4d-848b-08dc0d38dfc5.

[330] The turning point was undoubtedly the 2019 constitutional crisis. On the 30 January the Constitutional Court issued a landmark decision affirming its competence to review the constitutionality of constitutional amendments. Just 2 weeks after, nine of the 13 seats of the Slovak Constitutional Court became vacant as a consequence of the blockade of the parliamentary majority led by the Smer Party, trying to push the candidacy of the right-wing populist Robert Fico as President of the Constitutional Court. The deadlock was resolved by the election, in March 2019, of a liberal pro-European president, Zuzana Čaputová. Following the election, Fico renounced to his plan and three constitutional judges were appointed, putting an end to the Constitutional Court paralysis. The full composition of the Constitutional Court was restored only in October 2019. For a commentary to the Constitutional Court decision see: Lalik (2020).

of 340 judgments rendered against Slovakia, the CCSK is cited in 272, a percentage of roughly 80%.[331] Even more significant is the figure for the average number of citations per judgment, which is 17.5, the highest among all the courts considered in this work.

The temporal distribution of citations shows, especially in the last decade, a reduction in the absolute number of CCSK citations per year (see Fig. 4.10), that largely coincided with a reduction in the overall number of judgments pronounced against Slovakia, something which may indicate the good functioning of the Slovakian machinery for fundamental rights protection. Given these statistical evidences, it cannot come as a surprise that the ECtHR has consistently affirmed that the Slovak constitutional appeal constitutes in principle an effective remedy whose exhaustion is required under Article 35 ECHR.[332]

A partial exception has been established by the Strasbourg Court with regard to the principle of reasonable duration of proceedings—the importance of which is preponderant in the case law against Slovakia, coming to the fore in no less than 72 judgments, roughly 25% of all the judgment in which the CCSK is cited.[333] Following an amendment to Article 127 of the Constitution, which came into force in January 2002, the Slovakian constitutional legislator gave the CCSK jurisdiction over complaints for excessive duration of proceedings, also granting it the power to impose peremptory time limits on the lower courts for the conclusion of proceedings, as well as the possibility of awarding compensation to the victim.[334] Despite that in the majority of the cases that have reached Strasbourg, the CCSK itself had recognised the excessive duration of the proceedings, the ECtHR declares the applications admissible because the compensation awarded by the CCSK is less than that calculated according to the ECHR parameters.[335] Substantively the Strasbourg Court simply assesses whether the criteria used by the CCSK to calculate compensation for the unreasonable duration of the trial, complies

[331] The search was conducted using the term 'constitutional court' which produced 270 results, and 'cour constitutionnelle' which produced 12 results, only one of which was not translated into English.

[332] Lastly see: *Visy v. Slovakia* (70288/13), 16/10/2018, para. 27.

[333] This data has been obtained using the HUDOC research tools. In particular, through combining the search in the judgments' text of the words "constitutional court" with the subject matter filter "(Article 6-1) Reasonable time".

[334] A brief chronology of the constitutional reform in question can be found in: *Ziacik v Slovakia* (43377/98), 27/01/2003, para. 25.

[335] See *ex multis*: *Palgutova v. Slovakia* (9818/02), 17/05/2005, para. 48; *Magura v. Slovakia* (44068/02), 13/06/2006, para. 34; *Cavajda v. Slovakia* (65416/01), 14/10/2008, para. 77; *Softel Spol S.R.O. v. Slovakia (No. 1)* (32427/06), 16/12/2008, para. 24; *Dvoracek and Dorackova v. Slovakia* (30754/04), 28/07/2009, para. 84; *Kis v. Slovakia* (3673/05), 13/10/2009, para. 7; *Fekiac and Fekiacova v. Slovakia* (39202/04), 11/10/2009, para. 10; *Petrincova v. Slovakia*, 11395/06, 08/12/2009; *Kucera v. Slovakia* (29749/05), 15/12/2009, para. 18; *Bíro v. Slovakia (No. 5)* (45109/06), 18/05/2010, para. 7; *Winkler v. Slovakia* (25416/07), 17/07/2012, para. 31.

with ECHR standards.[336] If not, the ECtHR declares a violation of Article 13 ECHR.[337] To put it otherwise, as the ECtHR case law currently stands, in applications alleging a breach of Article 6 ECHR, the Slovakian individual constitutional appeal represent an effective remedy under Article 35 ECHR but not under Article 13 ECHR.[338] This confusion seems to find its cause in the composite nature of the domestic system for remedying to failure to guarantee the right to an expedite trial; a situation which has also prompted the CCSK to intervene in proceedings before the Strasbourg Court with reports and even statements of its President,[339] or Vice President,[340] to clarify the nature of the Constitutional Court's scrutiny and the rules governing the admissibility of individual constitutional complaints.[341] In any case, such an approach by the Strasbourg Court generates doubts concerning the respect of the principle of subsidiarity, in fact the ECtHR *de facto* acts as a fourth instance with respect to the constitutional court, as the scope of its review is limited to assess whether the Constitutional Court correctly applied ECHR parameters as to the amount of economic compensation. Emblematic to this regard is the judgment in *Judt* where the Strasbourg Court declares admissible the application action brought despite the fact that the Constitutional Court awarded the applicant €740 as compensation for the excessive length of its proceedings, and then condemns the Slovak state to pay as compensation a further €1000.[342] Finally, even though, as we have just seen, one of the main structural problems in Slovakia are the excessive delays of ordinary proceedings, the Strasbourg Court has never condemned the Slovak state for the excessive length of the constitutional trial.[343]

There are instead a few rulings applying Article 6 ECHR to constitutional proceedings, the most notable being undoubtedly that on the *Harabin* case. The delicate political context in which the Strasbourg Court was called upon to intervene, a clash between the judiciary and the government,[344] leads the ECtHR to make it clear from

---

[336]The Strasbourg Court itself explains in detail the reasons justifying such an examination in: *Istvan and Istvanova* v. *Slovakia* (30189/07), 12/06/2012, paras. 69–75.

[337]See *Bublakova v. Slovakia* (17763/07), 15/02/2011, para. 31.

[338]Lastly see: *Balogh and Others v. Slovakia*, (35142/15), 31/08/2018, in particular, paras 51–66.

[339]*Zoltán Varga v. Slovakia* (58361/12), (25592/16), (27176/16), 20/07/2021, paras 77–81.

[340]*Engelhardt v. Slovakia* (12085/16), 31/08/2018, para. 26.

[341]*Istvan and Istvanova v. Slovakia*, paras 36–44. The same report is referred to by the ECtHR also in two successive judgments. See: *Komanicky v. Slovakia (No. 6)* (40437/07), 12/06/2012, paras 34–42; *Horváth v. Slovakia* (5515/09), 27/11/2012, paras 40–43.

[342]It should be noted incidentally that the ECtHR judgment was delivered 3 years after the constitutional's and that Judge Casadevall's dissenting opinion criticises the majority for having failed to compensate the applicant also for the protraction of the proceedings in Strasbourg. See, *Judt v. Slovakia* (70985/01), 09/10/2007, *Dissenting Opinion of Judge Casadevall*, paras. 2–3.

[343]On the contrary, the only judgment that we have retrieved declared the application manifestly unfounded because the trial had lasted 1 year and 4 months. See *Komanicky v. Slovakia (No. 3)* (72092/01), 17/06/2008.

[344]For an interesting framing of the *Harabin* affair within the broader framework of the attacks on the presidents of the supreme courts of Central and Eastern Europe, see the Dutch judge's essay to the Strasbourg Court: Schukking (2018).

the outset that the purpose of its judgment was exclusively to assess the fairness of the disciplinary proceedings against the applicant, the President of the Slovakian Supreme Court, that took place before the CCSK.[345] On this point, the ECtHR finds that the right to an impartial judge of the applicant was violated because two judges of the CCSK, despite having been validly recused by the applicant in previous proceedings, took part in the disciplinary proceedings against him. The judgment affirmed that the reasons invoked by the CCSK, namely the fact that the disciplinary proceedings against Supreme Court judges are reserved to the competence of the plenary, could not justify the participation of the two judges.[346] In order to reinforce this conclusion, the judgment notes that also six judges of the CCSK annotated a dissenting opinion arguing that the plenary would have been lawfully composed even without the previously recused judges.[347]

The *Čičmanec* judgment instead concerns the principle of adversarial process and essentially affirmed that the written observations of the judge whose decision is impugned before the CCSK must be communicated to the applicant.[348] Even if the judgment does not fully clarify whether this obligation arises from the fact that in Slovak constitutional proceedings the court that issued the impugned decision is a party in the constitutional proceedings, taking into account its established case law on the issue,[349] it can be safely concluded that this obligation can be extended to all constitutional proceedings.

On the subject of constitutional due process in the broader sense, another issue that comes to the fore is the possibility of extending the faculty of cross-examination to intervening third parties. In *Lopez Gujo*, the applicant, a father alleging to be the victim of a child abduction, after having succeeded in obtaining the return of his daughter from the Slovak Supreme Court, had his decision annulled by the CCSK, appealed by the mother. However, the Constitutional Court had failed to notify the father of the constitutional appeal and thus could not intervene in the trial. The ECtHR recognises the decisive importance of the fact that although the appllicant had an interest in it, the trial before the CCSK took place without his participation, and the violation of Article 8 ECHR ultimately seems to be determined by this procedural omission.[350] Following the judgment, the CCSK changed its practice and started, in child abduction cases, to notifying the appeal to the parent against whom the appeal was brought and allowing him/her to file written observations, without,

[345] *Harabin v. Slovakia* (58688/11), 20/11/2012, para. 113.

[346] Ibidem, para. 141.

[347] Ibidem, para. 50.

[348] *Čičmanec v. Slovakia* (65302/11), 28/06/2016, paras. 63–65.

[349] In particular see: *Gaspari v. Slovenia*; *Juričić v. Croatia*; *Gramaxo Rozeira v. Portugal*.

[350] It must be pointed out that, although the applicant had also invoked Article 6 ECHR, the judgment addresses the issue only from the angle of the right to respect for family life. See *López Gujó v. Slovakia* (10280/12), 03/06/2014, paras. 103–112.

however, being able to intervene directly in the proceedings.[351] Further evidence of the constant attention of the CCSK to ECtHR case law is provided by a series of judgments on the calculation of time limits for filing a constitutional appeal. More precisely, the practice of the CCSK to calculate separately for each decision of ordinary tribunals the time-limit to file a constitutional appeal under Article 127 of the Slovak Constitution. This jurisprudential orientation induced applicant to introduce concomitantly a cassation appeal before the Supreme Court and a constitutional appeal in order to not lose the possibility of challenging the substantive aspects of inferior courts' decisions.[352] In a first judgment of 2011 (*Stavebna Spolocnost Tatry Poprad*), the ECtHR censured this method of calculation for depriving applicants of access to the constitutional court. Similarly, in the *Zborovsky* judgment—decided one year later—the Strasbourg Court again condemned Slovakia, while recognising that in the meantime the CCSK had amended its practice in order to bring it in line with Article 6 requirements.[353] To this respect, it should be noted that this solution was proposed by the ECtHR in a judgement against Czechia—the already mentioned *Zvolsky et Zvolska* case—its reception by the CCSK hence constitutes further proof of its great attention to Strasbourg jurisprudence.

This high level of compliance with ECHR standards, seems to induce the Strasbourg Court to frequently rely on the conventionality review carried out by the CCSK, correspondingly narrowing the scope of its review. In *Schwarch, for* example, the ECtHR states that '[s]ince in its judgment of 30 March 2010 the Constitutional Court expressly acknowledged a breach of the applicant's right under Article 5 § 4 to a speedy review of the lawfulness of his detention, the only issue which arises in that respect in the present case is whether the redress afforded to him can be considered as appropriate',[354] without verifying whether this assessment by the CCSK corresponded to the ECHR criteria.[355] The high level of convergence of the two jurisprudences is well evidenced also in the judgment on the *Trade Union of the Police in the Slovak Republic and Others* case, where the ECtHR fully confirms the conventionality judgement made by the CCSK, which found the

[351] See *Frisancho Perea v. Slovakia* (383/13), 21/07/2015, para. 39. In fact, as can be learnt from the judgment, the CCSK cannot admit third-party intervention because it is not provided for in the Constitutional Court Act (para. 24).

[352] *Stavebna Spolocnost Tatry Poprad, S.R.O. v. Slovakia* (7261/06), 03/05/2011, paras. 18–19.

[353] *Zborovsky v. Slovakia* (14325/08), 23/10/2012, para. 34. In similar terms see also: *Franek v. Slovakia* (14090/10), 11/02/2014, para. 31; *Kovárová v. Slovakia* (46564/10), 23/06/2015, para. 43. In particular the CCSK held that that if applicants comply the 2 months statutory limit with respect to the last Supreme Court decision "the time-limit would be considered as having been respected also in respect of the previous decision of the court of appeal".

[354] *Schwarch v. Slovakia* (64528/09), 14/01/2014, para. 28.

[355] A similar approach can be found in: *Yegorov v. Slovakia* (27112/11), 02/06/2015, paras. 130–131.

interference with the applicant's freedom of association and expression to be proportionate.[356] One cannot fail to emphasise that these two rights are those that are interpreted most extensively by the Strasbourg Court, in this sense a validation of a conventionality judgment on this matter acquires greater specific weight.[357]

In conclusion, the relationship between the ECHR and the CCSK, as observed from Strasbourg, appears to be characterised by a maximum degree of loyalty, especially on the CCSK side.[358] This allowed a maximisation of the impact of conventional case law on the functioning of the Slovak justice system, which ultimately appears to be due to the acceptance by the CCSK that the effects of a Strasbourg judgment extend beyond the individual case.[359] Also, this loyalty substantiated in a more active form of cooperation, in which the CCSK, through its President or Vice-President, directly intervened in proceeding pending in Strasbourg to help the ECtHR have the clearest possible picture of the domestic legal system.

4.15 The Slovenian Constitutional Court as Passive Receptor of ECHR Standards

Slovenia is the first of the former Yugoslav states to have ratified the European Convention on Human Rights, on 31 May 1994. This testifies, as it has been observed, to the strong commitment of this small northern Balkan state to respect for human rights.[360] Article 8 of the Slovenian Constitution gives all published and ratified international treaties direct applicability in the domestic legal system. Moreover, Article 153 of the Constitution specifies that the status of international norms is hierarchically superior to that of the law. As far as the ECHR and international human rights treaties are concerned, Art. 15(5) Constitution stipulates that no fundamental right recognised by a norm in force in the Slovene legal system may be restricted on the grounds that it is not recognised by the Constitution. In essence, this provision can be said to confer constitutional status to the ECHR and its Protocols.[361]

[356] *Trade Union of the Police in the Slovak Republic and Others v. Slovakia* (11828/08), 25/09/2012, para. 74.

[357] It should be noted, however, that the judgment was adopted by a majority of 5 votes to 2, and the two dissenting judges had a joint opinion annotated, in which they claim that the interference was disproportionate. See, Ibidem, *Dissenting Opinion of Judge Myjer Joined by Judge Gyulumyan.*

[358] Similar conclusions are reached by: Bobek and Kosar (2010), p. 157.

[359] On this point, see: Kryzanowska-Mierzewska (2008), p. 551.

[360] On the importance of the protection of fundamental rights in Slovenia, see: Zobec (2016), p. 432.

[361] See Zobec (2016), p. 429.

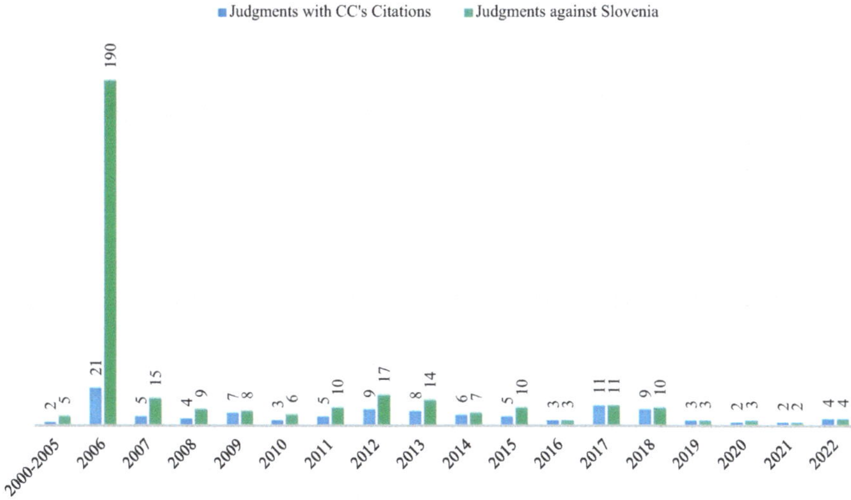

Fig. 4.11 Judgments with CCSL citations per year (2001—2022)

Concerning individual access to constitutional justice, Article 160 of the Constitution provides every individual with the right to bring an action before the Constitutional Court (hereinafter simply 'the CCSL') to complain about the unconstitutionality of an individualised act, be it a court judgment or an act of any other public authority. On the other hand, active conduct and omissions cannot be challenged; therefore, constitutional appeal has never been considered by the ECtHR an effective remedy in cases of unreasonable duration of proceedings.[362] To this regard, the Slovenian legislature in 2007, in order to remedy the backlog that was accumulating at the CCSL's registry, with a solution similar to the one adopted by the Spanish legislature, imposed stricter admissibility requirements for the constitutional appeal in Article 55b of the Constitutional Court Act, establishing two alternative criteria on the basis of which the CCSL assesses the possibility of accepting an appeal for decision: the seriousness of the injury complained of by the appellant, and the special constitutional relevance of the case.[363] Despite these limitations, coherently with its already examined position, the ECtHR has always maintained that applicants are required to lodge a constitutional complaint for

[362] See *Lukenda v. Slovenia* (23032/02), 06/10/2005, para. 65. For the development of domestic remedies for the reasonable length of proceedings, which in the current system no longer fall within the competence of the CCSL, see the judgment of the ECtHR in: *Sedminek v. Slovenia* (9842/07), 24/10/2013, paras 55–60; where a timely reconstruction of the discipline seen through the Strasbourg jurisprudence is offered.

[363] The English text of the standard can be found on the official website of the Slovenian CCSL at http://www.us-rs.si/media/constitutional.court.act.full.text.pdf).

domestic remedies to be considered exhausted for the purposes of Article 35 ECHR.[364] Concerning the requirement of the special constitutional importance, the ECtHR specifically affirmed that applicants cannot be considered to have failed to exhaust domestic remedies because they did not explicitly indicated to the Constitutional Court the constitutional significance of their case.[365]

The presence of both a subjective and objective criterion for declaring the inadmissibility of constitutional appeals results in a lower presence of the CCSL in the ECtHR jurisprudence compared to other courts that can receive individual complaints against mere conduct of the public administration such as the Spanish *Tribunal constitucional* or the German *Bundesverfassungsgerichthof.* In fact, out of a total of 328 judgments delivered against Slovenia, the CCSL is cited in 110, a percentage of just over 30%.[366] On the other hand, the average number of citations per judgment is comparable to that of the two constitutional courts mentioned above, being approximately 12.8 occurrences per judgment, as opposed to, for example, 12.7 occurrences for the *Bundesverfassungsgerichthof.*

Observing the graph of the temporal distribution of citations (Fig. 4.11), it is observable an increased interest from the part of the Strasbourg Court in Slovenian constitutional jurisprudence which manifested especially in the last 5 years, as the CCSL is now cited in almost all the augments delivered against Slovenia with an average of 25 citations per judgment. This data seems to confirm that the already observed switch in the posture of the Strasbourg Court towards constitutional case law is not limited to constitutional courts of established Western democracies.

As regards the applicability of Article 6 ECHR to constitutional proceedings the case law against Slovenia offers many interesting insights, ranging from the right to access to a court, to the principle of adversarial proceedings and the right to an impartial judge. Concerning the right to access to a court, we must first analyse the judgment in *Gros.*[367] Here, the applicant complained that the CCSL's rejection of its appeal for being out of time, violated its right to access to a court. In particular, the question concerned the subjective time limit of one year running from the moment in which the person learned of the occurrence of adverse consequences produced by the general measure to be impugned (Article 24(3) of the Constitutional Court Act). The ECtHR underlined that the applicant had justified its compliance with this subjective criterion with reasonable arguments, yet the CCSL "expected the applicant to show that he could not have done so earlier", without this expectation being

[364] Lastly see: *Rutar and Rutar Marketing D.O.O. v. Slovenia* (21164/20), 15/12/2022, paras. 39–44. Here the ECtHR also summarised its previous case-law on the effectiveness on the Slovenian constitutional appeal.

[365] Ibidem, para. 49.

[366] The 110 judgments were obtained by using the search string "constitutional court" which produced 106 results, supplemented by a search using the keyword "cour constitutionnelle" that produced 4 judgments that were not translated into English. See *Krisper v. Slovenia* (47825/99), 23/03/2006; *Mrkonjič v. Slovenia* (17360/02), 06/04/2006; *Digitel D.O.O. v. Slovenia* (70660/01), 15/06/2006; *Radojčič v. Slovenia* (4562/02), 13/07/2006.

[367] *Gros v. Slovenia* (45315/18), 07/07/2020.

based on any statutory requirement.[368] For this reason, the ECtHR declared that the CCSL imposed an excessive burden on the applicant which violated its right to access to the constitutional court. Essentially, the ECtHR is indicating to the CCSL the ECHR-compliant interpretation of the domestic procedural rules regulating the admissibility of constitutional complaints.

In *Tričković*, one of the first judgments delivered against Slovenia, the ECtHR was instead called upon to decide whether the CCSL had dealt with the applicant's case within a reasonable time.[369] With regard to this judgment, it should be emphasised that, although the Slovenian government had not objected to it, the ECtHR devoted a section of the judgment to examining the applicability of Article 6 ECHR to the constitutional proceeding,[370] this shows how in 2001, when *Tričković* was pronounced, the applicability of Article 6 ECHR to constitutional proceedings was not yet well consolidated. Despite a duration of the proceedings of only two years and seven months, the judgment examines in detail the activities carried out by the CCSL and concludes that, in light of the particular relevance of the case, the duration had not been excessive.[371] On the other hand, the judgment in *Hajrudinović*, which considers a duration of the constitutional proceeding of approximately three years to be excessive, may give rise to some perplexity.[372] The first reason for perplexity stems from the fact that the ECtHR fails to delimit, as is its custom, the period to be taken into consideration in assessing the reasonableness of the duration, limiting itself to stating the year 2000 as the date on which the constitutional appeal was lodged and quantifying the duration generically as "more than three years".[373] Such a statement, in relation to a duration that the same ECtHR has in other judgments held to be reasonable,[374] can only be explained in relation to the nature of the dispute, i.e. a dispute concerning the dismissal of the applicant. However, the lack of references to relevant precedents—including, for example, *Tsikakis c. Allemagne*,[375] and the lack of precision in stating the relevant temporal details makes the reasoning of the judgment hard to place it in the context of the previous case law on Article 6 ECHR.

---

[368] Ibidem, paras 28–30.

[369] *Tričković v. Slovenia* (39914/98), 12/06/2001.

[370] Ibidem, paras. 36–41.

[371] Ibidem, paras. 62–68.

[372] *Hajrudinović v. Slovenia* (69319/12), 21/05/2015.

[373] Ibidem, paras. 12, 37, 42.

[374] E.g. in *Kirsten v. Germany*, the HCHR had held that a constitutional trial duration within a range of 3 years and 6 months to 4 years and 8 months is in principle reasonable. See supra, Sect. 2.2, footnote 185.

[375] See: above, Sect. 3.2.

The judgment in *Švarc and Kavnik* deals instead with the question of the impartiality of the constitutional judge.[376] The appllicant, without having first raised the issue before the CCSL,[377] complained to the Strasbourg Court about the lack of impartiality of two of the three constitutional judges who had declared his appeal inadmissible for being manifestly unfounded. One of the judges composing the panel had in fact drafted an opinion, included in the applicant's case-file before the CCSL, at the request of the applicant's opponent in the proceedings, While the other, was a colleague of him at the University of Ljubljana. After declaring the doubts concerning the latter's judge impartiality to be completely unfounded,[378] the ECtHR focuses on the role of the former. In this regard, it notes that although there was no direct relationship between the opinion drafted before becoming a constitutional judge and the merits of the appeal, his mere involvement at an earlier stage of the same proceedings is sufficient to consider the appllicant's doubts well-founded.[379]

Also, on the subject of the impartiality of constitutional judges is the judgment in the *Hit D.D. Nova Gorica* case,[380] where, however, the issue is decidedly less controversial. In fact, one of the three judges of the panel that declared the inadmissibility of the constitutional appeal brought by the applicant, had also taken part as a judge in two different instances of the same proceedings. Although, from a simple reading of the facts of the case, the question seems to be decided *de plano*, the Strasbourg judgment nonetheless takes care to argue at length the reasons justifying the doubts as to the impartiality of the constitutional judge, showing how the affirmation of a judge's lack of impartiality, especially a constitutional one, can never be the result of a mechanical application of judicial precedents.

Concerning the principle of adversarial proceedings, in *Gaspari*, the Strasbourg Court sanctioned the CCSL for having failed to notify the applicant of the constitutional appeal lodged by the other party.[381] The judgment deserves to be noted above all because it shows that, despite the absence of a legal obligation, the CCSL followed the practice of notifying constitutional appeals to its counterparts—the notification in the case had failed due to an error in the address.[382]

---

[376] *Švarc and Kavnik v. Slovenia* (75617/01), 08/02/2007.

[377] The applicant had in fact only become aware of the composition of the panel at the time of the notification of the decision, but since Article 31 of the CCSL Act does not consider the drafting of a scientific opinion to be a valid ground for objection, the Court considers that such an objection cannot be considered effective for conventional purposes. Cf. ibidem., para. 27.

[378] Ibidem, para. 43.

[379] Ibidem, para. 44.

[380] *Hit D.D. Nova Gorica v. Slovenia* (50996/08), 05/06/2014.

[381] *Gaspari v. Slovenia* (21055/03), 21/07/2009.

[382] See, Ibidem., paras. 54–57; from which it can also be deduced that during the pendency of the conventional appeal, the Slovenian legislature introduced the obligation to notify the counterparties also for the Constitutional Court.

The most interesting element in the case law of the Strasbourg Court against Slovenia, at least for the purposes of this work, is the *Kurić and Others case.*[383] The case, in its essential lines,[384] concerned the deprivation of the right to citizenship of former citizens of the Federal Republic of Yugoslavia residing in Slovenia—but the problem also concerned the other republics of the former Yugoslavia—who found themselves stateless (the so-called *erased*) at the moment of the dissolution of the federation. Although, following a CCSL ruling, the Slovenian government had taken steps to recognise a right of permanent residence for those in this condition, the part of the constitutional ruling concerning the recognition of adequate compensation had remained unexecuted. Therefore, the Grand Chamber while positively noting the regularisation of the status of the *erased*, decided to adopt a pilot judgment under Rule 61 of the Court's Rules of Procedure in order to oblige the Slovenian State to provide for a compensation mechanism.[385] The judgment in *Kurić and Others* has been interpreted as a sign of the alliance between the Strasbourg Court and the CCSL, as the judgments of the two Courts seem to reinforce each other.[386] Indeed, it is difficult to imagine that in the absence of domestic constitutional jurisprudence affirming the necessity of providing for an adjustment of compensation to the *erased*, the ECtHR would have in any case adopted a pilot judgment, moreover of doubtful effectiveness in the concrete case. On the other hand, from the CCSL's point of view, the delivery of a pilot judgment meant a sanction of validity conferred to its ruling by an international tribunal, as well as a reminder that constitutional judgments should not be left unexecuted.[387]

In conclusion, the ECtHR jurisprudence examined in this paragraph shows a full subjection of the Slovenian constitutional process to the Strasbourg jurisprudence, signalled, *inter alia*, by the absence of any challenge by the Government to the applicability of Article 6 ECHR to constitutional jurisdiction. On the other hand, with the notable exception of the *Kurić and Others* judgment, there are no significant cases of dialogue between the two jurisdictions; nor it is possible to have insight from a reading of the ECtHR case law, about conventionality judgments carried out by the CCSL.[388]

[383] The case was first decided by the Third Chamber (13/07/2010), then, at the request of the Slovenian government, by the Grand Chamber (26/06/2012), and finally again by the Grand Chamber to verify the remedy (12/03/2014).

[384] For a more detailed reconstruction of the facts of the case see: Schneebaum (2014)

[385] See *Kurić and Others v. Slovenia* (26828/06), 26/06/2012, para. 415.

[386] Zobec (2016), p. 444.

[387] On the different extent of the obligation to execute a pilot judgment, see: Glas (2016), p. 59.

[388] Indeed, two cases of what could be called *weak review can be* found in this sense. The first is the *Matko* judgment (43393/98, 02/11/2006), in which the ECHR declares *en passant* the conventionality of the CCSB's new jurisprudence (paras. 66, 95). The second, more relevant, is the one contained in *Korelc* (*28456/03*, 12/05/2009) where the ECHR states that "Constitutional Court assessed the relevant facts in the light of the same criteria as the Court applies in similar cases" and that therefore the applicant's right to a fair trial was not violated (paras. 93–94).

4.16 The ECtHR Relationship with the Central Eastern European Constitutional Courts. Preliminary Conclusions

If we are to describe the relationship between the Strasbourg and CEE constitutional courts with a "one fits all" definition, the best one would be to label the relationship as one of faithful partnership. There are of course more than a couple of 'white flies', but in general CEE constitutional courts seem to have maintained the high degree of compliance with ECHR case law that characterised their jurisprudence in the first years after the democratic transition.[389] Consider for instance the 2022 judgment in *Alexandru Radu*, where the ECtHR took notes of how the Romanian Constitutional Court aligned the criminal procedure before the pre-trial judge with the exigencies of Article 6 ECHR[390]; or how the same Romanian court promptly executed the ECtHR judgement in the *N. (no.1)* case by declaring unconstitutional the provisions of the Civil Code incompatible with the ECHR.[391] Besides, CEE constitutional courts tend to abide by ECtHR judgments even if this implies changing their case law or practice. The Croatian Constitutional Court, for instance, changed its case law concerning procedural guarantees in eviction proceedings to implement the *dicta* of the ECtHR in *Ćosić* and *Paulić*.[392] Also, when it comes to the constitutional court's own procedure, the ECtHR did not shy away from ruling several times on similar applications in order to stimulate the constitutional court to change its practice.[393] However, sometimes this is not even necessary: as we have seen the Slovak Constitutional Court, for example, amended its method of calculation of the time limits for submitting a constitutional complaint to align it with the calculation

[389] For a comprehensive comparative review of the role of national constitutional courts in the implementation of the ECHR during democratic transitions see: Motoc and Ziemele (2016).

[390] *Alexandru-Radu Luca v. Romania* (20837/18), 14/06/2022.

[391] *N. v. Romania (No. 2)* (38048/18), 16/11/2021.

[392] See: *ĆosiĆ v. Croatia*, (28261/06) 15/01/2009; *PauliĆ v. Croatia* (3572/06), 22/10/2009. More generally, on the role of the Croatian Constitutional Court in ECHR implementation see: Turkovič and Omejec (2016).

[393] See, for example, the *judicial chain that* began with the *Pesa v. Croatia* (40523/08), 08/04/2010 consisting of 12 judgments with which the European Court of Human Rights is trying to induce the Croatian Constitutional Court to modify its practice of declaring inadmissible appeals for review of the legality of pre-trial detention solely on the ground that a new court order extending the duration of the detention has been made pending the appeal. See *Hadi v. Croatia* (42998/08), 01/07/2010; *Getos Magdic v. Croatia* (56305/08), 02/12/2010; *Bernobic v. Croatia* (57180/09), 21/06/2011; *Krnjak v. Croatia* (11228/10), 28/06/2011; *Trifkovič v. Croatia* (36653/09), 06/11/2012; *Osmanović v. Croatia* (67604/10), 06/11/2012; *Perica Oreb v. Croatia* (0824/09), 31/10/2013; *Margaretić v. Croatia* (16115/13), 05/06/2014; *V. R. v. Croatia* (55102/13), 13/10/2015; *Jović v. Croatia* (45593/13), 13/10/2015.

method contained in an ECtHR judgment delivered against another Respondent State.[394] That the CCSK is an enthusiastic supporter of the ECHR system also emerges from the various interventions of statements of its President,[395] or Vice President,[396] in the proceedings in Strasbourg to help the ECtHR have a clear picture of domestic law. This high degree of compliance from the part of constitutional courts is matched by an ECtHR jurisprudence which has progressively expanded the scope of Article 6 ECHR to include the most fundamental aspects of the constitutional justice system, from the constitutional courts' deliberative procedures,[397] to the procedure for the appointment and removal of constitutional judges.[398]

Another characteristic feature of the Strasbourg Court's relationship with CEE constitutional courts, especially compared with that with Western constitutional courts, is the lack of a fundamental rights dialogue intended as an exchange of views between the two courts on the content of a fundamental right.[399] Despite the fact that, except for the Bulgarian and Romanian courts, all CEE constitutional courts have an individual complaint mechanism and thus are routinely called to apply ECHR precedents in cases pending before them, they rarely challenge the ECtHR interpretation of fundamental rights. If we exclude the case of the Polish Constitutional Tribunal, which will be discussed afterwards, CEE constitutional courts are indeed mainly passive receptors of ECHR standards.[400] This passivity may be explained by two intertwined factors. On the one hand, many of the constitutional courts of the region still operate in "a politically precarious position",[401] which means that they have to defend their role as counter-majoritarian

[394] Amongst many see: *Kovárová v. Slovakia* (46564/10), 23/06/2015, para. 43. For another instance in which the Slovak Constitutional Court proactively implemented ECtHR judgments see: Petrov (2018), p. 514.

[395] *Zoltán Varga v. Slovakia* (58361/12, 25592/16, 27176/16), 20/07/2021, paras 77–81.

[396] *Engelhardt v. Slovakia* (12085/16), 31/08/2018, para. 26.

[397] *Marini v. Albania* (3738/02), 18/12/2007; *Avdić and Others v. Bosnia and Herzegovina* (28357/11 et al.), 19/11/2013

[398] The subjection of such procedures to the application of Article 6 ECHR depends exclusively on the presence, at the domestic level, of a judicial remedy to complain about possible irregularities, as required for all procedures concerning removal and appointment of public servants by the test developed by the Court in *Vilho Eskelinen T Vilho Eskelinen and Others v. Finland* (63235/00), 19/04/2007, paras. 61–62.

[399] Kosar and Petrov observe for instance that the Czech Constitutional Court is developing a more confident style of adjudication, defending Czech constitutional identity within the EU, however, this assertiveness did not manifest insofar within the ECHR system. See: Kosar and Petrov (2017), pp. 616–617.

[400] Ulfstein argues that such a passivity is ultimately detrimental to the well-functioning of the ECHR system, as national courts, and especially constitutionals ones, should act as "mediators" between national law and. See: Ulfstein (2016), p. 57.

[401] Sadurski (2009), p. 439. The persistent validity of this assessment is confirmed by all the main indexes for measuring democracy.

bulwarks in the constitutional order against attacks coming from the legislative and executive branches. It is thus obvious that courts in this position will tend to rely on, rather than challenge, the authority of Strasbourg's judgments.[402] Also, for countries wishing to enter the European Union, i.e. Albania, Bosnia and Herzegovina, Montenegro, North Macedonia, and Serbia, the compliance with, and faithful implementation of, ECtHR judgments is a criterion explicitly taken into account by the Commission in its pre-accession reports.[403] Just to give an example, in the 2023 Montenegro Report, the Commission has invited the Montenegrin Constitutional Court to ensure that the duration of constitutional proceedings remains in line with ECHR standards to guarantee that the "effectiveness of the constitutional complaint as a legal remedy in that country".[404] Hence, at least in countries with a genuine political will to enter the EU, this is another incentive for constitutional courts to avoid challenges to the Strasbourg Court's interpretative authority.[405]

Finally, to complete the picture of the relationship between the Strasbourg Court and the CEE constitutional courts is necessary to briefly consider the Strasbourg Court's relationship with populist captured constitutional courts, i.e. the Polish Constitutional Tribunal and the Hungarian Constitutional Court. The first thing to be said is that the ECtHR posture *vis-à-vis* those two courts has been radically different. On the one hand, with the landmark judgment in *Xero Flor v. Poland*, the ECtHR declared that the composition of the PCT was unlawful, as long as it included one of the three judges unlawfully elected in December 2015.[406] As well-known, the ruling triggered a harsh reaction from the PCT, which declared the

[402] Sadurski argues that this is the most significant institutional factor motivating constitutional courts to build 'a strong alliance' with the ECtHR. On the point see: Sadurski (2009), p. 438. For a detailed analysis on how the domestic political context can impact the constitutional courts implementation of ECtHR judgments see instead: Kosar and Petrov (2017), pp. 618–621.

[403] See, for instance, the Albania Report accompanying the 2023 Communication on EU Enlargement Policy, where it is positively noted that Albania "continues to ensure good cooperation with the European Court of Human Rights". See: SWD(2023) 690 final, *Albania 2023 Report*, 29. available at: https://neighbourhood-enlargement.ec.europa.eu/albania-report-2023_en. Conversely in 2023 Moldavia Report, the Commission criticise Moldavian authorities for their failure to implement ECtHR judgements concerning the rights of prisoners. See: *2023 Moldavia Report*.

[404] The Report is included in the 2023 Communication on EU Enlargement Policy. SEE: SWD (2023)*Montenegro 2023 Report*, 694 final, p. 40. Available at: https://neighbourhood-enlargement.ec.europa.eu/document/download/e09b27af-427a-440b-a47a-ed5254aec169_en?filename=SWD_2023_694%20Montenegro%20report.pdf.

[405] And it may also contribute to explain the enhanced assertiveness of the ECtHR case law with respect to CEE constitutional courts. For an overall assessment of the efficacy of the rule of law conditionality in the EU accession process see: Kochenov (2008).

[406] The innovative nature of this ruling cannot be overestimated, as it allows the Strasbourg Court to review the compatibility with the ECHR of judicial appointments—and removal—without the necessity to carry out the *Vilho Eskelinen* test.

unconstitutionality of Article 6 ECR inasmuch as it applies to constitutional courts.[407] Faced with such a serious challenge to its interpretative authority, the Strasbourg Court decided to adopt an even stronger stance, as it started to treat the judgments of the PCT adopted with the participation of the three unlawfully unelected judges as non-existent.[408] Conversely, the attitude of the Strasbourg Court following the illiberal turn in Hungary appears to be characterised by avoiding an open delegitimisation of the HCC. For instance, in a series of judgments finding a violation by Hungarian authorities of the applicant's freedom of expression, the Strasbourg Court engages with the relevant precedents of the HCC without pointing at the abusiveness of the HCC's interpretation or the fact that its composition does not comply with the rule of law principles.[409] It has to be noted that the HCC, insofar, never openly challenged the authority of the Strasbourg Court. This seems, in fact, to be part of a wider strategy of the HCC, which, in the EU context, has also carefully avoided entering into open confrontation with the Court of Justice.[410]

References

Alimehmeti E (2011) The evolution of the constitutional system in Albania. Academicus Int Sci J 3: 164–174

Antos M (2012) Constitutional complaint and its limits in Czech Republic. Charles University, Prague

Arato A (2016) Post sovereign constitution making: learning and legitimacy. Oxford University Press, Oxford

Attila Tóth G (ed) (2012) Constitution for a disunited nation: on Hungary's 2011 fundamental law. Central University Press, Budapest

Bárd K (2016) Hungary. The legal order of Hungary and the European convention on human rights. In: Motoc J, Ziemele I (eds) The impact of the ECHR on democratic change in central and Eastern Europe. Cambridge University Press, Cambridge, pp 176–200

Bánkuti M, Halmai G, Sheppele K (2012) Hungary's illiberal turn: disabling the constitution. J Democr 23:138–146

Bianku L (2016) Albania's long path towards European human rights standards. In: Motoc J, Ziemele I (eds) The impact of the ECHR on democratic change in central and Eastern Europe. Cambridge University Press, Cambridge, pp 13–38

Blaško M (2001a) Slovak Republic. In: Blackburn R, Polakiewicz J (eds) Fundamental rights in Europe. Oxford University Press, New York, pp 755–759

[407] Judgments of the Polish Constitutional Tribunal: No. K-6/21, of 24 November 2021; No. K-7/21 of 10 March 2022. The English translation of those judgments can be found on the website of the PCT at: https://trybunal.gov.pl/en/hearings/judgments?tx_ttnews%5Bpointer%5D=2&cHash=0c41b5df97798cc9782e6a06c4cae868.

[408] *M.L. v. Poland* (40119/21), 14/12/2023, para. 175.

[409] Despite the abusiveness of the HCC's interpretations and its capture by the ruling majority have been denounced by various parts. Amongst many see: Bánkuti et al. (2012), who talk of a "captured" constitutional court.

[410] See: Halmai (2022), available at: https://verfassungsblog.de/coping-strategies-of-the-hungarian-constitutional-court-since-2010/.

Blaško M (2001b) Slovakia. How the convention has helped Slovakia in its transition to a consolidated democracy. In: Motoc J, Ziemele I (eds) The impact of the ECHR on democratic change in central and Eastern Europe. Cambridge University Press, Cambridge, pp 401–424
Bobek M, Kosar D (2010) The application of European Union law and the law of the European convention of human rights in The Czech Republic and Slovakia: an overview. In: Martinico G, Pollicino O (eds) The National Judicial Treatment of the ECHR and EU Laws. A comparative constitutional perspective. Europa Law Publishing, Groningen, pp 157–190
Dedja B (2018) The role of constitutional court of Albania on the protection of human rights the Albanian perspective. Anayasa Yargısı 35:321–324
Duculescu V (2004) La réforme constitutionnelle en Roumanie et les exigences de l'intégration européenne. Revue Internationale de Droit Comparé 56:193–202
Ellis MS (2016) Purging the past: the current status of lustration Laws in the former communist bloc. Law Contemp Probl 59:181–196
Elster J (1991) Constitutionalism in Eastern Europe: an introduction. Univ Chic Law Rev 58:447–482
Favoreu L, Mastour W (1996) Les cours constitutionnelles. Presse Universitaire Française, Paris
Fromont (1996) La justice constitutionnelle dans le monde. Dalloz, Paris
Gárdos-Orosz F (2012) The Hungarian constitutional court in transition. From Actio Popularis to constitutional complaint. Acta Juridica Hungarica 53:302–315
Garlicki L, Kondak I (2016) Poland. Human rights between international and constitutional law. In: Motoc J, Ziemele I (eds) The impact of the ECHR on democratic change in central and Eastern Europe. Cambridge University Press, Cambridge, pp 308–309
Glas LR (2016) The functioning of the pilot-Judgement procedure of the European court of human rights in practice. Netherlands Q Human Rights 34:41–70
Jočienė D (2016) Lithuania. The European convention on human rights in the Lithuanian legal system: the lessons learned and perspectives for the future. In: Motoc J, Ziemele I (eds) The impact of the ECHR on democratic change in central and Eastern Europe. Cambridge University Press, Cambridge, pp 234–265
Kochenov D (2008) EU enlargement and the failure of conditionality: pre-accession conditionality in the field of democracy and the rule of law. Kluwer Law International, Alphen aan den Rijn
Keller H, Stone Sweet A (2008) A Europe of rights. The impact of the ECHR on national legal systems. Oxford Univerisity Press, New York
Kloth M (2010) Immunities and the right of access to court under article 6 of the European convention on human rights. Martinus Nijhoff, Leiden
Kosar D, Petrov J (2017) The strasburg system of human rights: the crucial role of the domestic level and the constitutional courts in particular. Zeitschrift für ausländisches öftentliches Recht und Völkerrecht 77:585–621
Kosař D, Vyhnánek V (2020) The constitutional court of Czechia. In: Bogdandy von A, Huber P (eds) The max Planck handbooks in European public law: volume III: constitutional adjudication: institutions. Oxford University Press, Oxford, pp 119–182
Kovacs K (2011) Cooperative decision-making: the relation between Hungary and Strasbourg. Vienna J Int Const Law 5:188–199
Kryzanowska-Mierzewska M (2008) The reception process in Poland and Slovakia. In: Keller H, Stone Sweet A (eds) A Europe of rights. Oxford University Press, Oxford, pp 531–602
Kūris E (2004) Constitutional justice in Lithuania: the first decade. Constitutional justice and the rule of law. Constitutional Court of the Republic of Lithuania, Vilnius
Lalik T (2020) The Slovak constitutional court on unconstitutional constitutional amendment (PL. ÚS 21/2014). Eur Const Law Rev 16:328–343
Leloup M (2023) The untapped potential of the systemic criterion in the ECJ's case law on judicial Independence. German Law J 24:995–110
Majerčík L (2016) Czech Republic: Strasbourg case law undisputed. In: Popelier et al (eds) Criticism of the European court of human rights. Intersentia, Cambridge, pp 131–153

Mercuri E, Anastasi A (2017) The reform of justice in Albania and the extension of the individual access in the constitutional court. In: Bozheku et al (eds) La riforma costituzionale "strutturale" del sistema della giustizia nella Repubblica d'Albania. Riflessioni a confronto con il sistema italiano. Nuova Cultura, Rome, pp 39–54

Mits M (2016) Latvia. Consolidating democratic changes in Latvia: and various roles of the European convention on human rights. In: Motoc J, Ziemele I (eds) The impact of the ECHR on democratic change in central and Eastern Europe. Cambridge University Press, Cambridge, pp 201–233

Morrison LF (1996) The constitution of Bosnia and Herzegovina. Const Comment 13:145–157

Murauskas D (2021) Legal developments during 30 years of Lithuanian Independence. In: Švedas G, Murauskas D (eds) Overview of legal accomplishment and challenges in Lithuania. Springer Publishing, Cham, pp 205–224

Olivetti M, Groppi T (2003) La giustizia constitutionale in Europa. Giuffrè, Milano

Omejec J (2016) A study on European constitutional court as the courts of human rights. Assessment, challenges, perspectives. In: SNU Asia Pacific Law Institute (ed) Global constitutionalism and multi-layered protection of human rights. Exploring the possibility of establishing a regional human rights mechanism in Asia. Constitutional Court of Korea, Seoul, pp 339–418

Papic T, Djeric V (2018) On the margins of consolidation: the constitutional court of Serbia. Hague J Rule Law 10:59–82

Pech L, Platon S (2018) Judicial independence under threat: the court of justice to the rescue in the ASJP case. Common Market Law Rev 55:1827–1854

Pech L, Wachowiec P, Mazur D (2021) Poland's rule of law breakdown: a five-year assessment of EU's (in)action. Hague J Rule Law 13:1–43

Pejchal A (2016) Czech Republic. Democratic tradition, legitimacy of confiscation, and translation of the case law of the ECtHR in the light of the convention in The Czech Republic. In: Motoc J, Ziemele I (eds) The impact of the ECHR on democratic change in central and Eastern Europe. Cambridge University Press, Cambridge, pp 136–152

Popović D, Marinković T (2016) The emergence of the human rights protection in Serbia under the European convention on human rights: the experience of the first ten years. In: Motoc J, Ziemele I (eds) The impact of the ECHR on democratic change in central and Eastern Europe. Cambridge University Press, Cambridge, pp 373–400

Petrov J (2018) Unpacking the partnership: typology of constitutional courts' roles in implementation of the European Court of Human Rights' case law. European Constitutional Law Rev 14: 499–531

Rainey B, McCormick P, Ovey C (2020) Jacobs, white, and Ovey: the European convention on human rights. Oxford University Press, Oxford

Sadurski W (2009) Partnering with Strasbourg: Constitutionalization of the European court of human rights, the accession of central and east European states to the Council of Europe, and the idea of pilot judgments. Hum Rights Law Rev 9:397–453

Sadusrki W (2008) Partnering with Strasbourg: Constitutionalization of the European Court of Human Rights, the Accession of Central and East European States to the Council of Europe, and the Idea of Pilot Judgments. EUI Working Papers, No. 33/2008, 17–21

Sadusrki W (2019) Poland's constitutional breakdown. Oxford University Press, Oxford

Schneebaum SM (2014) Introductory note to Kurić and others v. Slovenia & Kurić and others v. Slovenia (just satisfaction). Int Leg Mater 53:1073–1160

Schukking J (2018) Protection of human rights and the rule of law in Europe: a shared responsibility. Netherlands Q Human Rights 36:152–158

Simonelli MA (2019) Towards a theory of unconventional constitutional amendments. Some lessons from the Baka case. DPCE Online 39:1561–1577

Sólyom L (2020) The max Planck handbooks in European public law: volume III: constitutional adjudication: institutions. Oxford University Press, Oxford, pp 359–360

Sonnevend P, Jakab A, Csink L (2015) The constitution as an instrument of everyday party politics: the basic law of Hungary. In: Bogdandy von A, Sonnevend P (eds) Constitutional crisis in the European constitutional area. Hart Publishing, Oxford, pp 33–110

Szmulik B, Poglodek A (2016) The constitutional complaint in the polish supreme law. Espaço Jurídico J Law 17:29–46

Szwed M (2022) The polish constitutional tribunal crisis from the perspective of the European convention on human rights. Eur Const Law Rev 18:132–154

Trajkovska ML, Trajkovski I (2016) The impact of the European convention on human rights and the case law on the Republic of Macedonia. In: Motoc J, Ziemele I (eds) The impact of the ECHR on democratic change in central and Eastern Europe. Cambridge University Press, Cambridge, pp 266–288

Turkovič K, Omejec J (2016) Commitment to reform: assessing the impact of the ECtHR's case law on reinforcing democratisation efforts in Croatian legal order. In: Motoc J, Ziemele I (eds) The impact of the ECHR on democratic change in central and Eastern Europe. Cambridge University Press, Cambridge, pp 110–135

Ulfstein G (2016) The European Court of Human Rights and national courts: a constitutional relationship? In Anaradóttir O.M, Buyse A (eds.) Shifting centres of gravity in human rights protection. Routledge, London, pp 46–58

Vehabović F (2016) Impact of the case law of the European court of human rights on postconflict society of Bosnia and Herzegovina. In: Motoc J, Ziemele I (eds) The impact of the ECHR on democratic change in central and Eastern Europe. Cambridge University Press, Cambridge, pp 80–109

Vučinić NB (2016) Montenegro. The effect of the European convention on human rights on the legal system of Montenegro. In: Motoc J, Ziemele I (eds) The impact of the ECHR on democratic change in central and Eastern Europe. Cambridge University Press, Cambridge, pp 289–304

Vyhnánek L (2017) A holistic view of the Czech constitutional court approach to the ECtHR's case law. Heidelberg J Int Law 77:715–744

Ziemele I (2016) Conclusions. In: Motoc J, Ziemele I (eds) The impact of the ECHR on democratic change in central and Eastern Europe. Cambridge University Press, Cambridge, Judicial Perspectives, pp 493–495

Ziemele I, Spale A, Jurcēna L (2020) The constitutional court of the Republic of Latvia. In: Bogdandy von A, Huber P.M, Grabenwarter C (eds.) The max Planck handbooks in European public law 3. Oxford University Press, pp. 506-563

Zobec J (2016) Slovenia. Just a glass bead game? In: Motoc J, Ziemele I (eds) The impact of the ECHR on democratic change in central and Eastern Europe. Cambridge University Press, Cambridge, pp 425–456

Chapter 5
The ECtHR and National Constitutional Courts. A General Overview

5.1 The Factors Shaping the Relationship

At the beginning of this book, we described the relationship between the Strasbourg Court and European constitutional courts as a dynamic equilibrium in which both parties, while pursuing partially contradicting objectives—the uniform application of ECHR standards on the one hand and the defence of constitutional supremacy on the other—cooperate, with different degrees of enthusiasm to the smooth functioning of the European multilevel system of fundamental rights protection. The comparative analysis has illustrated how the relationship between the ECtHR and national constitutional courts is characterised by a dynamic interplay in which a plurality of variables can influence the type of relationship between Strasbourg and the national constitutional court.[1] Therefore, before dwelling on the techniques and strategies employed by the Strasbourg Court to dialogue with constitutional courts, it is useful to consider the relevance of each of those factors in determining the ECtHR attitude towards constitutional courts.

First of all, the analysis of the Court's jurisprudence *vis-à-vis* constitutional courts evidenced how the specific features of the national constitutional justice system are a major factor in shaping the relationship between the two levels. This is sufficiently clear after a mere reading of the quantitative data, which show that where an individual direct appeal is present in the constitutional justice system—and this remedy is considered an effective one by the ECtHR—the constitutional court is cited in almost every judgment: the percentages are above 95% for the Bosnian, the Spanish, the German and the Andorran constitutional courts, and above 80% for the constitutional courts of Croatia, Czechia, and Slovakia. Conversely, the lack of individual direct access to the Bulgarian, Italian, French, and Romanian

[1] For a wide-ranging comparative analysis of national dynamics in the ECHR system see: Popelier et al. (2016).

M. A. Simonelli, *The European Court of Human Rights and Constitutional Courts*, Ius Gentium: Comparative Perspectives on Law and Justice 120,
https://doi.org/10.1007/978-3-031-71268-5_5

constitutional jurisdictions, as well as the objective limitations of the Austrian, Belgian, Latvian, Portuguese and Slovenian individual constitutional appeals, results in those courts having fewer opportunities to rule on a case before an appeal is lodged in Strasbourg, and thus the percentage of citations in the ECtHR judgments of all these courts is below 50%. In other words, the first consequence of the presence of national restrictions on individual access to constitutional justice is that the ECtHR and the national constitutional court rarely deliver a decision on the same case. The effect on the relationship between the two courts of having fewer opportunities to interact seems to be ambivalent. Whilst it may be true that countries that do provide for individual access to constitutional court tend to have a lower percentage of condemnations by the Strasbourg Court,[2] limitations on individual access to constitutional court may on the other hand contribute to reducing the risk of jurisprudential conflicts. Be that as it may, the comparative analysis allows us to conclude that the tensions in the relationship between the ECtHR and national constitutional courts are not dependent on the presence of an individual constitutional appeal, as the harshest confrontations to Strasbourg's authority came from the Italian and Polish constitutional courts, both lacking a full constitutional complaint and whose presence in the ECtHR case law is rather limited.[3]

The quantitative analysis also showed that the case law of constitutional courts with direct individual access receives greater consideration from the Strasbourg Court—as evidenced by the fact that the average number of citations per judgment is significantly higher for courts with individual access.[4] If we combine this data with the higher percentage of citations in the ECtHR case law of constitutional courts granting individual access, we can infer that those constitutional courts play a more prominent role as formants of the ECtHR jurisprudence. The qualitative analysis fully confirmed such a conclusion, evidencing that the vast majority of fundamental rights dialogues' occurred with constitutional courts with an individual complaint mechanism. Conversely, in spite of an overall receptive attitude towards the Strasbourg Court's case law—the observed influence of e.g. the Belgian, Hungarian,[5] Latvian, and Portuguese constitutional jurisprudence in the ECtHR definition of European fundamental rights standards appears to be marginal.

Lastly, even though it may be superfluous, it shall be emphasised that the presence in the national constitutional justice system of an individual constitutional complaint is a key factor in the relationship between the constitutional court and the

[2]Dürr (2014), pp. 67–89. The Author however refers to a study of the Venice Commission which merely states that States where "a full constitutional complaint mechanism exists have a lower number of complaints (in proportion to the number of their population". See: CDL-AD (2010), Study on Individual Access to Constitutional Justice, Adopted by the Venice Commission at its 85th Plenary Session (Venice, 17–18 December 2010), para. 5.

[3]See, above, Ch. 3.5 and 3.6.

[4]See, above, Ch. 2.4, Fig. 2.4.

[5]Evidently, this statement refers to the attitude of the Hungarian Constitutional Court until 2012, when the HCC was 'captured' by the Fidesz' ruling majority. See, above, Ch. 4.6, in particular fn 132.

Strasbourg Court, in as much as it implies the former subjection to the fair trial guarantees flowing from Article 6 ECHR. The comparative analysis indeed showed that constitutional courts with such an avenue of access are fully subjected to ECHR fair trial guarantees, with limited derogations allowed by the ECtHR.[6] Conversely, constitutional courts without individual direct access are de facto immune to the applicability of Article 6 ECHR.

Another feature of the national constitutional justice system that affects the way the Strasbourg Court interacts with national constitutional courts is the possibility or otherwise for national constitutional judges to annotate a dissenting opinion. In cases of bodies governed by the principle of collegiality, such as the French and Italian courts, the ECtHR cannot find argumentative support in separate opinions; therefore, it sometimes relies on previous constitutional precedents, as well exemplified in the *De Tommaso* case, where the Strasbourg Court extensively cited the Italian constitutional jurisprudence, even mentioning a precedent dating as back as 1956, essentially because it fitted well within its reasoning. In contrast, in the judgments against Bulgaria, Germany, Hungary, Slovakia, and especially Spain,[7] it is not uncommon to find references to separate opinions attached to the decision of the constitutional court in the applicant's case that support the Strasbourg Court's reasoning. The possibility to ground the legitimacy of a ruling on an opinion held by national constitutional judges enhances the persuasive force of the ECtHR decision while strengthening at the same time the position of the minority judges, triggering a virtuous circle conducive to shared European fundamental rights standards.

A second factor affecting how the Strasbourg Court deals with constitutional jurisprudence is the national constitutional court's posture towards the ECtHR case law. The comparative analysis, in particular, evidenced the Strasbourg Court's sensitivity to constitutional judges' principled refusal to abide by ECtHR standards. Independently of whether these episodes of disobedience took more softened forms, as seen concerning the limits to freedom of expression in the Spanish case, or harsher ones, and this is undoubtedly the case for the *G.I.E.M* saga with Italy, the reaction of the European Court has been essentially the same: paying greater attention to constitutional jurisprudence.[8] The validity of this statement is subject to a significant precondition, i.e. that the Strasbourg Court considers the disobedience to be in good faith, i.e. whether its genuine intent is to promote an alternative interpretation of fundamental rights compatible with the ECHR values. When this is not the case, as

---

[6]See, below Sect. 5.3.2.

[7]See *Haidn v. Germany*, para. 96; *Stubing v. Germany* (43547/08), 12/04/2012, para. 66; *Vera Fernandez-Huidobro* (74181/01), 06/01/2010, para. 122; *Vaquero Hernandez v. Spain* (38715/06), 26/10/2010, para. 82; *Muñoz Díaz v. Spain* (49151/07), 08/12/2009, paras. 17–20; *Moreno Gomez v. Spain*, para. 39; *Miragall Escolano v. Spain*, para. 20. *Unión Alimentaria Sanders S.A. v. Spain* (11681/85), 07/07/1989, para. 19; *Gomez de Liano y Botella v. Spain* (21369/04), 22/07/2008, para. 27.

[8]The quantitative analysis also confirmed this trend, as following episodes of rebellion by constitutional courts is clearly observable an increase in the average number of constitutional precedents citations in the ECthR judgments.

illustrated emblematically by the Polish case, the Strasbourg Court is ready to go as far as to deny the constitutional court the status of legitimate interlocutor. A comparable attitude is identifiable in the most recent case law against Hungary, where the ECtHR appears to deliberately ignore the jurisprudence of the captured HCC and prospectively cast doubts about the effectiveness of its role as fundamental rights' guardian.[9]

Conversely, the Strasbourg Court's attitude towards national constitutional courts does not seem to be influenced by the latter degree of engagement with the ECtHR case law. Constitutional courts that routinely cite ECtHR jurisprudence, such as the Belgian and Portuguese ones, in fact, do not appear to receive greater consideration than constitutional jurisdictions that apparently ignore ECHR-made standards, like the French Constitutional Council. To this regard, it is worth noting that both the quantitative and qualitative analysis evidenced a shift in the most recent ECtHR case law, with the Strasbourg Court now devoting more attention to previously 'neglected' constitutional courts, like the Belgian, Italian, Portuguese and Romanian ones. In this sense, it appears that the ECtHR is taking into account scholars' criticism, accusing it of refraining from engaging constructively in dialogue with national courts as, more generally, we have observed an increasing presence of constitutional jurisprudence in the ECtHR case law.

As a last point before moving on to analyse the argumentation techniques employed by the ECtHR in interacting with constitutional precedents, we have to answer one of the questions posed in the Introduction, namely whether is identifiable an east-west cleavage in the way the Strasbourg Court interacts with constitutional courts. At the outset, it must be noted that most Western constitutional courts do not grant individual access through a full individual complaint, meaning that their role in fundamental rights protection is more limited compared to CEE courts that, in large majority, do grant such an avenue of access. This results, as the quantitative research has shown,[10] in a more reduced presence of the former courts in the ECtHR case law, and hence also a reduction of the possibility of dialogues. In any case, as the regards the attituded of the ECtHR in those dialogues in particular concerning the width of the margin of appreciation awarded to constitutional courts, our analysis did not evidence any double standard in the ECtHR case law, as the extent of the constitutional court's margin appears to be determined primarily by the subject matter pending before the Court. As a fair approximation, it can be affirmed that in rights with a political dimension, such as freedom of expression or freedom of association, the national margin of appreciation seems almost to disappear, as the ECtHR often substitutes its own balancing to that carried out by the constitutional court.[11]

Where instead, it is possible to identify a clear divide between Western and Eastern Constitutional Courts in the scope of applicability of Article 6 ECHR. As a matter of fact, concerning CEE constitutional courts the ECtHR has expanded the

[9] See in particular the judgment in Bancsók and László Magyar v. Hungary (No. 2).

[10] See, above, Ch. 1.4.

[11] See, below Sect. 5.2.2.

applicability of Article 6 to cover virtually any aspect of the constitutional justice system, even going as far as to review the conventionality of the deliberative procedures used by constitutional courts. The ECHR has 'dared' to practice such interference on only two occasions, against the constitutional courts of Albania,[12] and Bosnia Herzegovina.[13] Both cases concerned deadlocks in the constitutional court's decision-making capacity—the Rules of Procedure did not provide for mechanisms to reach a decision in the case of a tie—and were sanctioned by the ECtHR, which held that such blockages were in breach of Article 6. In the Albanian case, the Court's judgment even abstractly assesses the conventionality of the Albanian Constitutional Court Law, suggesting its amendment.[14] Another aspect of constitutional justice that has fallen under the scrutiny of the ECtHR is the procedure for the appointment and removal of constitutional judges.[15] The Strasbourg Court has exercised this review on only four occasions all concerning CEE constitutional courts: *Harabin v. Slovakia, Juričić v. Croatia,* and *Xero Flor v. Poland*, concerning the appointment procedure,[16] and in *Ivanovski v. The Former Yugoslav Republic of Macedonia*,[17] concerning the removal of a constitutional judge.[18] For this enhanced activism of the Strasbourg Court is, at least in part, liable for the initial lack of consolidated practice in CEE constitutional justice systems and the absence of an established constitutional jurisprudence, as demonstrated by the fact that of all the continuous changes of procedural rules before the Croatian, Czech, Slovak constitutional courts prompted by Strasbourg's case law, the last one occurred almost a decade ago.[19] Be that as it may, it appears that the Strasbourg Court has fully exploited the capital of legitimacy and political leverage at its disposal to convert Article 6 ECHR into a powerful tool in its hands to assess the compatibility of national constitutional justice systems not only with fair trial guarantees but also with the rule of law principles derived from an innovative interpretation of Article 6 ECHR. Admittedly, Article 6 ECHR has been applied as

---

[12] *Marini v. Albania* (3738/02), 18/12/2007.

[13] *Avdić and Others v. Bosnia and Herzegovina* (28357/11, 31549/11, 39295/11), 19/11/2013.

[14] *Marini v. Albania*, para. 123.

[15] The subjection of such procedures to the application of Article 6 ECHR depends exclusively on the presence, at the domestic level, of a judicial remedy to complain about possible irregularities, as required for all procedures concerning removal and appointment of public servants by the test developed by the Court in *Vilho Eskelinen T Vilho Eskelinen and Others v. Finland* (63235/00), 19/04/2007, paras. 61–62.

[16] *Harabin v. Slovakia* (58688/11), 20/11/2012; *Juričić v. Croatia* (58222/09), 26/07/2011.

[17] *Ivanovski v. The Former Yugoslav Republic of Macedonia* (29908/11), 21/01/2016.

[18] However, it must be underlined that in none of those cases, the ECtHR ordered the reopening of the appointment procedure or the reinstatement of the constitutional judge, as it did for instance in *Olexander Volkov v. Ukraine* for a judge of the Supreme Court. See: *Oleksandr Volkov v. Ukraine*, 21722/11, 09/01/2013.

[19] For the Czech Constitutional Court see: *Vodarenska Akciova Spolecnost A.S. v. Czech Republic* (73577/01), 24/02/2004, para. 35; *Soudek v. Czech Republic* (56526/00), 15/03/2005, para. 21; *Marík v. Czech Republic* (73116/01), 12/04/2005, para. 16. For the Slovak one instead see, *Zborovsky v. Slovakia* (14325/08), 23/10/2012, para. 53, and *Kovárová v. Slovakia*, para. 43.

a rule of law tool also against Western democracies, as in the *Lorenzo Bragado* case, hence it seems that this divergence in the scope of applicability of Article 6 is ultimately dependent on contingent circumstances, i.e. the democratic erosion which has affected more seriously Central Eastern European democracies rather than western ones.

However, it is not only that the scope of the ECtHR review seems to be wider concerning CEE courts; the tone of the Strasbourg also seems more assertive towards them. The jurisprudence where this is more visible is probably that against Bosnia and Herzegovina,[20] given the peculiarity of the composition of the Bosnian Constitutional Court,[21] but it is also possible to find harsh criticism of other CEE constitutional courts' judgments, in particular when they are interpreting the ECHR. Consider, for instance, the 2022 judgment in *Dragan Kovačević v. Croatia* which affirms that "the Constitutional Court did not give any meaningful reasons for its decision",[22] or the 2018 judgment in *Novotny v. Czech Republic* where the ECtHR even criticizes the Czech Constitutional Court for failing "to take into account not only its own jurisprudence [...]but also the Court's judgment in Paulík".[23] In conclusion, it may not be possible to speak about the existence of double standards, but a closer analysis reveals how the Strasbourg Court tone is more assertive when dialoguing with CEE constitutional courts

5.2 The Patterns and Techniques of the ECtHR Engagement with Constitutional Precedents

One of the stated objectives of this book was to illustrate the patterns and techniques followed by the Strasbourg Court to deal with constitutional precedents. In this regard, the first macro-distinction that has to be made is between the cases in which the ECtHR judgment is in line with the constitutional precedent and cases in which the Strasbourg Court instead delivers a ruling contradicting the national constitutional jurisprudence. Concerning the first type of situations, although it may be *prima facie* counter-intuitive, when there is harmony between the case law of the two courts, the Strasbourg Court normally condemns the Respondent State because

[20] See, for instance, *Muslija v. Bosnia and Herzegovina* (32042/11), 14/01/2014, in particular para. 38. Here, the Strasbourg Court straightforwardly affirms that the Bosnian Constitutional Court failed to correctly apply a conventional precedent.

[21] We remind that, according to Article VI.1(a), three judges of the Bosnian Constitutional Court are selected by the President of the European Court of Human Rights.

[22] *Dragan Kovačević v. Croatia* (49281/15), 12/05/2022, para. 83.

[23] *Novotny v. Czech Republic* (16314/13), 07/06/2018, para. 48. In similar terms see also: Milenković v. Serbia (50124/13), 01/03/2016, para. 48; Társásag a Szabadságjogokért v. Hungary (37374/05), 14/04/2009, para. 28

the applicant could not benefit from the constitutional judgment.[24] This leads us to consider the issue of the enforcement of constitutional judgments.

5.2.1 Techniques of Cooperation. The Enforcement of Constitutional Judgments

By enforcement of constitutional judgment, we mean here the practice followed by the Strasbourg Court of inferring a violation of the ECHR mainly or even exclusively on the ground that national authorities have failed to execute a decision of the constitutional court. Where the enforcement of a constitutional judgment is explicitly requested by the applicant, since the right to a fair trial also includes the right to the execution of a favourable decision, the identification of an enforcement is an operation without discretion.[25] In cases where, on the other hand, such a request is not present, the surest indication that the Strasbourg judges are applying the *dictum of* a constitutional judgment is represented by the fact that the ECtHR reasoning relies heavily on the relevant constitutional precedent.[26] In some instances, the ECtHR may only rely exclusively on the constitutional judgment, as it did for example in *Milojević* and *Others v. Serbia*, where the ECtHR simply affirmed that since the constitutional had adjudicated on an identical issue, finding a violation of Article 6 ECHR, and there was "no reason to depart from the reasoning of the Constitutional Court" Article 6 was violated also in the applicant's case.[27]

The most far-reaching—and effective—technique of enforcement is represented by the adoption of a pilot judgment replicating the decision of the constitutional court. From the domestic perspective, constitutional courts indeed benefit from the endorsement of the Strasbourg Court, as the execution of their judgments becomes the content of an obligation imposed on the national authorities by public international law.[28] From the Strasbourg perspective, anchoring the prescription of general measures to the Member States on a solid domestic basis instead enhances the legitimacy of the Strasbourg Court's "meddling in what national legislation should or should not do".[29] Nevertheless, the Strasbourg Court adopted a pilot judgment to enforce a constitutional judgment only on three occasions, notably in *Broniowski*

---

[24] Only in a small number of cases does the Court align with the constitutional jurisprudence without condemning the Respondent State. Among them see: *Trade Union of the Police in the Slovak Republic and Others v. Slovakia* (11828/08), 25/09/2012, para. 74; *Travaš v. Croatia* (75581/13), 04/10/2016, para. 113; *Milanković and Bošnjak v. Croatia*, (37762/12, 23530/13), 26/04/2016, para. 157; *Muršič v. Croatia* [GC] (7334/13), 20/10/2016, para. 170.

[25] See *Vidal Escoll and Guillan Gonzalez v. Andorra*, 38196/05, 29/07/2008.

[26] A palpable example of the above can be found in: *Milejović and Others v. Serbia* (43519/07, 43524/07, 45247/07), 12/01/2016, paras 83–84; *Raudevs v. Latvia*, 24086/03, 17/12/2013, para. 72.

[27] *Milejović and Others v. Serbia* (43519/07, 43524/07, 45247/07), 12/01/2016, para. 84.

[28] On the different extent of the obligation to execute a pilot judgment, see: Glas (2016), p. 59.

[29] Sadurski (2009), p. 438.

v. Poland, *Hutten-Czapska v. Poland*, and *Kurić and Others v. Slovenia*.[30] In other instances, the ECtHR simply recommended to the Respondent State, pursuant to Article 46 ECHR, the implementation of a constitutional judgment, but without transposing this recommendation into the operative part of the judgment.[31] Partially different are the situations in which the Strasbourg Court notes the lack of legislative implementation of a declaration of unconstitutionality: in these cases, the ECtHR has deemed the constitutional ruling to be binding on national courts in any case, even in cases pending on the date the unconstitutionality was pronounced,[32] or has censured the Parliament for its inaction.[33]

For the majority of judgments, however, the scope of such enforcement is limited to the applicant's situation, such as in cases where the ECtHR judgement merely finds a breach of the Convention in the failure to execute an order issued by the constitutional court to a lower court, e.g. the order to conclude the proceedings within a set time limit or to conduct an effective into the applicant's allegations.[34] Equally interesting are the judgments in which the ECtHR, endorsing a principle affirmed in a constitutional judgment, ends up applying it retroactively.[35] The retrospective application may indeed allow affording protection—through the award of economic compensation—to legal situations that could not otherwise be redressed, e.g. because the applicant's situation has become *res judicata* according to domestic rules.[36] A similar effect occurs when the ECtHR condemns the respondent State because the ordinary courts court applied a rule declared unconstitutional to the applicant's case, failing to verify the effects of the declaration of unconstitutionality on the applicant's case.[37] In other words, by doing so, the ECtHR frames its role as a temporal modulator of constitutional judgments, amplifying the latter effects beyond the limits imposed by domestic law and,[38] at the same time, vesting its own rulings with the legitimacy deriving from the constitutional court decision.

---

[30] *Broniowski v. Poland* [GC] (31443/96), 22/06/2004; *Hutten-Czapska v. Poland* [GC] (35014/97), 22/02/2005; *Kurić and Others v. Slovenia* [GC] (26828/06), 26/06/2012;

[31] *N. v. Romania (No. 2) (38048/18)*, 16/11/2021, para. 84; *Baralija v. Bosnia and* Herzegovina (30100/18), 29/10/2019; para. 62; *Spahić and Others v. Bosnia and Herzegovina* (20514/15, 20528/15, 20774/15, et al.), 14/11/2017, para. 33; *Kunić and Others v. Bosnia and Herzegovina* [GC] (68955/12 et al.), 29/03/2006, para. 230.

[32] *Kędzior v. Poland* (45026/07), 16/10/2012, para. 88.

[33] *Joanna Szulc v. Poland* (43932/08), 13/11/2012, para. 93.

[34] Concerning the failure to respect time limits see, *Kaic and Others v. Croatia* (22014/04), 17/07/2008, para. 43; *Vujcic v. Croatia* (33867/06), 25/06/2009, para. 40; *Lonza v. Croatia* (14062/07), 01/04/2010, para. 36; *Zaicevs v. Latvia*, (65022/01), 31/07/2007, para. 56. On the order to conduct an effective investigation see instead, *Baranin and Vukčeviç v. Montenegro* (24655/18, 24656/18), 11/03/2021, paras 142–149.

[35] *Ferencne Kovacs v. Hungary* (19325/09), 20/12/2011, para. 19.

[36] *Zustović v. Croatia* (27903/15), 22/04/2021, paras 104–106; *Wegera v. Poland* (141/07), 14/01/2010, para. 74.

[37] *Barac and Others v. Montenegro* (47974/06), 13/12/2011.

[38] Sometimes with not entirely convincing results. See to this regard the Dissenting Opinion of Judges Kalaydjieva and De Gaetano in, *Barac and Others v. Montenegro*.

Finally, it should be underscored that these different techniques for binding together the ECtHR judgment and the constitutional one have been employed by the Court only in relation to judgments of CEE constitutional courts. On the one hand, this surely points to the difficulties those courts experienced, and in some cases are facing, in their respective political environments, to secure the execution of their judgments.[39] On the other, given the openness of the majority CEE legal systems to the ECHR law, those judgments constitute further evidence that the constitutional links, both "institutional", such as the pilot judgment procedure, and jurisprudential, as the modulation of the temporal effects, between the Strasbourg Court and CEE constitutional courts are stricter than with the Western ones. Consider, for example, the pilot judgment in *Scordino v. Italy (no. 1)* concerning the systemic denial by Italian authorities of a reasonable amount of compensation to subjects of expropriation proceedings.[40] Here, the Strasbourg Court refrained from affirming that Italian authorities have not acknowledged the existence of a systemic failure, even though it underlines that with two judgments the ICC had affirmed the necessity for the Italian parliament to pass a law to award "substantial compensation" to subjects of expropriation proceedings. Consequently, when inviting the Italian authorities to "above all, remove every obstacle to the award of compensation bearing a reasonable relation to the value of the expropriated property" the Strasbourg Court does not make reference to the ICC's judgments.[41]

5.2.2 *Patterns of Disagreement*

As regards instead the situations in which the Strasbourg Court's judgment is conflict with the national constitutional court's, it is possible to identify a series of patterns that the ECtHR follow in its reasoning, in order to enhance the persuasiveness of its judgment. It may be worth signalling that cases of contradiction between the ECtHR and the constitutional court almost inevitably correspond to a condemnation of the Respondent State. As a second preliminary remark, it must be emphasised that the Strasbourg Court tend to hide rather than expose conflicts with constitutional courts. However, especially when the national government supports his submission with constitutional case law, the ECtHR cannot refrain from engaging with it. In such a situation, what Strasbourg judges then attempt to do is to downplay the conflict, focussing instead on elements of harmony.

[39] For a comparative overview see: Pócza et al. (2024).

[40] *Scordino v. Italy (no. 1)* [GC], (36813/97), 29/03/2006.

[41] The circumstances of the case were significantly more complex, as a previous law recognising applicants the right of compensation of the full market value, has been declared unconstitutional by the ICC. See: Ibidem, paras 50–61. However, this only confirms the Grand Chamber's increased sensitivity as it avoided entering into an interpretation of domestic constitutional case law.

One technique to reach this effect, which the ECtHR is adopting with increasing frequency, is to mention, when present, the dissenting opinions of national constitutional judges.[42] Significantly, this technique was first employed in the highly contested judgment in *Ruiz Mateos v. Spain*, where the Court held applicable Article 6 to incidental proceedings before the Spanish Constitutional Tribunal.[43] Highlighting the presence amongst national constitutional judges of an interpretation aligned with that proposed by the ECtHR indeed aims at enhancing its legitimacy, thus promoting its implementation. Normally the citations consist just of a brief exposition of the main argument of the dissenting opinion made in the factual part of the judgment.[44] More rarely, the Strasbourg Court refers to the arguments of dissenting constitutional judges to support the finding of a violation, as simply signalling the presence of dissenting opinions attached to the constitutional judgement may serve to undermine its conclusions, especially if the judgment has been adopted with a thin majority.[45]

---

[42] In the case law analysed we have retrieved 73 judgments referring to dissenting opinions of constitutional judges, of this 27 have been delivered in the last 5 years see: *Elmazova And Others v. North Macedonia* (11811/20, 13550/20) 13/12/2022; *Sevdari v. Albania* (40662/19), 13/12/2022; *Pejřilová v. The Czech Republic* (14889/19), 08/12/2022; *Garrido Herrero v. Spain* (61019/19), 11/10/2022; *Besnik Cani v. Albania* (37474/20), 04/10/2022; *Stăvilă v. Romania* (23126/16), 01/03/2022; *Šeks v. Croatia* (39325/20), 03/02/2022; *Baljak and Others v. Croatia* (41295/19), 25/11/2021; *Laçi v. Albania* (28142/17), 19/10/2021; *Xero Flor W Polsce Sp. Z O. O. v. Poland*; *Avřička and Others v. The Czech Republic* [GC] (47621/13, 3867/14, 73094/14 et al.), 08/04/2021; *Ghailan And Others v. Spain* (36366/14), 23/03/2021; *Benitez Moriana and Iñigo Fernandez v. Spain* (36537/15, 36539/15), 09/03/2021; *Xhoxhaj v. Albania* (15227/19), 09/02/2021; *Shiksaitov v. Slovakia* (56751/16, 33762/17), 10/12/2020; *Project-Trade D.O.O. v. Croatia* (1920/14), 19/11/2020; *Gil Sanjuan v. Spain* (48297/15), 26/05/2020; *Kostov and Others v. Bulgaria* (66581/12, 25054/15), 14/05/2020; *Strezovski and Others v. North Macedonia* (14460/16, 14958/16, 14962/16 et al.), 27/02/2020; *Magyar Kétfarkú Kutya Párt v. Hungary* [GC] (201/17), 20/01/2020; *Otegi Mondragon and Others v. Spain* (4184/15, 4317/15, 4323/15 et al.), 06/11/2018; *S. S. v. Slovenia* (40938/16), 30/10/2018; *Arrozpide Sarasola and Others v. Spain* (65101/16, 73789/16, 73902/16), 23/10/2018; *Frroku v. Albania* (47403/15), 18/09/2018; *Benedik v. Slovenia* (62357/14), 24/04/2018; *Čeferin v. Slovenia* (40975/08), 16/01/2018; *Cuenca Zarzoso v. Spain* (23383/12), 16/01/2018.

[43] See: *Ruiz-Mateos v. Spain*, (12952/87), 23/06/1993, para. 19. The two constitutional judges dissenting however only argued that the adoption of a law-decree for the expropriation of the applicant's company had deprived him of the right to access a Court. As of 1 January 2023, Strasbourg has cited dissenting opinions of Spanish constitutional judges on 14 occasions, the highest figure amongst the constitutional courts considered. For a complete list of those judgments see, above, Ch. 3.7, at fn 317.

[44] In *Benedik v. Slovenia,* for instance, the space devoted to the analysis of the dissenting opinions is even bigger than reserved to the judgment of the constitutional court. See, *Benedik v. Slovenia* (62357/14), 24/04/2018, paras 30–34.

[45] Consider in this regard the ruling of the Hungarian Constitutional Court on the termination of the mandate of the President and Vice President of the Supreme Court, adopted with an 8–7 majority. In both circumstances, the Strasbourg underlines this circumstance, illustrating the content of the minority judges' dissenting opinions. See *Erményi v. Hungary* (22254/14), 22/11/2016, para. 10; *Baka v. Hungary* [GC] (20261/12), 23/06/2016, para. 56.

An alternative technique that the ECtHR uses to contradict a constitutional judgment is to exploit an apparent contradiction within the constitutional jurisprudence. Especially significant in this regard is the judgment in *De Tommaso v. Italy*, where the Strasbourg Court to emphasise the overall harmony of the two jurisprudences, engaged in an extensive analysis of the ICC's case law, even remounting to the second judgment in the history of the ICC, dating from 1956.[46] In some instances, the ECtHR even went as far as to openly affirm the existence of a contradiction within the constitutional case law,[47] or criticise the constitutional court for its unmotivated departure from its own established case law.[48] Similar statements, however, present the obvious risk of misinterpreting constitutional jurisprudence, as well as that of generating amongst national constitutional judges the perception that the ECtHR considers itself to be the ultimate interpreter of constitutional law.[49] Finally, less controversial are the judgments in which the Strasbourg Court simply indicates to the constitutional court which ECtHR precedent it had misapplied.[50]

A second set of situations which is interesting to analyse is when the Strasbourg Court reviews the proportionality analysis carried out by the national constitutional court. Preliminarily, it must be observed that the subject matter seems to be a decisive criterion in the ECtHR delimitation of the extent of the margin of appreciation awarded to constitutional courts.[51] Concerning the restrictions on the external dimension of the freedom of religion, the margin of appreciation awarded to constitutional courts appears to be maximum. The judgments on the ban of the full-face veil in Belgium and France constitute the most evident example that in the limitation of freedom of religion in public places, national authorities enjoy a wide margin of appreciation.[52] A similar deference towards constitutional court's case law, is observable in cases against Germany,[53] as well as in the much criticised *Ebrahimian v. France* case,[54] all confirming the proportionality assessment of the

[46] See, *De Tommaso v. Italy* [GC] (43395/09), 23/02/2017, paras. 45–61.

[47] *Novotny v. Czech Republic* (16314/13), 07/06/2018, para. 48.

[48] *Mugoša v. Montenegro* (76522/12), 21/06/2016, para. 53. Similarly see: *Bigović v. Montenegro* (48343/16), 19/03/2019.

[49] Similars concerns are expressed by the concurring judges in: *Novotny v. Czech Republic*, Concurring Opinion of Judge Koskelo and Eicke, paras 3–4.

[50] *Muslija v. Bosnia and Herzegovina* (32042/11), 14/01/2014, para. 38; *Milenković v. Serbia* (50124/13), 01/03/2016, para. 48. However, it must be noted that the ECtHR, in these pronouncements, does not seem to allow for a conventionally compliant solution other than the one identified in its precedent, which ultimately seems at odds with the principle of subsidiarity.

[51] For a more detailed assessment of the criteria adopted by the Strasbourg Court in deterring the states' margin of appreciation see: Arnardóttir (2017), pp. 9–35.

[52] *Dakir v. Belgique* (4619/12), 11/07/2017; *Belcacemi et Oussar v. Belgique* (37798/13), 11/07/2017; *S.A.S. v. France* (43835/11), 01/07/2014.

[53] *Siebenhaar v. Germany* (18136/02), 03/02/2011, *Obst v. Germany* (425/03), 23/09/2010.

[54] *Ebrahimian v. France* (64846/11), 26/11/2015.

constitutional court and consequently denying the existence of a breach of Article 9 ECHR.[55]

On the other side of the spectrum, there are fundamental rights connected to the public sphere, such as Article 10, 11, and Article 3 Protocol 1 ECHR. Those rights are indeed amongst those that the Strasbourg Court interpret more extensively, generally conferring them a broader meaning than that maintained by national constitutional courts. In the interpretation of those rights, the ECtHR systematically disregarded the balancing carried out by constitutional courts,[56] up to a point that, to borrow Judge Loucaides' words, "it left nothing to the latter's margin of appreciation".[57]

Another issue on which the margin of appreciation of constitutional courts is essentially nullified is the award of compensation for Article 6 violations. Emblematic to this regard is the judgment in *Schvarc v. Slovakia*,[58] where the Court notes that the Slovakian Constitutional Court has recognised that there was a breach of the applicant's right to a speedy review of the legality of its detention and has awarded him compensation. Nevertheless, it went on to find a breach of Article 5(4) ECHR on the grounds that the compensation was not sufficient, only to finally award the applicant 500 euros more. This is not the only case in which the Strasbourg Court has delivered a judgement only to increase the compensation provided by the constitutional court, as this issue even generated a consistent strand of case law.[59] Those judgments ultimately seem at odds with the principle of subsidiarity, as they indicate that the ECtHR intends to maintain close scrutiny over how national constitutional courts apply ECHR economic parameters.[60]

---

[55] As a matter of fact, together with Article 4 and Article 7, Article 9 is the least violated provision of the ECHR, the Court having declared its breach in only 121 occasions (as of 1 January 2023).

[56] See, *Österreichische Vereinigung Zur Erhaltung, Stärkung und Schaffung v. Austria* (39534/07), 28/11/2013; *Association of Citizens Radko and Paunkowski v. The Former Yugoslav Republic of Macedonia* (74651/01), 15/01/2009; *Öllinger v. Austria* (76900/01), 29/06/2006; *United Macedonian Organization Ilinden - Pirin and Others v. Bulgaria* (59489/00), 20/10/2005.

[57] See, *Öllinger v. Austria*, Loucaides Dissenting, para. 1(f).

[58] *Schvarc v. Slovakia* (64528/09), 14/01/2014.

[59] Lastly see, *Dragan Kovačević v. Croatia* (49281/15), 12/05/2022, paras. 80–84; where the Court affirmed that the decision to not award cost to the applicant violated Article 6 ECHR. For the other judgments in this case law see, above, Ch. 3.4, fn 69.

[60] Sometimes they even cast serious doubts as to their utility. In *Judt v. Slovakia*, for instance, the Strasbourg Court took 6 years to find a breach of the applicant's right to a trial of reasonable duration because the CCSK only awarded him € 740. Yet, the Strasbourg Court took almost 6 years to award € 1000. It should be noted incidentally that Judge Casadevall's dissenting opinion criticises the majority for the insufficient amount of compensation awarded and for having failed to compensate the applicant also for the protraction of the proceedings in Strasbourg. See, *Judt v. Slovakia* (70985/01), 09/10/2007, *Dissenting Opinion of Judge Casadevall*, paras. 2–3.

5.3 The Procedural Subordination of Constitutional Justice to Article 6 Guarantees

5.3.1 The Effectiveness of the Constitutional Complaint. The Key Factor to Determine the Degree of Subordination to Article 6 Exigencies

The affirmation that a constitutional complaint may be an effective legal remedy in cases of fundamental rights violation predates the application of Article 6 to constitutional proceedings, as it was first affirmed in 1986.[61] In this sense, it should be remarked that despite the two concepts being strictly interrelated, the applicability of Article 6 ECHR to constitutional proceedings is not dependent upon the circumstance that the proceeding in question constitutes an effective remedy under Article 35 ECHR. Conversely, if the constitutional complaint is effective for ECHR purposes, the constitutional court will have to respect fair trial guarantees flowing from Article 6 of the Convention when dealing with it. This is why constitutional courts with a full individual complaint mechanism are more subject, as the case law analysis evidenced, to the application of Article 6 ECHR guarantees than constitutional courts with limited individual access.

The general position of the Strasbourg Court is that in Member States where a constitutional complaint is present, "it is incumbent on the aggrieved individual to test the extent of that protection".[62] However, as the Strasbourg Court itself admits, this requirement—and the whole set of rules concerning the exhaustion of domestic remedies—is to be applied "with some degree of flexibility and without excessive formalism".[63] There are indeed a series of circumstances that, according to the Strasbourg Court, may exonerate applicants to previously introduce a constitutional complaint. The first is when the constitutional court did not adopt any decision indicating the availability of the complaint to redress the applicant's situation. The approach of the Strasbourg Court is exemplified in the *Vincic and Others v. Serbia*, where the Court held that the Serbian individual constitutional complaint was to be considered an effective remedy starting from the first August 2008, i.e. the date of the first substantive judgment of the CCSB adjudicating on a constitutional complaint.[64] Conversely, in a series of cases against Montenegro, it repeatedly denied that the Montenegrin constitutional complaint was an effective remedy for cases of excessive duration of proceedings, because according to the Constitutional Court Act, it could only be introduced against a decision of public authorities, i.e. not

---

[61] In a cases decided that year the Commission declared an application inadmissible because the applicant's constitutional complaint was declared inadmissible by the BVG for being lodged out of time. See, *W. v Germany* [dec.] (10785/84), 18/07/1986.

[62] *Vinčić and Others v. Serbia* (44698/06), 01/12/2009, para. 51.

[63] Amongst many see, for example, *Vučković and Others v. Serbia* [GC] (17153/11), 25/03/2014, para. 76.

[64] *Vinčić and Others v. Serbia*, para. 51.

simple inaction, and the Government was not able to indicate any decision of the constitutional court holding otherwise.[65]

Second, the Court on some occasions also reviewed whether contextual political circumstances deprive the constitutional remedy of its effectiveness. In the 2023 judgement in *Walesa v. Poland*, for instance, the Court declared that the applicant was dispensed from submitting a constitutional complaint to the PCT in light of "the general context in which the Constitutional Court had operated since the end of 2015".[66] Lastly, also the applicant's personal situation may be taken into account by the Court to dispense her/him from the obligation to exhaust the constitutional complaint. In *M.S. v. Croatia (no. 2)*, considering that the government did not indicate any constitutional court's decision in cases similar to that of the applicant, the ECtHR held that the vulnerable position of the applicant—interned against her will in a psychiatric hospital—dispensed her from the obligation to submit a constitutional complaint.[67]

Concerning the requirements that a constitutional complaint must fulfil in order to be considered a remedy to be exhausted under Article 35 ECHR, these are essentially three: it must be directly available to individuals; it must have the capacity of preventing or redressing an ECHR violation; and it must offer reasonable prospect of success.[68] Concerning the direct availability to individuals, this condition implies that incidental questions of constitutionality are not effective remedies under Article 35 ECHR. In the first place this means that, as the ECtHR case law currently stands, individuals from Bulgaria, France, Italy, and Romania are never required to bring their cases to their respective constitutional jurisdictions before going to Strasbourg. The requirement of direct availability also implies that in cases of MPs, they must be able to bring their case autonomously to the constitutional court, so that constitutional complaints that can only be submitted by a minimum number of MPs are not effective under Article 35 ECHR.[69]

As regards the capacity to prevent or redress a violation, the first thing to be pointed out is that the ECtHR evaluates this requirement using as the main criterion the powers of the constitutional court as resulting from the domestic legal

---

[65] See: Novović v. Montenegro (13210/05), 23/10/2012, para. 45; Stakić v. Montenegro (49320/07), 02/10/2012, para. 41; Zivaljević v. Montenegro (17229/04), 08/03/2011, para. 68.

[66] *Walesa v. Poland* (50849/21), 23/11/2023, paras 152–154.

[67] *M.S. v. Croatia (no. 2)* (75450/12),19/02/2015, paras 122–123. Similarly see, *Tokić and Others v. Bosnia and Herzegovina* (12455/04, 14140/05, 12906/06 et al.), 08/07/2008, para. 59. It may be worth noting an almost paradoxical effect of this casuistic-oriented case law. In fact, the Croatian Government continues to argue in cases before the ECtHR that the individual constitutional complaint is not an effective remedy for Article 35 ECHR. See: *Trivkanović v. Croatia (no. 2)* (49083/18), 18/11/2021, paras 63–68; *Čolić v. Croatia* (49083/18), 18/11/2021, paras 26–31; *F. O. v. Croatia* (29555/13), 22/04/2021, paras 62–66; *Zustović v. Croatia* (27903/15), 22/04/2021, paras 58–64; *Smiljanić v. Croatia* (35983/14), 25/03/2021, paras 56–59; *Sabalić v. Croatia* (50231/13), 14/01/2021, paras 79–81.

[68] See, *mutatis mutandis*, *Pallanich v. Austria*, (30160/96), 30/01/2001, para. 26.

[69] *Petkov and Others v. Bulgaria*, (77568/01, 178/02, 505/02), 11/06/2009, paras 82–83.

framework. For example, in cases concerning excessive delays of proceedings under Article 5(4) or 6 ECHR, a constitutional remedy is effective only if the constitutional court can award compensation to the applicant,[70] or can effectively adopt measures capable of accelerating the proceeding.[71] Similarly, as regards constitutional complaints concerning non-enforcement of judicial decisions, the constitutional court must be capable of adopting measures to secure the enforcement or to award redress, as merely declaratory decisions would not be considered an effecter remedy under Article 35 ECHR.[72] Outside those cases, is in principle sufficient that the constitutional court's judgment favourable to the applicant may result in the reopening of this case before ordinary courts. Sometimes the ECtHR may also take into account also the substantive constitutional case law to assess the capacity of the constitutional remedy to redress the applicant's situation. A similar attitude is discernible in the case law on the effectiveness of the Hungarian constitutional complaint. The current position of the Strasbourg Court on the issue, is a remedy whose exhaustion is required under Article 35 ECHR upon the condition that ECHR rights are "equally protected by the Fundamental Law of Hungary".[73] This formula resumes the Strasbourg Court's stance since 2017, consisting of declaring admissible applications despite the applicants' failure to submit a constitutional complaint because the government was not able to indicate in the constitutional case law any judgment demonstrating that the HCC had afforded protection to situations similar to that of the applicant.[74]

Lastly, concerning the reasonable prospect of success, it has to be first underscored that this concept does not refer to its rate of success, as even the Spanish *recurso de amparo* and the German *Verfassungsbeschwerde* are considered effective remedies by the ECtHR despite their rate of success being lower than 1%.[75] In the same sense, the Strasbourg Court has clarified that both objective and subjective admissibility requirements do not deprive a constitutional complaint of its effectiveness.[76] Concerning in particular subjective requirements, such as that envisaged at Article 55(2a) of the Slovenian Constitutional Court Act, allowing the CCSL to declare inadmissible complaints on the ground that no significant consequences have been incurred by the alleged victim of the fundamental rights violation, the

[70] *Sürmeli v. Germany* [GC] (75529/01), 08/06/2006.

[71] However, when the constitutional court order is not capable of actually accelerating the proceeding, a constitutional complaint to seek such an acceleratory order will be considered ineffective. *Kunić and Others v. Bosnia and Herzegovina* (68955/12, 7270/15, 7286/15 et al.), 14/11/2017, paras 20–21.

[72] *Karanovic v. Bosnia and Herzegovina* (39462/03), 20/11/2007.

[73] *Bancsók and László Magyar v. Hungary (No. 2)* (52374/15, 53364/15), 28/10/2021, para. 24.

[74] See, *Sándor Varga and Others v. Hungary* (39734/15, 35530/16, 26804/18), 17/06/2021, para. 34; *Király and Dömötör v. Hungary* (10851/13), 17/01/2017, paras 47–49.

[75] See, above, fn 8.

[76] See, *Rutar and Rutar Marketing D.O.O. v. Slovenia* (21164/20), 15/12/2022, paras. 39–44. The case law on the issue is limited, as both types of requirements are more often assessed under the prism of Article 6 ECHR, as possible violations of the right to access to a court.

Strasbourg Court, in accordance with the principle of subsidiarity, held that applicants are required "to use a constitutional complaint even in cases that fall within the aforementioned section 55.a(2)", inasmuch the constitutional court could still declare those complaints admissible for presenting a special constitutional significance.[77] Therefore, to prove that the constitutional complaint does not offer reasonable prospects of success the applicant will have to show that "the issues raised by his or her case had previously been consistently considered by the Constitutional Court as not being capable of raising an important constitutional question".[78] What instead renders a constitutional complaint ineffective is the discretional power of the constitutional court in the decision on whether the institution of constitutional proceedings following the reception of a request in that sense by applicants.[79]

Before moving on to analyse how the Court applies Article 6 guarantees to constitutional proceedings, it may be useful to provide a brief comparative overview of which individual constitutional complaints are in principle considered effective remedies under Article 35 ECHR. The Strasbourg Court has explicitly declared that are remedies whose exhaustion is in principle required the full complaint mechanisms present in the constitutional justice system of: Albania,[80] Croatia,[81] Montenegro,[82] North Macedonia,[83] Serbia,[84] Slovenia,[85] and Slovakia.[86] No similar statements have been retrieved concerning the Bosnian, German, Hungarian, Lithuanian and Spanish constitutional complaints. In the case of the Bosnian constitutional complaint, this seems ultimately due to the difficulties the CCBH experiences in obtaining the enforcement of its judgments.[87] In the German and Spanish cases, the reason for this absence may be attributed to the low rate of success of the respective individual appeals. In contrast, it has already been underlined the reasons prompting the Court to exonerate applicants from submitting a complaint to the Hungarian Constitutional Court. Finally, in the case of Lithuania, the individual

---

[77] Ibidem, para. 45.

[78] *Kneževič and Others v. Slovenia* [dec.] (51388/13), 19/09/2017, para. 31. Cited in: Ibidem.

[79] See, *Horvat v. Croatia* (51585/99), 26/07/2001, paras 41–45; *Futterer v. Croatia* (52634/99), 20/12/2001, para. 22; *Mikulič v. Croatia* (53176/99), 07/02/02, para. 70; *Delic v. Croatia* (48771/99), 27/06/2002, para. 111; *Rados and Others v. Croatia* (45435/99), 07/11/2002, para. 79.

[80] *Fullani v. Albania* (dec.) (4586/18), 20/09/2022, para. 79.

[81] *Pavlović and Others v. Croatia* (13274/11), 02/04/2015, para. 32 and the case law thereby cited.

[82] *Siništaj and Others v. Montenegro* (1451/10, 7260/10, 7382/10), 24/11/2015, para. 123.

[83] The individual constitutional complaint is available, and thus effective, only for possible breach of the rights enshrined in Articles 9, 10, 11 and 14 of the ECHR.

[84] *Vinčić and Others v. Serbia*, para. 51.

[85] *Rutar and Rutar Marketing D.O.O. v. Slovenia*, para. 39.

[86] *Visy v. Slovakia* (70288/13), 16/10/2018, para. 27.

[87] See, for instance, *Tokić and Others v. Bosnia and* Herzegovina, para. 58–60.

constitutional complaint was introduced only in 2019, and the Strasbourg Court has not yet had the opportunity to pronounce on its effectiveness.[88]

As regards instead normative individual complaints, their effectiveness varies significantly in each legal system in which they are present. In the case of the Latvian individual complaint, the Strasbourg Court in 2020 introduced a presumption of effectiveness affirming that "where it is arguable that the individual decision, in respect of which the violation is alleged, was based on an unconstitutional legal provision, the Constitutional Court should be given an opportunity to address the matter".[89] In the case of the Portuguese constitutional complaint, the Court instead held that is an effective remedy only to challenge the unconstitutionality of a norm or a normative interpretation.[90] Finally, concerning the Polish constitutional complaint, the only circumstance in which is considered an effective remedy is when "the alleged violation of the Convention resulted from the direct application of a legal provision considered by the complainant to be unconstitutional".[91] However, after the ECtHR rulings in the Polish constitutional crisis,[92] it is unclear whether the Polish constitutional complaint may constitute an effective remedy under any circumstance.

5.3.2 *The Application of Article 6 to Constitutional Proceedings*

The results of the analysis of the ECtHR's case law citing constitutional courts allow us to safely conclude that the Court has completed its enterprise of rationalisating constitutional justice systems that commenced 30 years ago.[93] Indeed, the Court is applying all the constitutive elements of the right to a fair trial under Article 6 to constitutional proceedings. Although in some cases the ECHR continues to operate the formula elaborated in *Pammel* according to which the right to a fair trial 'cannot be construed in the same way for a constitutional court as for an ordinary court'[94], in the majority of cases the ECtHR seems almost to ignore the fact that the trial takes place before a constitutional court. Thanks to the high number of Strasbourg's judgments applying Article 6 to constitutional proceedings, it is also possible to identify the core elements of the right to a fair constitutional trial.

[88] However, in light of the principles illustrated it can be safely concluded that, starting from its entry into force, is a remedy whose exhaustion is required to comply with the rule of exhaustion of domestic remedies. See, above, Ch. 3.8, fn 188.

[89] *Zirnite* v. *Latvia* (69019/11), 11/06/2020, para. 69.

[90] Lastly see: *Dos Santos Calado and Others v. Portugal* (55997/14, 68143/16, 78841/16), 31/03/2020, para. 85.

[91] See, amongst many, *Sosinowska v. Poland* (10247/09), 18/10/2011, para. 54.

[92] See, above, fn 99.

[93] Burgorgue Larsen (2004), pp. 31–34.

[94] *Pammel v. Germany*, para. 68.

The first element to be considered is the right to access the constitutional court. In this respect, the Strasbourg Court has constantly stated, first in admissibility decisions,[95] and more recently in its case law on the merits,[96] that in principle the Convention does not guarantee the "right to access to a court with competence to invalidate or override a law". However, when a constitutional complaint is present, access to it must be guaranteed, even though with some differences compared with access to an ordinary court. The Strasbourg Court has indeed made it clear that decisions of inadmissibility can also be made by referring exclusively to the legal provisions that form their legal basis, thus without any obligation to give reasons.[97] Yet, if the constitutional court renders a reasoned decision, the ECtHR considers itself competent to review the reasons for the refusal. This review has been exercised with particular intensity in respect of the Czech, Slovenian, and Slovak constitutional courts:[98] this jurisprudence essentially evidences that excessive formalisms may impair the essence of the right to access to court and thus constitute a violation of Article 6 ECHR.[99] A far-reaching application of this principle is contained in *Lorenzo Bragado* v. Spain, where the ECtHR held that the inadmissibility decisions of the applicant's amparo for being lodged out of time, violated his right to access to a court in light of "the evident general importance of the matter, the apparent novelty or rareness of the legal issues raised before the Constitutional Court, and the particular circumstances of the case and with due regard to the aims of legal certainty and the proper administration of justice".[100] What this judgment seems ultimately to imply is that in highly significant cases, procedural constraints should not preclude the constitutional court from delivering a decision.

In the ECtHR's interpretation, the right to a court also includes the right "to have a final determination on a matter submitted to a court".[101] It is in fact under this aspect of the right to a fair trial that the Court sanctioned the Albanian and Montenegrin

---

[95] Ibrido (2016), p. 9.

[96] *Kristiana LTD v. Lithuania* (36184/13), 06/02/2018, para. 123.

[97] *Arribas Anton v. Spain* (16563/11), 20/01/2015, para. 47.

[98] See above, Sects. 3.4, 4.13 and 4.14, respectively.

[99] See *Stavebna Spolocnost Tatry Poprad, S.R.O. v. Slovakia* (7261/06), 03/05/2011, paras 18–19; *Zvolsky and Zvolska v. Czech Republic* (46129/99), 12/11/2002; *Beleš et autres v. Czech Republic* (47273/99), 12/11/2002, paras 63–66; *Vodarenska Akciova Spolecnost A.S. v. Czech Republic* (73577/01), 24/02/2004, para. 35; *Soudek v. Czech Republic* (56526/00), 15/03/2005, para. 21; *Marík v. Czech Republic* (73116/01), 12/04/2005, para. 16; *Turek v. Czech Republic* (73403/01), 21/06/2005, para. 32; *Páleník v. Czech Republic* (64737/01), 21/06/2005, para. 28; *Pillmann v. Czech Republic* (15333/02), 27/09/2005, para. 21; *Šroub v. Czech Republic* (5424/03), 17/01/2006, para. 22; *Friedrich v. Czech Republic* (12108/03), 26/10/2006, para. 20; *Ješina v. Czech Republic* (18806/02), 26/07/2007, para. 26; *Glaser v. Czech Republic* (55179/00), 24/02/2008, para. 34; *Horení v. Czech Republic* (31806/02), 06/03/2008, para. 28; *Drahorad et Drahoradova v. Czech Republic* (10254/03), 20/03/2008, para. 25; *Mourek v. Czech Republic* (17999/03), 03/04/2008, para. 19.

[100] *Lorenzo Bragado and Others v. Spain* (53193/21, 53707/21, 53848/21 et al.), 22/06/2023, para. 145.

[101] *Marini v. Albania* (3738/02), 18/12/2007, para. 120.

courts for the lack of anti-deadlock mechanism in the case of a tie.[102] The ECtHR also clarified that, whilst in principle constitutional courts are not required to award the costs of the procedure to applicants, the denial of the compensation of legal expenses sustained may result in a violation of the right to a court.[103]

Strictly connected with the right to access a court is the issue of the right to submit a question of constitutionality. Also to this regard, the Court affirmed that "the Convention does not guarantee, as such, any right to have a case referred by a domestic court to another national or international authority for a preliminary ruling".[104] The case law of the ECtHR on the point appears to be well consolidated, as it essentially simply requires the referring court to show to have considered the applicant's request, and the relevant threshold to establish a breach seems rather high.[105] The Court in fact found a violation of Article 6 ECHR on the ground that an ordinary judge refused to refer a question to the constitutional court on only one occasion, in the judgment in *Xero Flor v. Poland*. However, as also Judge Wojtyczek highlighted, the finding of a violation in this case is hardly compatible with the ECtHR case law, as three different levels of domestic courts considered the question and rejected it.[106] This is why, also considering the specific context in which the judgment was delivered, the passage of the judgment affirming that if "a party to civil proceedings raises a constitutional issue of importance for the determination of a case and requests that this issue be referred to the Constitutional Court for examination, a domestic court has to provide specific reasons justifying its refusal to refer the question",[107] is unlikely to indicate a switch in the ECtHR case law in the sense of imposing higher standards of reasoning for the refusal of referring question of constitutionality by ordinary judges.

Of all the aspects of the right to a fair constitutional trial, the right to a trial of reasonable duration constitutes by far the most applied to the constitutionality judgment. A diachronic analysis of the judgments on the subject allows us to appreciate the consolidation of the Strasbourg jurisprudence. The ECtHR seems indeed to have gradually abandoned, over the years, a purely casuistic approach in assessing the reasonable duration of constitutional trials. In the first decade of this century, the ECtHR carried out an individualised assessment of each constitutional

[102] *Avdić and Others v. Bosnia and Herzegovina* (28357/11, 31549/1139295/11 et al.),19/11/2013; *Marini v. Albania* (3738/02), *18/12/2007.*

[103] *Dragan Kovačević v. Croatia* (49281/15), 12/05/2022, paras. 80–84.

[104] Recently see, *Šaltinytė v. Lithuania* (32934/19), 26/10/2021, para. 88.

[105] See, Ibidem, paras 88–92. Also see, *Coeme and Others v. Belgium* (32492/96, 32547/96, 32548/96), 22/06/2000, para. 114–117; *Wynen and Centre Hospitalier Interrégional Edith-Cavell v. Belgium* (32576/96), 05/11/2002, paras 39–43; *Hodos et autres v. Romania* (29968/96), 21/05/2002, para. 57; *Ciobanu v. Romania* (29053/95), 16/07/2002, para. 41; *Maatescu et autres v. Romania* (30698/96), 22/10/2002, para. 37; *Iosif et Autres v. Romania* (10443/03), 20/12/2007, para. 73.

[106] *Xero Flor w Polsce sp. z o.o. v. Poland*, Partly Concurring Partly Disseting Opinion of Judge Wojtyczek, paras 9–10.

[107] Ibidem, para. 171.

proceeding to evaluate whether the constitutional court's conduct was reproachable in some regard.[108] Already in 2007, however, in the judgment in *Kirsten v. Germany,*[109] the Strasbourg Court appears to be moving towards a more principled approach, as it affirmed that in the range between 3 years and 6 months and 4 years and 8 months proceedings before the BVG should be considered of reasonable duration. The validity of this statement was circumscribed by the addition that was true "particularly in the unique context of the German reunification".[110] Nevertheless, one can infer from that judgment that, beyond that threshold, operates a rebuttable presumption that the duration is excessive: as a matter of fact, there have been no cases in which a constitutional trial lasting more than 5 years has been found to be reasonable.

On the other hand, since the judgment in *Komanicky v. Slovakia*—in which the ECtHR declared manifestly unfounded an application alleging the unreasonable duration of a constitutional trial lasting 1 year and 4 months—a presumption of non-excessive duration can be considered to operate for constitutional proceedings lasting less than 3 years.[111] In subsequent judgments, the ECtHR continued to declare appeals against constitutional trials lasting less than 3 years manifestly unfounded, thus confirming the existence of a strong presumption of reasonableness.[112] Conversely, for trials lasting between 3 years and 4 years and 6 months, the Strasbourg Court still carries out a detailed individual examination of the circumstances of the case.[113]

Whilst the criteria set out above may be recognised as useful guidelines that constitutional courts may take into account to avoid being sanctioned in Strasbourg, given the Strasbourg Court's eminently casuistic approach it is obvious that the Court does not feel bound by them. There are indeed a variety of factors that may reduce the maximum permissible duration of a constitutional proceeding. If for instance the case is concluded with an inadmissibility decision, a duration of 2 years and 8 months has been considered excessive.[114] Similarly, in the absence of any documented procedural activity on the part of the constitutional court, a duration of 3 years and 6 months is considered unreasonable.[115] Also, the nature of the violation complained of by the applicant appears to play a decisive role: in cases concerning the right of parents to obtain custody of their children, a duration of

---

[108] See, for instance, *Tričković v. Slovenia*, where the Court thoroughly analysed the CCSL's behaviour even though the latter court only took 2 years and 7 months to deliver a judgment in the applicant's case. See, *Tričković v. Slovenia* (39914/98), 12/06/2001, paras. 36–41.

[109] *Kirsten v. Germany,* 19124/02, 15/02/2007.

[110] Ibidem, para. 46.

[111] *Komanicky v. Slovakia (No. 3)* 72092/01, 17/06/2008.

[112] *Prezec v. Croatia* (48185/07), 15/10/2009, para. 42; *Tešić v. Serbia* (4678/07, 50591/12), 11/02/2014, para. 77.

[113] *Posedel-Jelinovic v. Croatia* (35915/02), 24/11/2005, paras. 24–26.

[114] *Hauser-Sporn v. Austria* (37301/13), 07/12/2006, paras. 36–40. Similarly, for a term of 3 years and 1 month see: *Rosa Marques et autres v. Portugal* (48187/99), 25/07/2002, para. 29.

[115] *Pitra v. Croatia* (41075/02), 16/06/2005, para. 21.

1 year and 7 months could be considered unreasonable according to ECHR standards, in light of the importance of what is at stake for the applicant.[116] In the same sense, a duration of 3 years and 6 months of a trial before the Croatian Constitutional Court is judged by the ECHR to be excessive despite the ECHR itself recognising the complexity of the dispute, considering the importance of the case for the applicant, who sought to rescue the possession of its flat.[117] Also, another element capable of influencing the determination of the reasonableness of the duration of constitutional proceedings is the overall duration of domestic proceedings. If these have been already excessively long, this seems to impose a special duty on the constitutional court to act with special celerity. If it fails to do so, the European Court of Human Rights may censure the work of the constitutional court, although it does not always specify to which specific body the violation is attributable.[118]

About the concept of impartiality of the constitutional judge, an overall reading of the case law of the ECtHR allows some general principles to be derived. As a preliminary remark, it shall be underscored that the Strasbourg Court never declared a constitutional judge to be impartial, but in some cases it affirmed that the appearance of impartiality was violated. The factor to which the Court attributes decisive weight is whether the constitutional judge has performed other functions within the same proceedings.[119] This prohibition appears to be almost absolute in scope, being applicable to cases where the constitutional judge has drafted a scientific opinion in favour of one of the parties to the proceedings, which has no bearing on the merits of the case decided by the constitutional court,[120] or cases where the contact with the other party was of limited duration and dating back in time.[121] Obviously, respect for the principle of impartiality prevents any participation as a judge, even for a single hearing, at another stage of the proceedings.[122] From a procedural point of view, the ECtHR imposes that the judge whose recusation is sought, must not rule on the request presented against him/her.[123] On the other hand, the contacts a constitutional judge has had with lower courts' judges do not appear to be relevant, as one of the main roles of a constitutional court is to overrule decisions of the lower courts and therefore this cannot be considered to affect the impartiality of the constitutional judge.[124] Overall, it appears that in the assessment of the impartiality of the constitutional judge, the Court maintains a rigid separation between previous participation in another stage of the proceedings, even just as an independent expert, which is

---

[116] *Kuhlen-Rafsandjani v. Germany* (21980/06, 26944/07, 36948/08), 20/01/2011, para. 83.

[117] *Butkovic v. Croatia* (32264/03), 24/05/2007 para. 27.

[118] *Diaz Aparicio v. Spain* (49468/99), 11/10/2001, paras. 21–22; *Pištorová v. Czech* Republic (73578/01), 26/10/2004, para. 28.

[119] *Hit D.D. Nova Gorica v. Slovenia* (50996/08), 05/06/2014.

[120] See *Švarc and Kavnik v. Slovenia* (75617/01), 08/02/2007.

[121] *Meznaric v. Croatia* (71615/01), 15/07/2005, paras. 34–35.

[122] *Liga Portoguesa de Futebol Profissional v. Portugal* (4687/11), 17/05/2016.

[123] *A.K. v. Liechtenstein (no. 2)*, 10722/13, 18/02/2016, para. 91.

[124] *Steck-Risch and Others v. Liechtenstein* (63151/00), 19/05/2005, paras. 46–50.

consistently considered in breach of judicial impartiality, and relationships outside the proceedings concerning the applicant, where the applicant has the burden of proving that those are capable of affecting the impartiality of the constitutional judge.[125] It is instead worth remarking that in no judgments the Strasbourg Court assessed possible breaches of the right to an independent constitutional judge.

As for the principle of adversarial proceedings,[126] the scope of application of Article 6 appears to be of similar breadth in constitutional and ordinary proceedings. Indeed, no exceptions whatsoever to the application of this principle have been found in the ECtHR jurisprudence examined. In constitutional proceedings, this right primarily implies the right to be informed and to be able to comment on any document contained in the file.[127] This right extends not only to documents produced by the opposing party,[128] but also to the observations of the judge *a quo*,[129] to the pleadings of the prosecution,[130] and even to information requested by the constitutional court concerning objective facts, such as the duration of the preliminary investigation or the participation of public entities in the legislative proceedings, although it may be argued that this is indisputable information that as such may be excluded from the duty to notification.[131] Finally, failure to respect the adversarial principle generates a violation of Article 6 ECHR even independently of the production of a concrete prejudice for the applicant.[132] The principle of adversarial proceedings, also implies the right to intervene in constitutional proceedings, and as such must be extended to counter-interested third parties. In two similar rulings, the Strasbourg Court has indeed found a violation of Article 8 ECHR provoked by the failure of national authorities to guarantee the applicants right to the custody of their children. For what concerns us the most, in both cases the Slovak Constitutional Court had not notified to the applicant the introduction of a constitutional appeal regarding the custody of their child.[133] Even though the ECtHR did not

[125] *Švarc and Kavnik v. Slovenia* (75617/01), 08/02/2007.

[126] This right guarantees that the parties to criminal or civil proceedings must in principle have the opportunity not only to make known any evidence needed for their claims to succeed, but also to have knowledge of, and comment on, all evidence adduced, or observations filed, with a view to influencing the court's decision. See, *Krčmář and Others v. Czech Republic* (35376/97), 03/03/2000, para. 40.

[127] See *Krčmar and Others v. Czech Republic* (35376/97), 03/03/2000, para. 43.

[128] *Gaspari v. Slovenia* (21055/03), 21/07/2009, paras. 54–57.

[129] See *Vokoun v. Czech Republic* (20728/05), 03/07/2008, para. 27; *Kysilková and Kysilka v. Czech Republic* (17273/03), 10/02/2011, para. 39; *Janyr v Czech Republic* (42937/08), 31/10/2013.

[130] See *Feliciano Bichao v. Portugal* (40225/04), 20/11/2007, paras. 25, 37.

[131] On the first example see: *Benet Praha Spol S.R.O. v. Czech Republic* (33908/04, 7937/05, 25249/05), 24/02/2011, paras 141–143; on the second: *Gramaxo Rozeira v. Portugal* (21976/09), 21/01/2014, para. 37.

[132] *Milatová et al v. Czech Republic* (61811/00), 21/06/2005, para. 65; *Mareš v. Czech Republic* (1414/03), 26/10/2006, para. 30; *Hubka v. Czech Republic* (500/06), 03/02/2011, para. 36; *Palšovič v. Czech Republic* (39278/04), 03/02/2011, para. 31.

[133] See *López Gujó v. Slovakia* (10280/12), 03/06/2014, paras 103–11; *Frisancho Perea v. Slovakia* (383/13), 21/07/2015, para. 39.

deal with the part of the application concerning Article 6, as it considered sufficient having established a breach of Article 8, it can be inferred that the failure to notify the introduction of a constitutional appeal to the persons with a direct interest in its outcome and who have participated in the ordinary proceedings, could lead to a violation of Article 6.

The last element of the right to a fair constitutional process to be considered is the right to a public hearing. First of all, in order to find a violation, the ECHR requires the applicant to make an explicit request, as the right to a public hearing is a right that can be waived.[134] Conversely, if the appellant makes such a request, the fairness of the proceedings requires that, in principle, a public hearing must be held to hear the appellant's arguments.[135] A careful reading of ECtHR case-law evidences the difference existing between full constitutional complaints and other constitutional proceedings of a predominantly objective character, such as questions of constitutionality and normative complaints. With regard to the latter, the Strasbourg Court affirmed in fact that if the proceedings are aimed exclusively at ascertaining the unconstitutionality of a rule, the applicant does not have a right to be heard.[136] Conversely, in full constitutional complaints, or when the constitutional court rules as a unique instance, a public hearing must be in principle celebrated.[137]

As a last point, it must be underlined that the applicability of Article 6 ECHR is not limited to individual constitutional complaints, even the vast majority of judgments applying Article 6 actually concerns individual complaints, as the Strasbourg Court has held it applicable to questions of constitutionality, conflict of attributions between the powers of the State,[138] and did not exclude its applicability for impeachment proceedings—upon the condition that the constitutional court has the power to adopt sanctions of criminal nature.[139] The only competence which is still exempt from the application of Article 6 ECHR seems to be electoral disputes concerning the right to stand for elections. The authority on the subject is represented by the landmark judgment in the case of *Pierre Bloch v. France*, in which the ECHR stated that Article 6 ECHR did not apply to electoral disputes because they are not aimed at determining the civil rights and duties of the applicant.[140] Except for this

---

[134] *Pauger v. Austria* (16717/90), 208/05/1997, paras. 60–61; *Gorraiz Lizarraga v. Spain* (62543/00), 27/04/2004.

[135] *Selmani and Others v. The Former Yugoslav Republic of Macedonia* (67259/14), 09/02/2017, paras. 37–39.

[136] *Meimanis v. Latvia* (70597/11), 21/07/2015, para. 44; *Selmani and Others v. The Former Yugoslav Republic of Macedonia*, para. 40.

[137] *Selmani and Others v. The Former Yugoslav Republic of Macedonia* (67259/14), 09/02/2017, paras 41–42.

[138] On this point, the copious case law against Italy must be mentioned: See, *Cordova (no. 1) v. Italy* (40877/98), 30/01/2003; *Cordova (no. 2) v. Italy* (45649/99), 30/01/2003; *C.G.I.L. and Cofferati v. Italy* (46967/07), 24/02/2009; *Onorato v. Italy* (26218/06), 24/05/2011; *Belpietro v. Italy* (43612/10), 24/09/2013.

[139] See *Paksas v. Lithuania* (34932/04), 06/01/2011.

[140] *Pierre Bloch v. France* (24194/94), 21/10/97.

significant exception, it appears that virtually no constitutional proceeding, as long as it foresees the presence of individual parties, is in principle immune from Strasbourg's scrutiny.

5.4 Interaction Outside Article 34 ECHR Proceedings. Informal Dialogue and the Potential of Protocol 16

This book has considered the interactions occurring between the Strasbourg Court and national constitutional courts only from the privileged perspective of the ECtHR case law in individual applications brought pursuant to Article 34 ECHR. Despite this being the main institutional channel of judicial communication between the two levels of jurisdiction, it should not be forgotten that there are also other formal and informal networks in which judicial dialogue, in the broadest sense of the term, occurs. As a preliminary consideration, it is worth observing that, as of 1 January 2024, seven judges in the current composition of the Court previously served as constitutional judges,[141] evidencing that the links between the two levels are in many cases also personal ones.[142] Concerning more formal forums of dialogues, European constitutional courts and the Strasbourg Court participate in the Joint Council of Constitutional Justice, established by the Venice Commission to steer cooperation between constitutional courts and CoE Bodies. The Joint Council meets once a year and it is preceded by a seminar during which the relevant case-law of national constitutional courts is presented by liaison officers. The Venice Commission also provides a wide range of services to both constitutional courts and Strasbourg Court. In particular the publication of the Bulletin on Constitutional Jurisprudence, following relevant developments in constitutional law, and the CODICES database providing English translation of national legislation and constitutional case law from all the Venice Commission Member States.[143] Also, conferences and seminars involving judges from both national constitutional courts and the Strasbourg Court are regularly organised by judges' networks, European universities, and by the ECtHR

[141] Those are: Kateřina Šimáčková former judge at CCCZ (2013–2021), Ana Maria Guerra Martins former judge of the PTC (2007–2016); Gabriele Kucsko-Stadlmayer Substitute Member of the VGH (1995–2015); Egidijus Kūris justice and President of the CCLT (1999–2008); Péter Paczolay former President of the HCC (2008–2015); Georges Ravarani, Former Vice President of the Luxembourg Constitutional Court (2008–2015); and Faris Vehabović, former member of the CCBH (2007–2012).

[142] In the case of Lithuania, this seems to have had a visible impact on the ECtHR case law, as the presence of a former constitutional judge seems to have produced an increase in the attention the Court dedicates to the CCLT case law in its judgments. See, above, Sect. 3.8.

[143] The vast majority of the legislation analysed in the present book has been consulted in this database.

itself.[144] These events facilitate a more informal exchange of legal insights, promote a shared understanding of fundamental rights principles, and contribute to strengthening the cooperation between constitutional and European judges.

Besides, some European constitutional courts also have the opportunity to request an advisory opinion concerning the ECHR interpretation to the Strasbourg Court under Protocol 16 ECHR. The stated aim of this Protocol, according to its Preamble, is to "enhance the interaction between the Court and the national authorities", whilst its underlying idea is to allow the ECtHR to take control of its docket, by reducing the number of cases reaching Strasbourg in the long term.[145] The request for an advisory opinion, presented by a superior jurisdiction of a Member State,[146] is received by a panel of five judges of the Grand Chamber, if the panel accepts the request, the Grand Chamber shall deliver an advisory opinion.[147] Protocol 16 entered into force in August 2018, after the tenth Member State ratified. As to 1 January 2024, when more than 10 years have elapsed since the Protocol was opened for signature, only a minority of CoE Member States, 22, ratified it. In particular, Austria, Bulgaria, Czechia, Germany, Hungary, Latvia, Liechtenstein Poland, Portugal, Serbia, and Spain, just to cite the States covered by our research, are not even signatories of this Protocol 16 ECHR. This stalemate in the ratification process, which may be interpreted as a signal of a generalised 'integration fatigue', renders any prognostic conclusions on the future effectiveness of this mechanism uncertain.[148]

However, for what it concerns more closely our purposes, it must be signalled that Article 10 of the Protocol leaves the Member States free to decide which national courts are empowered to submit a request for an advisory opinion to the Strasbourg Court, and thus also to deny constitutional courts this possibility. Amongst the current Parties of the Protocol, Ukraine for instance decided to not allow the constitutional court to request an advisory opinion.[149] In Italy, which signed the Protocol in 2013 but did not ratify it yet, the last ratification proposal remitted to the

[144] Particularly significant is the seminar "Dialogue between judges" organised each year by the Strasbourg Court in occasion of the opening of the judicial year. As the title of the seminar suggests, the themes are especially focused on the relationship between the Strasbourg Court and national courts, e.g. the 2024 seminar theme was "Revisiting subsidiarity in the age of shared responsibility". See, https://www.echr.coe.int/opening-of-the-judicial-year. All the websites were last accessed on the 30 of June 2024.

[145] Well before it entered into force, the capacity of Protocol 16 to reach those objectives was seriously questioned in academic scholarship, arguing that the risks for the efficient delivery of the Court adjudicatory function overweight the potential benefits of this constitutionalising function. See, in particular, Dzehtsiarou and O'Meara (2014).

[146] See, Article 10 Protocol 16 ECHR.

[147] See, Article 2 Protocol 16 ECHR.

[148] Also, as of 1 January 2024, the Grand Chamber only decided 20 such requests, which seems to indicate a scarce recourse to the instrument by national courts.

[149] See,Declaration contained in the instrument of ratification deposited on 22 March 2018, available at: https://www.coe.int/en/web/conventions/full-list?module=declarations-by-treaty&numSte=214&codeNature=3&codePays=U.

ICC the decision as to whether to consider itself legitimated to request an advisory opinion.[150] In any case, also taking into account constitutional courts' behaviour in submitting the preliminary reference procedure to the CJEU, consisting of a generalised reluctancy to use the instrument,[151] it seems unlikely that Protocol 16 will become a significant channel of the dialogue between the two levels of jurisdiction.[152]

References

Arnardóttir OM (2017) The "procedural turn" under the European Convention on Human Rights and presumptions of Convention compliance. Int J Const Law 15:9–35

Burgorgue Larsen L (2004) L'autonomie constitutionnelle aux prises avec la Convention européenne. Revue Belge de droit constitutionnel 1:31–64

Dürr SR (2014) Individual access to constitutional courts as an effective remedy against human rights violations in Europe - The contribution of the Venice Commission. J Law Politics 258(88):67–89

Dzehtsiarou K, O'Meara N (2014) Advisory jurisdiction and the European court of human rights: a magic bullet for dialogue and docket-control? Leg Stud 34:444–468

Glas LR (2016) The functioning of the pilot-judgment procedure of the European court of human rights in practice. 34. Netherlands Q Human Rights 34:41–70

Greco C (2022) Il protocollo n. 16 allegato alla Cedu e la funzione consultiva della Corte Europea dei diritti dell'uomo anche alla luce della futura e ancora incerta ratifica italiana. Cuadernos de Derecho Transnacional 14:313–333

Ibrido R (2016) Intorno all'equo processo costituzionale: il problema dell'operatività dell'art. 6 CEDU nei giudizi dinanzi ai tribunali costituzionali. Rivista AIC 1:1–32

Martinico G (2016) Italy: between constitutional openness and resistance. In: Popelier P et al (eds) Criticism of the European court of human rights. Shifting the convention system: counter-dynamics at the national and EU level. Intersentia, Cambridge, pp 177–198

Pivoda M (2023) Constitutional courts asking questions: a deliberative potential of preliminary reference mechanism. Camb Yearb Eur Legal Stud:1–20

Pócza K, Csapodi M, Dobos GA (2024) Constitutional review and judicial-legislative relations in new democracies. In: Pócza K (ed) Constitutional review in central and Eastern Europe. Judicial-legislative relations in comparative perspective. Routledge, London, pp 1–27

Popelier P, Lambrecht S, Lemmens K (2016) Criticism of the European court of human rights. Shifting the convention system: counter-dynamics at the national and EU level. Intersentia, Cambridge

Sadurski W (2009) Partnering with Strasbourg: Constitutionalization of the European court of human rights, the accession of central and east European states to the Council of Europe, and the idea of pilot judgments. Hum Rights Law Rev 9:397–453

[150] See, Greco (2022), fn 102.

[151] However an increasing trend in the constitutional courts referral of preliminary questions to the Court of Justice has been noted in recent years. See, Pivoda (2023), p. 8.

[152] As of 1 January 2024, only the Armenian Constitutional Court has requested an advisory opinion to the Strasbourg Court. See, *Advisory opinion concerning the use of the "blanket reference" or "legislation by reference" technique in the definition of an offence and the standards of comparison between the criminal law in force at the time of the commission of the offence and the amended criminal law*, 29/05/2020.

Chapter 6
Concluding Remarks

6.1 Pulling the Threads Together. The Strasbourg Self-Understanding of Its Role vis-à-vis Constitutional Courts

As we approach the conclusion of this book, it is time to pull the threads of our analysis together by considering the issues we laid out in the Introduction, starting with our first purpose: providing a general overview of the relationship between the ECtHR and national constitutional courts as seen from the Strasbourg standpoint. The first thing to be said in this regard is that the picture resulting from a comprehensive reading of the ECtHR case law in the different national political contexts and institutional set-ups is composite and multifaceted, advising against the opportunity of formulating statements of universal validity. With this caveat in mind, if we are to describe the Strasbourg Court's attitude *vis-à-vis* constitutional courts in a sentence, it can be affirmed that it is characterised by an authoritative revendication of its position as *primus inter pares* in the European legal order rather than the recognition of its subsidiary role with respect to constitutional courts. Both in fundamental rights' dialogues and in the review of constitutional courts' procedural performance, even in the presence of a consolidated domestic practice or jurisprudence,[1] the Strasbourg Court indeed assertively applies ECtHR standards, *de facto* claiming its prerogative to the last word.

There is, of course, substantive evidence that the ECtHR is adapting its case law to the entry into force of Protocol 15—which establishes subsidiarity and margin of appreciation as pillars of the European human rights architecture, as it is now taking

[1] Consider, for instance, the dialogue on freedom of expression with the Spanish Constitutional Tribunal or the case law concerning the insufficient amount of compensation for excessive duration of proceedings awarded by the Croatian Constitutional Court. See, above, respectively at Sects. 3.7 and 4.4, in particular fn 70.

M. A. Simonelli, *The European Court of Human Rights and Constitutional Courts*,
Ius Gentium: Comparative Perspectives on Law and Justice 120,
https://doi.org/10.1007/978-3-031-71268-5_6

more seriously the limitations of its supervisory role and refraining from manifestly too rigid applications of its standards.[2] There are also clear signals that the ECtHR is shifting towards a procedural assessment of human rights violations,[3] e.g. the judgment on the ban on abortion in Poland,[4] which omits any substantive analysis of the restrictions and focuses exclusively on the legality of the composition of the Constitutional Tribunal. Nevertheless, its most recent case law demonstrates that the Strasbourg Court is unwilling to abandon its role as supreme interpreter of European fundamental rights and guardian of democracy in the new "age of subsidiarity".[5]

At the same time, it is indisputable that constitutional courts, in the last decade, have been challenging this positioning of the Strasbourg Court with increasing frequency. Especially Western constitutional courts have indeed 'rebelled' against ECtHR judgments that they perceive as overstepping the boundaries of the ECtHR jurisdiction and not considering the specificities of each national legal system.[6] The Strasbourg Court seems aware of this mounting discontent amongst constitutional courts and is starting to take action. More specifically, in its most recent case law, national constitutional jurisprudence appears to play a more significant role as formant of ECtHR standards: it has indeed been observed a generalised increase both in the percentage of judgments with constitutional courts' citations and in the average number of citations in each ECtHR judgment. In a nutshell, it is thus possible to describe the relationship between Strasbourg and national constitutional courts as a synallagmatic one, where one party—constitutional courts— provides obedience and cooperation to the other—the Strasbourg Court—only as long as it is receiving back deference in issues identified as part of the national constitutional traditions. However, when this discontent, articulated in a principled disobedience, is transformed into an open, unprincipled challenge, as in the December 2021 judgment of the Polish Constitutional Tribunal, the reaction of the ECtHR has been firm, going as far as to deny the PCT the status of legitimate interlocutor.

Much more straightforward is the answer to the second declared purpose of this book, namely assessing the extent of constitutional courts' subordination to Article 6 guarantees. For constitutional courts with a full complaint mechanism, the Court

[2] Emblematic in this regard is the 2023 Grand Chamber in *Grosam v. the Czech Republic*, in which the Grand Chamber, overturning the decision of the First Section, declared that the latter "exceeded the powers conferred on the Court by Articles 32 and 34 of Convention" for not complying with the rules delimiting the material scope of its jurisdiction. See: *Grosam v. the Czech Republic* (19,750/13), 01/06/2023, paras 91–97.

[3] The proceduralization of the ECtHR is considered by scholars one of the most evident signs that the Strasbourg Court is embracing the new subsidiarity age inaugurated by the Brighton Declartation. See, Kleinlein (2019), pp. 91–92.

[4] *M.L. v. Poland* (40,119/21), 14/12/2023.

[5] The expression is taken from Robert Spano, former ECtHR judge, who argued that the entry force of Protocol 15 ECHR would have marked a new era in the ECHR system. See: Spano (2014).

[6] Some of these critics are partially echoed in academic scholarship, which has lamented the ECtHR's excessive ambiguity in defining the margin of appreciation doctrine. See, amongst many others, Kratochvíl (2011).

operates *de facto* as an additional instance, capable of scrutinising every aspect of the constitutional courts' procedural performance, from the decision to not admit a case to the voting procedure.[7] Conversely, constitutional courts that can only be reached indirectly via a question of constitutionality can more easily escape the application of Article 6. Nonetheless, this does not imply that those constitutional courts are immune from Strasbourg scrutiny. Despite the letter of Article 6 ECHR circumscribes the applicability of Article 6 to proceedings aimed at the determination of civil rights or criminal charges, since the landmark judgment in *Ruiz Mateos v. Spain*, the ECtHR has expanded the notion of civil rights under the Convention in a far-reaching manner so that it can now be safely affirmed that Article 6 applies to any constitutional dispute capable of affecting the outcome of the applicant's case.[8] However, concerning the incidental question of constitutionality, given that the Strasbourg Court only once -in the peculiar context of the Polish rule of law crisis—has affirmed that the refusal to submit a preliminary question to the constitutional court may amount to a violation of the right of access to a court, there are only a few cases in which the ECtHR has applied fair trial guarantees in incidental proceedings.

What it is interesting to note concerning the application of Article 6 ECHR is rather how the ECtHR has progressively transformed this provision into a rule of law tool. In particular, through an expansive interpretation of the *Vilho Eskelinen* test, the Court has held applicable Article 6 to procedures for the appointment and removal of ordinary (*Baka v. Hungary*), and constitutional judges (*Juričić v. Croatia*), judicial councils' members (*Lorenzo Bragado and Others v. Spain*), and public prosecutors (*Kovesi v. Romania*). All these cases have in common that the Strasbourg Court finds a violation of Article 6 ECHR on the grounds that a procedural guarantee was omitted, i.e., the right to access a court to challenge the removal or appointment decision.[9] However, both the benefits for the applicant and the spill-over effects of declaring a breach of Article 6 in those proceedings are by itself limited. On the one hand, only on one occasion the Strasbourg Court ordered the reinstatement of the applicant in the position he previously occupied,[10] and it never instated, or even recommended, the Respondent state to proceed to or repeat the appointment in question. As to the possibility of pecuniary compensation to represent an adequate redress, it is significant that both in *Kovesi v. Romania* and *Lorenzo Bragado and Others v. Spain*,[11] the applicants did not seek monetary satisfaction, which shows that are the same applicants that presented their cases as constitutional litigation.

[7] See, Sect. 5.3.2.

[8] *Ruiz Mateos v. Spain* (12,952/87), 23/06/1993.

[9] In this sense, then, those cases seem to confirm the procedural shift in the ECtHR case law.

[10] See, above, Sect. 4.1.2, fn 37.

[11] The applicant in *Lorenzo Bragado and Others* actually claimed the symbolic sum of one euro as compensation for non-pecuniary damage, which the Court however refused to award. Nor the Court awarded applicants compensation for legal costs, as they were not properly justified. See, *Lorenzo Bragado and Others v. Spain*, paras 152–157.

On the other hand, those judgements do not elaborate on the guarantees that must accompany removal and appointment procedures that may serve as guidelines for other Member States, but merely identify a breach of the applicant's right to a fair trial, provoked by the lack of an avenue to challenge the contested decision or by the constitutional court's dismissal of the applicant's case. At best, they can be thus interpreted as an invitation to the constitutional court to fulfil its role as rule of law bulwark and not refrain from adjudicating politically contentious cases.

Much more incisive is instead the approach adopted by the ECtHR in *Xero Flor v. Poland.*[12] The Court here employed Article 6, in its facet of the right to a tribunal established by law, as a yardstick to review the compatibility with the rule of law standards of the rules governing the appointment of constitutional judges. What is most striking about this case is that the ECtHR seems to have abandoned its traditional casuistic approach in favour of one which is mainly focused on the legislative framework. Even more striking are, however, the conclusions the Court has drawn from its judgment in *Xero Flor*. In its 2023 judgment in *M.L. v. Poland* the Court, instead of carrying out a much-awaited proportionality assessment delimitating the margin of appreciation awarded to Member States in restricting on the right to abortion,[13] found a violation of Article 8 ECHR on the grounds that the restriction was not prescribed by law as it was constituted by a judgment adopted by an unlawfully composed bench of the PCT. It is worth remarking in this regard that the PCT did not even intervene in the applicant's proceedings but pronounced a declaration of unconstitutionality in the context of an action of unconstitutionality proposed by the Polish parliament, *de facto* rendering it impossible to terminate a pregnancy in Poland lawfully. Such a bold approach of the Strasbourg Court can probably be better understood if considered together with the CJEU rule of law jurisprudence. After the landmark judgment in *Associação Sindical dos Juízes Portugueses*,[14] the CJEU indeed intensified its scrutiny over how Member States organise their judiciaries, often relying on ECtHR-made standards concerning the right to an independent and impartial tribunal.[15] It is thus possible to infer that the Strasbourg Court exploited the political leverage represented by the endorsement coming from Luxembourg to enhance the constitutional tone of its case law.

Yet, it should be underlined that the CJEU has insofar refrained from declaring a national court unlawfully composed. On the contrary, despite strong academic

---

[12] The judgment forms part of the rule of law jurisprudence inaugurated by the Strasbourg Court in *Guðmundur Andri Ástráðsson v. Iceland.* For a commentary on this judgment see, Karlsson (2022).

[13] See, Zabrocka (2023), The ML v Poland 'landmark' judgment on reproductive rights and the ENNHRI third-party intervention: How 'landmark' is it in reality?. Oxford Human Rights Hub, 31 January 2024. Available at: https://ohrh.law.ox.ac.uk/the-ml-v-poland-landmark-judgment-on-reproductive-rights-and-the-ennhri-third-party-intervention-how-landmark-is-it-inreality/#:~:text=On%2014%20December%202,023%2C%20in,)%20%5B168%2D176%5D. All the links were last accessed on the 30 of June 2024.

[14] Case C-64/16, *Associação Sindical dos Juízes Portugueses v Tribunal de Contas*, Judgment of the Grand Chamber of the Court of 27 February 2018, EU:C:2017:395.

[15] For a critical view on this point, see, Bustos Gisbert (2022), p. 606.

criticism,[16] the CJEU is allowing tribunals composed of judges whose appointments had been declared incompatible with the rule of law requirements to legitimately participate in the EU legal system.[17] Further, the Strasbourg Court is substantially deprived of any meaningful tool to ensure compliance with its judgments and has to externalise the implementation of its judgments to national constitutional courts. Ultimately, without adequate support from constitutional courts and the CJEU, a case law arrogating itself the power to establish the legality of national courts' composition is, in the long run, untenable.[18] Against this backdrop, it appears more promising for the Strasbourg Court to offer to national judges, as suggested by some scholars, the possibility to defend their prerogatives by conferring a subjective right to judicial independence upon them.[19] Be that as it may, this expansive application of Article 6 constitutes the most decisive evidence of an ongoing constitutionalising trend in the ECtHR case law. This is why tracking the evolution of this case law will be crucial to determining the future role of the Strasburg Court in the European legal order.

6.2 *Quo Vadis* Strasbourg?

At the beginning of this book, we affirmed that the Strasbourg Court's transformation into a European constitutional court would only be possible as long as national constitutional courts allow this transformation to happen. This statement implicitly reflected the conviction, widely shared in academic scholarship, that looking at the ECtHR competencies resulting from the Convention and its Protocols, the Strasbourg Court could hardly be assimilated into a constitutional court. There are indeed many strong reasons supporting this conclusion: first and foremost, the Strasbourg Court lacks explicit power to invalidate normative acts for incompatibility with the ECHR, and second, it does not have any competence related to the vertical and horizontal separation of powers in the ECHR system.[20] To put it otherwise, the

[16] See Pech L, Platon S (2021). How not to deal with Poland's fake judges' requests for a preliminary ruling: A critical analysis of AG Bobek's proposal in Case C-132/20. Verfassungsblog, 28 July 2021. Available at: https://verfassungsblog.de/how-not-to-deal-with-polands-fake-judges-requests-for-a-preliminary-ruling/.

[17] Grabowska-Moroz (2023), pp. 809–812.

[18] Especially if, as the First Section of the Court did in *Grosam v. Czech Republic*, the Strasbourg Court carries out this assessment overstretching or even disregarding the rules of engagement of its jurisdiction. See, Bobek and Kosař (2023).

[19] Leloup (2021), in particular pp. 419–421. The Author argues that the Strasbourg Court should follow the example of the UN Human Rights Committee and of the Inter-American Court of Human Rights and read such a subjective right into Article 6 ECHR, which is framed in very similar terms to Article 14(1) ICCPR and Article 8(1) of the Inter-American Convention on Human Rights.

[20] These two powers can indeed be considered the essential minimal features of a European model of constitutional court. Amongst many see, Stone Sweet (2012).

ECtHR treaty mandate is crystal clear: assessing whether, in individual cases, national legal systems have adequately protected human rights.

This notwithstanding, especially during the first decade of the current century, there has been an intense debate concerning the constitutional nature of the ECtHR.[21] Such a debate was prompted by a series of successive institutional and jurisprudential changes in the ECHR system affecting the role and functioning of the Strasbourg Court.[22] It is sufficient to remind, on the side of institutional change, the introduction of the requirement of the 'significant disadvantage' to bring a case before Strasbourg, and on the other, a gradual shift towards a procedural review in the ECtHR case law.[23] The combined effects of those changes led many authors to affirm that the Strasbourg Court's role was shifting away from that of a court of last instance for redressing individual injustices to a jurisdiction whose main function was to elaborate and guarantee the European standards on fundamental rights.

Even if this debate has long lost its centrality in academic scholarship, the comparative analysis has evidenced how the Strasbourg Court has managed to build a strong constitutional relationship with national constitutional courts, especially with CEE ones. The Strasbourg Court has indeed developed various cooperation mechanisms with the constitutional courts of the region, helping those courts establish their authority in their respective legal systems whilst providing authoritative interpretations of fundamental rights standards. In particular, the ECtHR has recognised those courts' role as ultimate protectors of fundamental rights at the domestic level. In this regard, it must be underscored that the Court has declared the 'full' constitutional complaints present in most CEE States to be, in principle, remedies of mandatory exhaustion under Article 35 ECHR.[24] This affirmation, which embodies the principle of subsidiarity governing the ECHR system, signals that the Strasbourg Court trusts the ECHR review carried out by national constitutional judges and will refrain from adjudicating cases that the national constitutional court has not previously examined. However, this does not constitute a blank check: in some cases, indeed, the ECtHR has even assumed the role of the constitutional judge, especially in cases of systemic failures in the execution of constitutional judgments either through pilot judgments, as in the Polish case, or with 'ordinary' ones as the ECtHR t did in cases against Croatia[25] and Bosnia and Herzegovina.[26] In some instances, the Strasbourg Court even acted as a modulator of the temporal effects of constitutional judgments, as it did in *Zaicevs v. Latvia*, where it conferred

[21] It shall be in particularly mentioned the position of the former ECtHR president Luzius Wildhaber which famously affirmed that he saw the Strasbourg Court "pretty much as a European constitutional court". See: Bruinsma and Parmentier (2003), p. 185. For a reconstruction of the debate see: Harmsen (2007).

[22] See, above, Sect. 2.1.

[23] Arnardóttir (2017).

[24] Conversely, it has refrained from doing so concerning the German and Spanish constitutional complaints. See, above, Sect. 5.3.1.

[25] See, above, Sect. 4.2, fn 96.

[26] See, above, Sect. 4.2.

retroactive effects, overturning *res judicata*, to a decision of the Latvian Constitutional Court.[27] In parallel, it can be affirmed that CEE constitutional courts loyally cooperate with the Strasbourg Court, and so far, they have not opposed this ECtHR case law with a marked constitutional tone. On the contrary, our investigation has evidenced a sort of passivity on the side of CEE courts that, with the significant exception of the 'captured' constitutional court of Poland, have never entered into a confrontation with the Strasbourg Court. Even the Czech Constitutional Court, which is becoming an increasingly assertive actor in the European scenario[28]—ready to declare an CJEU judgment *ultra-vires*—[29] never openly confronted the ECtHR,[30] although the Strasbourg Court has never refrained from censoring its jurisprudence, e.g. concerning the admissibility criteria for constitutional complaints adopted by the CCCZ.[31] All in all, paraphrasing an anecdote recounted by Sadurski, it can be affirmed that CEE constitutional judges seem fine with the idea of having another constitutional court in their countries.[32]

The same cannot be said for Western constitutional courts. There are, in fact, a variety of factors limiting the extent of such a strict constitutional relationship. First, Western constitutional courts operate in relatively friendly political systems and comparatively consolidated democracies. Hence, their need to rely on the Strasbourg Court to establish their authority and secure the execution of their judgement is reduced with respect to CEE constitutional courts. Second, the constitutional courts of Western Europe have well-established case law on fundamental rights, thus reducing the necessity to turn to Strasbourg to seek guidance. Besides, as well-exemplified by the *Varvara* saga with the Italian Constitutional Court,[33] or the 'dialogue' with the Spanish Constitutional Tribunal on freedom of expression,[34] if the two courts maintain two apparently irreconcilable views, the presence of an established case law may represent an obstacle in the implementation of the ECHR, as it requires an additional argumentative effort on the Strasbourg's side in order to persuade the constitutional court to change its case law to bring it in line with ECHR standards. Another significant factor is that, unlike CEE constitutional courts, most

---

[27] See, above, Sect. 4.7.

[28] Kosar and Petrov (2017), p. 616.

[29] Czech Constitutional Court, judgment of 31.1.2012, Pl. ÚS 5/12. See, ibid., fn 151.

[30] On the opposite, the Czech Constitutional Court remains one of the more enthusiastic promoters of the ECHR. Emblematically the CCC maintained the ECHR constitutional status even after a constitutional amendment explicitly affirmed that international human rights Treaties would only enjoy priority of application over primary legislation. In its landmark Euro-Amendment judgment, the CCC affirmed that "no amendment to the Constitution can be interpreted in such a way that it would result in limiting an already achieved procedural level of protection for fundamental rights and freedoms", thus recognising the Strasbourg Court as a constitutive part of the constitutional system for fundamental rights protection. See: Kosař and Vyhnánek (2020), p. 173.

[31] See, above, Sect. 4.5.

[32] Sadurski (2009), p. 452.

[33] See, above, Sect. 3.5.

[34] See, above, Sect. 3.7.

Western constitutional courts do not grant individual access, thus reducing the opportunities for building a close relationship between the two levels.[35] Also, in this respect, then, the national constitutional justice system can be deemed a key factor in shaping the relationship with the Strasbourg Court. As a concluding remark, we could thus merely repeat the observation made by David Kosař some 12 years ago that the ECtHR "has become more constitutional than before",[36] but with a small addition. Under the existing Treaty framework, and given the current European political scenario, it is rather unlikely that this constitutionalising process will go any further.

At this point, we may be expected to predict the future evolution of the role of the Strasbourg Court in the European legal order. The first thing to be said is that not only the future of the ECtHR, but even its very existence, seems to always have had a question mark over its head.[37] Indeed, by enlarging the spectrum of the analysis to the political environment in which the Strasbourg Court operates, there are at least two intertwined factors that point in two opposite directions. First, one is obliged to note how, in the last decade, political parties with a nationalist platform have been obtaining electoral success all across Europe. Those parties oppose any advancement in the European integration process and challenge the legitimacy of supranational and international organisations. Even though the main target of those parties is the European Union, the ECtHR system has also been affected by the recrudescence of nationalist politics. In the last decade, national governments showed little appetite for further integration within the CoE,[38] as demonstrated, for example, by the difficulties in ratifying Protocols 15 and 16 ECHR.[39] Also, in the same time span, a generalised increase in the number of unexecuted key ECtHR judgments has been observed,[40] evidencing a growing malaise towards Strasbourg's interferences in

[35] In this sense, it can be observed that the presence of an individual constitutional complaint may reduce the possibility of jurisprudential clashes between the ECtHR and the constitutional court as it should allow a divergence to emerge more rapidly.

[36] Kosař (2012).

[37] Even the most enthusiastic supporters of the Strasbourg Court have noted how, since its foundation, there has always been an ongoing debate about the necessity to reform the ECtHR system to ensure its survival. See, Vučinić (2011), pp. 190–192.

[38] Trubowitz and Burgoon (2023) have demonstrated a correlation between the presence in the domestic arena of political parties with a nationalist agenda and the willingness of national governments to further international integration.

[39] As well known, it took 8 years for all the CoE Member States to ratify Protocol 15, although its overall effect can be said to limit rather than expand the Strasbourg Court's jurisdiction. Protocol 16 instead has been insofar ratified only by a minority of Member States, 21. The status of ratification can be consulted at: https://www.coe.int/en/web/conventions/full-list?module=signatures-by-treaty&treatynum=214.

[40] Stafford and Jaraczewski calculate that of the leading judgments delivered against Bulgaria, Italy, Poland, Romania, and Spain from 2012 to 2022, more than 50% remained unexecuted. Significantly are calling on the European Commission to consider the non-implementation of ECtHR judgments as a negative element in its Rule of Law Reports. Stafford G, Jaraczewski, J (2022) Taking European Judgments Seriously: A Call for the EU Commission to Take Into Account the

domestic politics. Finally, in the long run, the presence within the CoE perimeter of nationalist governments may affect the Strasbourg Court from within, as they will keep selecting friendly nominees to the EC, thus threatening to neutralise its supervisory role.[41]

A second counteracting factor is that amidst the processes of democratic erosion—a collateral effect of the emergence of nationalist parties—that have interested virtually every European country, the Strasbourg Court's role in upholding democratic standards has become increasingly critical. The most decisive proof of this regard is the European Court of Justice's explicit and extensive reliance on ECtHR-made standards in its rule of law jurisprudence. This transposition converts the ECtHR case law into directly enforceable standards, irradiating its effects well beyond the reach of the Strasbourg Court, which, unlike its EU homologue, lacks the judicial instruments to obtain *ex-post* compliance with its rulings. Second, we have observed that when the independence of national judges and constitutional courts is threatened, individual judges have frequently turned to Strasbourg seeking support.[42] Providing a timely answer to those requests is quintessential to guarantee effective international protection, yet the rules of engagement of the ECtHR jurisdiction often represent an obstacle. In this sense, the advisory opinion mechanism of Protocol 16 may allow the Court to intervene more rapidly, yet as we have seen, constitutional courts are displaying a reticence to use this instrument.[43] Once again, the only way to overcome those structural limitations seems to be to strengthen cooperation with national constitutional courts, which can act as proxy-agent of the ECtHR in domestic cases and may directly ask it to intervene in the case.

In conclusion, such a plurality of factors with different signs would reduce any predictions on the future role of the Strasburg Court to little more than wishful thinking. All that can be affirmed is that if the Strasbourg Court is to direct the European judicial concerto, it will need to move in syntony with the other members of the orchestra.

References

Arnardóttir OM (2017) The "procedural turn" under the European convention on human rights and presumptions of convention compliance. Int J Const Law 15:9–35

Bobek M, Kosař D (2023) When a minority of the European court of human rights declares its own court to be ultra vires. Eur Law Rev 48:281–312

Non-Implementation of European Court Judgments in its Rule of Law Reports. VerfassungsBlog, 24 January 2022. Available at: https://verfassungsblog.de/taking-european-judgments-seriously/ , DOI: 10.17176/20220125-060258-0.

[41] On this point see: Bobek and Kosař (2023), pp. 208–209.

[42] All the rule of law cases discussed above (see, above, fn 9) were indeed initiated by judges themselves.

[43] See, above, Sect. 5.4.

Bruinsma F, Parmentier S (2003) Interview with Mr Luzius Wildhaber, president of the ECHR. Netherlands Q Human Rights 21:185–202

Bustos Gisbert R (2022) Judicial Independence in European constitutional law. Eur Const Law Rev 18:591–620

Grabowska-Moroz B (2023) Judicial dialogue about judicial independence in times of rule of law backsliding: Getin Noble Bank. Common Market Law Rev 60:797–818

Harmsen R (2007) The European court of human rights as a 'constitutional court': definitional debates and the dynamics of reform. In: Morison J et al (eds) Judges, transition and the human rights. Oxford University Press, Oxford, pp 33–53

Karlsson LG (2022) The emergence of the established "by law" criterion for reviewing European judicial appointments. German Law J 23:1051–1070

Kleinlein T (2019) The procedural approach of the European court of human rights: between subsidiarity and dynamic evolution. Int Comp Law Q 68:91–110

Kosař D (2012) Policing separation of powers: a new role for the European court of human rights? Eur Const Law Rev 8:33–62

Kosar D, Petrov J (2017) The architecture of the Strasbourg system of human rights: the crucial role of the domestic level and the constitutional courts in particular. Zeitschrift für ausländisches öffentliches Recht und Völkerrecht 77:585–621

Kosař D, Vyhnánek L (2020) The constitutional court of Czechia. In: von Bogdandy A et al (eds) The max Planck handbooks in European public law: volume III: constitutional adjudication: institutions. Oxford University Press, Oxford, pp 120–181

Kratochvíl (2011) The inflation of the margin of appreciation by the European court of human rights. Netherlands Q Human Rights 29:324–357

Leloup M (2021) Who safeguards the guardians? A subjective right of judges to their independence under article 6(1) ECHR. Eur Const Law Rev 17:394–421

Sadurski W (2009) Partnering with Strasbourg: Constitutionalisation of the European court of human rights, the accession of central and east European states to the Council of Europe, and the idea of pilot judgments. Hum Rights Law Rev 9:397–453

Spano R (2014) Universality or diversity of human rights? Strasbourg in the age of subsidiarity. Hum Rights Law Rev 14:487–502

Stone Sweet A (2012) Constitutional courts. In: Oxford handbook of comparative constitutional law. Oxford University Press, Oxford, pp 816–830

Trubowitz P, Burgoon B (2023) Geopolitics and democracy. The Western Liberal order from foundation to fracture. Oxford University Press, Oxford

Vučinić N (2011) The future. In: Sharpe J (ed) The conscience of Europe: 50 years of the European court of human rights. Third Millennium Publishing, London, pp 190–205

List of Cases

16 Austrian Communes and Some of Their Councillors v. Austria (5767/72, 5767/72, 5922/72, 5929/72, 5930/72, 5931/72, 5953/72, 5954/72, 5955/72, 5956/72, 5957/72, 5984/73, 5985/73, 5986/73, 5987/73, 5988/73, 6011/73), 31/05/1974
A.K. v. Liechtenstein (38191/12), 09/07/2015
A.K. v. Liechtenstein [no. 2] (10722/13), 18/02/2016
Abramiuc v. Romania (37411/02), 24/02/2009
Achache v. France (16043/03), 03/10/2006
Ādamsons v. Latvia (3669/03), 14/06/2008
Advance Pharma Sp. Z.O.O. v. Poland (1469/20), 03/02/2022
Affaire Becker v. Germany (45448/99), 26/09/2002
Affaire Epple v. Germany (77909/01), 24/03/2005
Affaire Hesse Anger v. Germany (45835/99), 06/02/2003
Akbay and Others v. Germany (40495/15, 37273/15, 40913/15), 15/10/2020
Aktiva DOO v. Serbia (23079/11), 19/01/2021
Al Husin v. Bosnia and Herzegovina (3727/08), 07/02/2012
Al Husin v. Bosnia and Herzegovina [No. 2] (10112/16), 25/06/2019
Alexandru-Radu Luca v. Romania (20837/18), 14/06/2022
Almeida Leitão Bento Fernandes v. Portugal (25790/11), 12/03/2015
Anchugov and Gladkov v Russia (11157/04, 15162/05), 04/07/2013
Annen v. Germany (3690/10), 26/11/2015
Apostol v. Georgia (40765/02), 28/11/2006
Arribas Anton v. Spain (16563/11), 20/01/2015
Arrozpide Sarasola and Others v. Spain (65101/16, 73789/16, 73902/16), 23/10/2018
Asan Rushiti v. Austria (28389/95), 21/03/2000
Asanović v. Montenegro (52415/18), 20/05/2021
Association of Citizens Radko and Paunkowski v. The Former Yugoslav Republic of Macedonia (74651/01), 15/01/2009
ATV ZRT v. Hungary (61178/14), 28/04/2020.

M. A. Simonelli, *The European Court of Human Rights and Constitutional Courts*,
Ius Gentium: Comparative Perspectives on Law and Justice 120,
https://doi.org/10.1007/978-3-031-71268-5

Avdić and Others v. Bosnia and Herzegovina (28357/11, 31549/11, 39295/11), 19/11/2013
Avram v. Romania (25339/03), 18/10/2011
Avřička And Others v. The Czech Republic [GC] (47621/13, 3867/14, 73094/14 at alt.), 08/04/2021
Baka v. Hungary (20261/12), 27/05/2014
Baka v. Hungary [GC] (20261/12), 23/06/2016
Baljak and Others v. Croatia (41295/19), 25/11/2021
Ballhausen v. Germany (1479/08), 23/04/2009
Bancsók and László Magyar v. Hungary [No. 2] (52374/15, 53364/15), 28/10/2021
Barac and Others v. Montenegro (47974/06), 13/12/2011.
Baralija v. Bosnia and Herzegovina (30100/18), 29/10/2019
Baranin and Vukčeviç v. Montenegro (24655/18, 24656/18), 11/03/2021
Barberà, Messegué and Jabardo v. Spain (10590/83), 06/12/1988.
Baumann v. France (33592/96), 22/05/2001
Bayer v. Germany (8453/04), 16/07/2009
Bayer v. Germany (8453/04), 16/07/2009
Belcacemi et Oussar v. Belgium (37798/13), 11/07/2017
Beleš et autres v. Czech Republic (47273/99), 12/11/2002
Belpietro v. Italy (43612/10), 24/09/2013
Belvedere Alberghiera v. Italy (31524/96), 30/05/2000
Benedik v. Slovenia (62357/14), 24/04/2018
Benet Praha Spol S.R.O. v. Czech Republic (33908/04, 7937/05, 25249/05), 24/02/2011
Benitez Moriana and Iñigo Fernandez v. Spain (36537/15, 36539/15), 09/03/2021
Bergmann v. Germany (23279/14), 07/01/2016
Bernobic v. Croatia (57180/09), 21/06/2011
Bērzins and Others v. Latvia (73105/12), 21/09/2021
Besnik Cani V. Albania (37474/20), 04/10/2022
Bigović v. Montenegro (48343/16), 19/03/2019
Bíro v. Slovakia [No. 5] (45109/06), 18/05/2010
Bjelic v. Montenegro and Serbia (11890/05), 28/04/2009
Bock v. Germany (11118/84), 29/03/1989
Boucke v. Montenegro (26945/06), 21/02/2012
Bozic v. Croatia (22457/02), 29/06/2006
Broniowski v. Poland (31443/96), 22/06/2004
Brozicek v. Italy (10964/84), 19/12/1989
Bublakova v. Slovakia (17763/07), 15/02/2011
Buccholz v. Germany (7759/77), 06/05/81
Bugajny and Others v. Poland (22531/05), 06/11/2007
Bujac v Romania (37217/03), 02/11/2010
Butkovic v. Croatia (32264/03), 24/05/2007
C.G.I.L. and Cofferati v. Italy (46967/07), 24/02/2009
Cabourdin v. France (60796/00), 11/04/2006
Campos Costa et autres v. Portugal (10172/04), 30/10/2007

Carbonara and Ventura v. Italy (24638/94), 30/05/2000
Cardot v. France (11069/84), 19/03/1991
Cavajda v. Slovakia (65416/01), 14/10/2008
Čeferin v. Slovenia (40975/08), 16/01/2018
Çela v. Albania (73274/17), 29/11/2022
Chassagnou v. France (25088/94, 28331/95, 28443/95), 29/04/1999
Čičmanec v. Slovakia (65302/11), 28/06/2016
Ciobanu v. Romania (29053/95), 16/07/2002
Coban v. Spain [dec] (17060/02), 25/09/2006
Coeme and Others v. Belgium (32492/96, 32492/96, 32547/96, 32548/96, 33209/96, 33210/96), 22/06/2000
Cofferati v. Italy (46967/07) 24/02/2009
Čolić v. Croatia (49083/18), 18/11/2021
Cordella v. Italy (54414/13), (54264/15), 24/01/2019.
Cordova (no. 1) v. Italy (40877/98), 30/01/2003
Cordova (no. 2) v. Italy (45649/99), 30/01/2003
Čović v. Bosnia and Herzegovina (61287/12), 03/10/2017
ĆosiĆ v. Croatia (28261/06), 15/01/2009
Croatian Golf Federation v. Croatia (66994/14), 17/12/2020
Cuenca Zarzoso v. Spain (23383/12), 16/01/2018
Cupara v. Serbia (34683/08), 12/07/2016
D. E. v. Germany (1126/05), 16/07/2009
Dakir v. Belgium (4619/12), 11/07/2017
De Jorio v. Italy (73936/01), 03/06/2004
De Tommaso v. Italy [GC] (43395/09), 23/02/2017
Del Río Prada v. Spain (42750/09), 21/10/2013
Delic v. Croatia (48771/99), 27/06/2002
Deumeland v. Germany (9384/81), 29/05/1986
Di Donato and Others v. Italy (41513/98), 26/04/2001
Diaz Aparicio v. Spain (49468/99), 11/10/2001
Digitel D.O.O. v. Slovenia (70660/01), 15/06/2006
Dolińska-Ficek and Ozimek v. Poland (49868/19, 57511/19), 08/11/2021
Dos Santos Calado and Others v. Portugal (55997/14, 68143/16, 78841/16), 31/03/2020,
Dotta v. Italy [dec.] (38399/97), 07/09/1999
Dragan Kovačević v. Croatia (49281/15), 12/05/2022
Dragicevic v. Croatia (11814/02), 09/12/2004
Dragovic v. Croatia (5705/02), 28/2004
Drahorad et Drahoradova v. Czech Republic (10254/03), 20/03/2008
Ducret v. France (40191/02), 12/06/2007
Dvoracek and Dorackova v. Slovakia (30754/04), 28/07/2009
Ebrahimian v. France (64846/11), 26/11/2015
Ēcis v. Latvia (12879/09), 10/01/2019
Eisenstecken v. Austria (29477/95), 03/10/2000
Elmazova And Others V. North Macedonia (11811/20, 13550/20) 13/12/2022

Engelhardt v. Slovakia (12085/16), 31/08/2018
Erményi v. Hungary (22254/14), 22/11/2016
F.O. v. Croatia (29555/13), 22/04/2021
Farfmeier v. Austria (16841/90), 23/10/1995
Fekiac and Fekiacova v. Slovakia (39202/04), 11/10/2009
Feliciano Bichao v. Portugal (40225/04), 20/11/2007
Ferencne Kovacs v. Hungary (19325/09), 20/12/2011
Fernández Martínez v. Spain (56030/07), 12/6/2014
Fernández-Molina González et autres v. Spain [dec.] (64359/01), 08/10/2002.
Ferré Gisbert v. Spain (39590/05), 13/10/2009
Fesar v. Czech Republic (76576/01), 13/11/2008
Fischer v. Austria (16922/90), 26/04/1995
Fragoso Dacosta v. Spain (27926/21), 08/06/2023
Franek v. Slovakia (14090/10), 11/02/2014
Franz Fischer v. Austria (37950/97), 29/05/2001
Friedrich v. Czech Republic (12108/03), 26/10/2006
Frisancho Perea v. Slovakia (383/13), 21/07/2015
Frodl v. Austria (20201/04), 08/04/2010
Frroku v. Albania (47403/15), 18/09/2018
Fullani v. Albania [dec.] (4586/18), 20/09/2022
Futterer v. Croatia (52634/99), 20/12/2001
G.B. v. Austria (11084/02, 15306/02), 02/06/2005
G.I.E.M. S.R.L. and Others v. Italy [GC] (1828/06, 34163/07, 19029/11), 28/06/2018.
Gáll v. Hungary (49570/11), 25/06/2013
García Mateos v. Spain (38285/09), 19/02/2013
Garrido Herrero v. Spain (61019/19), 11/10/2022
Gas and Dubois v. France (25951/07), 15/03/12
Gaspari v. Slovenia (21055/03), 21/07/2009
Gast and Popp v. Germany (29357/95), 25/02/2000
Getos Magdic v. Croatia (56305/08), 02/12/2010
Ghailan and Others v. Spain (36366/14) 23/03/2021
Giancarlo Lombardo v. Italy (12490/86), 26/11/1992
Gil Sanjuan v. Spain (48297/15), 26/05/2020
Gjyli v. Albania (32907/07), 29/09/2009
Glaser v. Czech Republic (55179/00), 24/02/2008
Glavinić and Marković v. Croatia (11388/15, 25605/15), 30/07/2020
Glien v. Germany (7345/12), 28/11/2013
Gomez de Liano y Botella v. Spain (21369/04), 22/07/2008
Gonzalez Doria Duran de Quiroga v. Spain (59072/00), 28/10/2003
Goretzki v. Germany [dec.] (52447/99), 24/01/2002
Gorraiz Lizarraga v. Spain (62543/00), 27/04/2004
Gouveia Gomes Fernandes et Freitas e Costa v. Portugal (1529/08), 29/03/2011
Gradinger v. Austria (15963/90), 23/10/1995
Gramaxo Rozeira v. Portugal (21976/09), 21/01/2014

Gromzig v. Germany (13791/06), 04/02/2010
Gros v. Slovenia (45315/18), 07/07/2020.
Grzęda v. Poland (43572/18), 15/03/2022
Grzywaczewski v. Poland (18364/06), 31/05/2012
Guzzardi v. Italy, Plenary (7367/76), 06/11/1980
Hadi v. Croatia (42998/08), 01/07/2010
Haidn v. Germany (6587/04), 13/01/2011
Hajdukovic v. Croatia (38303/02), 12/04/2007
Hajrudinović v. Slovenia (69319/12), 21/05/2015
Hamalainen v. Finland (37359/09), 16/07/2014
Hanan v. Germany [GC] (4871/16), 16/02/2021
Harabin v. Slovakia (58688/11), 20/11/2012
Hauser-Sporn v. Austria (37301/13), 07/12/2006
Herbai v. Hungary (11608/15), 05/11/2019
Herrmann v. Germany (9300/07), 20/01/2011
Herrmann v. Germany [GC] (9300/07), 26/06/2012
Hirst v. United Kingdom (74025/01), 06/10/2005
Hit D.D. Nova Gorica v. Slovenia (50996/08), 05/06/2014
Hodos et autres v. Romania (29968/96), 21/05/2002
Hoffer and Annen v. Germany (397/07, 2322/07), 13/01/2011
Horení v. Czech Republic (31806/02), 06/03/2008
Horvat v. Croatia (51585/99), 26/07/2001
Horváth v. Slovakia (5515/09), 27/11/2012
Hubka v. Czech Republic (500/06), 03/02/2011
Hutten-Czapska v. Poland (35014/97), 22/02/2005
Ilnseher v Germany [GC] (10211/12, 27505/14), 04/12/2018
Ilnseher v. Germany [GC] (10211/12, 27505/14), 04/12/2018
Iosif et Autres v. Romania (10443/03), 20/12/2007
Istvan and Istvanova v. Slovakia (30189/07), 12/06/2012
Ivanovski v. The Former Yugoslav Republic of Macedonia
Oleksandr Volkov v. Ukraine (29908/11), 21/01/2016
Jacupovic v. Croatia (12419/04), 31/07/2007
Janyr v. Czech Republic (42937/08), 31/10/2013
Jarrand v. France (56138/16), 09/12/2021
Ješina v. Czech Republic (18806/02), 26/07/2007
Jevtovic v. Serbia (29896/14), 03/12/2019
Joanna Szulc v. Poland (43932/08), 13/11/2012
Jović v. Croatia (45593/13), 13/10/2015
Judt v. Slovakia (70985/01), 09/10/2007
Juričić v. Croatia (58222/09), 26/07/2011
Kaemena and Thonebohn v. Germany (45749/06), (51115/06), 22/01/2009
Kaic and Others v. Croatia (22014/04), 17/07/2008
Kallweit v. Germany (17792/07), 13/01/2011
Kaperzynski v. Poland (43206/07), 03/04/2012
Karácsony and Others v. Hungary [GC] (42461/13, 44357/13), 17/05/2016

Karanovic v. Bosnia and Herzegovina (39462/03), 20/11/2007
Kędzior v. Poland (45026/07), 16/10/2012
Király and Dömötör v. Hungary (10851/13), 17/01/2017
Kirinčić and Others v. Croatia (31386/17), 30/07/2020
Kirsten v. Germany (19124/02), 15/02/2007
Kis v. Slovakia (3673/05), 13/10/2009
Klasen v. Germany (75204/01), 05/10/2006
Klein v. Germany (33379/96), 27/07/2000
Klug v. Austria (33928/05), 15/01/2009
Kneževič and Others v. Slovenia [dec.] (51388/13), 19/09/2017
Komanicky v. Slovakia (No. 3) (72092/01), 17/06/2008
Komanicky v. Slovakia (No. 6) (40437/07), 12/06/2012
Konolos v. Romania (26600/02), 07/02/2008
Könyv Tár and Others v. Hungary (21623/13), 16/10/2018
Kostov and Others v. Bulgaria (66581/12, 25054/15), 14/05/2020
Kovárová v. Slovakia (46564/10), 23/06/2015
Kozak v. Poland (13102/02), 02/03/2010
Krčmar and Others v. Czech Republic (35376/97), 03/03/2000
Krisper v. Slovénie (47825/99), 23/03/2006
Kristiana LTD v. Lithuania (36184/13), 06/02/2018
Krnjak v. Croatia (11228/10), 28/06/2011
Kronfeldner v. Germany (21906/09), 19/01/2012
Kucera v. Slovakia (29749/05), 15/12/2009
Kugler v. Austria (65631/01), 14/10/2010
Kuhlen-Rafsandjani v. Germany (21980/06, 26944/07, 36948/08), 20/01/2011
Kunić and Others v. Bosnia and Herzegovina [GC] (68955/12 et al.), 29/03/2006
Kunić and Others v. Bosnia and Herzegovina (68955/12, 7270/15, 7286/15 et al.), 14/11/2017
Kurić and Others v. Slovenia [GC] (26828/06), 26/06/2012
Kysilková and Kysilka v. Czech Republic (17273/03), 10/02/2011
L. and V. v. Austria (39392/98), (39829/98), 09/01/2003
Laçi v. Albania (28142/17), 19/10/2021
Laranjeira Marques Da Silva v. Portugal (16983/06), 19/01/2010
Lawless v. Ireland (332/57), 14/11/1960
Lecarpentier et autre v. France (67847/01), 14/02/06
Leela Forderkreis E.V. and Others v. Germany (58911/00), 06/11/2008
Lesnina D.D. v. Croatia (18421/05), 25/10/2007
Letica v. Croatia (27846/05), 18/10/2007
Liebscher v. Austria (5434/17), 06/04/2021
Liga Portoguesa de Futebol Profissional v. Portugal (4687/11), 17/05/2016
Lilly France (no. 2) v. France (20429/07), 25/11/2010.
Lonza v. Croatia (14062/07), 01/04/2010
Lopes Gomes Da Silva v. Portugal (37698/97), 28/09/2000
López Gujó v. Slovakia (10280/12), 03/06/2014
López Ostra v. Spain (16798/90), 09/12/1994

Lopez Sole y Martin de Vargas v. Spain (61133/00), 28/10/03
Lorenzo Bragado and Others v. Spain (53193/21, 53707/21, 53848/21 et al.), 22/06/2023
Lukenda v Slovenia (23032/02), 06/10/2005
Luli and Others v. Albania (64480/09, 64482/09, 12874/10) 01/04/2014
M. v. Germany (19359/04), 17/12/2009.
M.H. and Others v. Croatia (15670/18, 43115/18), 18/11/2021
M.L. v. Poland (40119/21), 14/12/2023
M.S. v. Croatia (no. 2) (75450/12), 19/02/2015
Maatescu et autres v. Romania (30698/96), 22/10/2002
Macinkovic v. Croatia (29759/03), 07/12/2006
Madzarovic and Others v. Montenegro (54839/17, 71093/17), 05/05/2020
Maggio v. Italy (357/07), 17/05/2011
Magura v. Slovakia (44068/02), 13/06/2006
Magyar Helsinki Bizottság v. Hungary (8030/11), 08/11/2016
Magyar Kétfarkú Kutya Párt v. Hungary [GC] (201/17), 20/01/2020
Mahmutovič v. Croatia (9505/03), 15/02/2007
Majski v. Croatia (33593/03), 01/06/2006
Marc Brauer v. Germany (24062/13), 01/09/2016.
Marcello Viola v. Italy (no. 2) (77633/16), 13/06/2019
Mareš v. Czech Republic (1414/03), 26/10/2006
Margaretić v. Croatia (16115/13), 05/06/2014
Marík v. Czech Republic (73116/01), 12/04/2005
Marini v. Albania (3738/02), 18/12/2007
Markus v. Latvia (17483/10), 11/06/2020
Martin v. Romania (14466/02), 10/03/2009
Martínez Martínez et Pino Manzano (61654/08), 03/07/2012.
Martinez-Martinez (21532/08), Court (Third Section), 18/10/2011.
Mautes v. Germany (20008/07), 13/01/2011
Medic v. Croatia (49916/07) 26/03/2009
Medžlis Islamske Zajednice Brčko v Bosnia and Herzegovina (7224/11), 03/11/2015
Medžlis Islamske Zajednice Brčko v Bosnia and Herzegovina (7224/11), 27/06/2017
Meimanis v. Latvia (70597/11), 21/07/2015
Melo Taddeu v. Portugal (27785/10) 23/10/2014
Mezey v. Hungary (7909/05), 14/10/2008
Meznaric v. Croatia (71615/01), 15/07/2005
Mihail Mihailhescu v. Romania (3795/15), 12/01/2021
Mijuskovic v. Montenegro (49337/07), 21/09/2010
Mikulič v. Croatia (53176/99), 07/02/02
Milanković and Bošnjak v. Croatia (37762/12),23530/13
Milatová et al. v. Czech Republic (61811/00), 21/06/2005
Milojević and Others v. Serbia (43519/07, 43524/07, 45247/07), 12/01/2016
Milenković v. Serbia (50124/13), 01/03/2016
Milićević v. Montenegro (27821/16), 06/11/2018,
Milovanovic v. Serbia (56065/10), 08/10/2019

Miragall Escolano and Others v. Spain (38366/97, 38688/97, 40777/98, 40843/98, 41015/98, 41400/98, 41446/98, 41484/98, 41487/98, 41509/98) 25/01/2000
Mishgjoni v. Albania (18381/05), 07/12/2010.
Mitrović v. Serbia (52142/12), 21/03/2017
Mourek v. Czech Republic (17999/03), 03/04/2008
Mrkonjič v. Slovénie (17360/02), 06/04/2006
Mugoša v. Montenegro (76522/12), 21/06/2016
Müller-Hartburg v. Austria (47195/06), 19/02/2013
Muñoz Díaz v. Spain (49151/07), 08/12/2009
Muršić v. Croatia [GC] (7334/13), 20/10/2016
Muslija v. Bosnia and Herzegovina (32042/11), 14/01/2014
Muzevic v. Croatia (39299/02), 16/11/2006
N. v. Romania (59152/08), 28/11/2017
N. v. Romania (No. 2) (38048/18), 16/11/2021
N.M. v France (66328/14), 03/02/2022
Nasr et Ghali v. Italy (44883/09), 23/02/2016
Nešic v. Montenegro (12131/18), 09/06/2020
Norbert Sikorski v. Poland (17599/05), 22/10/2009
Novkovic v. Croatia (43437/02), 05/04/207
Novotny v. Czech Republic (16314/13), 07/06/2018
Novović v. Montenegro (13210/05), 23/10/2012
O.H. v. Germany (4646/08), 24/11/2011
Obst v. Germany (425/03), 23/09/2010
Ohneberg v. Austria (10781/08), 18/09/2012
Oliari and others v. Italy (36030/11), 21/07/2015.
Olivares Zuniga v. Spain (11/18), 15/12/2022
Öllinger v. Austria (6900/01), 29/06/2006
Ommer v. Germany (No. 2) (26073/03), 13/11/2008.
Onorato v. Italy (26218/06), 24/05/2011
Orchowski v. Poland (17885/04), 22/10/2009
Oršuš and Others v. Croatia [GC] (15766/03), 16/03/2010
Ortenberg v. Austria (12884/87), 25/11/1994
Osmanović v. Croatia (67604/10), 06/11/2012
Österreichische Vereinigung Zur Erhaltung, Stärkung und Schaffung v. Austria (39534/07), 28/11/2013
Otegi Mondragon and Others v. Spain (4184/15, 4317/15, 4323/15 et alt.), 06/11/2018
Otegi Mondragon v. Spain (2034/07), 15/03/2011
P.B. and J.S. v. Austria (18984/02), 22/07/2010
P.N. v. Germany (74440/17), 11/06/2020 para
Padalevicius v. Lithuania (12278/03), 07/07/2009
Paksas v. Lithuania [GC] (34932/04), 06/01/2011
Pallanich v. Austria, (30160/96), 30/01/2001
Palaoro v. Austria (16718/90), 23/10/1995
Páleník v. Czech Republic (64737/01), 21/06/2005

Palgutova v. Slovakia (9818/02), 17/05/2005
Palšovič v. Czech Republic (39278/04), 03/02/2011
Pammel v. Germany (17820/91), 01/07/1997
Parlov Tkalcic v. Croatia (24810/06), 22/12/2009
Parrillo v. Italy [GC] (46470/11), 27/08/2015)
PauliĆ v. Croatia (3572/06), 22/10/2009
Pauger v. Austria (16717/90), 208/05/1997
Pavlović and Others v. Croatia (13274/11), 02/04/2015
Pejřilová v. The Czech Republic (14889/19), 08/12/2022
Pellon v. Spain (45238/99) 25/07/2002
Pérez de Rada Cavanilles v. Spain (28090/95), 28/10/1998
Perica Oreb v. Croatia (0824/09), 31/10/2013
Pesa v. Croatia (40523/08), 08/04/2010
Peter v. Germany (68919/10), 04/09/2014
Petkov and Others v. Bulgaria (7568/01, 178/02, 505/02), 11/06/2009
Petrovic v. Austria (20458/92), 27/03/1998
Petrovic v. Croatia (38292/02), 12/04/2007
Pierre Bloch v. France (24194/94), 21/10/1997
Pietrzak v. Poland (38185/02), 08/01/2008
Pillmann v. Czech Republic (15333/02), 27/09/2005
Pinto Coelho v. Portugal (28439/08), 28/06/2011
Pinto Coelho v. Portugal (No. 2) (48718/11), 22/03/2016
Pinto Coelho v. Portugal (No. 2) (8439/08), 28/06/2011
Pištorová v. Czech Republic (73578/01), 26/10/2004
Pitra v. Croatia (41075/02), 16/06/2005
Pocuca v. Croatia (38550/02), 29/06/2006
Popara v. Croatia (11072/03), 15/03/2007
Popovic and Others v. Serbia (26944/13, 14616/16, 14619/16), 30/06/2020
Posedel-Jelinovic v. Croatia (35915/02), 24/11/2005
Prado Bugallo v. Spain (58496/00), 18/02/2003
Pralica v. Bosnia and Herzegovina (38945/05), 27/01/2009
Pramstaller v. Austria (16713/90), 23/10/1995
Pranjić and Lukić v. Bosnia and Herzegovina (4938/16), 02/06/2020
Predil Anstalt S.A. v. Italy (dec.) (31993/96), 08/06/1999
Prezec v. Croatia (48185/07), 15/10/2009
Project-Trade D.O.O. v. Croatia (1920/14), 19/11/2020
Pronina v. Ukraine (63566/00), 18/07/2006
Prötsch v. Austria (15508/89), 15/11/1996
Publico - Comunicacao Social, S.A. et alt. v. Portugal (39324/07), 07/12/2010
Gouveia Gomes Fernandes et Freitas e Costa v. Portugal (1529/08), 29/03/2011
Conceicao Letria v. Portugal (4049/08), 12/04/2011
Q and R v Slovenia (19938/20), 08/02/2022
Qufaj Co. Sh.p.k. v. Albania (54268/00), 18/11/2004
R. R. v. Poland, (27617/04), 26/05/2011
R.H. v. Austria (7336/03), 19/01/2006

Radivoy Novakovic v. Croatia (43446/02), 12/04/2007
Radojčič v. Slovenia (4562/02), 13/07/2006
Rados and Others v. Croatia (45435/99), 07/11/2002
Raudevs v. Latvia (24086/03), 17/12/2013
Reczkowicz v. Poland (43447/19), 22/07/2021
Regálová v Czech Republic (40593/05), 03/07/2008
Renard et autres v. France (3569/12), 17/07/2015
Repcevirág Szövetkezet v. Hungary (70750/14),30/04/2019
Rimšēvičs v. Latvia (56425/18), 10/11/2022
Riza and Others v. Bulgaria (48555/10, 48377/10), 13/10/2015
Rizman v. Croatia (28704/06), 31/07/2008
Rodriguez Valin v. Spain (47792/99), 11/10/2001
Rolim Comercial, S.A. v. Portugal (16153/09), 16/04/2013
Rosa Marques et autres v. Portugal (48187/99), 25/07/2002
Roseiro Bento v. Portugal (29288/02), 18/04/2006
RSz v. Hungary (41838/11), 02/07/2013
Ruiz-Mateos v. Spain (12952/87), 23/06/1993
Rumpf v. Germany (46344/06), 02/09/2010
Rutar and Rutar Marketing D.O.O. v. Slovenia (21164/20), 15/12/2022
S.A.S. v. France (43835/11), 01/07/2014
S.H. and Others v. Austria [GC] (57813/00), 03/11/2011
S.L. v. Austria (45330/99), 09/01/2003
S.S. v. Slovenia (40938/16), 30/10/2018
Sabalić v. Croatia (50231/13), 14/01/2021
Sabou et Pircalab v. Romania (46572/99), 28/09/2004
Sailer v. Austria (38237/97), 06/06/2002
Saint-Adam et Millot v. France (72038/01), 02/05/2006;
Šaltinytė v. Lithuania (32934/19), 26/10/2021
Samija v. Croatia (14898/04), 07/12/2006
Sándor Varga and Others v. Hungary (39734/15, 35530/16, 26804/18), 17/06/2021.
Sandra Jankovic v. Croatia (38478/05), 05/03/2009
Šaranović v. Montenegro (31775/16), 05/03/2019
Savickis and Others v. Latvia [GC] (49270/11), 09/06/2022
Savičs v. Latvia (17892/03), 27/11/2012
Scalzo v. Italy (8790/21), 06/12/2022.
Schmautzer v. Austria (15523/89), 23/10/1995
Schmidt v. Austria (513/05), 17/07/2008
Schönbrod v. Germany (48038/06), 24/11/2011
Schummer v. Germany (No. 1) (27360/04, 42225/07), 13/01/2011
Schvarc v. Slovakia, (64528/09), 14/01/2014
Schwengel v. Germany [dec] (52442/99), 02/03/2000
Scordino v. Italy (No. 1) (36813/97), 29/03/2006
Sedminek v. Slovenia (9842/07), 24/10/2013
See, Gjyli v. Albania (32907/07), 29/09/2009
Sekanina v. Austria (13126/87), 25/08/1993

Šeks v. Croatia (39325/20), 03/02/2022
Selmani and Others v. The Former Yugoslav Republic of Macedonia (67259/14), 09/02/2017
Sérvulo & Associados - Sociedade de Advogados, RL and Others v. Portugal (27013/10), 03/09/2015
Sevdari v. Albania (40662/19), 13/12/2022
Shiksaitov v. Slovakia (56751/16, 33762/17), 10/12/2020
Siebenhaar v. Germany (18136/02), 03/02/2011
Sikic v. Croatia (9143/08), 15/07/2010
Siništaj and Others v. Montenegro (1451/10, 7260/10, 7382/10), 24/11/2015
Smiljanić v. Croatia (35983/14), 25/03/2021
Smoje v. Croatia (28074/03), 11/01/2007
Soares de Melo v. Portugal (72850/14), 16/02/2016
Šobota-Gajić v. Bosnia and Herzegovina (27966/06), 06/11/2007
Softel Spol S.R.O. v. Slovakia (No. 1) (32427/06), 16/12/2008
Sosinowska v. Poland (10247/09), 18/10/2011
Sostaric v. Croatia (39659/04), 12/04/2007
Soto Sanchez v. Spain (66990/01) 25/11/2003
Soudek v. Czech Republic (56526/00), 15/03/2005
Spahić and Others v. Bosnia and Herzegovina (20514/15, 20528/15, 20774/15, et al.), 14/11/2017
Špadijer v. Montenegro (31549/18), 09/11/2021
Šrouh v Czech Republic (5424/03), 17/01/2006
Stakić v. Montenegro (49320/07), 02/10/2012
Stallinger and Kuso v. Austria (14696/89, 14697/89), 23/04/1997
Stavebna Spolocnost Tatry Poprad, S.R.O. v. Slovakia (7261/06), 03/05/2011
Stăvilă v. Romania (23126/16), 01/03/2022
Steck-Risch and Others v. Liechtenstein (63151/00), 19/05/2005
Stefanetti and Others v. Italy (21838/10, 21849/10, 21852/10, 21855/10, 21860/10), 21863/10, 21869/10, 21870/10), 15/04/2014
Stern Taulats and Roura Capellera v. Spain (51168/15, 51186/15), 13/03/2018
Stevan Petrović v. Serbia (6097/16, 28999/19), 20/04/2021
Stojakovic v. Austria (30003/02), 09/11/2006
Strezovski and Others v. North Macedonia (14460/16, 14958/16, 14962/16 et alt.), 27/02/2020
Stubing v. Germany (43547/08), 12/04/2012
Sürmeli v. Germany [GC] (75529/01), 08/06/2006
Šury v. Czech Republic (16299/10), 13/10/2011
Süssmann v. Germany [GC] (20024/92), 16/09/1996
Švarc and Kavnik v. Slovenia (75617/01), 08/02/2007
Társásag a Szabadságjogokért v. Hungary (37374/05), 14/04/2009
Tavares De Almeida Fernandes and Almeida Fernandes v. Portugal (31566/13), 17/01/2017.
Tele 1 Privatfernseh v. Austria (32240/96), 21/09/2000
Terranova v. Italy (17156/90), 04/12/1995

Terzin-Laub v. Croatia (43362/02), 12/0472007
Tešić v. Serbia (4678/07, 50591/12), 11/02/2014
Tieze et Semerakova v. Czech Republic (26908/09, 30809/10), 13/10/2011
Tokić and Others v. Bosnia and Herzegovina (12455/04, 14140/05, 12906/06 et al.), 08/07/2008
Tomasic v. Croatia (21753/02), 19/10/2006
Topallaj v. Albania (32913/03), 21/04/2016
Trade Union of the Police in the Slovak Republic and Others v. Slovakia (11828/08), 25/09/2012
Travaš v. Croatia (75581/13), 04/10/2016
Tričković v. Slovenia (39914/98), 12/06/2001
Trifkovič v. Croatia (36653/09), 06/11/2012
Trivkanović v. Croatia (no. 2) (49083/18), 18/11/2021
Tsikakis v. Germany (1521/06), 10/02/2011
Tumeliai v. Lithuania (25545/14), 09/01/2018
Turek v. Czech Republic (73403/01), 21/06/2005
Ulemek v. Croatia (21613/16), 31/10/2019
Umlauft v. Austria (15527/89), 23/10/1995
Unión Alimentaria Sanders S.A. v. Spain (11681/85), 07/07/1989
United Communist Party of Turkey and Others v. Turkey (9392/92), 30/01/1998,
United Macedonian Organization Ilinden - Pirin and Others v. Bulgaria (59489/00), 20/10/2005
V.P. and F.D.R. v. Italy (44333/98),12/02/2002
V. R. v. Croatia (55102/13), 13/10/2015
Vajagic v. Croatia (30431/03), 20/07/2006
Valenzuela Contreras v. Spain (27671/95), 30/07/1998
Vallianatos v. Greece (29381/09), (2684/09), 07/11/2013
Vaquero Hernandez v. Spain (38715/06), 26/10/2010
Varvara v. Italy (17475/09), 29/10/2013
Vegotex International S.A. v. Belgium (49812/09), 03/11/2022
Vera Fernandez-Huidobro (74181/01), 06/01/2010
Vezon v. France (66018/01), 18/04/2006
Vidal Escoll et Guillan Gonzalez v. Andorre (38196/05), 29/07/2008
Vilho Eskelinen T Vilho Eskelinen and Others v. Finland (63235/00), 19/04/2007
Vinčić and Others v. Serbia (44698/06, 44700/06, 44722/06) 01/12/2009
Visy v. Slovakia (70288/13), 16/10/2018
Vodarenska Akciova Spolecnost A.S. v. Czech Republic (73577/01), 24/02/2004
Vokoun v. Czech Republic (20728/05), 03/07/2008
Von Hannover v. Germany (59320//00), 24/6/2004
Von Hannover v. Germany (No. 2) [GC] (40660/08, 60641/08), 07/02/2012
Vrioni and Others v. Albania (2141/03), 24/03/2009
Vučković and Others v. Serbia [GC] (17153/11), 25/03/2014
Vujcic v. Croatia (33867/06), 25/06/2009
Walesa v. Poland (50849/21), 23/11/2023
W. F. v. Austria (38275/97), 30/05/2002

W. v Germany [dec.] (10785/84), 18/07/1986
Wegera v. Poland (141/07), 14/01/2010
Weh v. Austria (38544/97), 08/04/2004
Wildgruber v. Germany (No. 2) (42402/05, 42423/05), 21/01/2010
Winkler v. Slovakia (25416/07), 17/07/2012
Woditschka and Wilfling v. Austria (69756/01), (6306/02), 21/10/2004
Wynen and Centre Hospitalier Interrégional Edith-Cavell v. Belgium (32576/96), 05/11/2002
X. c. Germany (441/58), 07/07/1959.
Xero Flor W Polsce Sp. Z O. O. v. Poland; *Avřička And Others v. The Czech Republic* [GC] (47621/13, 3867/14, 73094/14 et al.), 08/04/2021
Xhoxhaj v. Albania (15227/19), 09/02/2021
Yegorov v. Slovakia (27112/11), 02/06/2015
Zaicevs v. Latvia (65022/01), 31/07/2007
Zborovsky v. Slovakia (14325/08), 23/10/2012
Zdanoka v. Latvia (58278/00), 17/06/2004
Ziacik v Slovakia (43377/98), 27/01/2003
*Zielinski and Pradal & Gonzalez et alt. v. Franc*e (24846/94), (34165/96 to 34173/96), 28/10/1999
Zirnite v. Latvia (69019/11), 11/06/2020
Zivaljević v. Montenegro (17229/04), 08/03/2011
Zoltán Varga v. Slovakia (58361/12, 25592/16, 27176/16), 20/07/2021
Zovanovic v. Croatia (12877/02), 09/12/2004
Zumtobel v. Austria 1 (2235/86), 21/09/1993
Zustović v. Croatia (27903/15), 22/04/2021
Zvolsky and Zvolska v. Czech Republic (46129/99), 12/11/2002

SPRINGER NATURE

GPSR Compliance

The European Union's (EU) General Product Safety Regulation (GPSR) is a set of rules that requires consumer products to be safe and our obligations to ensure this.

If you have any concerns about our products, you can contact us on ProductSafety@springernature.com

In case Publisher is established outside the EU, the EU authorized representative is:

Springer Nature Customer Service Center GmbH
Europaplatz 3
69115 Heidelberg, Germany

The manufacturer's authorised representative in the EU is Springer Nature Customer Service Centre GmbH, Europaplatz 3, 69115 Heidelberg, Germany. If you have any concerns regarding our products, please contact ProductSafety@springernature.com

Printed and bound by CPI Group (UK) Ltd, Croydon, CR0 4YY
30/09/2026
02225584-0005